PUBLICATIONS OF THE NATIONAL BUREAU OF
ECONOMIC RESEARCH, INCORPORATED

No. 8

BUSINESS ANNALS

National Bureau of Economic Research, Inc.

Incorporated Under the Membership Corporations Laws of the State of New York, January 29, 1920

ITS ORGANIZATION AND PURPOSES

THE National Bureau of Economic Research was organized in 1920 in response to a growing demand for exact and impartial determinations of facts bearing on economic, social, and industrial problems.

It seeks not only to find facts and make them known, but to determine them in such manner and under such supervision as to make its findings carry conviction to Liberal and Conservative alike.

Entire control of the Bureau is vested in a Board of twenty directors, representing learned and scientific societies, financial, industrial, agricultural, commercial, labor, and technical organizations.

Rigid provisions in the Charter and By-Laws guard the Bureau from becoming a source of profit to its members, directors, or officers and from becoming an agency for propaganda. No report of the Research Staff may be published without the approval of the Directors and any Director who dissents from any finding approved by a majority of the Board may have such dissent published with the majority report.

The members of the Board of Directors are as follows:

DIRECTORS AT LARGE

T. S. ADAMS, Professor of Political Economy, Yale University, *Vice-President*.
JOHN R. COMMONS, Professor of Political Economy, University of Wisconsin.
JOHN P. FREY, Editor, International Molders' Journal, *Chairman of the Board*.
EDWIN F. GAY, Professor of Economic History, Harvard University, *Research Director*.
HARRY W. LAIDLER, Secretary, The League for Industrial Democracy.
GEORGE O. MAY, Senior Partner, Price, Waterhouse and Company, *President*.
ELWOOD MEAD, Commissioner of the Bureau of Reclamation.
WESLEY C. MITCHELL, Professor of Economics, Columbia University, *Research Director*.
DWIGHT W. MORROW, Member of firm of J. P. Morgan and Company.
GEORGE SOULE, Director, The Labor Bureau, Inc.
N. I. STONE, Industrial Consultant.
ALLYN A. YOUNG, Professor of Economics, Harvard University.

DIRECTORS BY APPOINTMENT

HUGH FRAYNE, American Federation of Labor.
DAVID FRIDAY, American Economic Association.
LEE GALLOWAY, American Management Association.
WALTER R. INGALLS, American Engineering Council.
GEORGE E. ROBERTS, American Bankers Association, *Treasurer*.
M. C. RORTY, American Statistical Association.
A. W. SHAW, National Publishers' Association.
GRAY SILVER, American Farm Bureau Federation.

OSWALD W. KNAUTH, *Recording Secretary*.   GUSTAV R. STAHL, *Executive Secretary*.

RESEARCH STAFF

EDWIN F. GAY, *Director*.
WILLFORD I. KING.
LEO WOLMAN.
FREDERICK C. MILLS.

WESLEY C. MITCHELL, *Director*.
FREDERICK R. MACAULAY.
HARRY JEROME.
WALTER F. WILLCOX.

WILLARD L. THORP.

BUSINESS ANNALS

United States, England, France, Germany, Austria, Russia, Sweden, Netherlands, Italy, Argentina, Brazil, Canada, South Africa, Australia, India, Japan, China

By
WILLARD LONG THORP
OF THE STAFF OF THE
NATIONAL BUREAU OF ECONOMIC RESEARCH

WITH AN
INTRODUCTORY CHAPTER

BY
WESLEY C. MITCHELL
DIRECTOR OF RESEARCH

AND A
FOREWORD

BY
EDWIN F. GAY
DIRECTOR OF RESEARCH

NEW YORK
NATIONAL BUREAU OF ECONOMIC
RESEARCH, INC.
1926

Copyright, 1926, by
NATIONAL BUREAU OF ECONOMIC RESEARCH, INC.
All rights reserved

Printed in the United States of America by
J. J. LITTLE AND IVES COMPANY, NEW YORK

FOREWORD

When the National Bureau of Economic Research, Incorporated, was established in 1920, its aim was to ascertain fundamental facts in the economic field, and to confine itself to stating these facts as objectively and dispassionately as possible. It hoped to contribute to the work of social disarmament by turning from the antagonisms of opinion to agreements upon facts. Men differ, often violently, in their philosophies of life, in their views as to the ends society should pursue, and as to the means best adapted to those ends. Until the knowledge of social behavior is greatly deepened and widely diffused, such opposing opinions will be honestly entertained and bitterly disputed. In so far, however, as the disputation turns upon the facts, and not merely upon their interpretation, it will be possible by the gradual extension of the field of exact knowledge ultimately to narrow the contentious field and correspondingly to enlarge the basis upon which useful social action may rest. The National Bureau, therefore, has chosen for its special province those economic and social problems which appear most susceptible of accurate or approximately reliable measurement, and it has elected for its audience those thoughtful citizens, of whatever persuasion or class, who esteem rational evidence, or who at least before drawing their own conclusions prefer in argument to come to agreement as to definitions and data.

The scientific method, then, of the National Bureau, is primarily that of quantitative measurement. But its public appeal is not merely to that limited number who delight in the refinements of statistics, but to the much larger group of intelligent men and women who realize that this choice of method means, not the evading of thorny social problems, but an attack upon them, persistently prosecuted, on one of their most vulnerable sides, that of cool and disinterested analysis. The supporters of the National Bureau have many differences of social viewpoint, but they are united in seeking the largest common ground of ascertainable truth.

In the confident belief that such a method and appeal would be a service to public discussion and to the advancement of economic science, and that in applying them it should commence at its own home, the National Bureau undertook from the outset to entrust the decision as to choice of topics of investigation and the review of its findings to the unfettered judgment of a board of directors deliberately selected to represent the significant divergencies of American opinion on economic problems. Its by-laws provide that all reports made by the expert staff shall be submitted before publication to the directors for criticism, and that a director who dissents from any method or finding approved by the majority of the board shall, if he so desires, have his dissenting view published in the report. Such a procedure, it should be frankly stated, was viewed with some misgiving by friends of the undertaking, but the operation of this board of review has in practice neither dampened the scientific spirit of the staff, nor resulted in any debilitating compromises in the statement of results. It has proved to be no hindrance, but rather a positive help. The occasional recorded dissents in the Bureau's publications have given continued assurance of the alertness of the directors, and a demonstration of that freedom from bias which it is the ambition of the Bureau to attain. In addition, the many unrecorded contributions of information and critical judgment from the varied experience and training of the directors have done much to improve the published work and have been welcomed by the scientific staff.

A first impression on seeing the title of the present book, *Business Annals,* might be that the National Bureau in entering the domain of history had swerved from its customary line of quantitative investigation. It is not here the place to discuss the relation to statistics, at least in the older and more general sense of the term, of careful description of economic phenomena. And it is not necessary to adduce the example of Herbert Spencer's elaborate tabular views of Descriptive Sociology, which he deemed so fundamental to social science that he made special provision in his will for their continuation. It will be sufficient to examine Professor Mitchell's Introduction in order to observe what illuminating statistical use can be made of the time-sequences so diligently collected and so compactly presented by Dr. Thorp in the body of this book. These sample observations of the "universe of cycles," 166 from 17 countries, yield highly suggestive preliminary statistical conclusions regarding the relative duration and frequency of the recurrent movements of prosperity and depression which characterize our existing economic organization.

FOREWORD

This collection of material might justly be regarded as a laboratory by-product. As the first studies of the National Bureau on Income in the United States were being completed, and even before the volume on *Business Cycles and Unemployment* had been undertaken at Mr. Hoover's request, the Executive Committee of the Bureau's board of directors had approved and authorized a comprehensive analysis of Business Cycles as its next main investigation. Professor Mitchell had already done what the Germans like to call "path-breaking" work in this field. His notable volume, *Business Cycles*, published in 1913 by the University of California, was out of print. But the new study, the directors agreed, should be more than a second edition of the earlier book. There was at the time, in 1921, an exceptionally widespread interest in the topic, stimulated naturally by the business depression of that year of distress; there was a considerable mass of new and valuable data, statistical and other, together with recent and improved statistical methods; and there were the available resources of the National Bureau, which, even though limited in extent for such a task, nevertheless furnished a better instrument than Professor Mitchell had possessed in his former, single-handed attack on the subject: there was finally, it may be permitted to add, the National Bureau's asset in Professor Mitchell himself with his ripened experience, ready to devote himself to that which the directors thought most timely and useful to undertake. It was therefore determined that a survey and analysis be made of Business Cycles, as wide and as thorough as the sources of information and the resources of the National Bureau would permit. As a part of the laboratory apparatus set up for the investigation, a detailed examination was undertaken of the past experiences of this and other countries when passing through the successive phases of cyclical changes. This information when collected, condensed, and tabulated by Dr. Thorp and his assistants, for Dr. Mitchell's use, was clearly of such value for other students and also for those of more general interests who would find convenient a handy compendium of this aspect of human history, that it was decided to publish the collection in the separate volume, here presented.

While in a sense the book is a by-product, it is also an integral part of the series on Business Cycles which the National Bureau has now in hand. It will be followed, in a few months, by Professor Mitchell's first volume on "The Problem and Its Setting." Another valuable collection of material, a full array of all the discoverable statistical series, many hitherto unpublished or, if printed, practically unknown, many more here, for the first time, brought accessibly together and critically annotated, is now almost completed, awaiting for publication the funds requisite for so costly a tabular work. The Bureau hopes that the next year will bring the publishing of Professor Mitchell's work in a second volume containing his analysis and conclusions from this wealth of material.

EDWIN F. GAY.

CONTENTS

	PAGE
FOREWORD, BY EDWIN F. GAY	5
INTRODUCTION. BUSINESS CYCLES AS REVEALED BY BUSINESS ANNALS, BY WESLEY C. MITCHELL	15
I. The Uses of Business Annals	15
II. The Scope of the Annals	17
III. The Trustworthiness of the Annals	20
IV. The Cyclical Character of Business Fluctuations	
1. The "Normal State of Trade" a Figment	31
2. Use of the Term "Cycle"	32
3. The Phases of Business Cycles	33
4. "Crises" and "Recessions"	34
5. The Uniformity and Variability of Business Cycles	37
V. The Duration of Business Cycles	
1. Current Estimates of Average Length	38
2. Measurements based upon the Annals	40
3. Frequency Distributions of the Measurements Based on the Annals	46
4. Relative Duration of Prosperity and Depression	62
5. Conclusions	67
VI. International Relationships among Business Cycles	
1. Other Problems on which the Annals throw Light	73
2. A Conspectus of Business Conditions in Different Countries	74
3. How Closely the Cycles Agree	88
4. Domestic and Foreign Factors in Business Cycles	96

BUSINESS ANNALS
By WILLARD L. THORP

PREFATORY NOTE	103
CHAPTER I. ANNALS OF THE UNITED STATES, 1790–1925	
Description	107
Annals	113
CHAPTER II. ANNALS OF ENGLAND, 1790–1925	
Description	146
Annals	150

CONTENTS

	PAGE
CHAPTER III. ANNALS OF FRANCE, 1840–1925	
Description	180
Annals	183
CHAPTER IV. ANNALS OF GERMANY, 1853–1925	
Description	200
Annals	204
CHAPTER V. ANNALS OF AUSTRIA, 1867–1925	
Description	219
Annals	222
CHAPTER VI. ANNALS OF RUSSIA, 1890–1925	
Description	234
Annals	237
CHAPTER VII. ANNALS OF SWEDEN, 1890–1925	
Description	245
Annals	247
CHAPTER VIII. ANNALS OF THE NETHERLANDS, 1890–1925	
Description	255
Annals	258
CHAPTER IX. ANNALS OF ITALY, 1890–1925	
Description	265
Annals	267
CHAPTER X. ANNALS OF ARGENTINE, 1890–1925	
Description	276
Annals	278
CHAPTER XI. ANNALS OF BRAZIL, 1890–1925	
Description	286
Annals	288
CHAPTER XII. ANNALS OF CANADA, 1890–1925	
Description	296
Annals	300
CHAPTER XIII. ANNALS OF SOUTH AFRICA, 1890–1925	
Description	308
Annals	311
CHAPTER XIV. ANNALS OF AUSTRALIA, 1890–1925	
Description	319
Annals	322

CONTENTS   11

                                                                    PAGE
CHAPTER XV.   ANNALS OF INDIA, 1890–1925
    Description   330
    Annals   333
CHAPTER XVI. ANNALS OF JAPAN, 1890–1925
    Description   341
    Annals   343
CHAPTER XVII. ANNALS OF CHINA, 1890–1925
    Description   351
    Annals   352
CHAPTER XVIII. BIBLIOGRAPHY   360

LIST OF TABLES

Table 1. Business Recessions in the United States and the Approximate Duration of Business Cycles, 1790-1925.   42

Table 2. Business Recessions in England and the Approximate Duration of Business Cycles, 1790-1925   44

Table 3. Data of Business Recessions in Fifteen Countries: various dates to 1925.   48

Table 4. Frequency Distributions of Business Cycles according to Duration in Years: Seventeen Countries, various dates to 1925 .   53

Table 5. Frequency Distributions of Business Cycles according to Approximate Duration by Countries, Groups of Countries, and Periods   54

Table 6. Relative Duration of Different Phases of Business Cycles: Seventeen Countries, 1890-1925   63

Table 7. Relative Duration of the Prosperity and Depression Phases in the Business Cycles of Seventeen Countries during Various Periods   65

Table 8. Relative Duration of the Prosperity and Depression Phases of Business Cycles in Periods of Rising and Declining Trends of Wholesale Prices: England and the United States, 1790-1925   66

Table 9. Relative Duration of Phases of Depression and Phases of Prosperity in Business Cycles Lasting Nine Years or More . .   67

Table 10. Conspection of Business Fluctuations in Various Countries   75

Table 11. Agreement and Difference of Phase in English, French, German, Austrian, and American Business Cycles   91

LIST OF CHARTS

	PAGE
Chart I. Business Fluctuations in the United States, as Shown by the Annals and by Two Statistical Indexes, 1875–1925	24
Chart II. Business Fluctuations in England, as Shown by the Annals and Dr. Dorothy S. Thomas' "Quarterly Index of British Cycles," 1855–1914	28
Chart III. Approximate Duration of Business Cycles, Arranged in Chronological Sequence	50
Chart IV. Percentage Distribution of Business Cycles in Various Countries and Various Periods According to their Approximate Duration in Years	56

    A. United States.
    B. England.
    C. United States and England.
    D. United States, England, France, Germany, and Austria: Before 1873.
    E. United States, England, France, Germany, and Austria: After 1873.
    F. United States, England, France, Germany, and Austria.
    G. Countries with Close Business Relations.
    H. Countries Relatively Independent of Each Other.
    I. Countries with Average Duration of 5.5 Years or More.
    J. Countries with Average Duration of 5.2 Years or Less: Excluding United States.
    K. Countries with Average Duration of 5.2 Years or Less: Including United States.
    L. Countries with Average Duration of 5.0 to 5.7 Years.
    M. Eight European Countries.
    N. Nine Non-European Countries.
    O. Five English-Speaking Countries.
    P. Twelve Non-English Speaking Countries.
    Q. All Countries except United States.
    R. All Countries.
    S. Eight European Countries: About 1890 to 1925.
    T. Eight Non-European Countries: About 1890 to 1925.
    U. Seven Industrial Countries: About 1890 to 1925.
    V. Ten Non-Industrial Countries: About 1890 to 1925.
    W. All Countries except United States: About 1890 to 1925.
    X. All Countries: About 1890 to 1925.

LIST OF CHARTS

PAGE

Chart V. Logarithmic Normal Curve fitted by Davies' Method to the Frequency Distribution of 166 Observations upon the Duration of Business Cycles 70

Chart VI. Conspectus of Business Cycles in Various Countries . . 94

BUSINESS ANNALS

INTRODUCTION

BUSINESS CYCLES AS REVEALED BY BUSINESS ANNALS.

BY WESLEY C. MITCHELL.[1]

I. The Uses of Business Annals.

For our work upon business cycles in the National Bureau of Economic Research we have made two collections of materials, which we think others will find useful.

One is a collection of statistics. We are assembling in a single source-book the widely scattered records of economic and social activities in Great Britain, France, Germany, the United States, and, to a limited extent, in other countries. We are going back to the earliest compilations of continuous series and coming down to the current year, making critical notes upon the character of the data, piecing together fragments, and presenting the figures by months or quarters whenever possible. When this collection is ready for use, we hope that we shall be enabled to publish it in two or more volumes.

The second collection, consisting of what we call "business annals", is presented in this book. Though less bulky than the statistics, these annals cover a wider area and a longer period. For the statistical record shrinks rapidly as we go back 25, 50, and 100 years; few indeed are the series extending to the earliest decades covered by our British and American annals. Another difference is that the annals sketch a general situation of which the statistics show certain parts in

---

[1] The writer has received much help from his colleagues in the National Bureau of Economic Research, especially Frederick C. Mills and Willard L. Thorp.

detail. Thus the two collections supplement each other:—one presents the most precise records kept of specific economic or social processes, the other traces the fluctuations in economic and social fortunes at large. Together they sum up much of the experience which may be made to light the path into the future.

The value of statistics for practical and theoretical uses is now widely recognized, and so too are the difficulties, dangers and limitations attending their use. Business annals are a less familiar form of record, and require an introduction showing how they are made, how far they may be trusted, and what they add to our knowledge.

One merit of the annals, simplicity, is obvious at first glance. They tell a story, tell it in the most straightforward way, and tell it without the use of symbols or strange terms. Men who lack the time, patience, or technical training to wring the meaning from statistical tables can use this record with ease.

The story which the annals tell concerns the vicissitudes of economic fortune through which 17 countries have passed in periods which range from 36 to 136 years. In the fewest possible words they trace the fluctuations in manufacturing, construction work, employment, domestic and foreign trade, prices, speculation, financial operations, and agriculture, so far as the facts can be gathered from available sources. Thus the annals cover the grand divisions of economic activity. They also note the most important events of a non-economic sort which presumably influence economic activity—the making of war and peace, diplomatic strains, domestic disorders, changes of political administration and economic policy, droughts, floods, earthquakes, epidemics among men or cattle, and the like.

Everyone who reads this story year after year for nation after nation will see running through all the episodes one of the problems of modern civilization. In no country covered by the annals—not in the most rapidly growing communities developing rich new lands, and not in the most conservative of old communities—does a period of economic prosperity ever last more than five or six years at a stretch. Each country has its seasons of prosperity, but these seasons always end in seasons of depression. In their turn, the periods of depression yield to new periods of prosperity. Economic experience is made up of such alternations of good and ill fortune and the transitions from one to the other. The alternations are more marked or more frequent in some countries than in others; but they occur everywhere. No country has yet learned to control them.

Upon the vexed question how these fluctuations come about, the annals throw no direct light. That problem is reserved for another volume, in which the National Bureau hopes to make what contributions it can toward a solution. But the annals establish certain facts about business fluctuations over a wider area and for a longer time than any other records. They show not only when periods of depression have begun in numerous countries, but also how long they have lasted, whether they have been severe or slight, confined to one country or spread over many. They show when revivals of activity have occurred and how these revivals have fared; they help us to find out how far the different branches of a country's business—particularly industry and trade, finance, and farming—have had common or diverse fortunes; they bring out the relations between the vicissitudes of business and the vicissitudes of politics and of natural processes.

While these annals were compiled primarily to throw light upon business cycles, they will prove useful for many other ends. Historians, political scientists, sociologists, and publicists frequently need to know the condition of business in certain times and countries. Statisticians dealing with time series will find that the annals provide an illuminating background for their special problems. Journalists who have to comment upon current developments, business men whose plans stretch into the future, indeed everyone who would control his expectations by experience, may profit by this condensed record of what has happened in the recent past. Those who are concerned with the spread of factory production and business enterprise over the world can see how far the economic fluctuations in Russia, Brazil, Argentina, South Africa, British India, Japan and China are being assimilated to the economic fluctuations in Western Europe and North America. The annals show us also how the great commercial nations share in each other's prosperity and suffer from each other's reverses—a matter which merits far more attention than it commonly receives in discussions of national policy.

II. The Scope of the Annals.

A few earlier efforts have been made to provide a record of the sort here set forth; but most of them have been restricted in scope and buried in technical books, journals or official documents.[1] Fuller accounts of business conditions in various countries, for various periods, have been included in many of the books dealing with the history or the theory of crises and depressions. But the reader who wished a wide view has had to do much hunting and piece together such scraps as he could collect. There have been gaps he could not fill. Nor has he been safe in trusting all that he found. Errors committed in certain early investigations have been taken over by writers upon the theory of business cycles, and supplemented by fresh errors due to the forcing of a stereotyped pattern upon variable facts. Those who have taken the precaution to consult two authorities have frequently ended in doubt; for the chronologies of business crises and depressions are seldom precisely alike.[2] To settle such doubts by appeal to the sources has been a laborious undertaking, for which few have had the time.

How much labor is required to compile a record which merits confidence can be inferred from the lists of official documents, reports, periodicals, pamphlets and books cited by Dr. Thorp and his assistants

---

[1] The use of condensed annals has been much commoner in political history than in economics. Quasi-annals are often found paralleling statistical tables, as in the "Annual Review" in the December number of the *Investor's Monthly Manual*, 1865 to date, London, and in Pixley and Abell's *Silver Circular*, London.

Annals for England for the period 1816-1841 were compiled by Thomas Michael Sadler, and reported in his biography by Robert M. Seeley, published in 1842. Annals covering the period 1821-1830 are given by William Smart in his most helpful *Economic Annals of the Nineteenth Century*, London, 1917, vol. ii, p. 571. The most extensive British annals are found in the *Final Report of the Royal Commission on Poor Law and Relief of Distress, 1909-1910* (Great Britain, Parliamentary Papers, 1909, vol. xxxvii, part vi, section 144, footnote). These annals cover the years from 1815 to 1907. Unfortunately, no source or authority is given, and a cloud is cast upon their reliability by several glaring inaccuracies, such as the placing of "Baring's crash" in 1894 instead of 1890.

For the United States, the longest table of annals is the table covering 1781 to 1922 in Otto C. Lightner's *History of Business Depressions*, New York, 1922, p. 123. These annals are phrased in meteorological terms, such as "stormy," "fair," "tornado." A brief but early series of annals, covering the years 1821 to 1832, is presented by the fiery William M. Gouge in his *Short History of Paper Money and Banking in the United States*, 4th ed., New York, 1840. Annals covering 1856 to 1893 appear in a broadside published by the *Financial Graphic*. More detailed annals for 1860 to 1922 are included in *Business Barometers* by Roger Babson, 16th ed., Wellesley Hills (Mass.), 1923.

At least two attempts have been made to compile comparable annals for several countries. The business annals of the United States, England, Germany and France, 1889-1911, are included in Wesley C. Mitchell's *Business Cycles*, Berkeley (Calif.), 1913, p. 88. The annals for the same four countries for 1867-1880 are presented by Warren M. Persons, P. M. Tuttle, and Edwin Frickey in the *Review of Economic Statistics*, preliminary volume ii, supplement, July, 1920.—Note by Willard L. Thorp.

[2] For example, the years of American depression listed by Mr. George H. Hull (*Industrial Depressions*, New York, 1911, pp. 50, 51) do not tally with the periods discussed by Mr. Otto C. Lightner in his *History of Business Depressions*, New York, 1922.

INTRODUCTION 19

as sources which they have used in dealing with the 17 countries covered.[1] Were all the publications which have been searched for information entered, the lists would be much longer. The work involves not merely much ransacking of sources likely and unlikely, but also careful weighing of the evidence. Pamphlets on questions of the day are valuable, particularly for our early years; but they often betray bias in the reporting of certain conditions. When the compiler finds differences in the views of contemporary observers, he may not be able to accept either view, or he may accept both; for sometimes the observers have different industries or different parts of a country in mind.

The American annals have been carried back to 1790, the first year after the adoption of the Constitution. To make possible international comparisons from the beginning of the American record, British annals have been compiled for the same period of 136 years. The lack of reliable sources, and, in Germany, lack of economic unity make it difficult to go back of 1840 in France, 1853 in Germany, and 1867 in Austria. The annals for these three countries are based upon drafts revised by foreign scholars, for whose generous coöperation the National Bureau expresses its hearty thanks—Professor Albert Aftalion of Paris, Dr. Robert R. Kuczynski of Berlin, and Dr. F. A. von Hayek of Vienna. To show the geographical spread of business fluctuations in recent times, it seemed desirable to add several other countries to the five included in the long-range studies. With 1890 as the starting point, Italy, the Netherlands, Sweden and Russia were chosen to represent diversified conditions in Europe. Dr. Robert F. Foerster has inspected the Italian annals, while the Russian annals were submitted to Professor N. D. Kondratieff, Director of the Conjuncture Institute of Moscow, and his colleagues Messrs. A. L. Vainstein and M. B. Ignatieff. Next, three large English-speaking colonies on three continents were included—Canada, Australia and South Africa. For expert help upon the records of the last mentioned country we are indebted to Dr. E. H. D. Arndt of Transvaal University College. To represent South America, Argentina and Brazil seemed fittest. Finally, the greatest of the Oriental civilizations were included—British India, Japan, and China.

[1] See the bibliography, Chapter xix, below.

III. The Trustworthiness of the Annals.

Despite the care exercised by the National Bureau's staff and the generous coöperation of foreign scholars, the compilers dare not believe the annals to be free from error. Indeed one who is fresh from the puzzling task of weighing many pieces of testimony, each tinted by its sponsor's personal equation, is likely to feel more uncertainty about his conclusions than does the reader. The compiler develops a standard of judgment more exacting than one who has not spent months upon such work. Results of the sort here put down in crisp phrases are as much subject to a margin of error as are statistical summaries. The analogy goes further. While no one acquainted with census enumerations (to take a familiar example) believes that we have a strictly accurate record of the growth of population in the United States since 1790, no competent critic doubts that the official figures give most valuable approximations to the unknown truth. These approximations are believed to be closer in some census years than others—the enumeration of 1870 for example seems to have been seriously defective in the Southern States. Further, the later results are certainly fuller than the earlier ones, and probably contain a lower percentage of error. So here. There are doubtless some errors in our results; these errors are doubtless more serious in some years than in others; the reliability of the results is less for the early periods than for the later periods in the same countries, and less for countries like China, Russia, or Italy than for countries like Germany, England and the United States. It is more difficult to detect the general drift of affairs in a country like British India with a wide diversity of conditions than in countries like Brazil or South Africa, where business seems to be dominated by a few well recorded factors. But, though keenly conscious of the fallibility of our sources and of our judgments concerning them, we believe that the annals form a valuable approximation to the truth.

Fortunately, there is a way of testing two samples of our results objectively. For varying periods of American and British experience, statisticians have compiled what are called "indexes of general business activity," or "indexes of the volume of trade." If these series deserve their names, the fluctuations which they show in economic activity and the business changes which our annals describe may be expected to run similar courses.

While Dr. Thorp and his assistants have made some use of

statistical tables in compiling their annals, and while the writers whose observations constitute their sources have done likewise, it is by no means a foregone conclusion that the annals and the indexes of business activity will agree closely. For the data used in making the indexes cover a much narrower range of economic activities than are represented in the annual business reviews of such sources as consular reports, the London *Economist,* Raffalovich's *Marché Financier,* or the *Financial Review.* Moreover, in so far as consuls, or editors, or our own compilers have used statistics in drawing their conclusions, they have used the data in unadjusted, or but slightly altered form. The statisticians who make business indexes, on the other hand, subject their data to an elaborate series of transformations. They compute and eliminate secular trends; often they eliminate also seasonal variations; in some cases they seek to eliminate the effects of price fluctuations. When they are combining several series, they may reduce the fluctuations of each to units of its standard deviation, and "weight" their average by the use of somewhat dubious data. As a final step they often "smooth" their curves. All these operations are quite different from those which a financial editor performs when he passes through his mind reports from many cities and many industries, and sets down his broad conclusion concerning the course of business as a whole. The statistical operations are more objective and more precise; but they deal with more limited data, and deal with them in a more circumscribed and mechanical fashion.

To all acquainted with the making of the two types of summaries, indeed, it will be clear that a comparison between the annals of business and the statistical indexes of general business activity is quite as much a test of the latter as of the former. The makers of the statistical indexes are usually careful to point out the limitations of their results, and eager to compare them with the results of other investigations. They recognize (1) that the original data are subject to varying margins of error; (2) that the technical methods of eliminating secular trends, seasonal fluctuations, and the effects of price variations are far from perfect; (3) that the residuals left in time series by these eliminations contain not merely the cyclical fluctuations, but also the effects of random factors peculiar to the series used. Even if a statistician had relatively abundant raw materials to work up, he would not claim that his results formed a strictly accurate record of changes in business conditions. In his eyes the best results he can get remain approximations, limited by the errors of the underlying data and the uncertainties of his technical methods.

But the most serious limitation is that the statistician who seeks to cover a considerable period can find but few time series fit for his purpose. The indexes of general business or volume of trade which run back of the great war must be made on one of two plans. Either they must be records of a single type of activity—like Mr. Carl Snyder's "clearings index of business"—or they must be made by averaging the fluctuations of groups of series which themselves change from time to time—like the American Telephone and Telegraph Company's "index of general business conditions," or Professor Warren M. Persons' "index of trade."

Now, no single type of transactions—not even such an inclusive type as the volume of checks cleared in all reporting towns outside of New York—can be taken to represent all the important phases of business activity. The payments made by check in the towns which have no clearing houses, and the payments made in coin and paper money may undergo fluctuations which differ in amplitude and timing from the fluctuations of clearings. That is merely a doubt concerning the faithfulness with which clearings represent changes in total payments. Far more important is the certainty that the volume of payments made by check within a given period undergoes fluctuations materially different from the fluctuations which are taking place in the volume of goods produced, shipped, or consumed, and different from the fluctuations in employment, the disbursing of income, and the purchasing of consumers' goods. Yet the latter processes are quite as much a part of the fluctuations of business as is the former.

The indexes made by averaging the fluctuations of several series represent a wider range of activities. But the activities which can be included are those for which a statistical record happens to have been made for a relatively long period—not the activities which a statistician would choose were he planning an index. Moreover, the changes in the lists of series which are available for successive decades raise grave questions about the comparability of the results for the earlier and the later years covered. Finally, there are puzzling questions about the interpretation of a composite made by averaging the fluctuations of series so different as (say) price indexes, values of goods imported, and tons of pig iron produced.

INTRODUCTION

What we have in our business annals and our indexes of general business conditions, then, are different approaches to the problem of recording the fluctuations of economic activities—approaches each of which has its uncertainties as well as its merits. We cannot expect them to agree perfectly. When they disagree we cannot say that the discrepancy necessarily means error in one or all; it may mean merely that the different activities reflected by the various approaches really did not change in quite the same way. But if we find a general consilience among the results we shall feel increased confidence in the reliability of both approaches, and may regard the occasional discrepancies as presenting genuine problems from the study of which fresh knowledge may be gained.

The charts which follow offer as graphic a comparison as can well be made between our annals and the leading American and British indexes of general trade which cover considerable periods. In the column for each year is entered a brief characterization of business conditions drawn from the annals, and above are plotted the index curves.[1] The curves show cyclical fluctuations above and below the moving base traced by the monthly ordinates of the secular trends of the time series used (corrected when necessary for seasonal variations). Since these ordinates are assigned the value of zero or 100 in the computations, they fall in the chart upon a horizontal line, which may be called the base.

In studying the charts, we must bear in mind that they do not do full justice either to the statistical method of presenting changes in business or to the annals. It is a commonplace that no statistical average represents adequately the array of data from which it is computed. Just so, the catchwords used to summarize the annals do not represent adequately Dr. Thorp's records. Much more than the charts show can be learned by examining the series combined to make the indexes of business conditions, and by reading the fuller form of the annals. In confining our comparison to the most abstract and symbolic summaries of the two sets of materials, we are imposing a severe test of conformity.

[1] For the methods followed in making the two American indexes used in Chart 1, see M. C. Rorty, "The Statistical Control of Business Activities," *Harvard Business Review*, January, 1923, vol. 1, pp. 154-166, and Carl Snyder, "A New Clearings Index of Business for Fifty Years," *Journal of the American Statistical Association*, September, 1924, vol. xix, pp. 329-335.

For the recent items in the two series, we are indebted respectively to Mr. Seymour L. Andrew, Chief Statistician of the American Telephone and Telegraph Company, and to Mr. Snyder of the Federal Reserve Bank of New York.

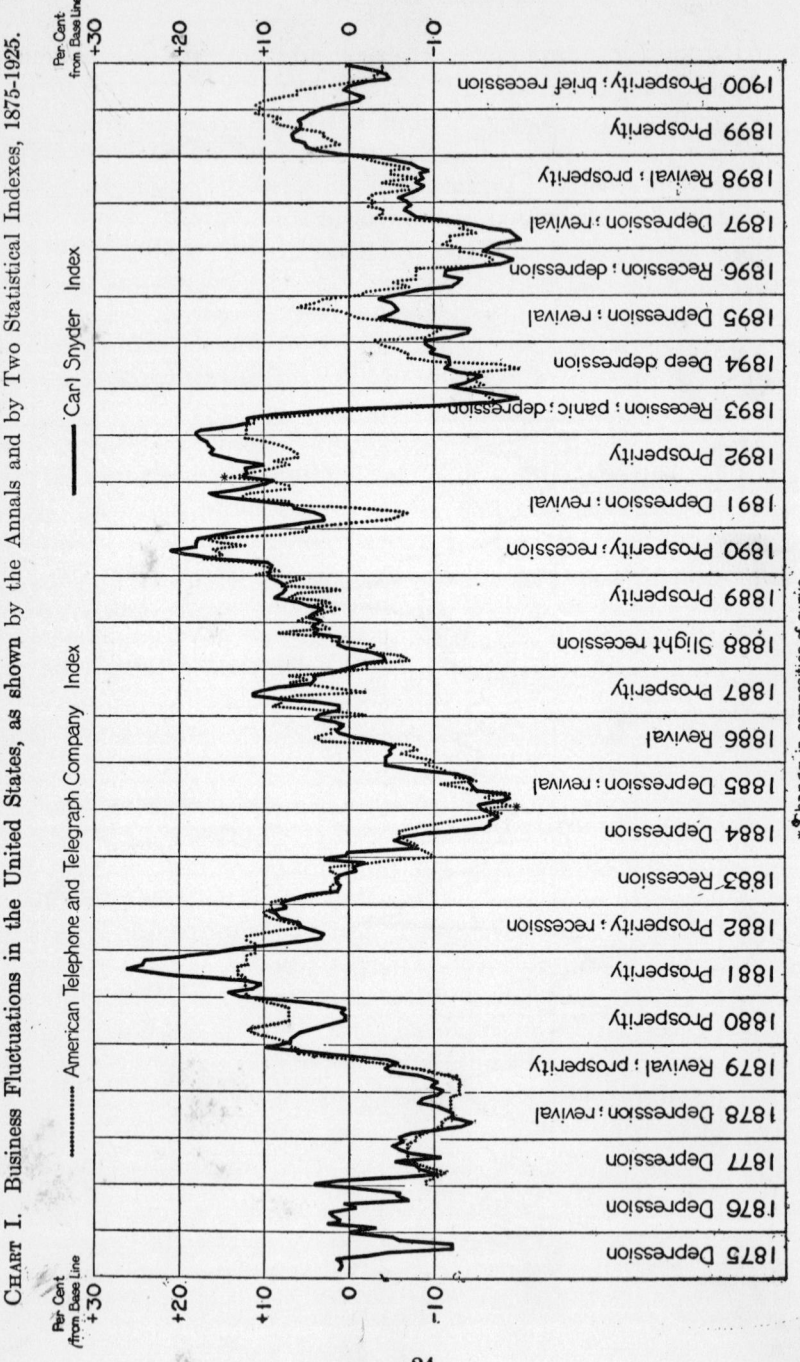

CHART I. Business Fluctuations in the United States, as shown by the Annals and by Two Statistical Indexes, 1875-1925.

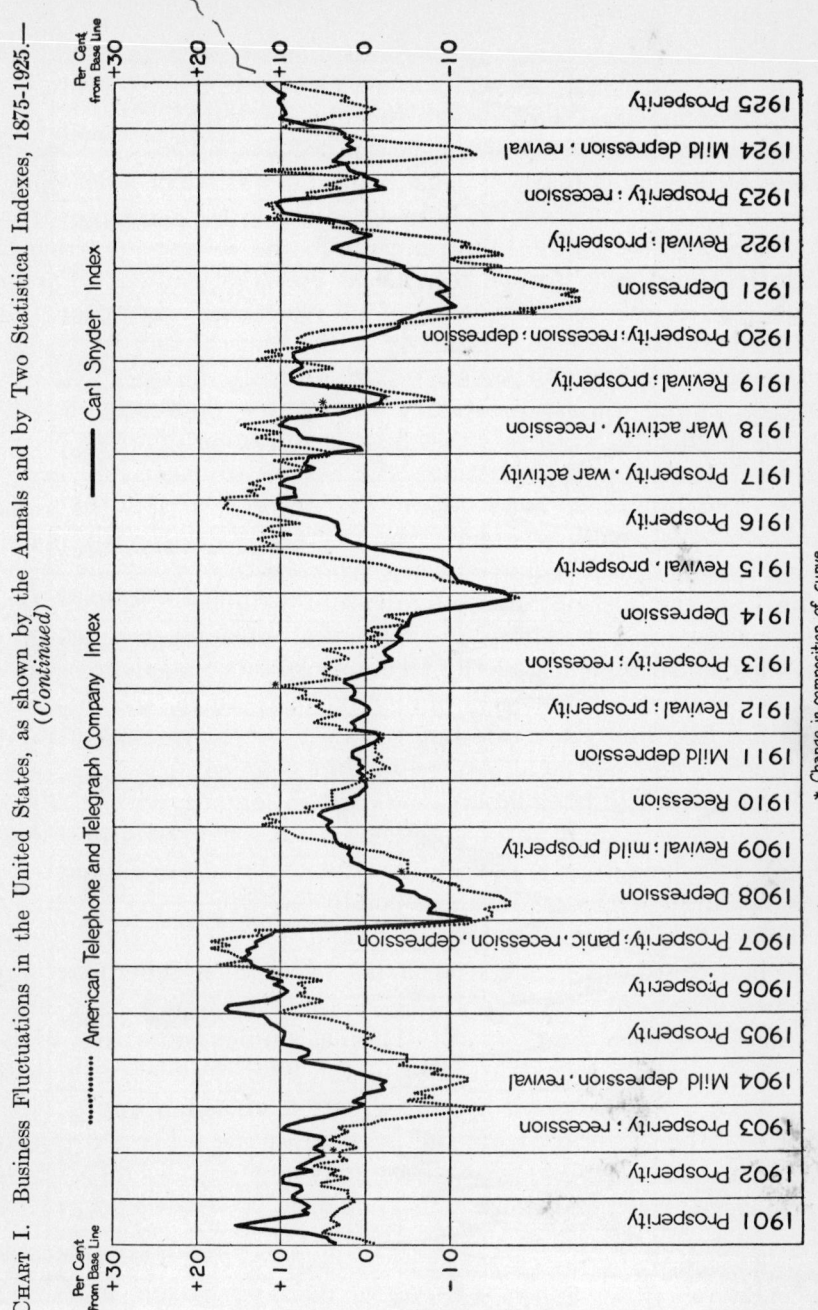

CHART I. Business Fluctuations in the United States, as shown by the Annals and by Two Statistical Indexes, 1875-1925.—(Continued)

On the American chart the correspondence between the annals and the two statistical indexes is very close. Indeed, there are no serious discrepancies. To be more specific, the annals show 13 business recessions, mild or severe, between 1875 and 1924. Every one of these recessions is marked in both of the statistical indexes by a decline in the curve. These declines are slight in the recessions which the annals describe as mild, and abrupt in the recessions which the annals (in their fuller form) describe as crises or panics.[1] Further, the two curves give joint evidence of no recessions other than those mentioned by the annals. Similarly with other phases of the successive cycles. When the annals report revivals the curves ascend; when the annals report prosperity the curves fluctuate on levels decidedly higher than in the preceding or following depressions, and when the annals report depressions the curves are relatively low.

The chief difference between the two records is that the annals show but vaguely and irregularly the degrees of prosperity and depression attained in successive cycles, whereas the curves necessarily deviate from the horizontal base by definite distances. Finally, there are indications in the American chart that business commentators are influenced in their use of the terms prosperity and depression by recent experience. From such subjective waverings, the statistical indices are exempt. But this point comes out more clearly in the British chart, and will be discussed in that connection.

For opportunity to compare the British annals with a British index, the National Bureau is indebted to Dr. Dorothy Swaine Thomas, who generously put at our disposal before publication a series showing changes in business conditions from 1855 to 1913 by quarters.[2] This index, like the "A. T. and T." index for the United States, is a composite made from a list of series which reflect various types of economic activity. Since these materials have grown more abundant with the years, Dr. Thomas's index represents British business as a whole more faithfully in the later decades than in the earlier ones. But of course the introduction of a new series with a numerical value different from the average of the other components of the index produces changes which may not correspond with the changes in business conditions.

[1] On the use of these three terms in the annals to suggest the varying character of the transitions from prosperity to depression, see below, pp. 34-37.
[2] See "An Index of British Business Cycles," by Dorothy S. Thomas, *Journal of the American Statistical Association*, March, 1926, vol. xxi, pp. 60-63.

INTRODUCTION 27

On the whole, the correspondence between the British annals and the British index is close, though not so close as in the American comparison. Dr. Thomas's curve usually rises when the annals report revival, stands high when the annals report prosperity, sinks when the annals report recession, and runs on a low level when the annals report depression. But there are exceptions to the rule which require comment.

(1) Judging from the curve, one would expect the annals to report a recession of British business in 1860-61. These years present an unusually mixed state of affairs. As a result of the American Civil War, the cotton textile industry suffered severely from scarcity of raw material. But reports from other trades do not indicate that there was a general recession of activity. On the contrary, most industries seem to have been very active. In the fuller form of the annals these facts are succinctly stated. For his two-word summary Dr. Thorp could find no phrase which seemed more accurate than "uneven prosperity", a phrase which he uses in all cases when most industries are thriving, but one or more important trades are depressed by special circumstances. The statistics available to Dr. Thomas for the 1860's are data in which the cotton industry counts heavily. Hence her curve drops abruptly.

(2) In 1874-75 the annals report depression while Dr. Thomas's curve, though declining, is still above the base line. In 1881, 1897-98 and 1910-11 the annals report "mild prosperity" or "prosperity", while Dr. Thomas's curve is slightly below or but slightly above the base line. Perhaps these differences between the statistical record and the annals are due in part to defects in the data at Dr. Thomas's disposal, or to the technical difficulties of eliminating secular trends. But it is probable that they indicate one of the characteristic defects of business annals. In judging current business conditions, everyone is influenced by comparisons with recent experience. When business has been notably good for several years, as it had been in England during the early 1870's, and then grows slack, a commentator will say that business is depressed, though the volume of trade still remains large. Similarly, after business has passed through a period of hard times, commentators are likely to hail as prosperity any substantial increase of activity. In short, men's judgments upon business conditions belong among the social phenomena which are influenced by business cycles. As a summary of current opinion about

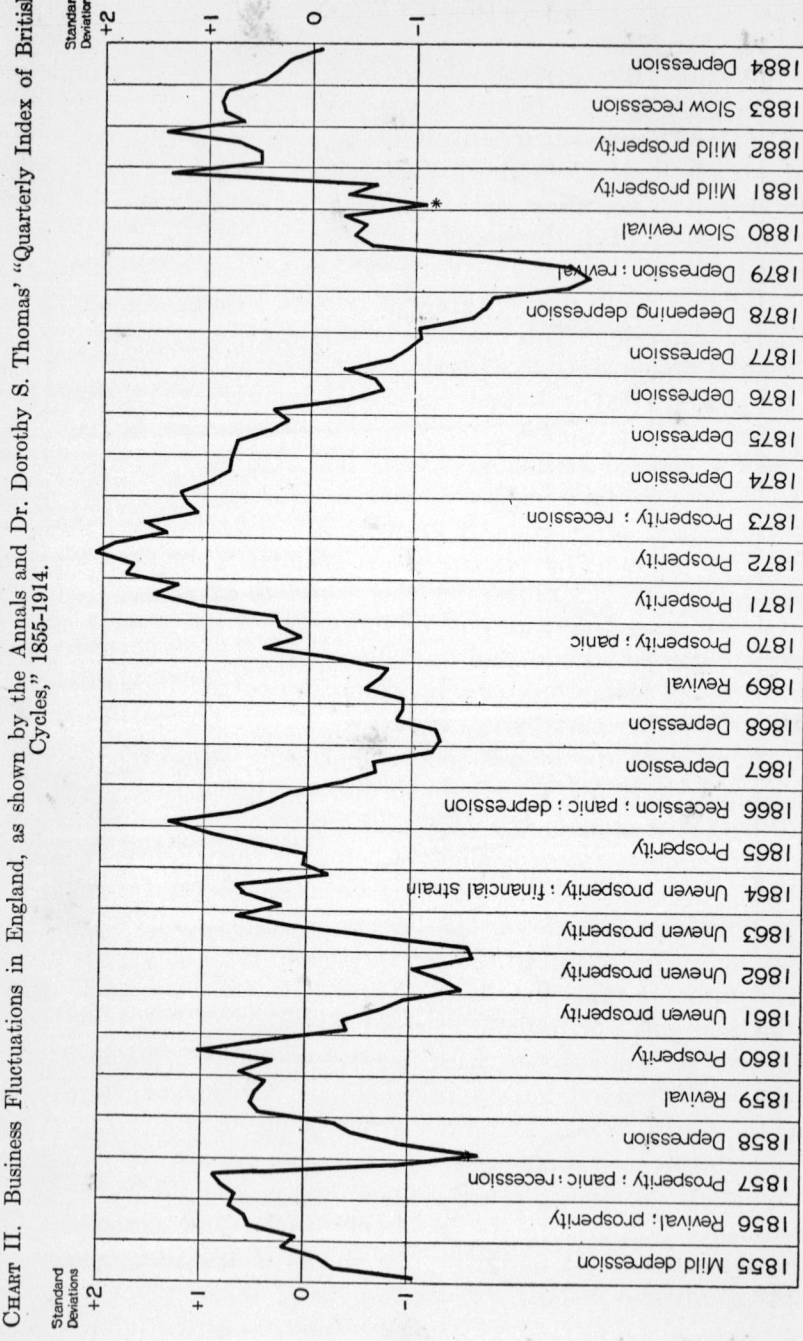

CHART II. Business Fluctuations in England, as shown by the Annals and Dr. Dorothy S. Thomas' "Quarterly Index of British Cycles," 1855-1914.

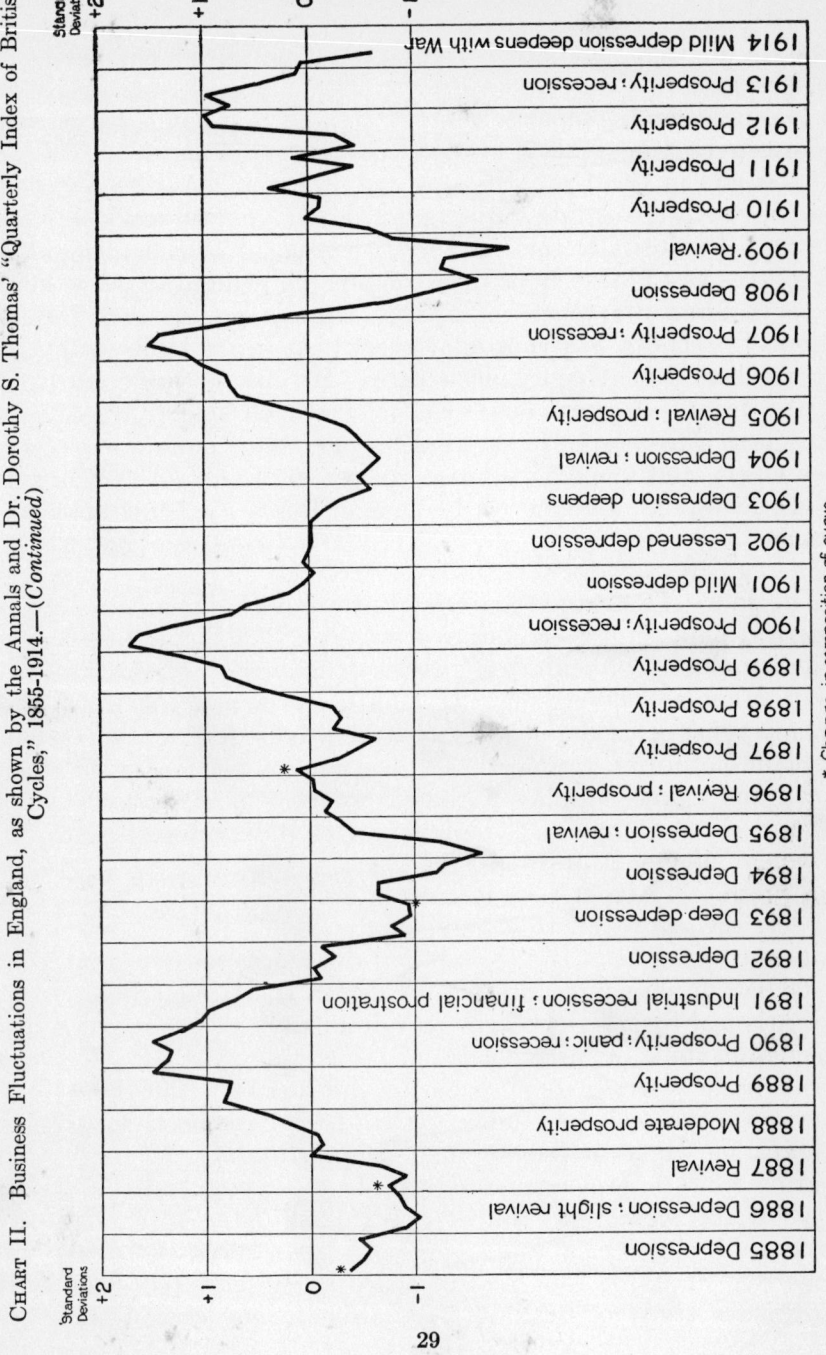

CHART II. Business Fluctuations in England, as shown by the Annals and Dr. Dorothy S. Thomas' "Quarterly Index of British Cycles," 1855-1914.—(Continued)

* Change in composition of curve

the state of trade, our annals reflect these subjective changes in the use of terms.

The preceding comparisons cover periods and countries in which business reporting is well developed. Presumably the annals for earlier years in the United States and England, and the annals for countries with a less integrated organization, contain a wider margin of error. But usually there is such a consensus of judgment among the sources as to leave little doubt about the general tenor of affairs. In years when differences of opinion appear among contemporary writers, Dr. Thorp has consulted every source available to him and has weighed the evidence with care. He has endeavored also to use the technical terms employed in characterizing different states of business as consistently as possible. Yet the results are subject to emendation, and readers who discover errors of any sort are urged to let the National Bureau of Economic Research benefit by their acumen.

The most satisfactory materials for studying business cycles are statistical data—not mere business indexes, like those shown in the preceding charts, but numerous series of materials, of the sort given in our other collection, showing month by month the fluctuations of many types of economic activity—the production of raw materials, the manufacture of producers' and consumers' goods, transportation by rail and water, supplies on hand, orders booked, sales by wholesale and retail merchants, employment in different trades, the disbursement of money incomes, the prices of all kinds of goods from farm produce to securities, interest rates, bank loans, deposits and reserves, the turnover of money, profits, bankruptcies, new investments and so on. But the periods and the places for which such data can be had in abundance are few. Even in the United States, where the statistical record is perhaps as full as anywhere, data have been collected on some of these heads only since the great war. Few even of the basic series extend back to the 1870's. Hardly a dozen American cycles can be studied by statistical methods with respect to more than three or four of their manifestations. In England the situation is much as it is in America. In other countries the number of cycles for which any but the scantiest data can be found is smaller still.

Narrow limits of time and of space are thus drawn around the quantitative study of business fluctuations. One cannot trace back business cycles to their beginnings in any country of Europe by the aid of figures. Nor can one trace in figures the spread of business cycles to countries which are just beginning to standardize their economic life on the European pattern. For the compilation of abundant statistics of business activities does not begin in any country until the business activities themselves have become highly organized. That comes later than business cycles.

According to the logic of the statistical method, this limitation of the number of cycles for which data have been preserved is most serious. The statistician's art, as practiced in the social sciences, consists in establishing generalizations about variable phenomena by the analysis of an array of cases. When his cases are few, no elaboration of technique can enable the statistician to generalize with security. Business cycles are both highly complex and highly variable phenomena, and statistical inferences concerning them must be taken as tentative until the number of cases available for analysis has grown decidedly larger than at present.

Under these circumstances it is well to learn all that we can from the annals of business. In countries like the United States and England these annals cover at least twice as many cycles as are covered by more than a few statistical series. In countries where statistics are in their infancy, the annals give us some insight into the course of developments. Precision, of course, cannot be had from descriptive accounts; but the annals speak in terms of more and less, they mark off turning points in business trends, they compare in general terms the contemporary fortunes of different countries. Taken, not as a rival, but as a supplement of statistical analysis, an attempt to find the characteristics of business cycles as shown by the longer and wider record of the annals has its value. Indeed, it will appear that there are certain fundamental problems concerning business cycles which can be answered more certainly by studying the annals than by analyzing the statistics now available.

IV. The Cyclical Character of Business Fluctuations.

1. THE "NORMAL STATE OF TRADE" A FIGMENT.

The broadest conclusion established by the long and wide experience covered by the annals is that there is no "normal state of trade". The phrase is common both in treatises upon economic theory and in the talk of business men. Yet the historical record shows no reality corresponding to this figment of the imagination.

If "normal" is interpreted to mean usual, prevailing, that which exists in the absence of grave "disturbing causes", the annals show that the only normal condition is a state of change—which is not what the phrase means to those who use it. From England in 1790 to China in 1925, from Sweden to Australia, the tables reveal incessant fluctuations. Frequently the word "prosperity" is used in the annals of some country for several years in succession. But "depression" occurs in series perhaps as often. And in a less condensed summary both of these catchwords would be qualified always, as they often are qualified even in these tables, by adjectives indicating that the prosperity or depression is waxing or waning.

If "normal" means, not that which usually does prevail, but that which we think should prevail, it is equally a figment—though one of a useful kind. There are good reasons for trying to decide what phase of business cycles is most conducive to social welfare; for seeking ways to make that phase last longer and to mitigate departures from it. But when such is the meaning in mind, a less ambiguous word than "normal" should be used.

An additional source of confusion and therefore an additional reason for avoiding the word is supplied by the slipshod practice of business-cycle statisticians, who sometimes write "normal" when they mean "average", and sometimes write "normal" when they mean the course marked by the ordinates of a secular trend.

2. Use of the Term "Cycle".

While the annals show that business is subject to continual fluctuations, they also show that in no country are the alternations of expansion and contraction highly regular. Is it justifiable, then, to speak of these fluctuations as business "cycles"?

That of course is a question regarding the proper use of a technical term. In 1922, President John C. Merriam of the Carnegie Institution called "A Conference on Cycles", in which representatives of several sciences discussed the cyclical phenomena with which they deal. To prevent misunderstandings the conferees needed a definition of cycles applicable alike in meteorology, botany, geology, paleontology, astronomy, geography and economics. Subsequent discussion showed that the definition given by the first speaker, Dr. F. E. Clements, commended itself to the others.

In general scientific use (said Dr. Clements) the word (cycle) denotes a recurrence of different phases of plus and minus departures, which are often susceptible of exact measurement. It has no necessary relation to a definite time interval, though this is frequently a characteristic of astronomical cycles. Apart from the familiar cycles of the day, the lunar month, and the year, the one best known is the sun-spot recurrence, to which the term cycle is almost universally applied. This furnishes convincing evidence that the significance of the term resides in the fact of recurrence rather than in that of the time interval, since the sun-spot cycle has varied in length from 7 to 17 years since 1788, while the minimum-maximum phase has ranged from 3 to 5 years and the maximum-minimum phase from 6 to 8 years since 1833. In consequence, it seems desirable to use cycle as the inclusive term for all recurrences that lend themselves to measurement, and period or periodicity for those with a definite time interval, recognizing, however, that there is no fixed line between the two.[1]

Now our annals show beyond doubt "a recurrence of different phases" in business activity, and these recurrences "lend themselves to measurement". Hence we have ample warrant in the usages of other sciences than economics for applying the term "cycles" to business fluctuations. But the term "periodicity" we should not use with reference to business cycles, or with reference to crises. For the time intervals between crises are far from regular. They vary, as will appear presently, even more than the length of sun-spot cycles.

3. THE PHASES OF BUSINESS CYCLES.

The different phases which recur in business activity are sometimes treated as only two—depression and prosperity. More often there are said to be three phases which recur in the order prosperity, crisis, depression.[2] But if the transition from prosperity to depression is recognized as a separate phase, it seems logical to give similar recognition to the transition from depression to prosperity. Then we

[1] "Report of a Conference on Cycles," *The Geographical Review*, Special Supplement, October, 1923, vol. xiii, pp. 657, 658.
[2] Compare for example, Dr. E. H. Vögel's description of a cycle, *Die Theorie des volkswirtschaftlichen Entwickelungsprozesses und das Krisenproblem*, Vienna, 1917, pp. 31, 32.

have a four-phase cycle of prosperity, crisis, depression, and revival.[1] Professor Warren M. Persons goes further still. By dividing the transition from prosperity to depression into "financial strain" and "industrial crisis", he gets five phases.[2]

This process of subdivision can be carried further indefinitely as statistics with brief time intervals become more abundant. And as knowledge of the subject grows and its practical applications become more important, there may be call for such refinements. As matters stand, however, four phases satisfy the needs of systematic inquiry. The separation of the phase of "financial strain" from that of "industrial crisis" rests on logical quite as much as upon chronological grounds, and is somewhat confusing in a cycle of recurrence in time. Phases of financial strain occur every now and then at other stages of the cycle than the transition from prosperity to depression, and industrial reactions have occurred when it is difficult to find any trace of preceding financial strain, for example, in the United States in 1923. But we are trenching upon a topic which requires separate treatment.

4. "Crises" and "Recessions".

Concerning only one of the four phases of the cycle here recognized are there doubts regarding its character, or its place in the order of recurrence. Rather curiously, this doubtful phase is the one which earliest attracted attention and which has been most studied.

Two quite distinct conceptions of business crises are current in recent books. Professor Aftalion, for example, defines the crisis as "the point of intersection . . . at which prosperity passes over into depression".[3] Professor Bouniatian, to give a corresponding example of the second usage, applies the term "to an organic disturbance of economic life, bringing upon a large number of enterprisers loss of fortune and income or complete economic ruin".[4]

From this difference of definition there follow differences in the lists of crisis recognized in various books, and hence differences in the

---

[1] These four phases were recognized and separately described as long ago as 1867 by John Mills, "On Credit Cycles, and the Origin of Commercial Panics," *Transactions of the Manchester Statistical Society*, 1867-68, pp. 5-40.
[2] See Professor Persons' numerous articles in the *Review of Economics Statistics*, and his *Measuring and Forecasting General Business Conditions*, New York, 1920, p. 34.
[3] Albert Aftalion, *Les Crises Périodiques de Surproduction*, Paris, 1913, vol. i, Preface, p. vi.
[4] Mentor Bouniatian, *Les Crises Économiques*, Paris, 1922, p. 31.

INTRODUCTION

average intervals asserted to lie between crises. Professor Lescure, who antedated Aftalion in defining crisis as the point of intersection between prosperity and depression, includes the crisis of 1913 in his historical section. But Bouniatian admits no crisis between 1907 and 1920, and quite consistently; for, as Lescure himself explains, there was no epidemic of bankruptcies in 1913.[1] Tugan-Baranovski goes even further than Bouniatian in stressing the violence of crises, and consequently in shortening his list of crisis dates. A crisis "breaks out like a tempest" in the midst of prosperity, "bringing bankruptcies, unemployment, misery, etc." With this conception in mind, he quite rightly says that England escaped a crisis in 1873, in 1882, in 1890, in 1900 and in 1907—though the "industrial cycle" shows itself in the evolution of English business in these later times "with the same neatness and clarity as before".[2]

Which of these two conceptions of the crisis fits better in a discussion of business cycles is easy to decide. What concerns such a discussion is the recurrence of certain phases of business activity. The transition from prosperity to depression is one of the regularly recurring phases, whether it is marked by "an organic disturbance of economic life", in Bouniatian's phrase, or whether financial strain is conspicuous by its absence.

But while there is no doubt about the reality of these transitions, there is grave doubt whether the word crisis should be retained to describe them. For with that word there is associated in the public mind, as in the minds of writers like Bouniatian and Tugan-Baranovski, the idea of financial strain. When such strain is scarcely perceptible, it is confusing to call the transition a crisis. Close study of the annals shows that transitions free from strain are frequent—perhaps more frequent than violent transitions. And there are cheering indications that the preponderance of mild transitions is growing greater.

To make the confusion worse, the annals report numerous cases of financial strain, not at the moment when prosperity is passing into depression, but in other phases of the cycle. "Financial stringency" and "bourse panics" are common phenomena in "booms", often occurring a year or two before the phase of expansion in general business ends. Less remembered, but not less important, are the

[1] Lescure, *Des Crises Générales et Périodiques de Surproduction*, 3rd ed., Paris, 1923, pp. 2 and 238-253; Bouniatian, as cited above, pp. 43, 44.
[2] Michel Tugan-Baranovski, *Les Crises Industrielles en Angleterre*, Paris, 1913, pp. 34, 150, 152, 166, 167, 174.

cases of financial strain coming in periods of depression. To cite a dozen examples, the annals make such reports for France in 1861, Germany in 1877, England in 1878, Argentina in 1891, Australia and Russia in 1892, Italy and the Netherlands in 1893, the United States in 1896 (as well as in 1819 and 1884), South Africa in 1898, Japan in 1901, and China in 1912. Often the sources from which the annals are drawn use the words "crisis" or "panic" in describing these episodes of depression, and sometimes they use "crisis" as equivalent to depression itself.

"Crisis", then, is a poor term to use in describing one of the four phases of business cycles. If it is to be retained, it must be defined in the colorless fashion of Lescure and Aftalion—as the mere point of intersection between prosperity and depression. But sad experience shows how much misunderstanding comes from the effort to use familiar words in new technical senses. Scientific writers can hardly expect that readers will purge their minds of old associations and form new ones at a terminologist's bidding.

One remedy for the ambiguity of "crisis" is to apply a qualifying adjective whenever the word is used. Thus Mr. Joseph Kitchin distinguishes between major and minor crises. But his major crises are in some cases such mild transitions that many writers refuse to call them crises at all. Such is the case with the American crises of 1882 and 1899 (*sic*, the date should be 1900), and the English crisis of 1913, all of which Mr. Kitchin labels "major".[1] Thus his conception of a major crisis is even more confusing to non-technical readers than the use of the unqualified term. If the ambiguity is to be remedied by applying adjectives, it seems best to use a pair that bear directly upon the ambiguous point. Thus the common expressions "mild crisis" and "severe crisis" are clear in intent and safe to use in descriptive work, such as business annals, provided there are not too many cases on the borderline between mildness and severity.

But no set of adjectives can make "crisis" a suitable name for the fourth phase of business cycles. Hardly can one say "depression, revival, prosperity, mild or severe crisis". The choice lies between retaining crisis defined in an unfamiliar way, or replacing it by some word corresponding to "revival", which is used to designate the upward turn of the cycle. This second alternative seems the lesser evil,

[1] See the "Dates of Major Crises" in Mr. Kitchin's paper, "Cycles and Trends in Economic Factors," *Review of Economic Statistics*, January, 1923, Prel. vol. v, pp. 10-16.

INTRODUCTION 37

especially in view of the fact that our theoretical and practical interests lie increasingly in those mild transitions from prosperity to depression which have been little attended to by theorists.

In this discussion, accordingly, business cycles are treated as having four phases—depression, revival, prosperity and recession. The word "crisis" is not dropped, but is used like the words "panic" or "boom" to indicate degrees of intensity. Every business cycle includes a phase of recession; this recession may or may not be marked by a crisis; the crisis, if there is one, may or may not degenerate into a panic. All the old and most of the recent books on the subject deal chiefly with crises, panics, and severe depressions; these annals endeavor to show also the mild recessions and the periods of dull business.

We have, indeed, gone far—we hope not too far—in calling attention to the mild recessions. Our aim has been to include all cases in which the evidence indicates a general slackening of activity, even though the slackening lasted but a few months, and did not reach grave proportions. Cases in point may be found in the American annals for 1888, 1900 and 1923. Other illustrations are Italy in 1900, England in 1803 and 1854, and the brief reaction in the majority of our 17 countries after the Armistice of 1918. On the other hand, we have tried not to include cases in which only one or two branches of business suffered a setback—such as the British case of 1860-61 already referred to, or the financial difficulties caused in London by the outbreak of war between France and Prussia in 1870.

5. The Uniformity and the Variability of Business Cycles.

Recurrence of depression, revival, prosperity and recession, time after time in land after land, may be the chief conclusion drawn from the experience packed into our annals; but a second conclusion is that no two recurrences in all the array seem precisely alike. Business cycles differ in their duration as wholes and in the relative duration of their component phases; they differ in industrial and geographical scope; they differ in intensity; they differ in the features which attain prominence; they differ in the quickness and the uniformity with which they sweep from one country to another.

This mixture of uniformity and variability in business cycles may seem disconcerting when stated so baldly. But we confront a similar mixture of fundamental similarity and detailed differences when we visualize men's faces, or consider their characters, or study any social phenomena. In all such cases, variability presents conceptual difficulties not to be glossed over, and difficulties of explanation not surmounted as yet. But uncounted ages ago men found that they could think of pines despite difference in the size, shape, location, color, roughness, and hardness of particular specimens; they could think of trees despite the differences among pines, maples and palms, and the difficulty of delimiting trees from shrubs. And within the past hundred years men have developed a technique for studying variations about a central tendency, a technique which reveals the existence of formerly unsuspected uniformities among variations themselves.

Differences among business cycles, then, afford no reason for doubting that these cycles constitute a valid species of phenomena. But the existence of such differences should put us on our guard against using concepts and methods of analysis appropriate only in work where differences among individuals of a given species either do not exist or can be precisely defined (as in geometry), or are not significant for the problems under consideration (as in certain branches of physics and chemistry). The student of business cycles should picture their characteristic differences as clearly as may be, measure them with what precision he can, and find how these differences are distributed around their central tendencies. While the annals are not quantitative in form, they can be used to some extent in treating this statistical problem.

V. The Duration of Business Cycles.

1. Current Estimates of Average Length.

The differences among business cycles which have attracted most attention are differences in duration. Quite naturally, the discoverers of the recurrence overstressed its uniformity in this respect as in others. Influenced by the dominant type of economic theory, these discoverers thought of a "normal" cycle and so simplified their problem—a practice still common. To cite an extreme example: in 1867 John Mills described the "credit cycle" as lasting ten years—three years of declining trade, three years of increasing trade, three years of over-excited trade, and one year of crisis.[1] Even the early statis-

[1] "On Credit Cycles and the Origin of Commercial Panics," *Transactions of the Manchester Statistical Society*, 1867–68, pp. 5–40. Compare the diagram of a cycle which Jevons gives in his *Primer of Political Economy*, New York, 1882, p. 121.

tical workers yielded to the lure of "normality." They were eager to establish the "periodicity of crises," which was suggested by such crisis dates as 1815, 1825, 1836, 1847, 1857 and 1866. This desire warped their selection and treatment of data. Jevons had an admirably candid mind; yet in 1875, when the sun-spot cycle was supposed to last 11.1 years, he was able to get from Thorold Rogers' *History of Agriculture and Prices in England* a period of 11 years in price fluctuations, and when the sun-spot cycle was revised to 10.45 years he was able to make the average interval between English crises 10.466 years.[1] To get this later result, Jevons purposely left out from his list of crises "a great commercial collapse in 1810-11 (which will not fit into the decennial series)"; he also omitted the crisis of 1873, and inserted a crisis in 1878, which other writers do not find.[2]

Jevons' way of reckoning the length of cycles by the intervals between crises, and of counting as crises periods of financial strain coming after booms, or recessions followed by long depressions, is still common among theoretical writers. The results they get are not in close agreement. Tugan-Baranovski takes 7 to 11 years as the limits of variation in the length of cycles and 10 years as the average duration. Bouniatian says that "under normal conditions" cycles last from 9 to 11 years, but adds that there is "a tendency toward a normal period of about 10 years". Cassel takes 1873, 1882, 1890, 1900, and 1907 as crisis years in Europe, and 1873, 1882, 1893, 1903, and 1907 as crisis years in the United States. Cassel himself strikes no average, but his dates give limits of 4 to 11 years and an average of 8½ years. Lavington also accepts 8 years as the average duration.

Slightly different is the method of reckoning cycles by the intervals between depressions. Otto C. Lightner records 18 depressions in American business from 1808 to 1921, not counting "minor" cases, with intervals ranging from 3 to 12 years and averaging 6⅔ years. George H. Hull, denying that depressions are periodic, counts 17 "industrial crises" in the United States from 1814 to 1907. His dates differ somewhat from Lightner's, having intervals ranging from 1 to 11 years, and averaging a little less than 6 years.

[1] Jevons withdrew his first paper from publication when he discovered "that periods of 3, 5, 7, 9, or even 13 years would agree with Professor Rogers' data just as well as a period of 11 years." See his *Investigations in Currency and Finance*, London, 1884, pp. 207, 225.

[2] See the three papers on crises reprinted in Jevons' *Investigations in Currency and Finance*, especially pp. 200-203, 225, 233.

With these results may be given two others of the same order of magnitude, but reached by quite different methods. Pigou, using British unemployment returns and measuring intervals between both the crests and the troughs of the industrial waves, gets a trifle less than 8 years as his average length. Henry L. Moore also gets 8 years as the standard length both of "generating" and of "derived economic cycles", but gets it from periodigram analysis of time-series.[1]

Other statistical workers have recently reached quite different conclusions. Thus Professor W. L. Crum made a periodigram analysis of monthly interest rates upon commercial paper in New York from 1866 to 1922 and found (somewhat doubtful) evidence of a period of 39-40 months in their fluctuations. At the same time Mr. Joseph Kitchin, after analyzing bank clearings, interest rates, and wholesale prices in Great Britain and the United States from 1890 to 1922, suggested that the cyclical fluctuations of trade are composed of minor cycles averaging 40 months in length, and major cycles, which are aggregates of two or less often, of three minor cycles.[2] Since the publication of these two papers in January, 1923, "the 40-month cycle" has enjoyed a considerable vogue among statisticians.

2. Measurements Based upon the Annals.

It is not necessary to examine narrowly the discrepancies among the results obtained by measuring the intervals between years of crisis or years of depression. They run back partly to differences in the countries and the periods covered, and partly to differences of opinion concerning the severity which entitles a particular disturbance to be called a true crisis or depression. Granted each author his own conception of what constitutes a cycle, his measurements are presumably correct for the land and period covered. By using the present annals, anyone so disposed might validate, and anyone so disposed might question any of the averages and limits of variations which have been derived in this way.

[1] See M. Tugan-Baranovski, *Les Crises Industrielles en Angleterre,* 1913, pp. 247, 248; M. Bouniatian, *Les Crises Économiques,* 1922, p. 42; G. Cassel, *The Theory of Social Economy,* 1924, p. 508; A. Aftalion, *Les Crises Périodiques de Surproduction,* 1913, vol. i, pp. 8-14; F. Lavington, *The Trade Cycle,* 1922, p. 14; O. C. Lightner, *History of Business Depressions,* 1922, table of contents; G. H. Hull, *Industrial Depressions,* 1911, pp. 54-57, and the chronological table, pp. 50, 51; A. C. Pigou, *The Economics of Welfare,* 1920, p. 804; Henry L. Moore, *Generating Economic Cycles,* 1923, pp. 15, 64.

[2] See W. L. Crum, "Cycles of Rates on Commercial Paper," *Review of Economic Statistics,* January, 1923, preliminary vol. v, pp. 17-28; Joseph Kitchin, "Cycles and Trends in Economic Factors," the same, pp. 10-16.

INTRODUCTION

But anyone who reads the annals closely, whatever the definition of crisis in his mind, will see that there is grave question regarding the unity of many of the 6-, or 8-, or 10-year cycles. Take as the simplest example Professor Cassel's list of crisis years in the United States: 1873, 1882, 1893, 1903 and 1907. One may argue that the annals justify these dates from Cassel's viewpoint. But the important point is that the cycle from 1882 to 1893 was punctuated by the recessions of 1888 and 1890, and that the cycle from 1893 to 1903 was punctuated by recessions both in 1896 and in 1900.

Now, the differences of opinion concerning the length of American cycles in this period turn less on the facts of business expansion and contraction than on what movements of expansion and contraction should be selected for treatment as business cycles. The older writers fastened upon the salient phenomena—severe crises and the rather long intervals between them—as requiring explanation. This tradition still rules in theoretical treatises. But as knowledge of business cycles grows, and as men seek to use this knowledge more effectively in interpreting current developments month by month, a more intensive treatment becomes both feasible and useful. Without denying the graver importance of the wider swings, we find ourselves involved much of the time in dealing with fluctuations of less amplitude, fluctuations which the theorists have passed over lightly. The same developments which make it wise to substitute the concept of recession for the concept of crisis make it wise to recognize the shorter segments into which the long swings are frequently divisible. This change reduces the typical duration of American cycles to roughly one-half of the estimate commonest among theoretical writers.

By way of illustration, we may compile from the American annals a list of recessions in the United States since 1790. In this list the recessions are characterized by phrases which indicate their severity, and leading features. Financial troubles occurring in the middle of depressions are not counted as recessions, but cases of this sort which have commonly been listed as crises are noted in the table.[1] In the early years the business fortunes of the northern states alone are followed; sometimes conditions were quite different in the agricultural south and west. Since the annals seldom permit a precise dating

[1] Other cases of financial troubles while business was depressed occurred in 1797, 1819, 1842, and 1914.

of recessions, the duration of successive cycles is reckoned to the nearest whole year.

TABLE 1

BUSINESS RECESSIONS IN THE UNITED STATES AND APPROXIMATE DURATION OF BUSINESS CYCLES, 1790–1925

		Duration of Cycles in Years			Duration of Cycles in Years
1796 *	Financial crisis, spring.....		1865	Recession, second quarter, close of Civil War	5
1802	Recession early in year....	6	1870	Recession, January	5
1807 *	Recession late in year.....	6	1873 *	Violent panic, September..	4
1812	Brief recession, June, War with England	5	1882	Recession late in year, financial panic in 1884 *....	9
1815 *	Crisis, March, following peace	3	1888	Slight recession, early in year	5
1822	Mild recession, May.......	7	1890	Financial crisis, autumn....	3
1825 *	Panic, autumn	3	1893 *	Severe panic, May........	2
1828	Recession, summer	3	1896	Recession early in year, financial stringency	3
1833	Recession, panic, autumn..	5	1900	Brief and slight recession, spring	4
1837 *	Panic, spring	4	1903 *	Financial strain, spring....	3
1839 *	Panic, October	3	1907 *	Severe crisis, autumn......	4
1845	Brief recession, May	6	1910	Mild recession, January....	2
1846	Mild recession early in year, War with Mexico	1	1913 *	Recession, summer	3
1847 *	Recession, financial panic, November	2	1918	Recession after Armistice, November	5
1853	Recession, last quarter....	6	1920 *	Severe crisis, May	2
1857 *	Recession, late spring, panic in August	4	1923	Mild recession, summer....	3
1860	Recession late in year, prospect of Civil War	3			

* The dates thus marked show the commonly accepted years of financial crises. Other dates frequently listed are 1819, a case of financial strain in a business depression, and 1890. The "rich man's panic" of 1903 is omitted in some lists.

To show the usual way of reckoning the length of cycles, the commonly accepted dates of crises in the United States are marked with asterisks. Anyone who checks these dates against those given in other books will find different ways of counting; for example, 1837-1839 is sometimes put down as a single crisis. But, taking the dates as marked, we have 14 cycles between 1796 and 1920, ranging from about 2 years (1837-39) to about 16 years (1857-1873) in length, and averaging 8 6/7 years. We can raise this average by omitting or combining some of the crises counted here, or reduce it by counting some

INTRODUCTION 43

of the other recessions as crises. At best there is a considerable margin for admissible difference of opinion.

When we drop the effort to discriminate the degrees of severity among crises and count all recessions, this margin of uncertainty becomes narrower, though it does not vanish. It is easier to recognize a change of direction in business movements than it is to determine how serious a change for the worse has been. Yet, another compiler drawing off a list of recessions from the most detailed form of our annals might give a slightly different set of dates, and one who made a fresh set of annals from the original sources might increase these differences somewhat. The broad results, however, seem well assured.

Counting business cycles now as the intervals between recessions, noting the quarters in which the turns came, and reckoning to the nearest whole year, we get the following results:

```
 1 cycle about 1 year long (1845-46)
 4 cycles   "   2 years  "
10   "      "   3   "    "
 5   "      "   4   "    "
 6   "      "   5   "    "
 4   "      "   6   "    "
 1   "      "   7   "    "   (1815-1822)
 0   "      "   8   "    "
 1   "      "   9   "    "   (1873-1882)
```

In all we have 32 cycles in 127 years, which yields an average length of not quite 4 years. The commonest length is about three years; and two-thirds of the cases fall within the limits of three to five years. There is no indication that the average duration of business cycles is changing. There were 16 cycles in the first 64 years covered by the table (1796-1860) and 16 cycles in the following 63 years (1860-1923). Of 3-year cycles, there were five in the first period and five in the second.

These results may be compared with similar summaries from the other country for which we have annals covering 136 years. The dates given by Bouniatian, who has written a history of English crises, are starred to show the conventional view of cycle chronology. His 16 dates mark off 15 cycles in the 127 years from 1793 to 1920— an average length of almost 8½ years. If 1913 be added to the list of crises, and it seems to belong there quite as much as certain dates which Bouniatian admits as turning-points unaccompanied by severe financial strain, there are 16 cycles, ranging in length from about 4 to about 13 years, and averaging not quite 8 years.

Of the cycles marked off by recessions, 22 are shown. Perhaps we should add recessions in 1814 after the first abdication of Napoleon, in 1861 when the American Civil War upset the cotton trade, and in 1870 when the Franco-Prussian War brought confusion to the financial markets. But in none of these cases does the evidence indicate a general slackening of trade. Even if these cases were counted, it would still appear that English business has experienced fewer recessions than American business during the same period of four generations.

Hence English cycles have been longer on the average than American cycles. Taking the dates entered in the table we get an average

TABLE 2

BUSINESS RECESSIONS IN ENGLAND AND APPROXIMATE DURATION OF BUSINESS CYCLES, 1790–1925

		Duration of Cycles in years			Duration of Cycles in years
1793	Recession, February, following financial pressure in 1792 *		1854	Recession, January, Crimean War	7
1797 *	Panic, February	4	1857 *	Financial panic, November	4
1803	Recession, May, renewal of war	6	1866 *	Severe financial crisis, first quarter, Overend-Gurney failure	8
1807	Mild recession	4	1873 *	Recession late in year	8
1810 *	Severe crisis, July	3	1883	Slow recession, early in year, perhaps beginning in 1882 *	9
1815 *	Crisis, autumn, following end of war	5			
1819 *	Recession, early spring	4	1890 *	Recession following financial crisis in November	8
1825 *	Recession, spring, followed by financial panic	6	1900 *	Recession, summer	10
1829	Recession, first quarter	4	1907 *	Recession, autumn, financial stringency	7
1831	Recession	2	1913	Recession, last quarter	6
1837	Recession early in year, following financial panic in 1836 *	6	1918	Recession on Armistice, November	5
1847 *	Financial panic, April, recession, summer	10	1920 *	Severe crisis, second quarter	2

* The dates thus marked show the crises recognized by Mentor Bouniatian, *Les Crises Économiques*, Paris, 1922, p. 43. Most authorities would include 1913, also, on the same grounds that lead Bouniatian to find crises in 1882 and 1900, although these years were not marked by severe financial strain.

INTRODUCTION 45

duration of 5¾ years in England, against 4 years in the United States. And the frequency of recessions has been diminishing in England, though not in this country. In the first half of the period covered (1793-1857), the average length of English cycles was nearly 5 years, in the second half (1857-1920) exactly 7 years.

But these averages are even less a guide to business forecasting in England than in America. It is difficult to find any regular order in the lengths of the successive cycles in either Table 1 or Table 2. When we tabulate the frequency of English cycles according to duration we find less concentration at the mode than in the corresponding American table. From 1793-1920 there were

2 cycles about 2 years long (1829-31, and 1918-20)
1   "   " 3   "   "   (1807-10)
5   "   " 4   "   "
2   "   " 5   "   "
4   "   " 6   "   "
2   "   " 7   "   "
3   "   " 8   "   "
1   "   " 9   "   "   (1873-83)
2   "   " 10   "   "   (1837-47, and 1890-1900)

Four-year cycles are most common in England, three-year cycles in the United States. One-half of the English cases are 4-6 years in length, while two-thirds of the American cases are grouped at 3-5 years.

On applying the same methods of analysis to the three other countries for which we have annals running back to the 1860's, 1850's, and 1840's, we find that in average duration their cycles are intermediate between the English and the American patterns. The average length works out as follows:

> 1838-1920—82 years
> France, 15 cycles, average length 5½ years.
> England, (1837-1920), 12 cycles, average length nearly 7 years.
> United States, (1837-1920), 22 cycles, average length 3¾ years.

1848-1925—77 years
   Germany, 15 cycles, average length 5 years.
   England (1847-1920), 11 cycles, average length 6⅔ years.
   United States (1847-1923), 19 cycles, average length 4 years.
1866-1922—56 years
   Austria, 10 cycles, average length 5.6 years.
   England (1866-1920), 8 cycles, average length 6¾ years.
   United States (1865-1923), 15 cycles, average length not quite 4 years.

If we split the periods covered by our annals for these three countries as nearly in the middle as possible, we find that the average length of business cycles has increased in France as in England, decreased slightly in Germany, and remained constant in Austria as in the United States. The figures are:

	First Half of Period				Second Half of Period			
	Dates	Number of Years	Number of Cycles	Average Duration	Dates	Number of Years	Number of Cycles	Average Duration
France	1838–76	38	8	4.75 yrs.	1876–1920	44	7	6.29 yrs.
Germany	1848–90	42	8	5.25 "	1890–1925	35	7	5.00 "
Austria	1866–94	28	5	5.60 "	1894–1922	28	5	5.60 "
England	1793–1857	64	13	4.92 "	1857–1920	63	9	7.00 "
United States	1796–1860	64	16	4.00 "	1860–1923	63	16	3.94 "

3. Frequency Distributions of the Measurements Based on the Annals.

A systematic summary of our evidence concerning the duration of business cycles is provided by the following exhibits. Table 3 is a companion piece to Tables 1 and 2. It shows the dates of recessions in fifteen countries as accurately as Dr. Thorp can determine them from the annals, and shows also the approximate duration of successive cycles reckoned to the nearest whole year. Chart III is a graphic version of Tables 1, 2 and 3. It uses lines of varying length to show the duration of business cycles in each of our countries, in chronological order.

INTRODUCTION 47

We can treat the observations upon the duration of business cycles assembled in this table and chart as the data of an historical inquiry, or as the data of a theoretical problem. In the first case we ask: What has been the duration of business cycles in the countries and during the periods for which we have annals? In the second case we ask: What expectations regarding the duration of business cycles are justified by the sample observations in hand?

As historical data, our observations probably contain inaccuracies. Conceiving a business recession as a decline in economic activity which follows a period of expansion and spreads over most of a country's industries, we have sought to find and date every recession which occurred in certain countries during certain periods. On the basis of these recession dates, we have measured the duration of successive cycles to the nearest whole year. Finally, we have struck averages from these measurements. Mistakes may have occurred in any of these steps. We may have omitted some recessions; we may have included some cases which do not fit our definition of recessions; we may have blundered in measuring or averaging. But so long as we are trying merely to report what has taken place in the past, these doubts concerning the accuracy of our work are all that need concern us. The historical record is fixed; it has its unique features and interest; in studying it we can indulge in no speculations.

A subtler problem and doubts of another order are presented when we treat our observations as data for drawing theoretical conclusions regarding the duration of business cycles at large. For this purpose, we must ask, not merely whether our observations are historically dependable, but also whether they constitute a representative sample of the phenomena measured. Are the observations sufficiently numerous? Are they sufficiently independent of each other? Ought we discard the observations upon cycles which we think have been cut short or prolonged by factors which have no organic relation to business activity?

In the sense in which the term is used here—recurrences of prosperity, recession, depression and revival in the business activities of countries taken as units—the total number of past business cycles may well be less than a thousand. For business cycles are phenomena peculiar to a certain form of economic organization which has been dominant even in Western Europe for less than two centuries, and for briefer periods in other regions. And the average cycle has lasted five years, if we may trust our data. Of the whole number of cases to date, the 166 cycles we have measured form a significant fraction. By compiling business annals for Norway, Belgium, Switzerland, Denmark, Spain, New Zealand and Chile we could probably get additional observations as satisfactory as some of those already included. Perhaps we could trace business cycles in Greece, Egypt, Turkey, some of the Balkan States, possibly Mexico, and additional countries

TABLE 3

DATES OF BUSINESS RECESSIONS IN FIFTEEN COUNTRIES: VARIOUS YEARS TO 1925

	France	Duration of Cycles in years		Austria	Duration of Cycles in years		Netherlands	Duration of Cycles in years
1838			1866			1891	early	
1847	early	9	1869	late	3	1901	early	10
1854	March	7	1873	summer	4	1907	autumn	7
1857	autumn	3	1884	early	11	1913	late	6
1860	autumn	3	1892	early	8	1917	early	3
1867	early	6	1894	early	2	1920	autumn	4
1870	July	3	1900	early	6		**Italy**	
1873	early	3	1908	early	8	1888	early	
1876	early	3	1912	autumn	5	1900	spring	12
1882	early	6	1918	October	6	1907	last quarter	8
1890	early	8	1922	autumn	4	1913	second half	6
1900	late summer	11				1918	October	5
1908	early	7		**Russia**		1920	early	1
1913	early summer	5	1891	early			**Argentina**	
1918	November	5	1899	third quarter	8	1890	first quarter	
1920	summer	2	1904	February	5	1892	autumn	3
	Germany		1908	early	4	1900	early	7
1848			1914	early	6	1908	early	8
1857	autumn	9	1917	March	3	1911	early	3
1866	June	9	1923	October	7	1913	early	2
1870	July	4	1925	late	2	1920	December	8
1873	autumn	3					**Brazil**	
1878	early	4				1889	November	
1880	early	2				1896	early	6
1882	summer	3		**Sweden**		1900	autumn	5
1890	early	8	1892	early		1907	autumn	7
1900	August	10	1901	early	9	1912	late	5
1904	summer	4	1907	late autumn	7	1918	November	6
1907	summer	3	1913	autumn	6	1920	autumn	2
1913	summer	6	1917		4	1924	second half	4
1918	November	5	1920	summer	3			
1922	summer	4						
1925	summer	3						

INTRODUCTION

TABLE 3—(Continued)
DATES OF BUSINESS RECESSIONS IN FIFTEEN COUNTRIES

	Canada	Duration of Cycles in years		Australia	Duration of Cycles in years		Japan	Duration of Cycles in years
1888			1890	January		1890	January	
1893	early	5	1901	January	11	1894	August	5
1900	autumn	7	1908	January	7	1897	autumn	3
1907	autumn	7	1913	January	5	1905	September	8
1913	second half	6	1914	autumn	2	1907	spring	2
1918	November	5	1920	November	6	1914	spring	7
1920	autumn	2	1924	January	3	1918	November	5
1924	spring	4				1920	March	1
	South Africa			India			China	
1890	September		1889					
1895	autumn	5	1896	summer	7	1888		
1899	October	4	1900	summer	4	1897		9
1903	early	3	1907	autumn	7	1900	May	3
1913		10	1914	August	7	1906		6
1918	late	5	1918	November	4	1910		4
1920	autumn	2	1920	May	2	1920	midyear	10

in Spanish America. Doubtless we might carry our observations further back in most of the seventeen countries which we have studied. But after we had pushed our investigations everywhere into the twilight zone where business cycles are doubtfully recognizable, we should still be dealing with relatively small numbers.

The observations are not all independent of each other. We shall see presently that the duration of business cycles in every country influences, and is influenced by, the duration of business cycles in other countries. Moreover, the non-business factors which affect the duration of business cycles often produce uniform results in several countries. To cite one example: 7 of our 17 countries had a two-year cycle at the end of the World War. One hundred and sixty-six observations, many of which come in clusters, are likely to show a less regular distribution around their central tendency than would 166 observations strictly independent of each other.

If we wish to find out what we can about the probable duration of future business cycles, we should discard observations upon cycles whose duration has been determined by factors of a kind not likely to be influential in the future. If the data for any country show

CHART III. Approximate Duration of Business Cycles, arranged in Chronological Sequence.

White inset figures indicate approximate duration in years.

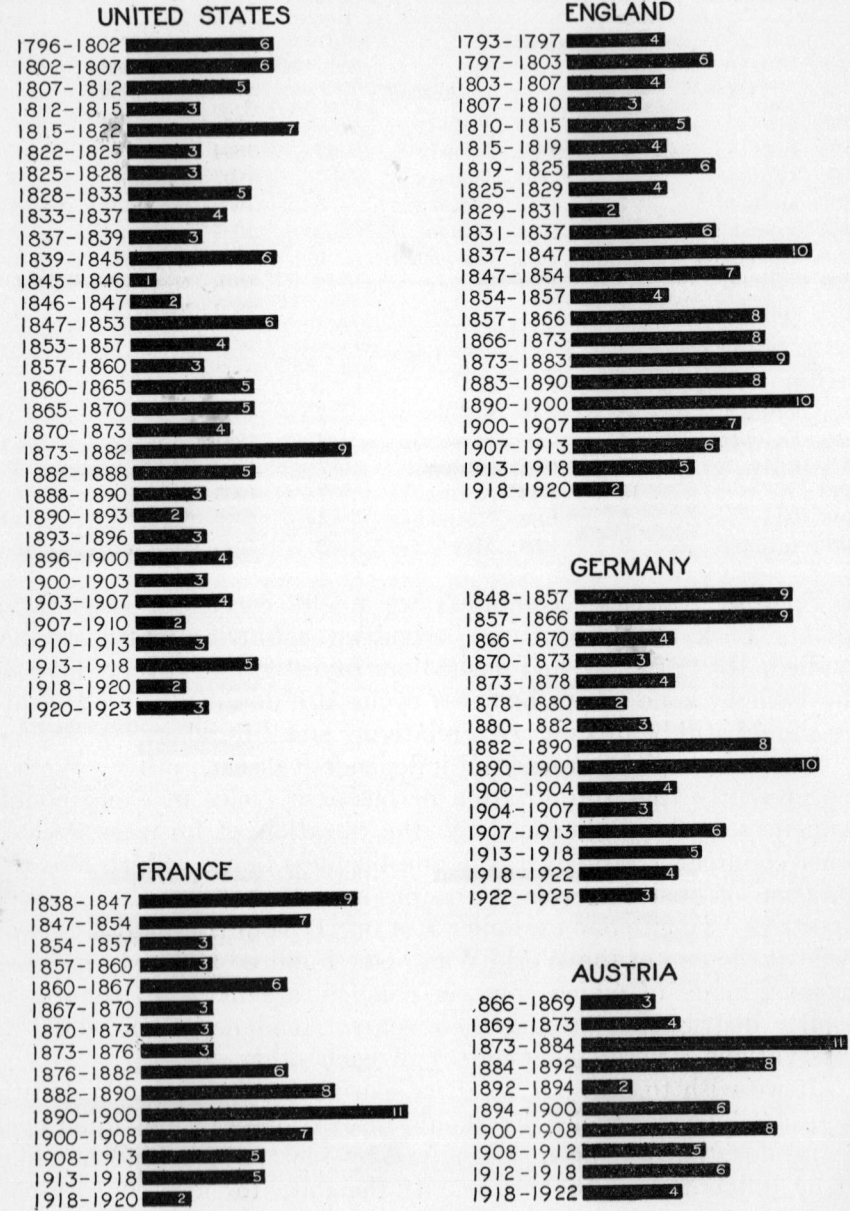

CHART III (*Continued*). Approximate Duration of Business Cycles, arranged in Chronological Sequence.
White inset figures indicate approximate duration in years.

RUSSIA
- 1891–1899 8
- 1899–1904 5
- 1904–1908 4
- 1908–1914 6
- 1914–1917 3
- 1917–1923 7
- 1923–1925 2

CANADA
- 1888–1893 5
- 1893–1900 7
- 1900–1907 7
- 1907–1913 6
- 1913–1918 5
- 1918–1920 2
- 1920–1924 4

SWEDEN
- 1892–1901 9
- 1901–1907 7
- 1907–1913 6
- 1913–1917 4
- 1917–1920 3

NETHERLANDS
- 1891–1901 10
- 1901–1907 7
- 1907–1913 6
- 1913–1917 3
- 1917–1920 4

ITALY
- 1888–1900 12
- 1900–1907 8
- 1907–1913 6
- 1913–1918 5
- 1918–1920 1

CHINA
- 1888–1897 9
- 1897–1900 3
- 1900–1906 6
- 1906–1910 4
- 1910–1920 10

ARGENTINA
- 1890–1892 3
- 1892–1900 7
- 1900–1908 8
- 1908–1911 3
- 1911–1913 2
- 1913–1920 8

SOUTH AFRICA
- 1890–1895 5
- 1895–1899 4
- 1899–1903 3
- 1903–1913 10
- 1913–1918 5
- 1918–1920 2

AUSTRALIA
- 1890–1901 11
- 1901–1908 7
- 1908–1913 5
- 1913–1914 2
- 1914–1920 6
- 1920–1924 3

INDIA
- 1889–1896 7
- 1896–1900 4
- 1900–1907 7
- 1907–1914 7
- 1914–1918 4
- 1918–1920 2

BRAZIL
- 1889–1896 6
- 1896–1900 5
- 1900–1907 7
- 1907–1912 5
- 1912–1918 6
- 1918–1920 2
- 1920–1924 4

JAPAN
- 1890–1894 5
- 1894–1897 3
- 1897–1905 8
- 1905–1907 2
- 1907–1914 7
- 1914–1918 5
- 1918–1920 1

unequivocal evidence of a change in the length of cycles, the later data are likely to be a safer guide to expectations than the earlier data, or the full array. But we have no warrant for discarding cases in which cycles seem to have been cut short or prolonged by wars, civil disorders, exceptional harvest conditions, or any other factor, unless we believe that such "disturbing circumstances" will not recur in the future as in the past. Even the man who has supposed that business cycles "tend" to have some standard period will probably conclude upon studying the present charts that he had better take the data as they come.

In fine, our observations form a fairly satisfactory basis for studying the duration of business cycles. Like all observations, their accuracy is open to question; but they have been made with care and their number is sufficient to allow errors to offset each other in some measure. We should be glad to have a larger sample; but the present one constitutes an appreciable fraction of its "universe." We need not reject any of the observations on the ground that the duration of certain cycles has been affected by "disturbing circumstances"; for we are interested in actual cycles in the actual world where "disturbing circumstances" are always present. We might expect a more regular distribution if all our observations were strictly independent of each other. But once again, as the world is constituted, inter-dependence in duration is characteristic of business cycles in different countries. A complete array of measurements for all past cycles would resemble our sample in this respect, and future cycles seem likely to show increasing inter-dependence in duration. Perhaps we should conceive of our distributions as made from a number of independent measurements smaller than the nominal count, but with the use of "weights" which total 166. Many cycles are weighted by one, while other cycles, which began and ended on the same dates in countries with close business relations, or dominated by the same non-business factors, are weighted by numbers running as high as seven.

To put our data in shape for analysis, we must disregard the chronological sequence of cycles of varying length, shown in Chart III, and rearrange all the cases in frequency tables of the sort already given for American and English cycles—tables which show the number of cycles of each recorded duration. That step is taken in Table 4. But the tabulations by separate countries have slight significance,

INTRODUCTION

except for England and the United States, because the number of cases is small (5-15 cycles). Hence Table 5 is made from Table 4, by combining the observations from single countries into various groups. To facilitate comparisons among the two dozen distributions here shown, all the samples are put in percentages. Chart IV is a graphic form of these percentage distributions.

TABLE 4

FREQUENCY DISTRIBUTION OF BUSINESS CYCLES ACCORDING TO DURATION IN YEARS

Data from Seventeen Countries. Various Dates to 1925.
Based upon Tables 1, 2 and 3.

Duration in Years	England 1793–1920	France 1838–1920	Germany 1848–1925	Austria 1866–1922	Italy 1888–1920	Netherlands 1891–1920	Sweden 1892–1920	Russia 1891–1925
1 year	..	..	..	..	1	..	..	..
2 years	2	1	1	1	..	..	..	1
3 "	1	5	4	1	..	1	1	1
4 "	5	..	4	2	..	1	1	1
5 "	2	2	1	1	1	..	..	1
6 "	4	2	1	2	1	1	1	1
7 "	2	2	..	..	..	1	1	1
8 "	3	1	1	2	1	..	..	1
9 "	1	1	2	..	..	..	1	..
10 "	2	.	1	..	..	1	..	..
11 "	..	1	..	1	..	..	..	..
12 "	..	..	..	..	1	..	..	..
Total number	22	15	15	10	5	5	5	7
Average duration in years	5.8	5.5	5.1	5.6	6.4	5.8	5.6	4.9

Duration in years	United States 1796–1923	Canada 1888–1924	Australia 1890–1924	South Africa 1890–1920	Argentina 1890–1920	Brazil 1889–1924	India 1889–1920	Japan 1890–1920	China 1888–1920
1 year	1	..	..	..	..	..	..	1	..
2 years	4	1	1	1	1	1	1	1	..
3 "	10	..	1	1	2	..	..	1	1
4 "	5	1	..	1	..	1	2	..	1
5 "	6	2	1	2	..	2	..	2	..
6 "	4	1	1	..	..	2	..	..	1
7 "	1	2	1	..	1	1	3	1	..
8 "	..	..	..	..	2	..	..	1	..
9 "	1	..	..	..	..	..	..	..	1
10 "	..	..	..	1	..	..	..	..	1
11 "	..	..	1	..	..	..	..	..	..
Total number	32	7	6	6	6	7	6	7	5
Average duration in years	4.0	5.1	5.7	5.0	5.0	5.0	5.2	4.3	6.4

TABLE 5
Frequency Distribution of Business Cycles According to Approximate Duration in Years: by Countries, Groups of Countries and Periods
(Based upon Table 4)

Duration in Years	United States		England		United States and England		United States, England, France, Germany and Austria						Duration in Years
							Before 1873		After 1873		Full Period		
	Number	Per Cent	Number	Per Cent	Number	Per Cent	Number	Per Cent	Number	Per Cent	Number	Per Cent	
1	1	3.1	..	...	1	1.9	1	2.1	..	...	1	1.1	1
2	4	12.5	2	9.1	6	11.1	2	4.3	7	14.9	9	9.6	2
3	10	31.2	1	4.5	11	20.4	12	25.5	9	19.1	21	22.4	3
4	5	15.6	5	22.7	10	18.5	10	21.3	6	12.8	16	17.0	4
5	6	18.8	2	9.1	8	14.8	5	10.6	7	14.9	12	12.8	5
6	4	12.5	4	18.2	8	14.8	8	17.0	5	10.6	13	13.8	6
7	1	3.1	2	9.1	3	5.6	3	6.4	2	4.3	5	5.3	7
8	..	...	3	13.6	3	5.6	2	4.3	5	10.6	7	7.4	8
9	1	3.1	1	4.5	2	3.7	3	6.4	2	4.3	5	5.3	9
10	..	...	2	9.1	2	3.7	1	2.1	2	4.3	3	3.2	10
11	..	...	..	...	..	...	..	...	2	4.3	2	2.1	11
Totals	32	100.0	22	100.0	54	100.0	47	100.0	47	100.0	94	100.0	Totals

Duration in Years	Countries with close business relations [1]		Countries relatively independent of each other [2]		Countries with average duration of 5.5 years or more [3]		Countries with average duration of 5.2 years or less [4]				Countries with average duration of 5.0 to 5.7 [5] years		Duration in Years
							Excluding United States		Including United States				
	Number	Per Cent	Number	Per Cent	Number	Per Cent	Number	Per Cent	Number	Per Cent	Number	Per Cent	
1	..	...	1	2.6	1	1.4	1	1.6	2	2.2	..	...	1
2	4	10.3	5	13.2	5	6.9	8	13.1	12	12.9	11	10.5	2
3	7	18.0	5	13.2	11	15.4	9	14.8	19	20.4	16	15.2	3
4	6	15.4	8	21.0	10	13.7	10	16.4	15	16.1	17	16.2	4
5	4	10.3	6	15.8	7	9.6	10	16.4	16	17.2	13	12.4	5
6	5	12.8	6	15.8	13	17.8	5	8.2	9	9.7	14	13.3	6
7	2	5.1	3	7.9	7	9.6	9	14.8	10	10.8	13	12.4	7
8	6	15.4	2	5.3	7	9.6	5	8.2	5	5.4	9	8.6	8
9	1	2.6	1	2.6	4	5.5	2	3.3	3	3.2	5	4.8	9
10	2	5.1	1	2.6	4	5.5	2	3.3	2	2.2	4	3.8	10
11	2	5.1	..	...	3	4.1	..	...	..	...	3	2.9	11
12	..	...	..	...	1	1.4	..	...	..	...	..	...	12
Totals	39	100.0	38	100.0	73	100.0	61	100.0	93	100.0	105	100.0	Totals

[1] England, France, Germany, and Austria, 1866–1920.
[2] England, 1793–1825; United States, 1825–1857; Germany, 1857–1890; Canada, 1888–1924; and Russia, 1891–1925.
[3] France, Austria, Sweden, England, Australia, Netherlands, Italy, and China.
[4] United States, Japan, Russia, South Africa, Argentina, Brazil, Canada, Germany, and India.
[5] South Africa, Argentina, Brazil, Canada, Germany, India, France, Austria, Sweden, England, and Australia.

INTRODUCTION

TABLE 5—(Continued)
Frequency Distribution of Business Cycles according to Approximate Duration in Years: by Countries, Groups of Countries and Periods
(Based upon Table 4)

Duration in Years	Eight European Countries		Nine Non-European Countries		Five English-Speaking Countries[1]		Twelve Non-English-Speaking Countries		All Countries except United States		All Countries		Duration in Years
	Number	Per Cent	Number	Per Cent	Number	Per Cent	Number	Per Cent	Number	Per Cent	Number	Per Cent	
1	1	1.2	2	2.4	1	1.4	2	2.2	2	1.5	3	1.8	1
2	6	7.1	11	13.4	9	12.5	8	8.6	13	9.7	17	10.2	2
3	14	16.7	16	19.5	13	17.8	17	18.3	20	14.9	30	18.1	3
4	14	16.7	11	13.4	12	16.4	13	14.0	20	14.9	25	15.1	4
5	8	9.5	15	18.3	13	17.8	10	10.8	17	12.7	23	13.9	5
6	13	15.5	9	11.0	10	13.7	12	12.9	18	13.4	22	13.3	6
7	7	8.3	10	12.2	6	8.2	11	11.8	16	11.9	17	10.2	7
8	9	10.7	3	3.7	3	4.1	9	9.7	12	9.0	12	7.2	8
9	5	6.0	2	2.4	2	2.7	5	5.4	6	4.5	7	4.2	9
10	4	4.8	2	2.4	3	4.1	3	3.2	6	4.5	6	3.6	10
11	2	2.4	1	1.2	1	1.4	2	2.2	3	2.2	3	1.8	11
12	1	1.2	..	...	..	...	1	1.1	1	0.7	1	0.6	12
Totals	84	100.0	82	100.0	73	100.0	93	100.0	134	100.0	166	100.0	Totals

Recent Cycles Only: About 1890 to 1925

Duration in Years	European and Non-European Countries				Industrial and Non-Industrial Countries				Totals excluding and including United States				Duration in Years
	Eight European Countries		Eight Non-European Countries[2]		Seven Industrial Countries[3]		Ten Non-Industrial Countries[4]		Excluding United States		Including United States		
	Number	Per Cent	Number	Per Cent	Number	Per Cent	Number	Per Cent	Number	Per Cent	Number	Per Cent	
1	1	2.2	1	2.0	..	...	2	3.2	2	2.1	2	1.9	1
2	3	6.7	7	14.0	5	11.6	8	12.9	10	10.5	13	12.4	2
3	6	13.3	6	12.0	9	20.9	7	11.3	12	12.6	16	15.2	3
4	7	15.6	6	12.0	8	18.6	7	11.3	13	13.7	15	14.3	4
5	6	13.3	9	18.0	5	11.6	11	17.7	15	15.8	16	15.2	5
6	8	17.8	5	10.0	6	14.0	7	11.3	13	13.7	13	12.4	6
7	5	11.1	9	18.0	4	9.3	10	16.1	14	14.7	14	13.3	7
8	3	6.7	3	6.0	1	2.3	5	8.1	6	6.3	6	5.7	8
9	1	2.2	1	2.0	1	2.3	1	1.6	2	2.1	2	1.9	9
10	3	6.7	2	4.0	3	7.0	2	3.2	5	5.3	5	4.8	10
11	1	2.2	1	2.0	1	2.3	1	1.6	2	2.1	2	1.9	11
12	1	2.2	..	...	..	...	1	1.6	1	1.1	1	1.0	12
Totals	45	100.0	50	100.0	43	100.0	62	100.0	95	100.0	105	100.0	Totals

[1] England, United States, Canada, Australia, South Africa.
[2] Not including United States.
[3] England, France, Germany, Austria, Netherlands, Sweden, United States.
[4] All other countries included in *Annals*.

56 BUSINESS ANNALS

CHART IV. Percentage Distribution of Business Cycles in Various Countries and Various Periods According to their Approximate Duration in Years.

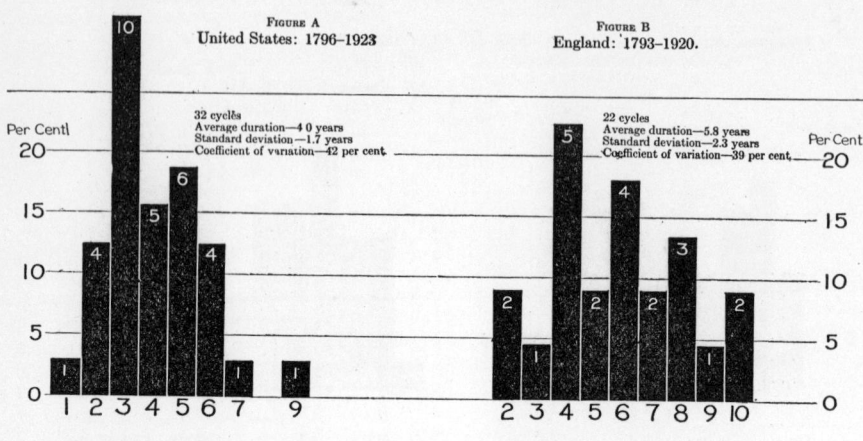
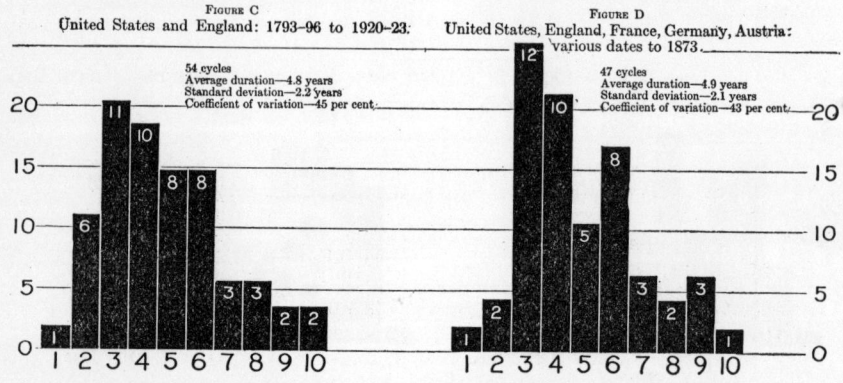
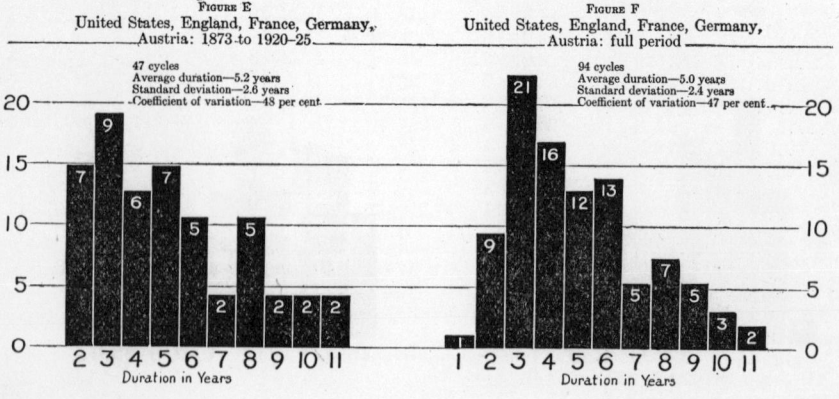

INTRODUCTION

CHART IV. Percentage Distribution of Business Cycles in Various Countries and Various Periods According to their Approximate Duration in Years.—(*Continued*)

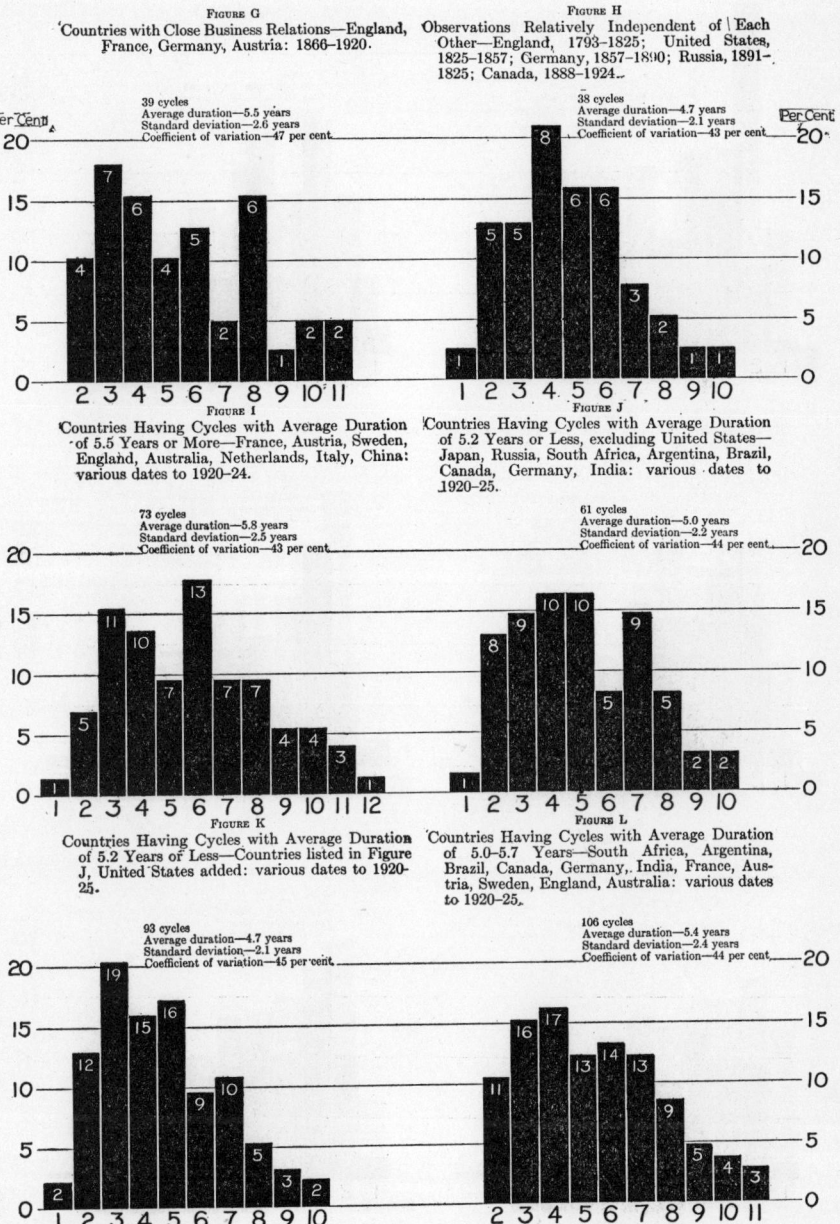

CHART IV. Percentage Distribution of Business Cycles in Various Countries and Various Periods According to their Approximate Duration in Years.—(*Continued*)

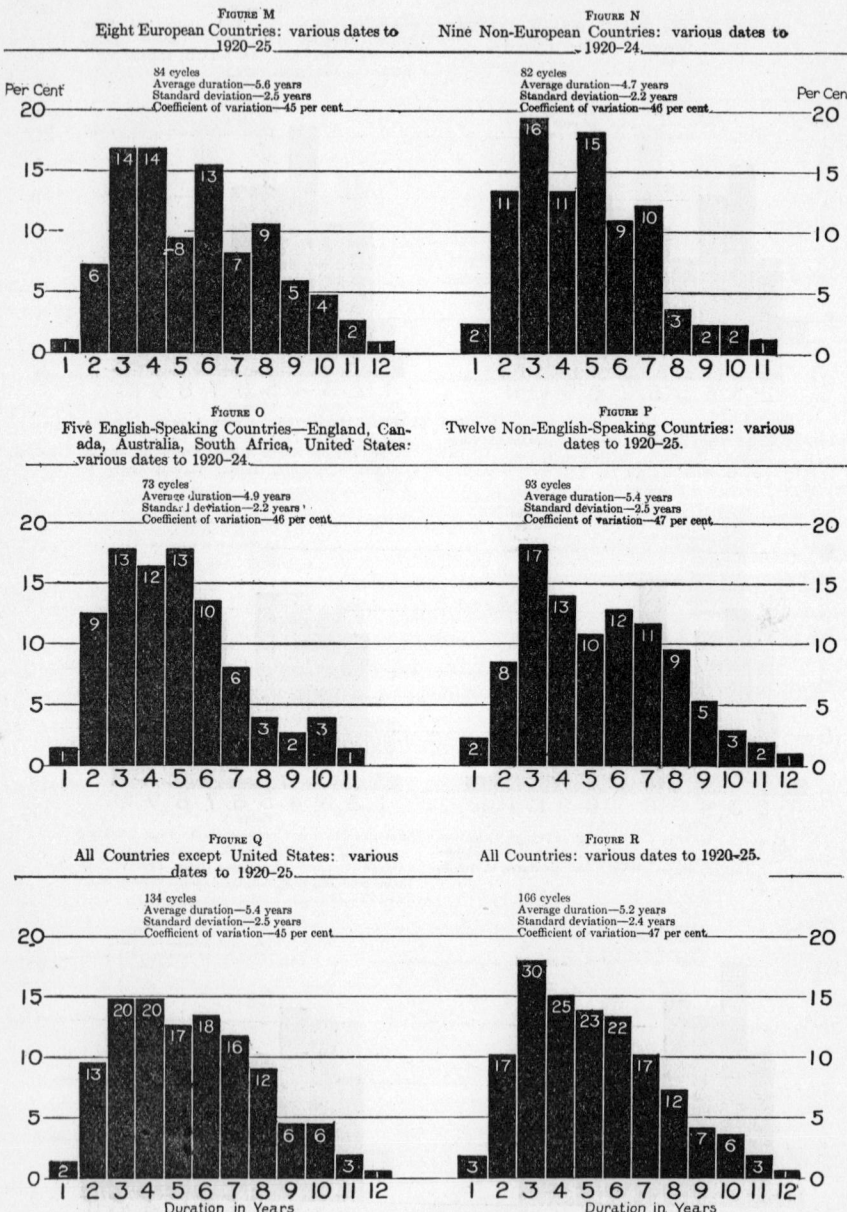

INTRODUCTION

CHART IV. Percentage Distribution of Business Cycles in Various Countries and Various Periods According to their Approximate Duration in Years.—(*Continued*)

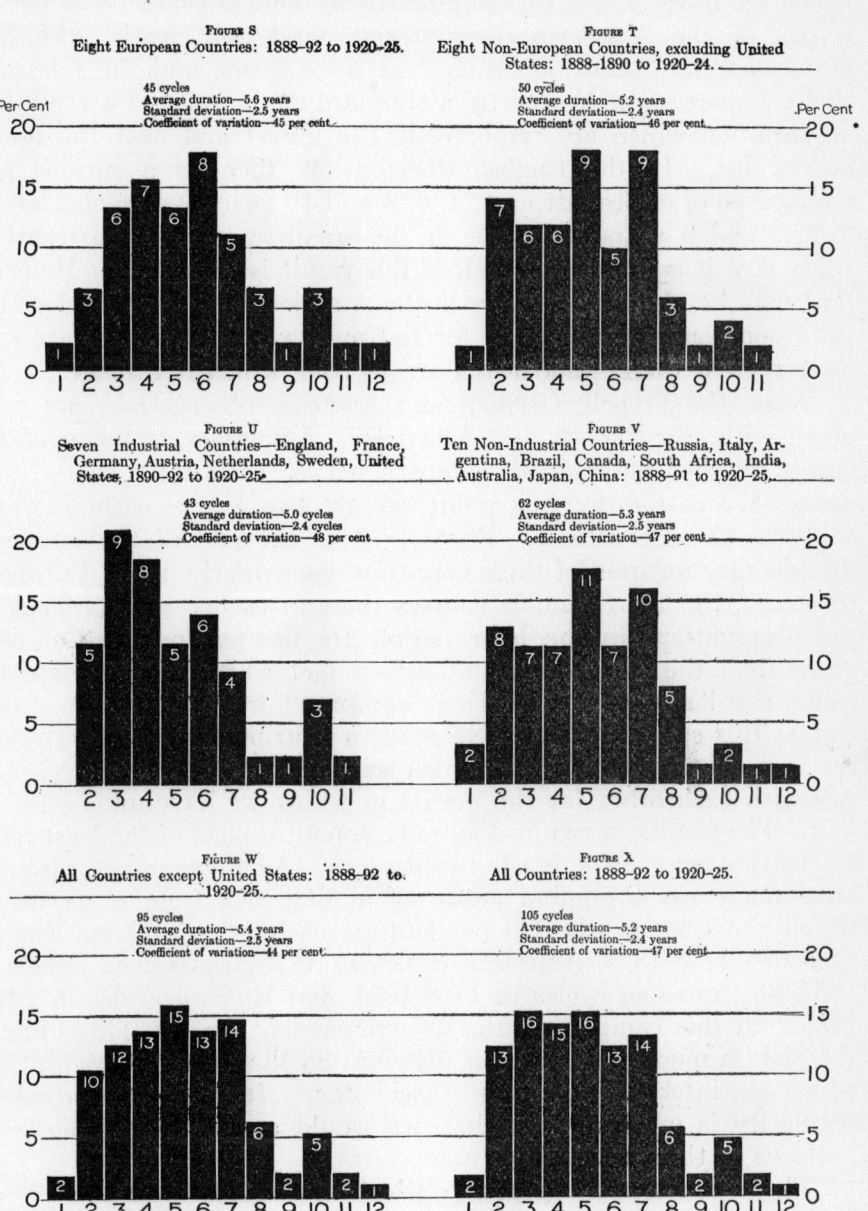

The first six figures in the chart deal with the five countries for which we have annals covering relatively long periods. The peculiarities of the American distribution stand out clearly—the pronounced mode, almost a "spike," at three years, and the relatively slight dispersion, indicated by a standard deviation and a coefficient of variation which are respectively the lowest and next the lowest in the list. In the English distribution, there is a curious predominance of cycles lasting 2, 4, 6, 8 and 10 years over cycles lasting 3, 5, 7 and 9 years. In view of the small number of observations (only 22), it is uncertain whether this result is significant. However that may be, the irregularities in the American and English distributions compensate each other for the most part, so that Figure C is more regular than either of the arrays from which it is made.

Next, the French, German and Austrian observations are combined with the English and American. Advantage is taken of the larger number of cases to compare earlier with later cycles. By using 1873 as the dividing point, we get two groups each of which contains 47 observations. From 1873 to the end of the late war, the business fortunes of these countries, particularly of the European countries, ran more similar courses than in earlier years. That is, the observations in the later period are less independent of each other than the earlier observations—a fact which may explain the lesser regularity of Figure E as compared with Figure D. As a test of this suggestion we have made a distribution of the cycles in the four countries in our list which seem to have the closest business ties with each other for the period in which we have annals for all four. The results, shown in Figure G, constitute one of the least regular distributions in the whole twenty-four. As a companion piece we have made up a random group of similar size from observations which must be nearly independent of each other, taking English cycles in 1793-1825, American cycles in 1825-57, German cycles in 1857-90, Canadian cycles in 1888-1924, and Russian cycles in 1891-1925. In this comparison the 38 independent observations (Figure H) yield a much more regular distribution than the 39 observations which are inter-correlated with each other. Indeed, the contrast in regularity is more striking than we would expect from other comparisons of the sort.

There follow ten figures in which all of the observations are broken into parts on the basis of four criteria. First, the countries

INTRODUCTION

are grouped according to the average duration of their business cycles as given in our annals. Figure I shows the observations from countries with relatively long cycles, Figures J and K the observations from countries with relatively short cycles (excluding and including the United States), and Figure L the observations from countries with cycles of medium length. The latter group contains part of the observations used in Figure I and part of those used in Figure J. Second, the European and non-European observations are presented separately in Figures M and N. Third, the observations from five English-speaking and twelve non-English-speaking countries are shown. Fourth, Figure Q gives all the non-American observations for comparison with the American distribution of Figure A. Figure R sums up the whole body of data.

The final section of the chart is confined to recent cycles—those occurring since about 1890. Again the data are divided into groups: observations from European and non-European countries, from industrial and non-industrial countries; from all countries except and all including the United States.

When we review the whole array of distributions, we see that the diagrams and the differences among the diagrams are of a sort common in studies of social phenomena. As usually happens in such work, the small samples, especially when they contain inter-correlated observations, are rather irregular. But with increase in the size of the samples and in the independence of the observations, the distributions grow fairly regular, though not symmetrical.

The materials appear to be homogeneous, with the important exception already noted—the distribution of American business cycles in respect to length differs from the distribution of cycles in other countries. This difference stands out most sharply in the contrast between Figures A and Q. It is responsible for the double modes, separated by a lower point, in Figures O and X, and for the relatively high coefficients of variation in most of the groups combining American and foreign observations. In the samples drawn solely from foreign countries, the diagrams usually have a rounded top quite unlike the spike of Figure A. Combining the American with foreign observations generally produces an unambiguous mode at three years, but twice (Figures O and X) it produces the double mode already spoken of.

Barring out the twelve distributions into which American observations enter does not reduce the variety in the position of the crude modes. Two of the remaining dozen figures have modes at three years (G and P); two at three and four years (M and Q); and eight at 4, 5, or 6 years, if we may include here one double mode at 5 and 7 years (Figures T). By way of generalization we can hardly be more specific than to say that two thirds of the foreign cycles are concentrated in the interval three to seven years.

All of the distributions have rather high coefficients of variation (the standard deviations expressed as percentages of the arithmetic means). In other words, the observations do not cluster closely around their averages. These coefficients are least in the two distributions confined to single countries (Figures A and B), and greatest in the distributions made from American, British, French, German and Austrian observations since 1873 (Figure E). But the difference between the lowest and highest coefficients (39 and 48 per cent) is not great, and 14 of the 24 round off at 45, 46 or 47 per cent.

All the distributions are skewed positively. The range runs farther above the arithmetic mean than below it in every case, and in every case but Figure T the range also runs farther above the crude mode than below it. Moreover, the crude mode is less than the arithmetic mean in 16 cases, about equal to it in 7 cases, and clearly higher than the mean only in Figure T. One of the most significant distributions, Figure W, which includes all cycles since about 1890 in countries other than the United States, approaches symmetry; but the very broadest groups, Figures X (all recent cycles), Q (all foreign cycles), and R (all cycles) are decidedly, though not extremely, skewed.

Before attempting to interpret these frequency distributions, it is advisable to consider the relative duration of periods of prosperity and depression in business cycles, and the bearing of long-period trends of wholesale prices upon our problem.

4. The Relative Duration of Prosperity and Depression.

Dr. Thorp has made a special study of the annals to determine as accurately as possible how many months of the record for each country can be classed as prosperous and how many as depressed. Need-

INTRODUCTION

less to say, this task involved the continuous exercise of personal judgment.

As pointed out in the comparison between the annals and certain statistical indexes of business activity, contemporary observers are always influenced by recent experience in their use of the terms depression and prosperity. Hence, no rigid criterion of what constitutes business prosperity and depression can be evolved from, or read into, our sources. But that fact does not obstruct, it really facilitates, the task in hand. For we seek to compare the duration of the prosperous phase with that of the depressed phase within each cycle treated as a unit. That the prosperous phases of successive cycles in the same country and of synchronous cycles in different countries attain different degrees of intensity is a matter of deep interest, both practically and theoretically; but it is beside the present point.

Dr. Thorp's chief difficulty was that his sources seldom date the transitions from one phase of a cycle to the next phase. In trying to supply that omission in every case, he had to rely upon indications which are often faint. In detail his decisions must be subject to a wider margin of error than his measurements of the durations of whole cycles, since the recessions on which the latter measurements are based, are the phases which have attracted most attention. Hence it will be advisable to confine attention to his averages, covering several or many cycles, and to draw only broad conclusions.

Table 6 shows the form and drift of Dr. Thorp's tabulations. It

TABLE 6

Relative Duration of Different Phases of Business Cycles in Seventeen Countries, 1890–1925

	Months	Percentages
Months of prosperity	2,888	39.3
Months of recession and revival	1,756	23.9
Months of depression	2,700	36.8
Total	7,344	100.0

Years of prosperity per year of depression: 1.07.

appears that the phases of recession and revival put together make up rather less than one-quarter of the duration of recent cycles. But in view of the difficulty of saying just when revival has blossomed into prosperity, and just when recession has merged into depression, this conclusion should not be stressed heavily. However, if these decisions can be made on a substantially consistent basis, the comparison between the relative duration of the prosperous and depressed phases of the cycles will not be compromised.[1] What the table indicates is that in this period of 36 years the prosperous phases averaged somewhat longer than the depressed phases.

Similar averages showing the relative duration of prosperity and depression for particular countries and periods are given in Table 7. To get comparable results it has been necessary both to take periods which comprise whole cycles, and to make these periods as nearly synchronous as may be. For the results in any one country vary considerably from one period to another. For example, the English and American averages come out in three different periods as follows:

	Years of Prosperity per Year of Depression		Years of Prosperity per Year of Depression
England 1790–1925	1.11	United States 1790–1925	1.50
1890–1913	1.24	1890–1913	1.57
1890–1920	1.71	1890–1923	1.79

As a guide to future expectations, the averages which include the years of the great war seem less significant than the averages which we have for longer periods of time in five countries, or than the averages for 17 countries in the period from about 1890 to 1913.

The wide differences between the averages for the countries at the bottom and the top of the list in Table 7 show how much business conditions are affected by political turmoil and stability. Brazil, China, Russia and South Africa had grave troubles in the period for which we have compiled their annals, and Austria suffered from her proximity to the Balkan volcanoes. The other figures speak for themselves. But we should remember that the figures for each country speak that country's language. Swedish prosperity may differ from Canadian prosperity—the comparison made is between the prosperous and the depressed phases of Swedish cycles in one case, and between the prosperous and the depressed phases of Canadian cycles in the other case. It is risky to say that one of these countries has been more prosperous than the other, even in the period here covered. And it is easy to conceive that any country might change its ranking in such a list radically within a decade or two.

[1] Chart VI, below, shows for every cycle the quarters and years which Dr. Thorp has taken as marking off revival and recession.

TABLE 7

Relative Duration of the Prosperous and Depressed Phases in the Business Cycles of Seventeen Countries during Various Periods

	Period	Years of Prosperity per Year of Depression
United States	1790–1925	1.50
England	1790–1925	1.11
France	1840–1925	1.18
Germany	1853–1925	1.18
Austria	1866–1925	0.70

	Period	Years of Prosperity per Year of Depression	Period	Years of Prosperity per Year of Depression
Canada	1888–1924	1.86	1888–1913	2.08
United States	1890–1923	1.79	1890–1913	1.57
England	1890–1920	1.71	1890–1913	1.24
France	1890–1920	1.70	1890–1913	1.47
Australia	1890–1920	1.69	1890–1913	1.37
Sweden	1892–1920	1.67	1892–1913	1.89
Netherlands	1891–1920	1.61	1891–1913	1.59
India	1889–1920	1.43	1889–1914	1.26
Argentina	1890–1920	1.07	1890–1913	1.06
Japan	1890–1920	1.05	1890–1914	.75
Germany	1890–1925	1.03	1890–1913	1.14
Italy	1888–1920	.98	1888–1913	.90
South Africa	1890–1920	.89	1890–1913	.66
Russia	1891–1925	.81	1891–1914	1.09
China	1888–1920	.65	1888–1910	.57
Austria	1892–1922	.63	1892–1912	.73
Brazil	1889–1924	.45	1889–1912	.29
Seventeen Countries		1.14		1.08

One of the main reasons why these ratios of years of prosperity to years of depression are unstable is revealed by a further analysis of the long records for England and the United States. From various index numbers of prices, it is known that the long-period trend of the wholesale price level changed direction four times in the 130 years, 1790 to 1920. The turning points came at nearly the same dates in this country and England, save that our greenback prices reached their highest point just before the end of the Civil War in 1865, whereas in gold-standard nations prices continued to rise until

1873. Thus we have in both countries five periods of alternately declining and advancing price trends. From 1790 to 1814 wholesale prices rose unsteadily; from 1814 to 1849 wholesale prices declined unsteadily; from 1849 to 1865 in the United States and to 1873 in England wholesale prices rose unsteadily; from 1865 in the United States and 1873 in England prices declined unsteadily until 1896; from 1896 to 1920 they rose unsteadily. For the periods thus marked off, Dr. Thorp has obtained the following ratios of years of prosperity to years of depression:

TABLE 8

RELATIVE DURATION OF THE PROSPEROUS AND THE DEPRESSED PHASES OF BUSINESS CYCLES IN PERIODS OF RISING AND DECLINING TRENDS OF WHOLESALE PRICES: ENGLAND AND THE UNITED STATES, 1790–1925

England	Years of Prosperity per Year of Depression	United States	Years of Prosperity per Year of Depression
1790–1815 Prices rising	1.0	1790–1815 Prices rising	2.6
1815–1849 Prices falling	.9	1815–1849 Prices falling	.8
1849–1873 Prices rising	3.3	1849–1865 Prices rising	2.9
1873–1896 Prices falling	.4	1865–1896 Prices falling	.9
1896–1920 Prices rising	2.7	1896–1920 Prices rising	3.1

These results are so uniform and so striking as to leave little doubt that the secular trend of the wholesale price level is a factor of great moment in determining the characteristics of business cycles. That is no novel conclusion; but Dr. Thorp's data lend it new force and precision.

A final point established by study of the relative duration of the prosperous and the depressed phases of business cycles is that the very long cycles usually owe their length primarily to prolongation of depression. Among the 166 cycles we have measured there are 17 which lasted 9 years or more. The average of all our observations, it will be remembered, is 5.2 years. Dr. Thorp has made a special examination of these long cycles to determine when the revivals occurred, and how long were the periods of declining and of increasing activity. His results appear in Table 9.

Whereas the most inclusive average in Table 7 gives a ratio of 1.14 years of prosperity per year of depression, the present table gives a ratio of 0.79. In 11 of the 17 cycles the phase of depression

INTRODUCTION 67

is longer than the phase of prosperity. The longest period of prosperity found is 72 months; the longest periods of depression run 72, 76 and 100 months. Finally, the average phase of depression in these long cycles is nearly a year longer than the average phase of prosperity.

TABLE 9

RELATIVE DURATION OF PHASES OF DEPRESSION AND PHASES OF PROSPERITY IN BUSINESS
CYCLES LASTING NINE YEARS OR MORE

Length in Years	Country	Periods Covered by the Cycles	Year of Revival	Months of Depression	Months of Prosperity
12	Italy	1888, early–1900, early	1897	100	30
11	France	1890, early–1900, late	1895	60	42
11	Austria	1873–1884	1880	72	36
11	Australia	1890–1901	1896	62	48
10	England	1837, early–1847, April	1843	68	44
10	England	1890, Nov.–1900	1895	42	48
10	Germany	1890, early–1900, summer	1894, late	44	51
10	Netherlands	1891–1901	1896	48	48
10	South Africa	1903–1913	1909	60	36
10	China	1910–1920	1916	60	48
9	United States	1873–1882	1878	57	42
9	England	1873, late–1883, early	1880	69	24
9	France	1838–1847	1840	24	72
9	Germany	1848–1857	1853	54	42
9	Germany	1857–1866	1860	18	66
9	Sweden	1892–1901	1895	30	60
9	China	1888–1897	1895	76	12
			Total	944	749
			Average	55	44

Years of prosperity per year of depression: 0.79.

5. CONCLUSIONS.

1. Our measurements of the intervals between recessions do not bear precisely upon the obsolescent debate concerning the periodicity of crises. But measurements made from the annals upon the old plan would be as fatal to the hypothesis of periodicity as the measurements which we prefer. Indeed, counting from crisis to crisis would make the limits within which cycles vary even wider than does counting from recession to recession. The longest cycle shown by our annals —the Italian case of 1888-1900—would be extended from 12 to 19 years if we skipped the mild recession of 1900 and passed on to the

crisis of 1907. Perhaps still longer cycles might be found, were this method of counting systematically applied to all countries. Nor could the extension of the range in one direction be compensated by reduction at the other end of the scale. The shortest cycle could not be prolonged beyond two or three years, except by such violent procedures as telescoping the American panics of 1837 and 1839 into a single crisis.

Nor can we confirm the ingenious suggestion made by Professor H. S. Jevons and Mr. Joseph Kitchin, that long cycles are multiples of two or three short ones.[1] Were such the case, and were the short cycles 3⅓ or 3½ years long as these writers suppose, one would expect our frequency diagrams to show modes, primary or secondary, at 3, 7, and 10, or 11 years. None of them do so. There are diagrams with modes, pronounced or faint, at 3 and 7 years, and 4 and 8 years. But there are also diagrams with modes, pronounced or faint, at 3 and 4 years; 3 and 5 years; 3 and 6 years; 3 and 8 years; 3, 4, 6, and 8 years; 3, 5, and 7 years; 3, 5, and 10 years; 3, 6, and 10 years; 4 and 5 years; 4 and 6 years; 5 and 7 years, etc. More significant is the fact that as the size of the samples increases the minor modes tend to disappear, instead of tending to grow clearer. In the most inclusive sample of all (Figure R of Chart IV), there are no secondary modes.

While few if any recent writers maintain the hypothesis of periodicity in any form, many of them do give some average figure to represent the duration typical of business cycles. Such averages are adequate for certain purposes. But our results show that no average can suggest the facts about the duration of cycles which are most significant for theory and practice.

2. If there is any regularity in the sequence of cycles of different lengths, we have failed to find it. Chart III, which represents the duration of cycles taken in chronological order, shows the hazard of attempting to forecast how long the next cycle will last in any of our countries. Neither modal length, nor the duration of the preceding cycle is a safe guide.

3. A semblance of regularity does appear, however, when we disregard chronological sequence and group our observations in frequency tables. And the regularity becomes more marked as the size

[1] See Herbert Stanley Jevons, *The Sun's Heat and Solar Activity*, London, 1910, and Joseph Kitchin, "Cycles and Trends in Economic Factors," *Review of Economic Statistics*, January, 1923, Preliminary vol. v, pp. 10-16.

of the sample increases, that is, as the number of independent observations upon the duration of business cycles becomes greater.

The regularity which emerges, consists, not in the preponderance of cycles of any given duration, but in the way in which cycles of different durations group themselves about their central tendency. The distribution is of a type found in many studies of biological and social phenomena. It is not symmetrical, but skewed positively. In all the groups into which we have divided the observations for analysis, the range runs farther above than below the arithmetic mean, and in two-thirds of the groups the crude mode is less than the arithmetic mean.

4. American cycles have a shorter average duration than those of any other country studied. The averages of 32 American and of 134 foreign measurements are 4.0 and 5.4 years respectively. The shortest average duration found in any foreign country is 4.3 years in Japan, where 7 cycles occurred in approximately the period covered by 10 American cycles. The American distribution shows a pronounced mode at 3 years; the most inclusive of the foreign distributions shows a rounded top with equal numbers of cases at 3 and 4 years, and no marked decline in numbers before 8 years.

The peculiarity of the American cycles cannot be due to the "newness" of the country; for Canadian, Australian, and South African cycles conform more closely to the European type. Nor have we reason to believe that in our American sources the standard of business reports concerning recessions is peculiar. Certainly the differences between the duration of American and English cycles shown by our annals since the 1870's are matched by corresponding differences between the American and English indexes of business activity, shown for these years in an earlier section. Our confidence in the American measurements is further confirmed by the fact that several statisticians, dealing with various time series, have called attention to the prominence of a 40-month cycle in American business fluctuations. While the annals support this statistical finding on the basis of descriptive materials, they start a new problem by indicating that the predominance of 3-year cycles in recent years has been confined to the United States.[1]

5. While our frequency distributions lack the symmetry of the

---

[1] Table 3 shows that France had a remarkable run of 3-year cycles in 1854-1876. Since the latter date, however, we find that in France only 1 cycle out of 7 has been so brief.

Gaussian normal curve, their form suggests fitting "a logarithmic normal curve; that is a Gaussian curve in which the successive units (standard deviations) of the horizontal scale are readjusted to distances having a constant ratio rather than a constant difference."[1] This experiment has been tried upon Figure R of Chart 4—the distri-

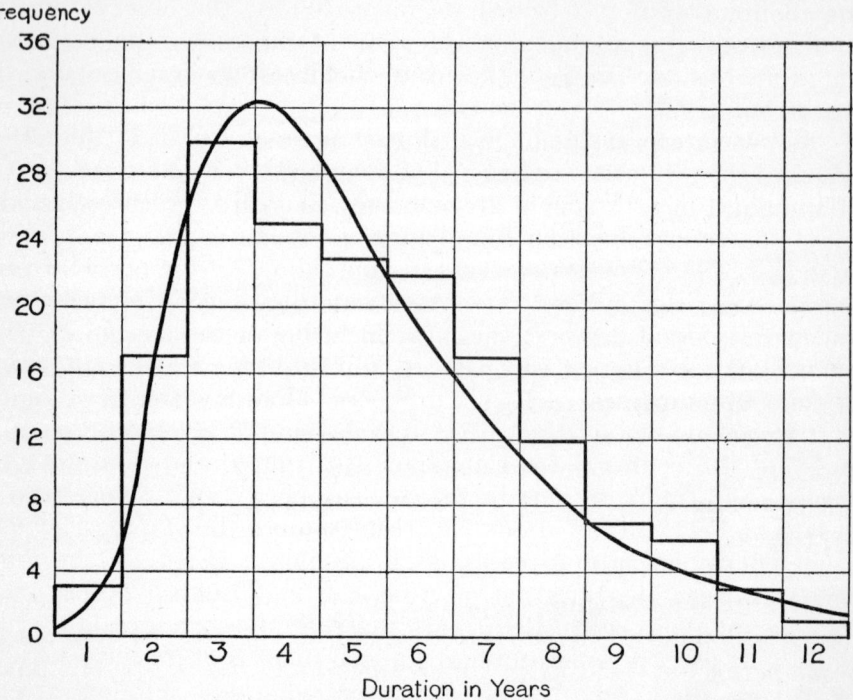

CHART V. Logarithmic Normal Curve Fitted by Davies' Method to the Frequency Distribution of 166 Observations upon the Duration of Business Cycles.

bution which includes all of our 166 observations. Chart V shows that the fit of the logarithmic normal curve to the data is on the whole rather close.[2]

From this fact we infer that, like other biological and social phenomena whose distributions are well described by some form of the

---

[1] See George R. Davies, "The Logarithmic Curve of Distribution," *Journal of the American Statistical Association*, December, 1925, vol. xx, pp. 467–480. Dr. Thorp has adopted Professor Davies' method in making the chart which follows.

[2] When the cycles now running in our 17 countries are ended, the new batch of observations promises to modify the distribution of Chart V somewhat. Five years have already elapsed since the latest recession in three of our countries, and six years in seven countries.

INTRODUCTION

normal curve, the durations of business cycles may be regarded as the net resultants of a multitude of factors which are largely independent of each other. If there is any dominant factor or set of factors, which tends to produce cycles of uniform duration, its influence is greatly modified by a host of other factors combined in ways which vary endlessly. This conclusion has an important bearing upon the theory of business cycles and the methods by which that theory may be improved.

6. Regarding the relative duration of the several phases which make up business cycles, the annals yield certain fragmentary, but significant, results.

As we interpret them, the phases of recession and revival are relatively brief. Put together, they account for only one-quarter of the duration of business cycles on the average. Of the remaining three-quarters, the prosperous phase occupies a somewhat longer time than the phase of depression. But the ratio of months of prosperity to months of depression varies widely from country to country, and within any country it varies widely from cycle to cycle. Consequently, the average ratios approach stability only when long periods of time and many countries are included. Perhaps the most significant figures are those for the United States and England in 1790-1925, and for all our 17 countries in 1890-1913. These three results come out respectively 1.50, 1.11 and 1.08 years of prosperity per year of depression.

Both the English and the American records indicate that the relative duration of the prosperous and depressed phases of business cycles is dominated by the secular trend of wholesale prices. In the three periods of rising price trends since 1790, the prosperous phases of the cycles have been prolonged and the depressed phases have been relatively brief. In the three periods of declining price trends, the prosperous phases of the cycles have been relatively brief and the depressed phases prolonged. While the observations upon which these conclusions rest are subject to a margin of uncertainty in every cycle considered, random errors could hardly produce such uniform results as we find.

Finally, it appears that the depressed phases of business cycles are susceptible of greater prolongation than the prosperous phases. Whereas our averages including many cycles all show a slight preponderance of years of prosperity over years of depression, our long cycles as a group show a marked preponderance of years of depression over years of prosperity.

In weighing the conclusions drawn in this section, one should bear in mind certain features of the data and methods used.

No selection or "adjustment" has been practiced upon the observations. The "abnormal cases"—if that phrase has an intelligible meaning—are included with the "normal". Every reader of the annals will note how frequently foreign wars and domestic turmoil, harvest fluctuations, epidemics, floods and earthquakes have checked or reënforced the tides of business activity. A tendency toward alternations of prosperity and depression must have considerable constancy and energy to stamp its pattern upon economic history in a world where other factors of most unequal power are constantly present, and where one or other of these factors, singly or in combination, rises to dominance at irregular intervals.

Our measurements are based solely upon the intervals between recessions. It would be desirable to check the results by a second set, based on the intervals between revivals. We have not attempted such a check, because business commentators have paid less attention to the upward than to the downward turning points of business cycles. The materials for making the second set of measurements are less full and reliable than the materials we have exploited. If a second set as satisfactory as the first could be made, the frequency distributions it yielded would doubtless differ in numberless details from the frequency distributions here presented. But we have no reason to believe that the broad conclusions suggested by the new frequency distributions would run counter to the conclusions we have drawn.

The year is too large a unit for measuring business cycles. Our results have the crudity of an effort to ascertain the stature distribution of men, women and children from measurements made in feet. In statistical work with time series, it is often possible to substitute the more appropriate unit of a month. But such investigations of business fluctuations are confined to those narrow limits of time, place, and type of business for which elaborate numerical data have been collected. In a problem which requires a considerable array of cases to yield significant results, the cruder but more numerous measures afforded by business annals have their advantages. And the preceding comparison between the business annals and the business indexes for the United States and England favor the view that the results to

INTRODUCTION

which the annals point would be supported by statistical analysis, did the numerical data cover a longer period.

VI. International Relationships Among Business Cycles.

1. OTHER PROBLEMS UPON WHICH THE ANNALS THROW LIGHT.

Despite their brevity, the running accounts found in the following chapters on business conditions in various countries can be made to throw light upon many aspects of business cycles besides their duration. For example, variations in the intensity of different periods of prosperity and depression, in the severity of successive recessions, and in the character of successive revivals are here revealed, though they are not expressed in quantitative terms. The relations between the intensity of business fluctuations and their duration also appear, as well as the relations between intensity in one phase of a cycle and intensity in succeeding phases. So, too, the annals afford many insights into the complexities of business expansion and contraction. Often they show what branches of trade led a certain movement and what branches lagged behind, what parts of a country benefited or suffered most in a given cycle. The exceedingly mixed relations between business conditions and agricultural fortunes receive much attention. In one sense every cycle is a unique historical episode; the annals bring out many of the idiosyncrasies of particular cases, as well as the features which recur in case after case.

All these are matters which one will notice upon casual reading, but about which one can learn much more by systematic comparisons of the annals for different countries and different times. In the treatise upon *Business Cycles*, which the National Bureau has under way, we plan to make continual use of this collection, which, as said at the outset, covers a period longer and an area wider than we can cover, save in the most fragmentary way, in our collection of statistical data.

The present introduction, then, falls far short of developing the full significance of the materials contained in later chapters. But there is one more problem which must be discussed, both because of its relation to the duration of business cycles, and because of its large significance.

2. A Conspectus of Business Conditions in Different Countries.

Opinions differ widely concerning the relations between the economic fortunes of different countries. One prevalent view, often implied in discussions of public policy though seldom avowed openly, is that competition for foreign markets and foreign investments makes one nation's gain another nation's loss. A second view is that small countries with a vast commerce—England, the Netherlands, Belgium, Sweden and Norway—experience prosperity or depression as world business quickens or slackens; but that nations with a continental spread need feel slight concern about foreign factors—to them internal development is of overshadowing importance. There is still a third view, that business enterprise has been silently establishing a "world economy", a "commercial league of nations", in which all the members prosper or suffer together.

Needless to say, the annals do not give clear proof or disproof of any of these contentions. But they do indicate a trend in the direction of "world economy".

To facilitate international comparisons of economic fortunes, the annals of all the countries studied have been compressed into a single table. This conspectus begins with the United States and England in 1790, adds France in 1840, Germany in 1853, Austria in 1867, and 12 other countries in 1890. For the last generation it affords a fair view of world experience. The entries have the bleakness of statistical averages; they do not indicate the complexity of conditions prevailing every year within each country. For most purposes the fuller form of the annals given on later pages should be used rather than the conspectus. But it is only as we concentrate in each country upon the net resultant of its diverse conditions that we can gain a clear view of the international similarities and diversities. Even the conspectus is not simple enough to tell its own story; it needs to be analyzed and summarized, as the reader who looks it over will agree.

INTRODUCTION

TABLE 10
Conspectus of Business Fluctuations in Various Countries

	1790	1791	1792	1793
United States	Revival; prosperity	Prosperity	Prosperity; financial distress	Prosperity
England	Moderate prosperity	Prosperity	Prosperity; financial strain	Recession; panic; depression

	1794	1795	1796	1797
United States	Uneven prosperity	Prosperity	Recession; depression	Depression; panic
England	Depression	Revival	Uneven prosperity	Recession; panic; depression

	1798	1799	1800	1801
United States	Depression	Revival	Prosperity	Mild prosperity
England	Depression	Depression	Depression	Depression; revival

	1802	1803	1804	1805
United States	Recession	Mild depression	Revival	Prosperity
England	Prosperity	Prosperity; recession	Mild depression	Revival

	1806	1807	1808	1809
United States	Prosperity	Prosperity; recession	Depression	Depression
England	Prosperity	Recession	Mild depression	Revival; prosperity

	1810	1811	1812	1813
United States	Revival	Moderate prosperity	Brief recession; uneven prosperity	Prosperity
England	Prosperity; recession	Deep depression	Revival	Prosperity

	1814	1815	1816	1817
United States	Prosperity; financial distress	Prosperity; panic; recession	Depression	Mild depression
England	Uneven prosperity	Boom; recession	Deep depression	Depression; revival

	1818	1819	1820	1821
United States	Mild depression	Severe depression; financial panic	Depression	Depression; revival
England	Prosperity	Recession; depression	Depression; slight revival	Slow revival

TABLE 10—(Continued)
Conspectus of Business Fluctuations in Various Countries

	1822	1823	1824	1825
United States	Mild recession	Revival	Prosperity	Prosperity; panic; recession
England	Revival; prosperity	Prosperity	Prosperity	Prosperity; recession; panic

	1826	1827	1828	1829
United States	Depression; revival	Moderate prosperity	Prosperity; recession	Depression; revival
England	Depression	Revival	Prosperity	Recession; depression

	1830	1831	1832	1833
United States	Moderate prosperity	Prosperity	Moderate prosperity	Prosperity; panic; recession
England	Slow revival	Recession; depression	Depression	Revival

	1834	1835	1836	1837
United States	Mild depression	Revival; prosperity	Prosperity	Prosperity; panic; recession; depression
England	Prosperity	Prosperity; stock exchange panic	Prosperity; financial panic	Recession; panic; depression

	1838	1839	1840	1841
United States	Depression; slight revival	Revival; panic; recession	Depression	Depression
England	Depression	Depression	Depression	Depression
France	....	....	Revival	Prosperity

	1842	1843	1844	1845
United States	Depression	Depression; revival	Revival; prosperity	Prosperity; brief recession
England	Depression	Revival	Mild prosperity	Prosperity
France	Prosperity	Prosperity	Prosperity	Prosperity; bourse panic

	1846	1847	1848	1849
United States	Recession; mild depression	Revival; prosperity; panic; recession	Mild depression; revival	Prosperity
England	Prosperity	Prosperity; panic; recession	Depression	Depression; revival
France	Prosperity	Recession; panic	Depression; panic	Depression

	1850	1851	1852	1853
United States	Prosperity	Prosperity	Prosperity	Prosperity; recession
England	Prosperity	Prosperity	Prosperity	Prosperity
France	Depression	Depression	Revival	Prosperity
Germany	....	....	....	Revival

INTRODUCTION

TABLE 10—(Continued)
CONSPECTUS OF BUSINESS FLUCTUATIONS IN VARIOUS COUNTRIES

	1854	1855	1856	1857
United States	Recession; depression	Depression; revival	Prosperity	Prosperity; panic; recession; depression
England	Recession	Mild depression	Revival; prosperity	Prosperity; panic; recession
France	Prosperity; brief recession	Prosperity	Brief recession	Moderate prosperity; panic; recession
Germany	Prosperity	Prosperity	Prosperity; bourse panic	Prosperity; panic; recession

	1858	1859	1860	1861
United States	Depression	Revival	Prosperity; recession	Mild depression; revival
England	Depression	Revival	Prosperity	Uneven prosperity
France	Depression	Revival	Prosperity; recession	Recession
Germany	Recession; depression	Depression	Revival	Mild prosperity

	1862	1863	1864	1865
United States	War activity	War activity	War activity	Boom; recession
England	Uneven prosperity	Uneven prosperity	Uneven prosperity; financial strain	Prosperity
France	Mild depression	Uneven depression	Depression; financial panic	Depression
Germany	Uneven prosperity	Moderate prosperity	Moderate prosperity	Prosperity

	1866	1867	1868	1869
United States	Mild depression	Depression	Revival	Prosperity; monetary difficulties
England	Recession; panic; depression	Depression	Depression	Revival
France	Revival	Recession; mild depression; bourse panic	Depression; revival	Prosperity; Prosperity bourse panic
Germany	Prosperity; recession; depression	Depression; revival	Revival	
Austria	....	Revival	Moderate prosperity	Prosperity; panic; recession

TABLE 10—(Continued)

CONSPECTUS OF BUSINESS FLUCTUATIONS IN VARIOUS COUNTRIES

	1870	1871	1872	1873
United States	Recession; mild depression	Revival; prosperity	Prosperity	Prosperity; panic; recession
England	Prosperity; panic	Prosperity	Prosperity	Prosperity; recession
France	Prosperity; recession; depression	Depression; panic	Revival	Recession; depression
Germany	Prosperity; brief recession	Prosperity	Prosperity	Prosperity; panic; recession; depression
Austria	Slow recession	Mild depression	Revival; prosperity	Prosperity; panic; recession

	1874	1875	1876	1877
United States	Depression	Depression	Depression	Depression
England	Depression	Depression	Depression	Depression
France	Mild depression	Revival	Gradual recession	Mild depression
Germany	Depression	Depression	Depression	Slow revival
Austria	Deep depression	Depression	Depression	Depression

	1878	1879	1880	1881
United States	Depression; revival	Revival; prosperity	Prosperity	Prosperity
England	Deepening depression	Depression; revival	Slow revival	Mild prosperity
France	Depression	Revival; bourse panic	Prosperity	Moderate prosperity
Germany	Recession; depression	Depression; revival	Recession; mild depression	Renewed revival
Austria	Depression	Depression	Revival	Mild prosperity

	1882	1883	1884	1885
United States	Prosperity; slight recession	Recession	Depression	Depression; revival
England	Mild prosperity	Slow recession	Depression	Depression
France	Recession; panic	Depression	Depression	Depression
Germany	Prosperity; recession	Mild depression	Depression	Depression
Austria	Moderate prosperity; bourse panic	Prosperity	Recession	Mild depression

	1886	1887	1888	1889
United States	Revival	Prosperity	Brief recession	Prosperity
England	Depression; slight revival	Revival	Moderate prosperity	Prosperity
France	Depression	Revival	Moderate prosperity	Moderate prosperity; financial strain
Germany	Depression; revival	Revival	Moderate prosperity	Prosperity
Austria	Depression; revival	Revival	Prosperity	Prosperity

TABLE 10—(Continued)
Conspectus of Business Fluctuations in Various Countries

	1890	1891	1892	1893
United States	Prosperity; recession	Depression; revival	Prosperity	Recession; panic; depression
England	Prosperity; panic; recession	Industrial recession; financial prostration	Depression	Deep depression
France	Recession; mild depression	Mild depression	Depression	Depression
Germany	Recession	Depression	Depression	Depression
Austria	Uneven prosperity	Prosperity	Recession	Revival
Russia	Mild prosperity	Recession, depression	Depression	Revival
Sweden	Prosperity	Prosperity	Recession, mild depression	Depression
Netherlands	Mild prosperity	Recession	Depression	Depression
Italy	Depression	Depression; panic	Depression	Depression; panic
Argentina	Recession; depression	Depression; panic	Revival, recession	Mild depression
Brazil	Depression	Depression	Uneven depression	Depression
Canada	Mild depression	Depression; revival	Mild prosperity	Recession; depression
South Africa	Prosperity; recession; depression	Depression	Rapid revival	Prosperity
Australia	Recession; depression	Depression	Depression	Depression; panic
India	Mild depression	Depression	Uneven depression	Depression
Japan	Recession; depression	Depression	Depression	Mild depression
China	Mild depression	Mild depression	Depression deepens	Depression

TABLE 10—(Continued)
CONSPECTUS OF BUSINESS FLUCTUATIONS IN VARIOUS COUNTRIES

	1894	1895	1896	1897
United States	Deep depression	Depression; revival	Recession; depression	Depression; revival
England	Depression	Depression; revival last half-year	Revival; prosperity	Prosperity
France	Depression	Depression; revival	Revival	Moderate prosperity
Germany	Depression; revival	Revival	Prosperity	Prosperity
Austria	Recession; mild depression	Mild depression	Mild depression	Mild depression
Russia	Prosperity	Prosperity	Prosperity	Prosperity
Sweden	Mild depression	Revival	Prosperity	Prosperity
Netherlands	Depression	Depression	Revival	Mild prosperity
Italy	Depression	Depression	Depression; slight revival	Revival
Argentina	Depression	Lessening depression	Revival	Revival retarded
Brazil	Revival	Mild prosperity	Recession; panic; depression	Depression; panic
Canada	Acute depression	Depression	Lessening depression	Revival
South Africa	Prosperity	Prosperity; recession	Depression	Depression
Australia	Depression	Depression; slight revival	Strong revival	Mild prosperity; agricultural depression
India	Uneven revival	Mild prosperity	Recession	Depression
Japan	Revival; recession	Revival	Prosperity	Prosperity; recession
China	Depression	Revival	Prosperity	Gradual recession

TABLE 10—(*Continued*)

CONSPECTUS OF BUSINESS FLUCTUATIONS IN VARIOUS COUNTRIES

	1898	1899	1900	1901
United States	Revival; prosperity	Prosperity	Prosperity, brief recession	Prosperity
England	Prosperity	Prosperity	Prosperity; recession, summer	Mild depression
France	Prosperity	Prosperity	Prosperity; recession	Depression
Germany	Prosperity	Prosperity	Prosperity; recession; depression	Depression
Austria	Mild depression; revival	Mild prosperity	Recession; depression	Depression
Russia	Prosperity	Prosperity; panic; recession	Recession; depression	Depression
Sweden	Prosperity	Prosperity	Prosperity	Recession; depression
Netherlands	Prosperity	Prosperity	Prosperity	Recession; mild depression
Italy	Uneven prosperity	Mild prosperity	Prosperity; brief recession	Prosperity
Argentina	Mild prosperity	Prosperity	Recession; depression	Depression
Brazil	Depression deepens	Depression; revival	Revival; panic; recession	Mild depression
Canada	Prosperity	Prosperity	Prosperity; slight recession	Revival; prosperity
South Africa	Depression	Revival; recession	Depression	Revival
Australia	Prosperity	Prosperity	Prosperity	Recession
India	Slow revival	Moderate prosperity	Recession	Depression
Japan	Depression	Depression	Deeper depression	Depression; financial panic, spring
China	Mild depression	Revival; prosperity	Prosperity; recession; depression	Depression; revival

BUSINESS ANNALS

TABLE 10—(*Continued*)

CONSPECTUS OF BUSINESS FLUCTUATIONS IN VARIOUS COUNTRIES

	1902	1903	1904	1905
United States	Prosperity	Prosperity; recession	Mild depression; revival	Prosperity
England	Lessened depression	Depression deepens	Revival	Revival; prosperity
France	Depression	Revival	Moderate prosperity	Prosperity
Germany	Depression	Revival	Mild prosperity; recession	Revival; prosperity
Austria	Depression	Depression; revival	Revival	Mild prosperity
Russia	Depression	Depression; revival	Recession; depression	Depression
Sweden	Depression	Revival	Mild prosperity	Prosperity
Netherlands	Depression	Depression	Revival; prosperity	Prosperity
Italy	Moderate prosperity	Prosperity	Prosperity	Prosperity
Argentina	Depression; revival	Prosperity	Prosperity	Prosperity
Brazil	Mild depression	Depression deepens	Depression	Depression
Canada	Prosperity; financial distress	Prosperity	Uneven prosperity	Full prosperity
South Africa	Prosperity	Recession	Depression	Depression
Australia	Mild depression	Deepening depression	Revival	Mild prosperity
India	Revival	Prosperity	Prosperity	Prosperity
Japan	Slow revival	Revival	Prosperity	Prosperity; recession; depression
China	Mild prosperity	Mild prosperity	Mild prosperity	Mild prosperity

INTRODUCTION

TABLE 10—(Continued)
Conspectus of Business Fluctuations in Various Countries

	1906	1907	1908	1909
United States	Prosperity	Prosperity; panic; recession; depression	Depression	Revival; mild prosperity
England	Prosperity	Prosperity; recession	Depression	Revival
France	Prosperity	Prosperity	Recession; mild depression	Revival
Germany	Prosperity	Prosperity; recession; depression	Depression	Depression; revival
Austria	Prosperity	Prosperity	Recession; depression	Depression
Russia	Depression; slight revival	Revival	Recession; depression	Depression; revival
Sweden	Prosperity	Prosperity; recession; panic	Depression	Depression
Netherlands	Prosperity	Prosperity	Depression; revival	Revival; prosperity
Italy	Prosperity	Prosperity; recession	Depression	Depression
Argentina	Prosperity	Prosperity	Mild recession	Revival; prosperity
Brazil	Slow revival	Revival; recession, autumn	Depression	Revival
Canada	Prosperity peak	Prosperity; panic; recession	Depression; revival	Revival
South Africa	Depression	Depression deepens	Depression lessens	Revival
Australia	Prosperity	Prosperity	Recession; mild depression	Rapid revival; prosperity
India	Prosperity	Prosperity; recession	Depression	Depression; slight revival
Japan	Revival; prosperity	Prosperity; panic; recession	Depression	Depression; revival
China	Recession	Depression	Depression	Revival

BUSINESS ANNALS

TABLE 10—(*Continued*)
CONSPECTUS OF BUSINESS FLUCTUATIONS IN VARIOUS COUNTRIES

	1910	1911	1912	1913
United States	Recession	Mild depression	Revival; prosperity	Prosperity; recession
England.....	Prosperity	Prosperity	Prosperity	Prosperity; recession, last quarter
France.......	Prosperity	Prosperity	Prosperity	Prosperity; recession
Germany....	Revival; prosperity	Prosperity	Prosperity	Prosperity; recession
Austria......	Depression	Revival	Prosperity; recession; depression	Depression; panic
Russia.......	Prosperity	Prosperity	Prosperity	Prosperity except on bourse
Sweden......	Revival	Prosperity	Prosperity	Prosperity; slight recession
Netherlands..	Prosperity	Prosperity	Prosperity	Recession
Italy........	Mild depression	Revival halted, autumn	Uneven prosperity	Mild prosperity; recession
Argentina....	Prosperity	Recession; mild depression	Depression; revival, autumn	Recession
Brazil.......	Prosperity	Prosperity	Prosperity	Uneven prosperity
Canada......	Prosperity	Prosperity	Prosperity	Prosperity; recession
South Africa.	Prosperity	Prosperity	Prosperity	Uneven recession
Australia....	Prosperity	Prosperity	Prosperity	Mild recession
India........	Revival	Prosperity	Prosperity	Uneven prosperity
Japan.......	Revival; prosperity	Prosperity	Prosperity	Prosperity
China.......	Recession	Depression	Depression	Depression

TABLE 10—(*Continued*)
CONSPECTUS OF BUSINESS FLUCTUATIONS IN VARIOUS COUNTRIES

	1914	1915	1916	1917
United States	Depression	Revival; prosperity	Prosperity	Prosperity; war activity
England	Mild depression, deepens with war	War activity	War activity	War activity
France	Depression	War activity	War activity	War activity
Germany	Mild depression; revival	War activity	War activity	War activity
Austria	Depression	War activity	War activity	War activity
Russia	Recession; panic; depression	Uneven depression	War activity	Recession; depression
Sweden	Recession; depression	Revival, prosperity	Prosperity	Recession
Netherlands	Recession; panic; depression	Revival; uneven prosperity	Moderate prosperity	Recession
Italy	Recession; panic; depression	Uneven depression	War activity	War activity
Argentina	Depression; panic	Uneven depression	Depression; slow revival	Revival
Brazil	Depression deepens	Depression; revival	Revival; prosperity	Prosperity
Canada	Depression deepening with war	Depression; revival	War activity	War activity
South Africa	Recession; depression	Slow revival	Rapid revival	Prosperity
Australia	Revival; recession	Mild depression; revival	War activity	War activity
India	Prosperity; recession	Depression	Revival	Prosperity
Japan	Recession; depression	Revival; prosperity	Prosperity	Uneven prosperity
China	Depression deepens	Depression	Revival; prosperity	Uneven prosperity

TABLE 10—(*Continued*)

CONSPECTUS OF BUSINESS FLUCTUATIONS IN VARIOUS COUNTRIES

	1918	1919	1920	1921
United States	War activity; recession	Revival; prosperity	Prosperity; recession; depression	Depression
England	War activity; recession	Revival; prosperity	Prosperity; recession; depression	Deep depression
France	War activity; stagnation	Depression; revival; boom	Prosperity; recession; depression	Depression; revival
Germany	War activity; disorganization, November	Depression	Depression	Revival, spring
Austria	War activity; chaos	Depression	Slow revival	Revival
Russia	Depression	Depression	Depression	Depression
Sweden	Depression	Depression; revival	Boom; recession; depression	Depression
Netherlands	Depression	Revival; prosperity	Prosperity; recession; depression	Depression
Italy	War activity; slight recession	Mild depression; revival	Recession; depression	Depression; panic
Argentina	Moderate prosperity	Prosperity	Prosperity; recession	Depression
Brazil	Prosperity; brief recession	Prosperity	Prosperity; recession; depression	Severe depression
Canada	War activity; recession	Revival; prosperity	Prosperity; recession	Depression
South Africa	Prosperity; recession	Revival; prosperity	Prosperity; recession; depression	Deep depression
Australia	War activity	Prosperity	Prosperity; recession	Depression
India	Prosperity; recession	Revival; prosperity	Prosperity; recession; depression	Depression
Japan	Uneven prosperity; recession	Depression; revival; prosperity	Prosperity; recession; depression	Depression
China	Uneven prosperity	Prosperity	Prosperity; recession; depression	Depression

TABLE 10—(Continued)
Conspectus of Business Fluctuations in Various Countries

	1922	1923	1924	1925 (Preliminary)
United States	Revival; prosperity	Prosperity; recession	Mild depression; revival	Prosperity
England	Depression	Depression	Lessening depression	Depression
France	Revival	Prosperity	Prosperity	Prosperity
Germany	Revival checked, summer; disorganization	Depression	Revival; temporary check, summer	Halting revival; recession
Austria	Uneven recession	Depression	Depression; financial strain	Depression
Russia	Depression; slight revival	Revival; recession, October	Mild depression; revival	Uneven prosperity; recession
Sweden	Depression; revival	Revival	Mild prosperity	Mild prosperity
Netherlands	Depression	Depression	Revival	Mild prosperity
Italy	Depression	Depression; revival	Moderate prosperity	Prosperity
Argentina	Depression	Lessening depression	Revival	Prosperity
Brazil	Lessening depression	Revival	Mild prosperity; recession	Depression
Canada	Depression; revival	Moderate prosperity	Recession; mild depression	Revival; prosperity
South Africa	Depression	Revival	Mild prosperity	Prosperity
Australia	Slow revival	Revival; mild prosperity	Mild recession	Revival; prosperity
India	Depression	Slow revival	Revival; mild prosperity	Mild prosperity
Japan	Depression	Depression	Depression	Depression; revival
China	Depression	Depression	Depression	Depression

3. How Closely the Cycles in Different Countries Agree.

Concerning the fact of fundamental interest in this inquiry, the conspectus of business conditions gives an exaggerated impression of century-long and world-wide similarity. Periods of prosperity, recession, depression and revival are here pictured as recurring in much the same way in every country and during every decade. The fuller form of the annals makes it clear, not only that this recurrence is nowhere the whole story of economic fluctuations, but also that it is farther from being the whole story in some countries than in others. The importance of business cycles as a factor in national life was less during the closing decades of the 18th century than during the opening decades of the 20th century in England and the United States. There is a similar difference between these two countries and China, Russia or Brazil at present. The more highly organized a country's business, the larger the proportion of its people who live by making and spending money incomes, the more important become the recurrent cycles of activity. Let us, however, take cyclical oscillations for granted, disregard their relative importance, and inquire what influence the cycles in one country exercise upon cycles in other countries.

It has long been recognized that the great financial crises have an international sweep. Thus the conspectus shows that England and the United States shared in the crises of 1815, 1825 and 1837; that England, the United States and France (which now is represented in the annals) shared in the crisis of 1847; that these three countries, and Germany also, shared in the panic of 1857; that England, the United States, France, Germany and Austria shared in varying degrees the crisis of 1873. To these familiar facts our annals add that all five countries had mild recessions in 1882-84. Of the 17 countries included in the annals after 1890, 10 had recessions in 1890-91, 15 had recessions in 1900-01, 15 in 1907-08, 12 in 1912-13, 11 in 1918, and 14 in 1920. Further, the countries which escaped a share in these world reactions usually owed their exemption to still worse fortune. Thus South Africa and Japan had no recession in 1900-01 because they were already suffering from depression. The three countries of our 17 which escaped in 1920 were Germany, Austria and Russia.

INTRODUCTION

Of course the experiences of the several countries were not identical in the years of crises and recessions. In the whole record there is no crisis which was equally severe everywhere. In 1873, for example, the United States, Germany and Austria suffered far more severely than England and France. In 1890, on the contrary, the financial strain was more severe in London than in New York or Berlin, while Vienna deferred its recession until 1892. The center of disturbance in 1900 seems to have been Germany; countries like the United States and Italy felt but repercussions of a foreign shock. In 1907 the gravest difficulties appeared in the United States. Probably the nearest approach to a severe world-wide crisis was made in 1920, and that case was obviously dominated by post-war re-adjustments. It is clear, however, that a financial crisis breaking out in any country of commercial importance produces financial strains in other countries, and that even mild recessions like those of 1882-83 and 1913 spread widely.

It has been less noticed that other phases of business cycles also propagate themselves. The long depressions of the 1870's, the checkered fortunes of the 1880's, the revival of the middle 1890's, the boom of 1906-7, the calmer prosperity of 1912, the hectic activity of the war years, and the severe depression after 1920 had much the same international character as the crises to which attention is commonly restricted.

Yet business cycles do not run a strictly parallel course in any two countries. Perhaps the best way to bring out the degree of likeness and difference in contemporary fortunes is to note the proportion of years in which conditions in different countries are described by the same terms in the conspectus, and the proportion of years in which conditions are described in unlike terms. An effort to carry out this plan shows that many years do not fall into either category. Business may be reviving in one country and already prosperous in another, depressed in one and entering depression in another; or conditions may be similar during the early part of a year and divergent in the closing months, or different at the start and convergent at the close. In such cases one cannot call the conditions quite similar or decidedly unlike. Thus it is necessary to recognize at least three types of relations between the synchronous phases of business cycles in different countries—agreement, partial agreement and opposition. Arbitrary definitions were adopted, and a statistical tabulation made of these relationships.[1]

Such a comparison of business conditions in the five countries for which we have annals running back of 1890 is provided by Table 11. Most of the comparisons here made show a preponderance of years in which the business cycles of the countries paired were passing through the same phases over years in which they were passing through opposite phases. The intimacy of relations is probably understated by the table; for it takes no account of the shifting relations of lead and lag in the influence exercised by business conditions in one country upon business conditions in the other country with which it is compared. As one would expect from England's position in international trade and finance, English cycles are more highly correlated with the cycles of other countries, than the cycles of other countries are correlated with each other. The closest agreements are found between English and French or English and German cycles; the loosest agreements are between Austrian and American cycles.

From the third section of the table, it appears that the international similarity of phase in business cycles increased on the whole with the passage of time. The breaking of economic bonds by the war, and the tardiness of their restoration after the Armistice, interfered with this process of synchronizing cycles. But the non-economic factors, which played so large a rôle after 1914, had much the same character and influenced business among all the belligerents in much the same way, so long as hostilities lasted. Since 1918, economic

---

[1] The rules followed by Dr. Thorp in preparing the data for the following table are as follows:

Agreement includes
1. Years in which two countries pass through the same phase or phases of a cycle.
2. Years in which two countries pass through at least two corresponding phases, though one may enter a third phase. Example: "Prosperity; recession" in one country, and "Prosperity; recession; depression" in another.

Partial agreement includes
Years in which two countries pass through phases of the cycle which succeed one another. Example: "Revival" in one country, and "Prosperity" in another; or "Recession" in one country, and "Recession; depression" in another.

Opposition of phases includes
Years in which opposite phases of cycles occur, whatever intermediate phases are noted. Example: "Prosperity; recession; depression" in one country, and "Depression; revival" in a second.

War activity is interpreted in this tabulation as corresponding to prosperity.
The relative severity of recessions in different countries is not taken into account.

TABLE 11

Agreement and Difference of Phase in English, French, German, Austrian and American Business Cycles

Various Periods

	Period Covered		Number of Years of			Percentage of Years of		
	Dates	Number of Years	Agreement in Phase	Partial agreement	Opposition in Phase	Agreement in Phase	Partial agreement	Opposition in Phase
I								
English and French cycles.	1867–1925	59	32	20	7	54	34	12
English and German cycles	" "	59	33	22	4	56	37	7
English and Austrian cycles	" "	59	27	21	11	46	36	19
English and American cycles	" "	59	28	18	13	47	31	22
French and German cycles.	" "	59	27	25	7	46	42	12
French and Austrian cycles	" "	59	19	21	19	32	36	32
French and American cycles	" "	59	23	23	13	39	39	22
German and Austrian cycles	" "	59	23	24	12	39	41	20
German and American cycles	" "	59	21	20	18	36	34	31
Austrian and American cycles	" "	59	18	23	18	31	39	31
II								
England and four other countries	1867–1925	236	120	81	35	51	34	15
Germany and four other countries	" "	236	104	91	41	44	39	17
France and four other countries	" "	236	101	89	46	43	38	19
United States and four other countries	" "	236	90	84	62	38	36	26
Austria and four other countries	" "	236	87	89	60	37	38	25
III								
English and American cycles	1790–1857	68	21	28	19	31	41	28
	1857–1925	68	33	21	14	49	31	21
English and French cycles..	1840–1882	43	12	17	14	28	40	33
	1883–1925	43	28	11	4	65	26	9
English and German cycles.	1853–1888	36	19	15	2	53	42	6
	1889–1925	37	21	13	3	57	35	8
English and Austrian cycles.	1867–1895	29	14	12	3	48	41	10
	1896–1925	30	13	9	8	43	30	27

fortunes have diverged widely. Presumably the business forces tending toward convergence are gradually resuming their wonted sway.

In treating the period when the annals include 17 countries, a more significant method of presenting the relations among their business cycles is feasible. For the cycles since 1890 have an international pattern simple enough to be carried in mind, and applied to the experience of one country after another. This pattern may be sketched as follows:

1st cycle, 1890-91 to 1900-01
   Recession in 1890-91; depression in 1891-95; revival in 1895-96; prosperity in 1896-00; recession in 1900-01.
2nd cycle, 1900-01 to 1907-08
   Recession in 1900-01; depression in 1901-03; revival in 1903-04; prosperity in 1905-07; recession in 1907-08.
3rd cycle, 1907-08 to 1913-14
   Recession in 1907-08; depression in 1908-09; revival in 1909-10; prosperity in 1910-13; recession in 1913-14.
4th cycle, 1913-14 to 1918
   Recession in 1913-14; depression in 1914-15; revival in 1915; prosperity in 1915-18; recession in 1918.
5th cycle, 1918 to 1920
   Recession in 1918; very brief and mild depression early in 1919; quick revival in 1919; prosperity in 1919-20; recession in 1920.
6th cycle, 1920 to —— (unfinished)
   Recession in 1920; severe depression in 1921-22; revival in 1922-23; mild prosperity in 1924-25.
During this period, of our 17 countries

Six have had 5 cycles and are now in a 6th: England, France, the Netherlands, Sweden, Italy and China.

Five have had 6 cycles and are now in a 7th: Austria, South Africa, Australia, Argentina and India.

Five have had 7 cycles and are now in an 8th: Germany, Russia, Canada, Brazil, and Japan.

One has had 10 cycles and is now in an 11th: the United States.

Thus no country in our list has had fewer business cycles since 1890 than the international pattern calls for; but the majority of countries have had one or two more than that number. These additional cycles seldom result from failure to participate in the international movements of activity and depression, but rather from the intercalation of what we may call domestic recessions between the dates of international recessions. To take the most striking case: the United States had its share in all the recessions of the international pattern; but it also had domestic recessions in 1893, 1896, 1903, 1910, and 1923. When a country skips an international recession, it is usually because that country has recently suffered a domestic recession. Thus business was already depressed in Japan and South Africa when the international recession of 1900 began; South Africa and China escaped the international recession of 1907 for similar reasons; so too the European neutrals had recessions in 1917 and not in 1918.

The countries whose business cycles diverge most from the international pattern are Italy before say 1907, Russia, South Africa, Brazil and China—all countries rather backward in economic organization and predominantly agricultural. The countries whose cycles have followed the international pattern most closely, on the other hand, are countries of highly developed industry, trade, and finance— England, France, Germany (until 1919), Sweden, and the Netherlands. Australia and Canada lag but a little behind these European powers in conformity. Austrian cycles were being assimilated closely to those of her western and northern neighbors in the decade before the war. Even British India and Japan have followed the European pattern of cycles without very striking divergencies.

Another way of summing up the international relationships of business cycles since 1890 is to run down the columns of entries in Table 10 for each year. There is no year of the 36 covered in which the same phase of the cycle prevailed in all of the 17 countries. Uniformity is approached, however, in 1893, 1899, 1906, 1908, 1912, 1916, 1920, and 1921; and in most years there is a marked preponderance of entries of similar tenor.

A graphic presentation of these facts is given by Chart VI. The irregular bands of white and of black which run vertically across the chart are not quite continuous in any year from 1890 to 1925. But the existence of a general trend toward uniformity of business fortunes is plain.

CHART VI. Conspectus of Business Cycles in Various Countries, 1790-1925.

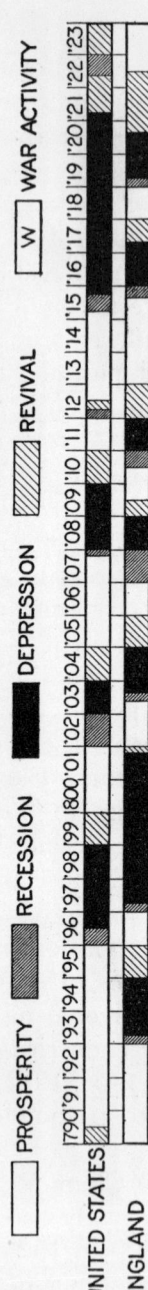
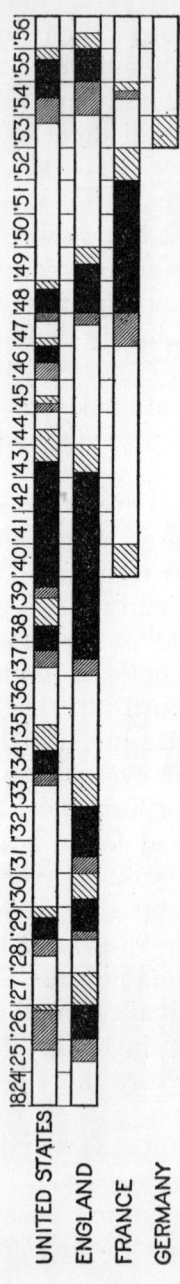

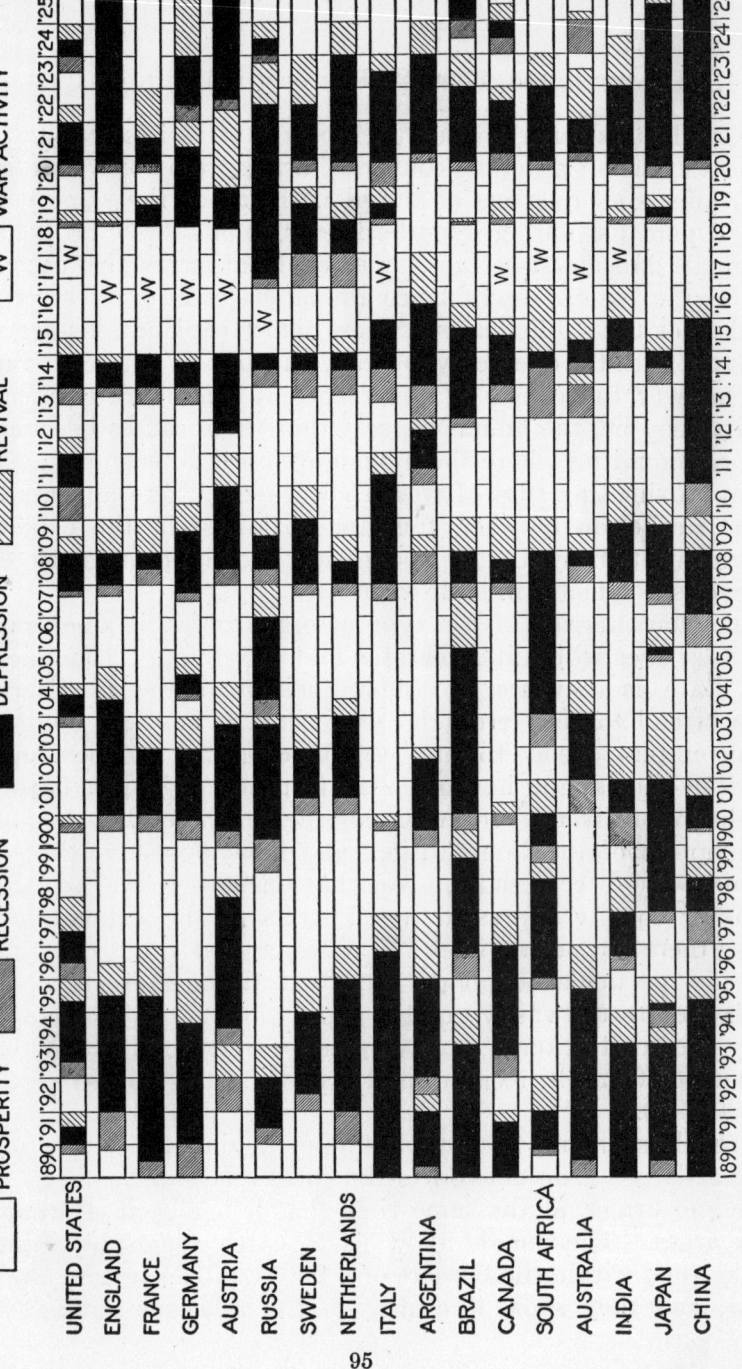

CHART VI. Conspectus of Business Cycles in Various Countries, 1790-1925—(Continued)

4. Domestic and Foreign Factors in Business Cycles.

Possibly this tendency to synchronize their phases, found in the business cycles of different countries, arises from some cosmic cause which affects all quarters of the globe in much the same way each year. Upon that daring hypothesis, our annals throw no light. But the annals do suggest certain tamer explanations, which account not only for the general resemblance among cycles in different countries, but also for their differences. These tamer explanations are not inconsistent with the cosmic hypothesis, but they do not depend upon it.

Whatever the causes of the recurrent fluctuations in economic activity may be, the annals suggest that these causes become active in all communities where there has developed an economic organization approximating that of western Europe. There appears to be a rough parallelism between the stage attained in the evolution of this organization by different countries, and the prominence of business cycles as a factor in their fortunes.

One characteristic of the type of organization in question is the wide area over which it integrates and coördinates economic activities. Bare as they are and short their span, the annals reveal a secular trend toward territorial expansion of business relations and a concomitant trend toward economic unity. For example, the American annals show how often the fortunes of the North, the South and the West diverged from one another in the earlier decades after the adoption of the Constitution, and how these divergencies have diminished in later decades. Not that business is ever equally prosperous or equally depressed in all states of the Union even now: always there are perceptible differences, and at times the differences are wide, particularly among the great farming "belts". Yet the annals picture the vastly greater population of today, spread over a vastly greater territory, as having more unity of fortune than had the people of the thirteen original states and the frontier settlements in 1790-1820.

Broadly speaking, the annals support a similar conclusion for the world at large. The network of business relations has been growing closer and firmer, at the same time that it has been stretching over wider areas. The annals allow us to catch some glimpses of this double trend within the borders of a few countries besides the United States, and they show it clearly in the relations among different countries. As American business is coming to have one story, diversified by agricultural episodes, so, before the war shattered international bonds for a time, world business seemed to be approaching the time when it too would have one story, diversified by political and social as well as agricultural episodes in different countries.

The basis of this trend toward unity of economic fortunes among communities organized on the European model is that each phase in a business cycle, as it develops in any area, tends to produce the same phase in all the areas with which the first has dealings.

Prosperity in one country stimulates demand for the products of other countries, and so quickens activities in the latter regions. Prosperity also lessens the energy with which merchants, financiers, and contractors seek competitive business in neutral markets, and so gives a better chance to the corresponding classes in countries where the domestic demand is less active. Further, prosperity, with its sanguine temper and its liberal profits, encourages investments abroad as well as at home, and the export of capital to other countries gives an impetus to their trade. A recession checks all these stimuli. A severe crisis in any important center produces quicker and graver results. Demands for financial assistance raise interest rates and reduce domestic lending power in other centers; apprehensions regarding the solvency of international houses may start demands for liquidation in many places; the losses which bankruptcies bring are likely to be felt by business enterprises the world over. So, too, with depressions and revival; wherever they prevail, they exert influences upon businss elsewhere which tend to produce depressions or revivals in all regions with which the center of disturbance trades.

Nor are these relations one-sided. The condition of business in every country not only influences, but is influenced by conditions in other countries. The trend toward international similarity of business cycles is enforced by an endless series of actions and re-actions among the influences exerted and experienced by all the nations which deal with each other.

Of course, the degree of influence exerted by business conditions in a given area upon business elsewhere depends upon the importance of that area in international commerce and finance. Similarly, the sensitiveness of business in a given area to the influence of business conditions elsewhere is least in communities like interior China, whose economic activities are mainly self-contained, and greatest in communities which depend largely upon foreign markets, foreign investments, and foreign sources of supply, like England. It is also clear that a country of the latter type will reflect world conditions more faithfully, the more widely its foreign interests are distributed.

While this line of analysis explains the tendency of business cycles in different countries to synchronize their phases, it does not hide the obstructions which this tendency meets.

In so far as the people in any country buy and sell, lend and borrow only among themselves, they are likely to have economic vicissitudes all their own. Agricultural communities which live largely on what they produce suffer more from acts of nature than farming populations which trade extensively; but they have little share in the world fluctuations of business. Even in countries where farmers are more business-like, we have noted that agriculture has a story of its own, dictated by the weather at home and abroad—a story which often differs from the story of mining, manufactures, transportation, wholesale trade, and finance.[1] Of course the agricultural story modifies the general tale. Fluctuations in the cost of raw materials and of foods, as well as fluctuations in the buying power of farm families, react upon the prosperity of other industries in proportion to the relative weight of agriculture in the country's total business. Hence, the larger the agricultural element in a given nation, the less likely are that nation's business cycles to fit neatly into the international pattern over a long series of years. For two nations with large farming interests are not likely to have closely similar harvest fluctuations year after year. The one development touching agriculture which most clearly tends toward unifying business fortunes is the decline in the proportion of families which depend on farming, and the concomitant increase in the proportion following industrial pursuits. Dr. Thorp's prefaces to the chapters of annals which follow show that this decline is world-wide.

While the rise of large-scale industry within a nation of cultivators, craftsmen and petty traders links its economic life to that of other nations, there may be a stage in this development when international influences seem to recede and domestic influences to grow more important. The first modern mines, factories, railways,

[1] In one way, the development of a "world market" for the great agricultural staples even increases the hazards of farming. A scanty yield of wheat in Canada, for example, need not cause a compensatory rise of prices.

and banks in such a country are likely to be foreign enterprises, dependent upon foreign investors for their capital and perhaps upon foreign customers for their markets. During that stage, such business as the outside world recognizes in the new-old country will be peculiarly sensitive to foreign fluctuations in finance and commerce. Meanwhile, if the new ventures prosper, natives of the country will learn to imitate modern methods and to consume modern products. Alongside the foreign-owned enterprises, domestic enterprises will multiply, drawing their capital from home sources and selling largely in the home market. After a time perhaps most of the early enterprises will be sold by their foreign owners to native business men. During this stage the country's business will seem to be emancipating itself from the domination of outside influences, and its business cycles will diverge more widely from the international pattern. But if the process of modernizing economic life continues until a considerable fraction of the population is affected, then a gradual reapproach toward world conditions will begin. Some such series of changes probably explains in part, but in part only, a curious feature of our Russian annals. In the earlier years covered by this record, Russian cycles followed the international pattern more closely than in the later years of the Tsarist regime.[1] Perhaps Chinese business will pass through similar stages in the not-distant future.

Besides differences in economic organization, in the proportion of people engaged in farming, and in harvest conditions, there is a host of more obvious causes of divergencies among business cycles, whether we consider successive cycles in the same country or synchronous cycles in different countries. Wars and civil disturbances play a prominent rôle in business annals, and that rôle is most erratic. Many of the differences of business fortune which the annals show seem ascribable to such factors; but we have had occasion to note that during its earlier stages, at least, the World War had a unifying effect upon conditions among both belligerents and neutrals. The after-effects of this war, however, were far from uniform in different nations. In the cycles of every country we can trace also the influence of changes in monetary conditions, banking organization and tariff acts domestic or foreign, if not the influence of changes in taxation, internal improvement plans and public regulation of business enter-

---

[1] For a fuller discussion of the relations between business cycles in Russia and in Western Europe, see S. A. Pervushin, *The Business Conjuncture*, Moscow, 1925, pp. 209-213. The writer is indebted to Dr. Simon Kuznets for a synopsis of Professor Pervushin's analysis.

prises. Besides these governmental matters, it seems probable that differences of national habit in respect to enterprise and thrift affect the frequency and violence of business oscillations. Still other matters which may count are changes in the methods of directing investments, the integration of industry, the organization of labor, the development of social insurance. But there is little point in extending a list of factors whose relative importance we cannot weigh.

This much seems clear: business activity is influenced by countless developments in the realms of nature, politics and science, as well as by developments within the realm of business itself; few of these developments occur at the same time, in the same form and on the same scale in all countries. Thus there is no difficulty in understanding why business cycles vary in many ways from nation to nation, though it is quite impossible as yet to assign its relative importance to each (perhaps to any) cause of divergence. One's final reflection may be that the quiet business forces working toward uniformity of fortunes must be powerful indeed to impress a common pattern upon the course of business cycles in many countries. And the increasing conformity to an international pattern which the annals reveal in recent years shows that the international influences are gaining in relative importance.

BUSINESS ANNALS

UNITED STATES	ITALY
ENGLAND	ARGENTINA
FRANCE	BRAZIL
GERMANY	CANADA
AUSTRIA	SOUTH AFRICA
RUSSIA	AUSTRALIA
SWEDEN	INDIA
NETHERLANDS	JAPAN
CHINA	

BY

WILLARD LONG THORP

ASSISTED BY

HILDEGARDE E. THORP

PREFATORY NOTE

Business Annals is an attempt to summarize and depict the business conditions in seventeen countries as they appeared to intelligent and expert observers. The chief sources are commercial and trade journals, reviews, magazines, and papers, consular and diplomatic reports, and government records. Doubtless the annals represent the years as contemporaries thought they were, rather than as statistical records later proved them to have been. Nevertheless, we have made considerable use of statistical material, and the analysts before us doubtless formed their opinions and views largely from such data. But we have tried to view the statistics through their eyes,—and describe the years as business men saw them at the time.

Each country has been studied as a separate unit. Therefore, prosperity in England is not comparable with prosperity in Russia, or India. It is impossible to impose similar standards of prosperity or depression on all countries or we might be forced to the conclusion, for example, that Russia and Argentina have never experienced prosperity. As a matter of fact, in the mind of the business man, a year is judged by comparison with previous years,—perhaps with the more recent years given extra weight. Prosperity and depression are therefore relative terms, and may vary in exact meaning between countries and between decades.

The annals consist of five paragraphs for each country for each year. The first paragraph is a phrase summarizing the year. Obviously, such a brief summary cannot provide more than a general impression of the year's record. Both industrially and geographically, quite different business conditions may exist within one country at the same time. But just as averages are attempts to picture varying observations by a single expression, so this phrase-summary is an endeavor to sound the dominant note of the year. In other words, it gives the central tendency, from which reviewers state exceptions. "Prosperity except in textiles" is obviously not complete prosperity, yet prosperity is, implicit in the statement, the dominant tendency. Although observers generally agree that 1925 was a prosperous year for the United States, they also note that, although construction activity reached new records, the textile industries were depressed, and that although the Florida boom created great activity in the South, parts of New England were virtually in a state of depression. The phrase-summary throws aside all qualifications, some of which are stated in the more detailed paragraphs of the annals.

There have been occasions in national history, when economic activity has been completely reorganized and dominated by the endeavor to win a war. In such cases, the annals describe the year as one of "war activity". It is only very recently, however, that nations have conducted their war-making so systematically. Earlier wars often had but slight immediate influence on the economic system.

The second paragraph of each annal refers to industrial, commercial, and labor conditions. It notes business activity, construction and manufacturing activity, employment, important strikes, movements in commodity prices, speculation in commodities, and foreign trade. For lack of other data, references to commodity price movements relate to wholesale prices, and are generally based on averages of quotations for many commodities. The description of foreign trade refers to changes in imports and exports, and often remarks on the "balance of trade". A favorable balance of trade is one in which the country's exports exceed its imports, and an unfavorable balance is one recording an excess of imports. Since fluctuations in the relationship between exports and imports are of considerable importance, significant changes in the balance are noted. When no comment is made it may be assumed that the balance is similar to that of the previous year. The balance of trade figures are based on merchandise shipments, and do not include "invisible" items, such as international loans, interest and capital payments, immigrant remittances, and shipping and insurance services.

The third paragraph describes conditions in the money, security, and foreign exchange markets. The phrases "money tight" or "money easy", are used in their technical senses, indicating that money is difficult or easy to borrow—i.e., interest rates are high or low. Foreign exchange is quoted in terms of its departure from the par of exchange with countries on the gold standard. "Exchange declines" may be interpreted, therefore, as meaning that the currency has fallen below the par of exchange, commanding less of the foreign currency than comparison of the nominal gold parities would justify. The absence of any specific reference to exchange or money in circulation may be assumed to indicate that there was no significant change during the year.

The fourth paragraph reports agricultural production and prices. Crops are included as of the years in which they are harvested. In general, harvest time in the Northern Hemisphere is in the autumn, in the Southern Hemisphere in the spring. It sometimes occurs, as in India in 1898, that the fourth paragraph reports "Abundant crops" while the fifth paragraph reports "Famine". Such cases are explained by the fact that the harvest was not reaped until autumn, whereas the famine existed in spring and summer. The agricultural prices given refer to those realized from the crops with which they are grouped.

The fifth paragraph refers to various non-economic phenomena which may have exerted influence upon the conditions of business. Political events, epidemics, and natural catastrophes are the chief subjects of note. It would be both impossible and absurd to include all the events which have influenced business conditions, but it is hoped that those of major importance are given.

In constructing the annals of certain countries, the writer has been fortunate in receiving the assistance of several scholars, for whose expert aid he is exceedingly grateful. They are in no way responsible for errors in detail, their assistance consisting rather in perfecting the general framework, and suggesting sources and improvements. Aid was given in the French annals by Professor Albert Aftalion, of the University of Paris; in the German annals by Dr. Robert C. Kuczynski, Editor of *Finanzpolitische Korrespondenz*, Berlin, and Dr. Franz A. von Hayek, of the University of Vienna; in the Austrian annals, by Dr. von Hayek; in the Russian annals, by Professor N. D. Kondratieff, and Messrs. A. L. Vainshtein and M. V. Ignatieff of the Conjuncture Institute, Moscow, and Dr. S. Guberman of the Institute of National Economy, Moscow; in the Italian annals, by Dr. von Hayek and Professor Robert F. Foerster of Princeton University; in the South African annals, by Professor E. H. D. Arndt of Transvaal University College. Monthly indices of commodity prices for the period, 1805-1824, were kindly placed at the disposal of the writer by Professor Walter B. Smith of Wellesley College. Suggestions and assistance by the members of the Board of Directors and of the Research Staff of the National Bureau of Economic Research have greatly improved the original manuscript. In particular, Dr. Fred R. Macaulay, in addition to offering many valuable suggestions, placed at the writer's disposal manuscript notes and unpublished statistical series which proved of great assistance in preparing the American annals. Finally, it is impossible to express adequately my indebtedness to the New York Public Library. The facilities for research and the skilled assistance provided by the staff of the Economics Division have been of the utmost importance in making this book possible.

Perhaps no one realizes the temerity of the undertaking as much as the writer. Economic histories have proven of surprisingly little assistance. Their concern lies more with long-term developments, or conspicuous events. Data on crises are abundant, but little is written concerning the intervening years. Contemporary observers are more given to discussing current conditions during periods of depression than during any other phase of the cycle. Later authors, reviewing the same general period, find the time of crisis of most interest. Periods of prosperity receive little published recognition, —except in the Annual Message of the President to Congress, in which all years appear as prosperous and abundant. The writer has attempted to exhaust the available sources. Every suggested title has been examined. Many proved to be sterile, those actually utilized being listed in Chapter XVIII. In spite of the extensive source-material, and the use of the utmost care in analysis, there must be many errors, both of commission and omission. It is the writer's desire to make the annals as accurate as possible. He earnestly requests any person who possesses further information on the subject-matter of the annals, to aid in bringing the record closer to the actual facts.

Although nearly one hundred periodicals were utilized in preparing the annals for 1925, there still remain many excellent sources which could not be employed, because they are not yet available (April, 1926). In particular, government reports are slow of publication. Consequently, the annals for 1925 must be regarded as preliminary. Final revised annals for 1925 and preliminary annals for 1926 will probably be published early in 1927 in the *News-Bulletin* of the National Bureau of Economic Research.

WILLARD L. THORP.

CHAPTER I.

THE ANNALS OF THE UNITED STATES OF AMERICA.

The second Continental Congress, representing thirteen colonies, declared independence of Great Britain on July 4, 1776. Since that time, the United States has extended its territory across North America, now occupying a band about 1,500 miles wide between Canada and Mexico. An extensive central plain is bounded on the east by the Appalachians and on the west by the Cordilleras. Historically, these mountain ranges have been very important in limiting and directing the development of the country. It was not until the early part of the nineteenth century that the barrier of the Appalachians was surmounted. The mineral discoveries in the West in the late 1840's stimulated settlement of that region. However, it was not until 1890, that the report of the Superintendent of the Census recorded the disappearance of the frontier.

The records of area and population of the United States for the period from 1790 to 1920 are shown in the following page. It is interesting to note in addition that the area covered by the Census of 1790, which was actually less than one-half the total claimed area, the remainder being so sparsely populated that it was impracticable to canvass it, included 43 per cent of the total population in the country in 1920. It is also interesting to note that 49.9 per cent of the ancestry of the total white population of 1920, was included in the enumeration of 1790.[1] Immigration to the United States has come in increasing waves. The first notable influx was in the late 1840's, and peaks thereafter were reached in 1873, 1882, 1892, 1907 and 1914. In 1905, the number of immigrants first exceeded one million persons. Since the war, governmental restriction has limited the number of aliens admitted.

[1] See Rossiter, William S., *Increase of Population in the United States 1910-1920*. (Census Monograph No. 1.) Washington, 1922. Appendix A. Although an estimate, this figure is substantiated by a close similarity between the results obtained by two relatively independent methods,—the first based upon net immigration and the net rate of increase of their descendants since 1790, the other on the natural rate of increase of the inhabitants recorded by the census of 1790 and their descendants.

108   BUSINESS ANNALS

Census Date	Population [a]	Land Area (square miles)	Persons per Square Mile	Population in Places of 8,000 Inhabitants or More (per cent)
Aug. 2, 1790	3,929,214	867,980	4.5	3.3
Aug. 4, 1800	5,308,483	867,980	6.1	4.0
Aug. 6, 1810	7,239,881	1,685,865 [b]	4.3	4.9
Aug. 7, 1820	9,638,453	1,753,588 [c]	5.5	4.9
June 1, 1830	12,866,020	1,753,588	7.3	6.7
June 1, 1840	17,069,453	1,753,588	9.7	8.5
June 1, 1850	23,191,876	2,944,337 [d]	7.9	12.5
June 1, 1860	31,443,321	2,973,965 [e]	10.6	16.1
June 1, 1870	39,818,449 [f]	2,973,965	13.4	20.9
June 1, 1880	50,155,783	2,973,965	16.9	22.7
June 1, 1890	62,947,714 [g]	2,973,965	21.2	29.0
June 1, 1900	75,994,575	2,974,159 [h]	25.6	32.9
April 15, 1910	91,972,266	2,973,890 [h]	30.9	38.7
Jan. 1, 1920	105,710,620	2,973,774 [h]	35.5	43.8

[a] United States Bureau of the Census, *Fourteenth Census: Population, 1920*. Washington, 1921.
[b] Includes Louisiana purchase.
[c] Includes Florida purchase.
[d] Includes Texas annexation, Oregon territory, and Mexican cession.
[e] Includes Gadsden purchase.
[f] Revised estimate. See *Census of 1890. Population*. Part I, pp. xi, xii, and xvi.
[g] Includes Indians and other persons in the Indian Territory and in reservations.
[h] Area change due to reclamation or reservoir construction.

The period of the annals has witnessed the evolution of the United States from a nation predominantly agricultural to one whose chief economic interest is manufacturing. In 1787, Tench Coxe estimated that less than one-eighth of the working population was engaged in manufacturing, fishing, navigation and trade—a category so broad

Census Year	Total	Percentage Distribution of Agricultural, Manufacturing, and Mining Products [a]		
		Value of Agricultural Products	Value Added by Manufacture	Value of Mineral Products
1850	100.0	71.5	26.5	1.9
1870	100.0	56.3	40.1	3.5
1899	100.0	45.6	46.7	7.7
1919	100.0	42.6	51.0	6.4

[a] Thorp, Willard L., *The Integration of Industrial Operation*. (Census Monograph No. 3.) Washington, 1924.

that it included everything except agriculture and the professions. The Census of 1820 reported 14 per cent of the population engaged in manufacturing and mechanical industries. The shift in the importance of agriculture, manufacturing, and mining since 1850 is shown in the preceding table. In 1900, the value added by manufacture first exceeded the value of agricultural products. However, it was not until 1920 that the gainfully employed in manufacturing exceeded those in agriculture.

The occupation distributions in 1910 and 1920 were as follows:

Occupation	Percentage Distribution of Gainfully Employed [a]	
	1910	1920
Agriculture	33.2	26.3
Manufacturing and Mining	30.3	33.4
Trade and Transportation	16.4	17.6
Other [b]	20.1	22.8
Total	100.0	100.0

[a] United States Bureau of the Census, *Fourteenth Census: Occupations.* Washington, 1923.
[b] Includes persons employed in public service, professions, domestic and personal service, and clerical work.

The United States produces an extraordinary variety of agricultural products. The opening of vast areas of land since 1850 caused a westward migration of farmers. The available supply of the more desirable land has been so diminished that, since 1900, further additions to the farm area have been at a much slower rate. The outstanding products are cereal grains and cotton. Each dominates a section of the country. They are important as export commodities. The leading crops in order of acreage are corn, wheat, oats, and cotton; in order of value, corn, cotton, wheat, and oats. American wheat reaches the market beginning with July; cotton beginning with August.

One explanation of the rapid economic development of the United States is doubtless its vast natural resources. Not only is there fertile soil, but all important mineral products except tin are found in large deposits. In its output of coal, iron, lead, and copper, the United States leads the world. It also ranks first in petroleum.

The industrial awakening of the United States proceeded at first at a much slower rate than did that of England, and the factory system really gained its first foothold during the years of embargo and the War of 1812. Further aid came from the first protective tariff, that of 1816. The manufacture of cotton and wool passed rapidly from the household to the mill; but the methods of domestic and neighborhood industry, even in these lines of manufacture, continued to predominate down to and including the decade between 1820 and 1830. It was not until 1840 that the factory method of manufacture penetrated to any considerable degree into widely varied industries, but it then began to force from the market the handmade products with which the community had hitherto supplied itself. By 1899, there were 207,514 establishments with 4,712,763 wage-earners. In 1920, the number of establishments had increased to 290,105, with 9,096,372 employees. Their activities are extremely varied, though the textile and iron and steel industries each recorded twice as many wage-earners as any other general group of industry.

In a country the size of the United States, the development of adequate transportation facilities is a matter of great importance. Numerous canals have been built, and the Great Lakes and the Mississippi River furnish excellent waterways. Moreover, railroad development has been such that, in 1920, the United States possessed 36 per cent of the mileage of the world. The expansion has been as follows:

Year [a]	Railway Mileage [b] (miles of line in operation)
1830	23
1840	2,818
1850	9,021
1860	30,626
1870	52,922
1880	93,262
1890	167,191
1900	198,964
1910	249,992 [c]
1920	263,821

[a] Prior to 1890, December 1; 1890 and thereafter, July 1.
[b] United States Bureau of Foreign and Domestic Commerce, *Statistical Abstract, 1923*. Washington, 1924.
[c] Switching and terminal companies excluded, 1910 and 1920.

The period of most rapid expansion of railroads was the 1880's. The rate of increase at the present time is very slight.

Foreign trade plays a less important part in the economic life of the United States than in that of most other countries. Estimates made by the Bureau of Foreign and Domestic Commerce place the proportion of goods actually exported to those which might have been exported at 9.6 per cent in 1914 and 8.5 per cent in 1923.[1] The significant changes in the nature of the exports and imports during the last hundred years are shown in the following table:

Yearly Average [b]

Per Cent of Total Value [a]

	Total	Crude Materials	Crude Foodstuffs	Manufactured Foodstuffs	Semi-manufactures	Finished Manufactures
Imports—						
1821	100.0	3.6	11.1	19.9	7.5	56.9
1850	100.0	6.8	10.4	12.4	15.1	54.9
1880-84	100.0	18.4	14.7	19.1	14.3	31.8
1900-04	100.0	32.2	12.6	12.8	16.7	25.1
1910-14	100.0	34.4	12.0	11.5	18.2	23.1
1921-24	100.0	35.5	10.9	13.9	17.6	21.5
Exports [c]—						
1821	100.0	60.5	4.8	19.5	9.4	5.7
1850	100.0	62.3	5.6	14.8	4.5	12.7
1880-84	100.0	32.2	24.1	24.7	4.4	14.1
1900-04	100.0	28.0	14.0	23.0	10.7	23.5
1910-14	100.0	33.1	5.9	13.8	16.0	30.7
1921-24	100.0	26.8	10.6	14.5	12.1	35.8

[a] United States Bureau of Foreign and Domestic Commerce, *Statistical Abstract,* 1921, and *Commerce Yearbook,* 1924, Washington.

[b] Beginning with 1915, foreign trade figures were for calendar years, previously for years ending June 30.

[c] Domestic exports only.

The notable changes in importance among the various groups have been, in imports, the increase in crude materials, such as silk and rubber, and the decline in the shipments of manufactured goods from other countries; in exports, the decrease in relative importance of crude materials, and marked increase in the sale of domestic manufactured goods in foreign markets. At all times, cotton has been the leading export, government records indicating that generally about two-thirds of the crop is shipped to foreign markets. Since the Civil War, foreign trade has claimed about one-fourth of the wheat crop each year. Leading imports, in order of importance in 1924, were sugar, silk, coffee, rubber, and newsprint paper. Leading exports were cotton, refined mineral oil, wheat and flour, automobiles, and machinery. Until the 1870's, imports generally exceeded exports. Since then, the balance has been usually favorable.

The banking system of the United States has passed through

[1] United States Bureau of Foreign and Domestic Commerce, *Trade Information Bulletin No. 387,* Washington, 1925.

many phases. Prior to the establishment of the National Banking System in 1862, two attempts had been made by the government to dominate the individual banks by means of a state bank, but currency and credit remained in the hands of private banks, and the money market was chaotic. The establishment of national banks introduced a degree of government supervision. It was not until the establishment of the Federal Reserve System in 1914, however, that the banks were brought into a unified system. The Federal Reserve Banks act as bankers' banks, and also control the currency to a large degree through the issue of Federal Reserve notes.

The earliest recorded depression in America came in New England in 1640, and followed a period of ten years of rapid growth. The severity of the early recession is described by Dr. Clark as follows: "When the check came, there was a sudden and disastrous fall in prices of land, produce and American commodities. Cattle a year previously worth $100, could not be sold for a fourth or fifth that sum, land was a drug on the market, and there was nothing to exchange for the foreign manufactures that still arrived." [1] The various colonies had independent periods of depression, but that which began at the end of the seventeenth century and continued into the eighteenth was felt generally. In 1750, a money panic caused a severe crisis in New England, and depression ensued. John Adams reports: "I am old enough to remember the war of 1745 and its end, the war of 1755 and its close, the war of 1775 and its termination, the war of 1812 and its pacification. Every one of these wars has been followed by a general distress, embarrassments of commerce, destruction of manufactures, fall of the price of produce and lands."

The ten years prior to the breaking out of the Revolutionary War were years of economic depression in nearly every colony. During the war, the natural economic activities of the country were of course seriously disrupted. Immediately after the war, in 1783, a short boom ensued, but like most post-war booms, soon collapsed. The depression which followed was most severe in 1785 and 1786. Shays's Rebellion, in 1786, indicates the distress felt in New England. Gradually, improvement appeared, and at the beginning of the annals, in 1790, the United States was approaching prosperity.

It should be noted that the annals which follow portray for the

[1] Clark, Victor S., *History of Manufactures in the United States, 1607-1860*. Washington, 1916. For an elaborate description, see Osgood, Herbert L., *The American Colonies in the Seventeenth Century*. 3 vols. New York, 1904-07.

THE ANNALS OF THE UNITED STATES OF AMERICA

very early years chiefly the conditions which prevailed in the New England and Middle Atlantic states. For the years of the Civil War, the records of both the northern and southern states are given.

1790 Revival; prosperity.

Rapid and steady increase in activity by summer, except in South; manufacturing expands; foreign trade recovers.

Federal government assumes state debts after heated controversy; funding scheme adopted, July.

Wheat crop abundant.

Rhode Island last state to ratify Constitution, May; unsuccessful Indian War in Northwest, autumn.

1791 Prosperity.

Increased activity; further expansion in manufacturing; many new projects launched; South depressed; foreign trade growing.

Money eases but tightens late in year; United States Bank organized, July; active speculation, especially in bank stock.

Poor wheat crop.

Disastrous Indian War; ten amendments to the Constitution declared in force, December.

1792 Prosperity; financial distress.

Continued activity and expansion, little affected by financial difficulties; South depressed; exports increase, marked decrease in imports.

Active speculation, especially in United States Bank stock, brings financial crisis and short panic, January; money eases, spring, and speculation again vigorous, autumn.

Excellent wheat crop.

Washington reëlected without opposition; United States Mint established, April; higher tariff, May; outbreak of Whiskey Rebellion.

1793 Prosperity.

Continued prosperity; rapid revival in South ascribed to invention of cotton gin; exports increase; import trade depressed.

Yellow fever and panic in Philadelphia, autumn; British attack American commerce.

1794 Uneven prosperity.

Continued activity despite many unfavorable circumstances; further improvement in South; foreign trade temporarily checked by Embargo, April and May.

Culmination of Whiskey Rebellion, Pennsylvania, after calling out of militia; Indian War concluded, autumn; Genet's recall requested.

1795 Prosperity.
Internal trade active; land speculation; many new companies formed; foreign trade booms.
Banks multiply rapidly.
Peace with Algiers; Spanish treaty opens Mississippi.

1796 Recession; depression.
Financial distress results in many failures and slackening of industrial activity; prosperity continues in South; further large increase in volume of foreign trade.
Money very tight; minor panic, spring.
John Adams, Federalist, elected President.

1797 Depression; panic.
Little activity in North, continued prosperity in South; falling prices; many failures; foreign trade restricted.
Money tight; little speculation; financial panic, autumn.
Abundant harvest.
Yellow fever epidemic, Philadelphia, autumn; difficulties with France and XYZ mission sent by Adams.

1798 Depression.
Continued depression in North with failures; yellow fever causes complete cessation of business in Philadelphia, June to November; prosperity in South; collapse of land speculation; slight increase in exports but further restriction of imports.
Money very tight.
Difficulties with France result in sea-fights and embargo, June; Alien and Sedition Laws enacted; active recruiting and expansion of army.

1799 Revival.
Marked improvement in Northern activity; continued prosperity, South; commodity prices high; recovery in foreign trade.
Money eases somewhat.
Poor harvest.
Civil unrest in Pennsylvania; continued diplomatic conflict with France.

1800 Prosperity.
Further improvement in industry despite many failures; South prosperous; reduced exports and large imports.
Rapid advance in security prices.
Excellent wheat crop; cotton crop nearly doubles; high wheat price.
Jefferson, Republican, elected after tie vote with Burr; government moved to Washington.

1801 Mild prosperity.
Quiet expansion in industry; commodity prices very high; big increase in foreign trade.
Continued advance in security prices.
Wheat price very high; further large increase in cotton crop.
Peace with France, February; war with Tripoli begins, June.

1802 Recession.
Activity slackens; commodity prices fall precipitately; foreign trade booms but declines after Peace of Amiens, especially imports.
Continued advance in security prices.
Excellent wheat crop, lower price; continued expansion in cotton yield.
Spain closes mouth of Mississippi, October.

1803 Mild depression.
Dullness prevails; commodity prices very low; foreign trade further reduced.
Security prices decline, January, but recover somewhat late in year.
Very low wheat price; fair cotton yield.
Louisiana purchase, April; vigorous campaign against Barbary pirates; yellow fever paralyzes New York City, autumn.

1804 Revival.
Rapid improvement; development and expansion of industry; commodity prices rise; foreign trade revives.
Banking mania begins in New England; severe decline in security prices.
Rising wheat price; good cotton yield.
Reëlection of Jefferson.

1805 Prosperity.
Widespread activity; many new companies formed; further advance in commodity prices; foreign trade booms.
Banks multiply; rapid extension of paper money circulation; continued decline in security prices.
High wheat price; good cotton crop.
Barbary pirates finally subdued, June; British blockade New York for inspection of ships.

1806 Prosperity.
Continued activity; active speculation; slight decline in commodity prices; further expansion in foreign trade.
Foreign gold and silver coins made legal tender, April; higher security prices.
Decline in price of wheat; good cotton crop.
European embargoes threaten foreign trade; non-importation act, April.

1807 Prosperity; recession.
Continued activity slackens late in year; marked steady drop in commodity prices; foreign trade reaches peak volume.
Recession in security prices.
Lower wheat price; poor cotton yield.
War with England threatens, summer; England tightens trade restrictions, November; rigid American embargo declared, December, completely checking foreign trade; Aaron Burr's attempt to establish Southern Empire fails; Fulton's *Clermont* achieves success.

1808 Depression.
Rigid embargo causes paralysis on coast, gradually spreading inland; severe distress in New England; further sharp decline in commodity prices to low point, third quarter; foreign trade completely checked.
Dull security market.
Very low wheat price; very poor cotton crop.
Madison, Republican, elected.

1809 Depression.
Continued distress; complete stagnation in New England, some revival elsewhere; many failures; rapid advance of commodity prices, first half-year; foreign trade improves with partial lifting of Embargo, March.
Money tight; legality of foreign coins terminated; bank crisis in New England; steady security prices.
Rising wheat price; larger cotton crop.
Growing opposition causes Non-Intercourse Acts against England and France to replace general embargo, May.

1810 Revival.
Rapid recovery in North, continued prosperity in South; further rise in commodity prices to peak, December; increase in foreign trade.
Money market stringency; period of rapid expansion of bank note currency begins; security market steady.
High wheat price; excellent cotton crop.
Embargoes end, May.

1811 Moderate prosperity.
Increased activity; temporary flurry with closing of United States Bank; declining commodity prices; foreign trade smaller.
Money tight; United States Bank closed, March; security prices decline.
High wheat price; poor cotton crop.
Non-Intercourse Act against Great Britain, March; Tippecanoe victory over Indians, November.

1812   Brief recession; uneven prosperity.

Outbreak of war, June, causes temporary check, followed by moderate activity, less in New England; depression in South; commodity prices low; foreign trade paralyzed.

Money very tight; financial distress in New England; rapid extension of bank notes; low security prices boom late in year.

Agriculture depressed; high wheat price; very small cotton crop.

More stringent embargo, April; war with Great Britain declared, June; English blockade coast; Canadian expedition fails; Madison reëlected.

1813   Prosperity.

Widespread activity and expansion of manufactures; New England less active; South depressed; extraordinary rise of commodity prices; foreign trade further restricted.

Many new banks formed; declining security prices.

Agriculture depressed; lower wheat price; small cotton crop.

Victories on Lake Erie and defeats at sea.

1814   Prosperity, financial distress.

Continued activity, little affected by financial difficulties; commodity prices very high; active speculation; South depressed; large imports, no exports.

Money tight; bank notes at large discount; suspension of specie payments by banks outside New England, August; further decline in security prices.

Agriculture depressed; very small cotton crop.

Naval victories; capture and burning of Washington by British, August; peace declared, December.

1815   Prosperity; panic; recession; depression.

Increased activity in manufactures checked, March, by flood of imports; distress in New England; recovery in South and West; commodity prices decline from peak, first quarter; continued speculation, especially in land; many failures; renewed activity in foreign trade.

Financial chaos, with bank notes at various rates of depreciation; money very tight; further decline in security prices.

Agriculture revives, with higher wheat price and enormous cotton crop.

Victory at New Orleans, January; war against Algiers, March.

1816   Depression.

Manufactures distressed; unemployment and many failures; sharp drop in commodity prices; prosperity in South; rapid sale of public lands; foreign trade active with enormous imports.

Temporary ease in money market, summer; continued depreciation of currency; security prices revive; second United States Bank organized, April.

Very high wheat price; rapid extension of cotton acreage, large crop.

New tariff, spring; Monroe, Republican, elected.

1817   Mild depression.

Manufactures continue inactive, despite some improvement ascribed to tariff; Southern prosperity maintained; commodity prices steady; active speculation; exports increase and imports decline sharply.

Bank of United States opened, January; nominal resumption of specie payments, February; active speculation in Bank stock causes rapid stock price rise which collapses, September.

Extremely high wheat price; large cotton crop.

Rapid western migration.

1818   Mild depression.

Dullness in manufactures, especially iron and steel industry; many failures; wild land and slave speculation in South causes severe crisis; hard times and distress in South and West; increased activity in foreign trade.

Credit contraction causes widespread financial difficulty; specie payments restricted by United States Bank, August, and suspended by many banks late in year; declining security prices, after United States Bank stock boom, summer.

High wheat price; very small cotton crop, high price.

1819   Severe depression; financial panic.

Further restriction of activity to complete stagnation; speculative purchase of public land extensive, spring; many failures and severe unemployment, last half-year; commodity prices decline rapidly; collapse in real estate values; marked reduction in foreign trade.

Financial panic and bank failures, May; money very tight; marked decline in security values.

Wheat crop below average, low price; high cotton price despite enormous crop.

Purchase of Florida, February; first immigration law passed.

1820 Depression.
Continued distress; many failures; further decline in commodity prices; foreign trade small.
Money continues tight; security prices reach bottom.
Very low wheat price; fair cotton crop, lower price.
Congress passes relief acts for holders of public land; political crisis ends in Missouri Compromise, March; Monroe reëlected.

1821 Depression; revival.
Dull business revives, spring; marked improvement by October; commodity prices reach bottom, second quarter, and then advance; foreign trade depressed, favorable balance.
Money easy; revival of security speculation.
Depression in agriculture; record low wheat price; larger cotton yield, good price.

1822 Revival; mild recession.
Continued improvement to May, when reaction sets in; commodity prices rise to peak, March, and then decline; many failures; unemployment increases; marked increase in imports creates unfavorable balance.
Money tightens, spring; security prices decline.
Higher wheat price; excellent cotton crop, sharp decline in price.

1823 Revival.
Marked improvement in business activity; commodity prices gradually decline; increased exports and smaller imports.
Financial expansion; slump in security prices, summer.
Fair wheat price; cotton crop failure, higher price.

1824 Prosperity.
Widespread activity; excited speculation; commodity prices rise after June; slight increase in foreign trade.
Bank mania; many new banks chartered with large capital flotations; money easy.
Lower wheat price; good cotton crop, very high price.
John Quincy Adams, Republican, elected after close contest; high tariff enacted.

1825 Prosperity; panic; recession.
Continued activity; commodity prices rise with feverish speculation to autumn, when they collapse, especially cotton and wool; activity slackens; severe unemployment late in year; record volume of foreign trade, with favorable balance.
Money tightens severely; panic, July; bank failures; security prices fall sharply.
Declining wheat price; good cotton crop, very low price.
Erie Canal completed.

1826 Depression; revival.
Dullness in trade and industry; slight revival toward end of year; lower commodity prices; small foreign trade, unfavorable balance.
Money very tight; bank failures, April; security market depressed.
Very low wheat price; excellent cotton crop, record low price.
England forbids United States trade with her colonies.

1827 Moderate prosperity.
Continued improvement in industry; rapid rise of commodity prices; some recovery in foreign trade.
Money eases; revival of speculation.
Low wheat price; poor cotton crop, low price.
United States issues counter-prohibition of trade with British colonies.

1828 Prosperity; recession.
Activity continued, but slackens in summer; credit restriction causes great distress among New England manufacturers; marked decline in commodity prices; further reduction in foreign trade.
Money plentiful to May, followed by severe stringency.
Fair wheat price; good cotton crop, low price.
Higher tariff enacted, May; Jackson, Democrat, elected; widespread distress in winter.

1829 Depression; revival.
Dullness yields to increased activity, autumn; commodity prices decline further; many failures, first half-year; foreign trade severely depressed.
Money eases after July; security prices decline.
High wheat price; large cotton crop, low price.
Revival in purchase of public land.

1830 Moderate prosperity.
Activity and progress; commodity prices reach low point; export trade revives but imports continue depressed.
Money very easy; President Jackson's message indicates hostility to the United States Bank, December.
Low wheat price; fair cotton crop, very low price.
Difficulties limiting trade with British colonies removed, October.

1831 Prosperity.
Further improvement in business and industry; commodity prices rise; foreign trade booms, especially imports, creating unfavorable balance.
Easy money tightens, October; security prices rise.
Short wheat crop, fair price; good cotton crop, low price.

1832 Moderate prosperity.

Continued activity hampered somewhat by financial strain; further advance in commodity prices; marked increase in export trade.

Money market somewhat tight, ascribed to extensive western loans; Jackson vetoes United States Bank charter renewal, July.

Short wheat crop, fair price; good cotton crop, rising price.

Cholera, summer; Ohio River flood; Black Hawk War; lower tariff enacted, July; Jackson reëlected.

1833 Prosperity; panic; recession.

Activity continues to autumn, then slackens; commercial distress; many failures; unemployment; commodity prices decline; some further increase in foreign trade.

Easier money becomes very tight; panic late in year; security prices decline; Jackson orders public funds distributed among banks, September; extraordinary contraction of credit by United States Bank.

Good crops; lower wheat, higher cotton price.

Further decrease in tariff; active public land dealings.

1834 Mild depression; revival.

Dullness; improvement marked, last quarter; declining commodity prices; great activity in foreign trade, chiefly due to increased cotton exports.

Money very tight, easing slowly; revision of money standard reduces amount of gold in dollar; dull stock market.

Good crops; lower wheat price, marked improvement in cotton market.

1835 Revival; prosperity.

Rapid improvement to great business activity; commodity prices rise rapidly; active speculation, especially in land; railroad construction and foreign trade boom.

Money easier, but tightens late in year; formation of many new banks; lower security prices.

Wheat crop failure, higher price; rapid rise in cotton price despite very large yield.

Seminole War begun; Texan War with Mexico commences; New York City fire, December.

1836 Prosperity.

Great activity; continued land speculation, especially in West and South; further strong rise in commodity prices; foreign trade exceedingly active, especially imports.

Money extremely tight; severe financial strain following Jackson's "Specie Circular", requiring payments to land agents in specie; expiration of United States Bank charter, March, and Pennsylvania charter obtained; national debt paid off.

Wheat shortage, due chiefly to the Hessian fly, very high price; excellent cotton yield, lower price.

Defense of the "Alamo" in Texas; Van Buren, Democrat, elected President.

1837 Prosperity; panic; recession; depression.

Great activity and excited speculation, first quarter, followed by slackening and depression; many failures; unemployment; complete collapse of cotton market, spring; commodity prices decline; foreign trade restricted.

Money very tight; panic begins, March, in New Orleans; worst in New York, May; general suspension of specie payments, high gold premium; over six hundred bank failures.

Good wheat crop, lower price; record cotton crop, low price.

Canadian insurrection receives much American sympathy.

1838 Depression; slight revival.

Stagnation gradually yields to improvement and increased activity, summer; commodity prices reach bottom and rise; many failures early in year; further decline in foreign trade.

Money eases; gradual resumption of specie payments by banks begins, May.

Fair wheat crop, lower price; poor cotton yield, high price.

Canadian raids necessitate statement of neutrality.

1839 Revival; panic; recession.

Continued improvement; revival of land speculation early in year; rapid decline to depression, autumn; many failures; commodity prices collapse after rapid rise; recovery in foreign trade.

Further resumption led by United States Bank, January; money market tightens to panic and bank failures, October; specie payments again suspended, except New England and New York, last quarter.

Excellent wheat harvest, record cotton crop; prices collapse.

War with England over boundary threatened, January.

1840　　Depression.

Stagnation; commodity prices decline rapidly; revival of export trade, very small imports, favorable balance.

Continued financial strain, especially in West; slowly easing money market; gold at premium; Sub-Treasury Bill passed; declining security prices.

Large wheat, fair cotton crop; stronger prices.

Harrison, Whig, elected.

1841　　Depression.

Dullness; commodity prices decline; many failures; improved imports and smaller exports cause return to unfavorable balance.

Money easier; attempt to open the Bank of the United States and make resumption general fails, February; many bank failures in West; Sub-Treasury scheme annulled; declining security prices, especially last quarter.

Good wheat, poor cotton crop; higher wheat price, lower cotton.

Tyler, Democrat, becomes President upon death of Harrison.

1842　　Depression.

Continued dullness; many failures, spring; marked decline in commodity prices, especially last half-year; foreign trade small.

Tight money eases; specie payments resumed in eastern cities, March; bank failures numerous; slower resumption with panics in interior, especially New Orleans, spring; securities reach bottom, February, and rise rapidly, second quarter.

Abundant crops, especially cotton; very low prices.

High tariff passed, August; Dorr's rebellion; Seminole War ended.

1843　　Depression; revival.

Inactivity gradually yields to improvement, summer, except in South; commodity prices reach low point and improve, autumn; excellent exports, small import trade.

Money easy; active speculation, security prices advancing to July.

Good cereal crops, especially corn; poor cotton yield; very low wheat price.

1844　　Revival; prosperity.

Continued improvement in manufacturing; prices of manufactured products rise, foodstuffs decline; cotton speculation appears; revived imports, exports dull.

Easy money tightens temporarily, February and August; further rise in security prices, spring; stock exchange panic after election.

Agriculture depressed; poor wheat and corn, excellent oats and cotton crops; severe fall in prices of agricultural commodities.

Polk, Democrat, elected President.

1845   Prosperity; brief recession.

General prosperity, aided by marked improvement in South; slump ascribed to political difficulties, May; return to activity, October; slight rise in commodity prices; exports increase, smaller imports.

Money tight; stock market depressed, summer, but revives with active railroad speculation late in year.

Excellent wheat, fair cotton and oats, and poor corn crops; rising prices; active wheat speculation, last quarter.

Annexation of Texas, March; Oregon trouble with England, April; New York City business section destroyed by fire, August.

1846   Recession; mild depression.

Slackening of activity to dullness; some advance of commodity prices; prosperity continues in South; smaller exports, larger imports.

Severe pressure in money market, May, and late in year; sub-treasuries established; security prices fall.

Large wheat, short cotton crop; agricultural prices rise late in year.

War with Mexico declared, May, followed by rapid successes; Oregon controversy settled, June; more liberal tariff becomes effective, December.

1847   Revival; prosperity; panic; recession.

Rapid improvement begins, January; great activity; full employment; high commodity prices; activity slackens with collapse of English exchange and cotton prices, November; large foreign trade.

Money eases with large importation of specie; panic, November; tight money and break in security prices.

Good wheat and oats, excellent corn and cotton crops; very high prices collapse late in year.

Further victories in Mexico; capture of Vera Cruz, March, and City of Mexico, September.

1848   Mild depression; revival.

Dullness in industry and trade; gradual improvement late in year with California boom; commodity prices decline; failures; foreign trade slackens, though exports of foodstuffs continue large.

Very tight money eases slightly; bonds advance late in year, stock prices decline; Mexico makes indemnity payments.

Record crops, very low prices.

Gold discoveries in California, January; treaty with Mexico, February; Taylor, Whig, elected.

1849 Prosperity.

Widespread activity in industry; California expansion and speculation; commodity prices reach minimum; very active railroad construction; foreign trade recovers.

Money eases, summer; rising security prices, first half-year.

Excellent crops except cotton; higher prices.

Cholera scare, summer.

1850 Prosperity.

Unusual activity and expansion; commodity prices advance; very active railroad construction; foreign trade booms, especially import trade.

Money easy; revival of stock market, especially railroad securities, late in year; influx of gold from California commences.

Fair wheat, poor cotton crops; good wheat price, very high cotton.

Fillmore, Whig, becomes President upon death of Taylor.

1851 Prosperity.

Continued activity despite failures, summer, due to collapse of speculation in California shipments; further advance in commodity prices; enormous expansion in foreign trade, especially exports.

Money tightens, July; railroad stock prices reach peak, May, decline sharply to September, and then partially recover.

Fair wheat, very large cotton crop; high wheat price, rapid decline in price of cotton.

1852 Prosperity.

Widespread activity and expansion; lower commodity prices; active speculation; real estate boom; large foreign trade.

Money easier; security prices rise; railroad stocks reach peak, end of year.

Good wheat and record cotton crops; much lower prices.

Pierce, Democrat, elected President.

1853 Prosperity; recession.

Continued activity and expansion, slackening last quarter; iron and steel industry severely depressed; commodity prices rise rapidly; very active railroad construction; extensive speculation; great activity in foreign trade.

Money tightens severely; panics and distress in interior cities; decline in railroad stock prices.

Record wheat, poor cotton crops; wheat price low.

1854 Recession; depression.

Declining industrial activity; unemployment appears, autumn; continued rise of commodity prices and feverish speculation to autumn; railroad construction halted; many failures; continued activity in foreign trade.

Schuyler frauds bared, July, precipitating stock exchange panic; money very tight; financial panic, September; many private bank failures; financial distress especially severe, San Francisco; railroad stock prices steady to June, and then collapse.

Very small wheat and cotton crops; wheat price rises strongly.

Japan opened to the United States.

1855 Depression; revival.

Dullness continues to autumn, when revival sets in; slack foreign trade, especially imports.

Money eases, but tightens, autumn; railroad securities reach low point and recover somewhat.

Excellent wheat, oats, corn and cotton crops; high prices.

Kansas election riots, March; Indian War, April.

1856 Prosperity.

General activity and expansion; revival in railroad construction; increased number of failures late in year; very active commodity speculation; foreign trade recovers with favorable balance.

Money very easy to autumn; severe stringency, November; excited and declining stock market with prices fairly steady and higher, summer.

Excellent wheat, small cotton crop; wheat price falls.

Civil War in Kansas over slavery; Buchanan, Democrat, elected President.

1857 Prosperity; panic; recession; depression.

Activity gives way to dullness, spring, and stagnation, autumn; commodity prices decline late in year; many failures; enormous foreign trade checked.

Money very tight; panic, August; runs on banks and bank failures, October; specie payment suspended, October to December; stock prices collapse with low point, October; bonds collapse temporarily, autumn.

Good wheat and cotton crops, lower prices.

Dred Scott decision, March; tariff reduced, March.

1858 Depression.

Dullness continues; many failures; commodity prices decline; further reduction in construction; foreign trade restricted.

Money eases; security markets depressed after temporary recovery, first quarter.

Excellent crops, low prices.

Atlantic submarine cable completed, August, but proves unsuccessful.

1859 Revival.

Gradual improvement; commodity prices steady; foreign trade very active.

Money easy; further decline in railroad stock prices to low point, August; lower bond prices.

Good wheat, enormous cotton crops; price for wheat low, high for cotton.

John Brown's raid on Harper's Ferry, October; gold stampede to Colorado.

1860 Prosperity; recession.

Continued activity, slackening late in year; foreign trade booms.

Money tight after easing, summer; financial panic, November, necessitates issuing of clearing house certificates; slight recovery in railroad stock prices to peak, September; bond prices advance to summer and then decline.

Good wheat and cotton crops, lower prices.

Lincoln, Republican, elected after heated campaign; secession of South Carolina, December.

1861 Mild depression; revival.

(North) Dullness, unemployment, and uncertainty give way to rapid revival of activity, autumn; commodity prices decline, but recover somewhat, last quarter; many failures early in year; foreign trade greatly reduced, especially exports, creating unfavorable balance.

Money eases gradually; stock market depressed after minor panic, April; banks suspend specie payments quietly at end of year; low bond prices.

Good wheat harvest, low price.

Higher tariff enacted, March; bombardment of Fort Sumter, April; battle of Bull Run, July; income tax established, August; *Trent* difficulty with England.

1861 War activity.

(South) Gradual slackening of ordinary trade activity; commodity prices rise, especially last half-year; foreign trade restricted by blockade.

Money tight; currency expansion; many banks suspend specie payments; gold goes to premium, last half-year.

Abundant crops, especially grain and sugar; large cotton yield.

Confederation formed and Constitution adopted, February; elaborate tariff system adopted.

1862 War activity.

(North) Marked activity in war industries; commodity prices rise, especially last half-year; speculation; foreign trade greatly restricted, favorable balance.

Money eases; greenbacks made legal tender, February; rapid increase in circulation and steady depreciation; stock market revives with rapid advance on stock and bond prices.

Fair wheat and corn, poor oats crops; rising prices.

Confederate victories predominate; higher tariff; New Orleans captured, April.

(South) War activity.

Wild business activity as commodity prices rise rapidly to peak, third quarter; foreign trade halted.

Money tight; continued expansion of currency and active counterfeiting; government bonds collapse, summer.

Poor crops, with extensive shift from cotton to cereal crops; very small cotton yield.

Compulsory military service law adopted, April; bread riots, Richmond, August.

1863 War activity.

(North) Continued widespread activity; commodity prices rise rapidly, first half-year; feverish speculation; foreign trade continues small.

Money plentiful but tightens, December; temporary improvement in currency, summer; National Bank Act passed, February; stock exchange and gold market very active; continued advance in stock prices; bond rise halted, March.

Fair wheat and oats crops, corn failure; high prices.

Emancipation proclamation, January; turning point, July, with Northern victories of Gettysburg and Vicksburg; North adopts conscription; draft riots in New York, July.

(South) War activity.

Calmer business activity as commodity prices decline; transportation facilities severely restricted.

Money tight; rapid rise in gold premium, August.

Large corn and wheat yields, especially Virginia.

1864   War activity.

(North) Activity overshadowed by tremendous rise in commodity prices; extensive speculation; some revival in import trade.

Money tight; financial and stock market panic, April; further decline in value of greenbacks to low point, July; trade in gold prohibited, June, and repealed, July; stock prices reach peak, April; bonds advance to peak, July.

Small wheat, fair oats, and good corn crops; high prices create agricultural prosperity.

Continued Northern victories; Sherman's march to the sea; Lincoln reëlected.

(South) War activity.

Dullness and depression in business; commodity prices decline, spring, but advance to record heights late in year.

Money tight; currency in circulation reduced one-third, February, but later expanded rapidly; government debts funded.

Excellent corn and wheat crops, but currency derangement makes farmers unwilling to sell.

Conscription Act extended, February.

1865   Boom; recession.

(North) Industry and trade expand rapidly at close of war; gradual decline to dullness, summer; commodity prices reach peak, first quarter, and then decline; active speculation; foreign trade revives.

Money tightens severely; improvement in currency, first half-year; tax imposed on state bank circulation; stock and bond prices decline, especially first quarter.

Very small wheat, excellent oats and corn crops; cotton crop one-half pre-war average; lower prices.

Lee surrenders, April; Lincoln assassinated and Johnson, Republican, becomes President, April; Southern blockade raised, June; war formally ended, August.

(South) Economic chaos with collapse of currency and government finance, March.

1866   Mild depression.

Dullness in trade; active manufacturing; unsteady declining commodity prices; revival of railroad construction; partial recovery in South; large foreign trade, but decreasing.

Money market somewhat easier; stocks depressed, despite several corners; low point in railroad stock and bond prices, March.

Poor wheat, excellent oats and corn crops; cotton yield very small, lower price; very high wheat price.

New Atlantic cable laid by *Great Eastern,* July.

1867 Depression.

Dullness in trade and industry; declining prices; unemployment; foreign trade smaller.

Tight money eases in summer; contraction of greenback currency; some revival on stock exchange late in year, steady prices.

Enormous increase in wheat crop, good oats, fair corn crop; some revival in cotton growing, much lower price; wheat price reaches record heights, second quarter, and then declines.

Alaska purchased, March.

1868 Revival.

Marked improvement; commodity prices relatively steady; slight further decline in foreign trade, especially exports.

Money tightens; gold premium advances to August, and then declines sharply; very active stock exchange with corners and contests between leading operators; rising stock and bond prices.

Record wheat and corn crops, poor oats yield; slight increase in cotton; lower wheat, higher cotton prices.

Impeachment of President Johnson fails, May; Reconstruction Amendment ratified, July; Grant, Republican, elected President.

1869 Prosperity; monetary difficulties.

Continued activity in spite of diminished profits; improvement in South; period of heavy railroad building begins; expanding foreign trade.

Money tight; stock exchange dull; gold cornered, price raised strongly to Black Friday panic, September, followed by rapid decline in gold premium; numerous bank failures; railroad stock prices advance to peak, June, and decline; bond prices lower.

Excellent wheat and oats, poor corn crops; cotton increases; very low wheat, high cotton price.

Trans-continental railroad opens for business, May.

1870 Recession; mild depression.

Quiet and dull year; failures; rapid decline of commodity prices; increased foreign trade, especially exports.

Money eases; gold premium low; stock market dead, with low prices; slow rise in bond prices.

Poor wheat crop; excellent corn yield; cotton crop reaches pre-war level; higher wheat, low cotton price.

Tariff duties lowered, July.

1871 Revival; prosperity.

Marked improvement in trade and industry; commodity price decline slackens; railroad construction reaches maximum rate; foreign trade booms.

Easy money tightens; stock exchange panic, October; United States loan negotiated in Europe; railroad stock prices steady; slow rise in bond prices continues.

Poor wheat and cotton, very poor corn crops; wheat price very high, cotton higher.

New tariff becomes effective, January; Tweed ring scandals exposed; Chicago fire, October.

1872 Prosperity.

Widespread activity, especially in iron and steel industry; slow advance of commodity prices; boom in building and railroad construction slackens; exports advance but little, enormous imports.

Money very tight; temporary ease in summer, but severe stringency in autumn; bank reserves deficient; stock exchange active; railroad stock prices decline, industrials rise; bond prices steady.

Fair wheat, good corn and cotton crops; high wheat, low corn prices, cotton high.

Income tax abolished; lower tariff enacted; general strike, New York, June; *Alabama* claims award favors United States, September; Boston fire, November; Grant reëlected.

1873 Prosperity; panic; recession; depression.

Activity continues, slackening to stagnation in last quarter; many failures; severe unemployment; commodity prices rise to second quarter and then decline rapidly; land speculation collapses; imports decline, large increase in exports.

Money very tight; Jay Cooke failure and collapse of railroad speculation precipitates panic, September; broker and bank failures; clearing house certificates issued and stock exchange closed for ten days; banks suspend currency payments to November; gold premium reaches new low level late in year; silver demonetized.

Good wheat and cotton, poor corn crops; high wheat, improved corn, and lower cotton prices.

Granger movement increases railroad difficulties.

1874　　Depression.

Stagnation in industry and trade; utter lack of enterprise; failures; unemployment; commodity prices decline; public improvements and railroad building checked; smaller foreign trade, favorable balance.

Money eases; Grant vetoes inflation bill; stock and bond markets dull, slowly rising prices.

Excellent wheat, good cotton, and very poor corn crops; wheat and cotton prices fall, corn rises.

Many states assume regulation of railroads; immigration greatly reduced.

1875　　Depression.

Poor year with little activity and many failures; further decline of commodity prices; marked reduction in foreign trade.

Money easy, except September when Bank of California fails; extreme depression of stock prices; speculation causes gold premium to advance; steady railroad stock prices, declining industrials, first half-year; marked improvement in bond prices; Resumption Act passed.

Poor wheat, record corn and cotton crops; low prices.

Higher tariff enacted.

1876　　Depression.

Continued inactivity in trade and industry; record number of failures; commodity prices decline slowly; dissolution of anthracite coal combination; railroad war between trunk lines; some recovery in exports, imports small.

Money exceedingly easy; tremendous decline in railroad stock prices after April; industrials slump, spring and autumn; bond prices steady; gold premium declines.

Poor crops; higher prices, except corn.

Hayes, Republican, elected over Tilden after deadlock.

1877　　Depression.

Continued stagnation in industry; many failures; more rapid decline of commodity prices; railroad strikes, July, necessitate military force; increased foreign trade.

Money very easy; revival on stock exchange, last half-year, stock prices reaching bottom, June; bond prices steady; steady decline in gold premium.

Large wheat and corn, poor cotton crops; higher prices.

"Molly Maguires" riot in coal districts; silver agitation in Congress, last quarter.

1878 Depression; revival.

Inactivity of first half-year gives way to improvement which becomes marked, last quarter; commodity prices decline, especially first half-year; active sales of railroad and public land; small imports, very large exports.

Money very easy; stocks dull with temporary revival, second quarter; bond price advance resumed; gold declines to par, December; Bland-Allison Act reinstates silver as legal tender, February.

Record crops and very low prices.

Yellow fever in South, autumn.

1879 Revival; prosperity.

Great activity, with rapid expansion in autumn; commodity prices rise from low point, first quarter; very active railroad construction; increase in foreign trade, especially imports.

Money easy; great advance in stock prices, especially last four months; further rise in bond prices; resumption of specie payments, January.

Enormous crops and high prices.

1880 Prosperity.

Rapid expansion of industry and trade; price decline in summer of little effect; speculation and corners in commodities; very active construction; great activity in foreign trade.

Money tightens, spring and autumn; stock market collapses, May, but recovers and booms after October, especially railroads; marked advance in bond prices.

Good wheat and corn, excellent cotton crops; prices decline, except corn.

Big increase in immigration; Garfield, Republican, elected.

1881 Prosperity.

Continued activity; enormous output of manufactured goods; large issues of new securities; active speculation; commodity prices rise sharply; slight decline in foreign trade.

Money tight; railroads reach peak, May, and industrials, June; bond prices advance to summer and then decline.

Wheat and corn crop failures, poor cotton yield; prices very high.

Garfield assassinated, July; Arthur, Republican, becomes President; increased immigration; severe drought.

1882   Prosperity; recession.

Continued great activity with slackening rate of expansion; railroad building peak; many new flotations; iron and steel industries depressed late in year; ironworkers' strike, third quarter; commodity prices decline slowly; imports boom but exports decline.

Money eases and tightens again in autumn; temporary boom in stock prices, summer; steady bond prices.

Record wheat and cotton, good corn crops; lower prices.

Severe Mississippi floods, spring; Chicago riots; immigration reaches peak.

1883   Recession.

Steadily increasing depression in industry and trade; many failures; curtailed production; lower wages and unemployment; commodity price decline continues; falling off in railroad construction; increased exports, smaller imports.

Money easy; slight decline in railroad stocks, marked in industrials; steady bond prices.

Poor wheat and cotton crops, fair corn; little change in prices.

New tariff into operation, July.

1884   Depression.

Stagnation in trade and industry; further decline in commodity prices; many failures; unemployment; reduction in volume of foreign trade.

Money tightens to panic, May; bank and broker failures; clearing house certificates issued; money eases; tremendous decline in stock prices, especially second quarter; after further advance, bond prices decline, second quarter.

Excellent wheat and corn, poor cotton crops; severe shrinkage in values, except cotton.

Coal strike, autumn; Cleveland, Democrat, elected.

1885   Depression; revival.

Continued dullness with slow improvement late in year, especially in iron and steel industries; commodity prices very low; many failures; further reduction in foreign trade.

Money easy; stock exchange revives, summer, with increasing prices, especially industrials; bond prices higher.

Wheat crop failure, corn and cotton records; wheat price advances, others decline.

Anti-Chinese riots begin; silver agitation.

1886   Revival.

Continued recovery, somewhat hampered by labor troubles; commodity prices decline slowly; railroad building revives; iron industry very active; some improvement in foreign trade.

Money easy; stock exchange active, last half-year, after temporary dullness; bond prices reach peak, July, and then decline.

Larger wheat, smaller corn and cotton crops; lower prices except corn.

Knights of Labor railroad strike, March; coal strike, March; Haymarket anarchist massacre, Chicago, May; Galveston flood.

1887   Prosperity.

Widespread activity with higher prices; tremendous railroad construction; western real estate boom; larger imports.

Money tightens; stock prices reach peak, May, and then decline; marked drop in bond prices to October.

Good wheat and cotton crops, corn failure; slightly higher prices.

Interstate Commerce Law goes into effect, April.

1888   Slight recession.

Quiet activity with less profit; cotton manufacturing prosperous, iron and steel depressed; formation of trusts; reduction in construction; unfavorable balance of trade with increased imports and smaller exports.

Money easy; stock prices reach bottom, spring, and then revive, especially industrials; some improvement in bond prices.

Poor wheat, fair cotton, and excellent corn crops; wheat price advances sharply, others decline.

Harrison, Republican, elected.

1889   Prosperity.

Enormous volume of activity; many records made, especially in cotton and iron; further slight decline in commodity prices; favorable balance with marked improvement in foreign trade.

Money tightens, last quarter; moderate activity on stock exchange with further advance in stock prices; bond prices reach peak, June.

Fair wheat, good cotton, and excellent corn crops; low prices.

Johnstown flood, June; trunk lines form "gentlemen's agreement".

1890 Prosperity; recession.

Great activity; gradual curtailment, last quarter; extensive railroad construction; many new enterprises; active real estate speculation; declining commodity prices; very active foreign trade.

Money very tight; financial strain, November, with failure of banks and brokers; stock prices reach peak in May and decline rapidly; falling bond prices.

Small wheat and corn crops, large cotton; good prices, especially corn.

Large immigration; McKinley tariff puts higher rates into effect, October; Sherman Silver Purchase Act passed, July; Sherman Anti-Trust Act passed, July.

1891 Depression; revival.

Dullness continues until August, when revival sets in; moderate improvement in business and industry; South continues depressed; many failures; further decline in commodity prices; foreign trade expands, especially exports.

Tight money eases late in year; some improvement in stocks, especially last half-year; bond prices reach low point, June.

Excellent crops; wheat price high, corn and cotton decline.

Peak immigration.

1892 Prosperity.

Great activity; manufacturing expansion; further decline in commodity prices; active foreign trade, especially imports.

Money eases, tightening late in year; railroad stocks decline from peak, March; industrial stocks advance steadily; bond prices steady.

Fair wheat and corn, poor cotton crops; wheat and corn prices decline, cotton rises.

Period of smaller immigration begins; continued silver agitation; Homestead riots at Carnegie mills, July; cholera panic, New York, September; quiet election of Cleveland.

1893 Recession; panic; depression.

Gradual decline to extreme depression, last half-year; business failures and railway receiverships; temporary recovery of commodity prices, spring, gives way to further decline; large imports, first half-year, but very small, last half-year; decline in exports.

Money very tight with stringency, summer, and ease late in year; violent panic, May; crisis most severe, August; stock prices collapse, autumn, especially industrials, which reach low point, August; bond prices collapse, summer, but recover later in year.

Wheat and corn crops very small, cotton fair; lower prices.

Silver Purchase Act repealed, August; Chicago World's Fair late in year.

1894 Deep depression.

Severe stagnation; widespread unemployment; bituminous coal strike, second quarter; railroad strike, June; many failures; further decline in commodity prices; reduction in foreign trade.

Money very easy; declining railroad stock prices, rising industrials; higher bond prices.

Average wheat crop with low price; corn failure, high price; large cotton crop and very low price.

Floods in Middle West and Pacific states; Coxey's armies of tramps, spring; lower tariff into operation, August.

1895 Depression; revival.

Dullness yields to gradual improvement, late spring; boom in iron and steel industry; continued numerous failures; commodity prices rise; revival of imports.

Money market easy to December; temporary boom advances industrial stocks to peak, June, and railroads, September; further advance in bond prices.

Excellent corn, good wheat, and short cotton crops; prices low, except cotton.

Diplomatic difficulties with Great Britain over Venezuela, December.

1896 Recession; depression.

Return to state of intense depression; severe unemployment; large increase in failures; marked decline in commodity prices; large expansion in exports and falling off in imports.

Money rates firm, tightening in autumn; temporary slump in stock prices, summer, especially industrials; bond prices fall sharply, third quarter, but then recover.

Small wheat, record corn, and fair cotton crops; prices low, except wheat.

Venezuela difficulty settled, January; political controversy over recognition of Cuba; Free Silver campaign results in victory for gold standard and McKinley, Republican.

1897 Depression; revival.

Dullness gradually yields to revival in spite of severe bituminous coal strike, third quarter; fewer failures; commodity prices reach bottom, third quarter; active foreign trade, imports boom prior to operation of tariff.

Money easy; higher stock prices, especially industrials; marked rise in bond prices.

Excellent wheat and cotton, good corn crops; higher wheat and corn prices, cotton lower.

Dingley tariff raises rates, August; severe Mississippi floods; yellow fever epidemic in South.

1898 Revival; prosperity.

Growing activity and rising prosperity; formation of many industrial combinations; slow rise in commodity prices; decline in imports, unprecedented exports.

Money easy; railroad stocks steady, industrials advance; bond prices collapse, spring, but then advance rapidly.

Record wheat and cotton, fair corn crops; "Leiter" corner on wheat collapses, June, and price declines; cotton and corn prices low.

Maine explosion, February; war declared with Spain, April; rapid victories; peace declared, August; Philippines, Hawaii, and other islands acquired.

1899 Prosperity.

Activity and expansion; extensive promotion and flotation of new securities; wages rise; rapid increase of commodity prices; larger foreign trade, especially imports.

Easy money tightens, summer; wild speculation on stock exchange sends stock prices to peak, June; panic, December, with important failures; bond prices reach peak, summer, and fall sharply.

Large crops and good prices.

Boom in immigration begins.

1900 Prosperity; brief recession.

Exceptional activity and progress; slight check to expansion appears, spring, and disappears late in year; decline in commodity prices, summer; iron and steel boom collapses, March; large foreign trade.

Money fairly easy; stock exchange quiet with declining prices to boom, last quarter; bond prices steady; gold standard formally established, March.

Good harvests, especially corn; prices higher.

Reëlection of McKinley.

1901 Prosperity.

Activity; many records for production established; transportation shortage, autumn; steel workers' strike, third quarter; copper market collapse, December; commodity prices decline to June, and then rise steadily; imports increase, exports decline slightly.

Money fairly easy; stock exchange panic, May, with Northern Pacific corner; great rise in railroad security prices, decline in industrials; slightly higher bond prices.

Record wheat crop, good cotton, and corn failure; wheat and cotton prices fair, corn very high.

U. S. Steel Corporation formed; McKinley assassinated and Roosevelt takes office, September.

1902 Prosperity.

Record volume of business; anthracite strike, May to October; traffic blockade, autumn; rising prices; imports increase, exports decline.

Money market gradually tightens; further rise in railroad stock prices to peak, September; industrials steady; declining bond prices.

Excellent wheat and cotton crops, record corn; prices fairly high, except cotton.

1903 Prosperity; recession.

Continued activity gradually retarded, autumn; coal famine, spring; many labor troubles; increased unemployment; commercial failures numerous; commodity prices reach peak early in year and then decline; imports decline after first quarter, exports large.

Money tight; severe decline of security prices to low points, railroads, September, and industrials, November; marked decline in bond prices to low point, September.

Good but smaller crops; prices higher.

Immigration very large.

1904 Mild depression; revival.

Inactivity and dullness to autumn when revival sets in; little movement of prices; big increase in imports, exports decline slightly.

Money easy; stock exchange buoyant with rapidly rising prices, last half-year; rising bond prices.

Record cotton, large corn and very poor wheat crop; collapse of Sully cotton corner, March, sends prices very low; corn price fair and wheat very high.

Some decline in immigration; World's Fair, St. Louis; Northern Securities decision, March; election of President Roosevelt calm, November.

1905 Prosperity.

Great activity and expansion; railroads and iron and steel industries very prosperous; severe freight congestion; rising commodity prices; foreign trade expands.

Money market tightens late in year; continued advance in stock prices despite temporary slump, second quarter; steady bond prices.

Large crops; good prices.

Increased immigration; yellow fever epidemic in South.

1906   Prosperity.

Continued activity and expansion; marked increases in wages; extensive car shortage; commodity price rise continued, last half-year; big increase in foreign trade.

Money tight, with extreme tension at times; security prices reach peak, January, and waver; declining bond prices.

Excellent harvests, record corn; prices slightly lower.

Large immigration; San Francisco earthquake and fire, April; intervention in Cuba, suppressing revolt, September.

1907   Prosperity; panic; recession; depression.

Continued great activity to autumn; business paralyzed with panic; gradual rise of commodity prices to sharp decline, last quarter; record imports and exports.

Money very tight, stringent in autumn; failure of Knickerbocker Trust Co., October, precipitates panic; banks suspend payments and clearing house certificates issued; stock exchange collapses, March and August; railroad and industrial stocks reach bottom, November; big drop in bond prices to low, November.

Fair crops, higher prices.

Record immigration.

1908   Depression.

Stagnation in industry and trade; many failures; severe unemployment; signs of improvement late in year; commodity prices reach bottom, summer; copper and cotton speculation; many railroad receiverships; foreign trade restricted.

Tight money eases; marked rise in both railroad and industrial stock prices; bond prices higher.

Good wheat and corn, large cotton crops; wheat and corn prices rise, cotton falls.

Marked decline in immigration; Taft, Republican, elected President, November.

1909   Revival; mild prosperity.

Sustained improvement as year progresses; marked rise in prices, especially last half-year; active construction slackens late in year; imports revive while exports decline.

Money tightens in autumn; further advance in stocks, railroads to peak, August, and industrials, September; bond prices rise to February, and slowly decline.

Excellent wheat, fair corn and poor cotton crops; wheat and cotton prices at record heights, corn good.

Payne tariff revises rates; revival in immigration.

THE ANNALS OF THE UNITED STATES OF AMERICA 141

1910   Recession.

Activity checked at beginning of year; decline to depression evident, last half-year, especially severe in iron and steel industry; commodity prices reach peak, spring, and then decline; further increase in foreign trade.

Money fairly tight; stock prices decline, especially railroads, to bottom, July; falling bond prices.

Fair wheat and cotton crops, record corn; wheat and corn prices lower, cotton higher.

Large immigration.

1911   Mild depression.

Dullness and inactivity; commodity prices reach bottom, May, and gradually rise; decrease in imports, increased exports.

Money very easy; slow rise in stock prices, first half-year, but slump, autumn; steady bond prices.

Poor wheat and corn crops, record cotton; high corn, good wheat, and very low cotton prices; hay crop smallest since 1895.

Extreme heat and drought; Standard Oil and American Tobacco dissolutions ordered, May; marked decline in immigration.

1912   Revival; prosperity.

Improvement, marked last half-year; many labor disputes; anthracite mining halted, April and May; commodity prices rise to May and then remain fixed; large increase in foreign trade.

Money easy, tightening severely, autumn; dull stock exchange revives to peaks, industrials, September and railroads, October; falling bond prices.

Large crops, record corn; wheat and corn prices fall, cotton rises.

Improved immigration; *Titanic* disaster, April; severe overflow of Mississippi; Presidential election with Roosevelt as "Bull Moose" won by Wilson, Democrat.

1913   Prosperity; recession.

Continued activity gradually yields to decline in volume of production; increasing unemployment; many failures; commodity prices steady; decline in imports, increased exports.

Money tight; stock prices slump, first half-year; marked fall in bond prices, first half-year; act establishing Federal Reserve System passed, December.

Large wheat and cotton, poor corn crops; higher prices, especially corn.

Income Tax Amendment ratified, May; Underwood tariff reduces rates, October; record immigration.

1914 Depression.

Conditions grow steadily worse to war; severe depression with little activity and extensive unemployment; many failures; commodity prices decline, temporary boom with war; decline in foreign trade, especially exports.

Money market easy to war; stringency yields gradually to ease; weak stock market collapses with war; exchange closed, July to December; bond prices collapse with war.

Large harvests, record wheat and cotton yields; high wheat and corn prices, cotton very low.

Trade Commission and Clayton Acts passed; intervention in Mexico, April; troops withdrawn late in year; United States neutrality declared in World War; with war, immigration halted; Panama Canal opened, August.

1915 Revival; prosperity.

Increased activity, beginning in industries manufacturing war materials; unemployment gradually disappears; many failures; depression continues in South until autumn; slight rise in prices accelerates, last quarter; enormous increase in exports.

Money easy; stock exchange revives, second quarter, with rapid rise in prices; unsteady bond prices rise sharply, last quarter; Anglo-French loan negotiated, October; foreign exchanges very favorable.

Record wheat, large corn, short cotton crop; lower wheat and corn prices, higher cotton.

Slow revival in immigration; extensive emigration; *Lusitania* sunk, May, followed by long series of diplomatic notes with Germany; Supreme Court upholds U. S. Steel Corporation, June.

1916 Prosperity.

Great activity and expanding trade; active employment and wage increases; many failures; rapidly rising commodity prices; commodity speculation; further enormous increase in foreign trade.

Money easy; many foreign loans; after temporary slump, railroad stock prices rise to peak, October, and industrials, November; further improvement in bond prices.

Small wheat and cotton, large corn yields; rapidly rising prices.

Submarine activity of Germany provokes further correspondence; invasion of New Mexico by Villa results in calling of troops to border; act creating Shipping Board passed, September; Wilson reëlected.

THE ANNALS OF THE UNITED STATES OF AMERICA 143

1917 Prosperity; war activity.

Continued activity, with reorganization of industry for war; shortage of fuel and labor, and freight congestion; commodity prices rise, first half-year; government price-fixing policy adopted, August; active foreign trade.

Money tightens; tremendous fall in prices of railroad stocks; industrials decline last half-year; bond prices fall from peak, January; Liberty Loans floated; embargo on gold exports, September.

Large harvests except wheat; high prices.

Germany announces unrestricted submarine warfare, January; United States enters war, April; Compulsory Military Service Act passed, May; embargo on exports, July; government assumes control of railroads, December.

1918 War activity; recession.

Continued activity; rising commodity prices, despite government control over major products; labor troubles; government operation of railways effected, January; confusion with armistice; foreign trade expansion halted.

Money very tight; some recovery in stock prices, slump after Armistice; declining bond prices recover sharply, last quarter; flotation of new securities restricted; Pitman Act authorizes sale of silver, April.

Excellent wheat, good cotton and poor corn crops; prices stabilized, except corn which rises.

Extensive conscription, and shipment of men to Europe progresses rapidly; strict conservation of food and fuel; armistice, November; control of most prices ends with year.

1919 Revival; prosperity.

Uncertainty gives way to extraordinary activity, late spring; building revival; enormous output of new securities; speculation; steel, coal, and railroad shopmen's strikes, autumn; commodity prices rise; active foreign trade.

Money eases slightly but tightens late in year; stock exchange booms, railroads reaching peak, May, and industrials, November; falling bond prices; embargo on gold exports removed, June.

Large wheat, fair cotton and corn crops; prices very high.

Revival in immigration; Versailles Treaty, June; controversy over entrance into League of Nations.

1920   Prosperity; recession; depression.

Great activity; decline, late spring; stagnation and severe unemployment late in year; commodity prices reach peak, May, and decline rapidly; unprecedented cancellations; foreign trade very large, but imports decline, last half-year.

Money extremely tight, most stringent in autumn; tremendous decline in prices of industrial stocks, railroads steady; bond prices reach low point, May, and recover sharply.

Good cotton and corn crops, poor wheat; high prices decline rapidly.

Prohibition Amendment becomes effective, January; Transportation Act, February, provides for return of railroads to private control; ratification of Women's Suffrage Amendment announced, August; election of Harding, Republican, November; large immigration.

1921   Depression.

Stagnation in many industries; severe unemployment worst, summer; many failures; marked decline in commodity prices; severe depression in foreign trade.

Money eases; further decline in security prices to railroad stock low, June, and industrial, August, followed by recovery; bond prices rise rapidly.

Poor crops, cotton failure; prices decline, except cotton which rises.

Marked reduction in immigration; disarmament conference.

1922   Revival; prosperity.

Gradual but steady recovery; rapid improvement in employment; railroad shopmen's strike, July; coal strikes, April to September; construction and automobile booms; steady rise in commodity prices; revival in imports, but exports decline.

Money easy; stock prices rise, railroad stocks and bonds reaching peak, June, and declining.

Fair wheat, poor cotton and corn crops; prices higher.

Federal Child Labor Tax Law declared unconstitutional, May; Fordney Tariff raises rates, September.

1923   Prosperity; recession.

Activity and record production recede mildly, summer; full employment; commodity prices rise to peak, April, and then fall; further revival in foreign trade.

Money easy; industrial stocks reach peak, March; decline in stock markets checked late in year; bond market steady after decline, first half-year; English debt arrangement completed.

Fair wheat, larger cotton and corn crops; prices improve, except wheat.

U. S. Steel Corporation abolishes twelve-hour day; Harding dies and Coolidge becomes President, August.

1924   Mild depression; revival.

Further decline in production to dullness; revived activity, third quarter; gradual fall in commodity prices to April, followed by gradual rise; increased exports, decreased imports.

Money easy; decline in stock prices checked, late spring; rapid revival in security markets, last quarter; bond prices higher.

Larger crops and higher prices, except cotton.

Cabinet officials involved in oil scandals; hotly contested election against Davis and LaFollette won by Coolidge; immigration restriction extended, July.

1925   Prosperity.

Marked activity and expansion despite brief hesitation, second quarter; full employment; record volume of construction; active real estate speculation, especially Florida; textile industries depressed; anthracite coal strike begins, September; steady commodity prices except for temporary decline, spring; increased foreign trade, especially imports.

Rise in money rates, especially first and last quarters; active stock market with notable advance in prices, except for slumps, March and November; rising bond prices, especially first half-year; extensive foreign loans.

Very small wheat, fair oats, and large corn and cotton crops; high wheat, low corn and cotton prices.

Belgian debt funded, August; attempt to arrange French debt fails, October; Italian debt funded, November.

CHAPTER II.

THE ANNALS OF ENGLAND.

The United Kingdom is the name used to denote England, Wales, Scotland, Ireland (now North Ireland only), the Isle of Man and the Channel Islands—in all, the island group a few miles off the west coast of Europe. Great Britain includes the three regions on the largest island, England, Wales, and Scotland. These annals pertain chiefly to England, occupying the south, a densely populated highly developed area. The coast line is a succession of large inlets making excellent harbors. There are hills and highlands, but no mountains.

The area of the United Kingdom is 94,101 square miles, of England and Wales, 58,340. The census records of the population of England and Wales indicate a rapid and steady growth. They are as follows: [a]

Census Date	Population	Persons Per Square Mile	Per Cent Urban [b]
March 10, 1801	8,892,536	152	... [c]
May 27, 1811	10,164,256	174	... [c]
May 28, 1821	12,000,236	206	... [c]
May 30, 1831	13,896,797	238	... [c]
June 7, 1841	15,914,148	273	... [c]
March 31, 1851 [d]	17,927,609	307	50.2 [e]
April 8, 1861	20,066,224	344	54.6 [e]
April 3, 1871	22,712,266	389	61.8 [e]
April 4, 1881	25,974,439	445	67.9
April 6, 1891	29,002,525	497	72.0
April 1, 1901	32,527,843	558	77.0
April 3, 1911	36,070,492	618	78.1
June 20, 1921	37,886,699	649 [f]	79.3

[a] Data from various census records published by the General Register Office. Especially Great Britain General Register Office, *General Report, 1921.* London, 1925.
[b] As constituted at each census.
[c] No data available.
[d] Beginning with 1851, includes army at home, men on shore belonging to the royal navy or to the merchant service, and all persons on board vessels in port on census night or arriving the following day.
[e] Approximations.
[f] Computed from population and area given above.

Although the high density of the population may be accounted for in part by the concentration about London, other sections, such as the lowlands of south Lancashire, are practically one vast town. There has been a steady flow of emigrants from the United Kingdom for over a century. Periods of largest emigration were the late forties and early fifties, the decade of the eighties, and the twentieth century, except the years of the war. The peak was reached in 1913, when nearly one-half million persons left for non-European countries.

Although agriculture was for many centuries the dominating industry in England, it is completely overshadowed to-day by manufacturing activity. Because of a reclassification of the occupational grouping used by the census, earlier comparisons cannot be made, but the distribution of the working population, twelve years of age and over, in 1921, follows:

Industry	Per Cent of Total [a]
Agriculture	7.3
Mining and Quarrying	6.2
Manufacturing and Construction	36.1
Trade and Transportation	19.8
Other [b]	30.6
Total	100.0

[a] Computed from data in Great Britain General Register Office, *Census of 1291. Occupation Tables.* London, 1924.
[b] Includes persons engaged in fishing, public administration, defense, professions, entertainment and sport, personal service, clerical and draughting work, and other activities.

Some indication of the progressive decline in the importance of agriculture to the point indicated above is given in the following table:

Census Year	Percentage of Total Males 10 Years and Over Engaged in Agriculture [a]
1851	23.5 [b]
1861	21.2 [b]
1871	16.8 [b]
1881	13.8
1891	11.6
1901	9.5
1911	9.2

[a] Great Britain General Register Office, *Census of 1911. General Report.* London, 1917. p. 113.
[b] Includes "retired".

During the last sixty years, there has been little change in the total farm land in use in Great Britain, which forms about 70 per cent of the total area. However, there has been a steady tendency to increase the land used as permanent pasture and decrease the acreage sown in crops. In terms of acreage used, the leading crops historically of Great Britain may be ranked as follows: wheat, oats, barley and potatoes. The high point in wheat acreage was reached in 1869, official records having first been kept in 1866, and this acreage has steadily declined to about one-half its then recorded area. Oats, on the other hand, has held its acreage, and for the last forty years has actually employed a larger area than wheat. The crops are harvested chiefly in the autumn.

Manufacturing has become England's leading economic activity. An earlier table brought out its present importance. Some idea of the rate and periods of growth can be obtained from the data given below, since a large part of the manufactured goods enters into export trade.

Year	Total Exports [a] (official values) [c]	Exports of British Produce [b] (real values) [d]
	Millions of pounds sterling	
1780	11	..
1790	18	..
1800	34	..
1810	44	48
1820	49	36
1830	70	38
1840	116	51
1850	197	71
1860	...	136
1870	...	200
1880	...	223
1890	...	264
1900	...	291 [e]
1910	...	430
1920	...	1,334

[a] Great Britain Custom House Statistical Office, *Customs Tariffs of the United Kingdom from 1800 to 1897.* (Great Britain, Parliamentary Papers, 1898, vol. xxxiv. [c. 8706]) London, 1897. p. 46.

[b] Source given above and Great Britain Board of Trade, Statistical Department, *Statistical Abstract*, 1850-1922. London.

[c] The "official" values of exports were based upon the old rates or valuation of goods as laid down in the Books of Rates of Charles II and George I.

[d] "Real" value prior to 1853 is declared value, since which time it is based on the "prices of the day".

[e] Value of ships and boats (new) with their machinery made for foreign owners first included in totals.

The most important manufacturing industries of England are metal work and textiles. The textile industry had already begun to assume modern form at the time of the beginning of the annals. In 1835, the Chief Inspectors of Factories and Workshops reported 2,641 textile factories in England and Wales, employing 294,933 persons.

Mining holds a more important place in England's life than in that of most countries. The coal output dominates the industry, accounting for 93 per cent of the value of all mining and quarried products in 1923.

The above figures indicate the advance of Great Britain's foreign trade as well as her manufacturing. On the basis of "official values" prior to 1853, exports customarily exceeded imports. However, with the adoption of "real values", the balance was reversed and imports have always far exceeded exports since then. The leading imports are cotton, meat, wheat, and flour. The leading exports are cotton goods, coal, iron, and steel.

At the time of the beginning of the annals, England was just awakening to the need for good roads. In many regions, communication was extremely difficult, but the last decade of the eighteenth century saw the government encouraging the building of new roads. On many highways the payment of toll was exacted, and it was not until 1895 that these barriers were completely removed. The development of railways in England and Wales is shown by the following table:

December 31	Railway Mileage [a]
1843	2,031
1850	6,621
1860	10,433
1870	11,043
1880	12,656
1890	14,119
1910	16,148

[a] Great Britain Committee of the Privy Council for Trade and Foreign Plantations, *Report to the Lords, 1854,* and Great Britain Board of Trade, Statistical Department, *Statistical Abstract,* 1860-1922. London.

The banking system of Great Britain is built around the Bank of England. Most of the regular banking business is handled by large joint-stock and private banks, having many branches. The Bank of England controls the issue of bank notes. The notations in the annals concerning foreign exchange beginning 1914, refer to English exchange in New York.

There had been many serious periods of crisis and distress for English trade and industry before 1790, when our annals begin. In most cases, these were not general, and were closely connected with important political events. Four panics are notable in the seventeenth century,—1640, when Charles I financed his Scottish war by force; 1667, following the great London fire of September, 1666; 1672, arising from the Dutch war; and 1696, just after the formation of the Bank of England. In 1708, political troubles led to credit difficulties. This was soon followed by a period of unprecedented speculation,—the South Sea bubble burst in 1720. A long depression and slow recovery followed, undisturbed until 1745, when the Scotch Prince Charles invaded England as far as Derby, and caused a currency, bank, and stock exchange collapse. In 1763, the boom which followed the ending of the Seven Years' war collapsed. A short depression and rapid revival continued to 1772, when the failure of an important banking house caused a severe panic, the worst since the bursting of the South Sea bubble. The war with the American colonies caused a depression in trade. An excited boom followed the end of the war, but collapsed in 1783 with a financial panic. It is after the recovery from the ensuing depression that the annals begin.

It should be noted that in the section of the annals devoted to agricultural conditions, references to the "crop" or "harvest" refer to the wheat harvest, and references to "crops" are to wheat, oats, and barley unless otherwise stated.

1790   Moderate prosperity.
        Improved domestic trade; higher commodity prices; marked increase in foreign trade.
        Money easy.
        Poor harvest, high price for wheat.
        Spain yields Vancouver Island after diplomatic strain, October.

1791   Prosperity.
        Activity and expansion in trade and industry; increase in foreign trade continued, especially exports.
        Money easy.
        Abundant harvest with low price causes agricultural distress.
        Corn Law with higher duty passed; new French protective tariff.

1792 Prosperity; financial strain.
Continued prosperity and expansion in trade; speculation; imports decline but exports increase strongly.
Easy money tightens, autumn; security prices high.
Crop failure with higher price.
Mobilization of forces in preparation for war, December.

1793 Recession; panic; depression.
Slackening of activity to stagnation, spring; many failures, especially second quarter; commodity prices advance sharply to peak, spring, and then decline; reduction in foreign trade, chiefly exports.
Very tight money eases, summer; panic, February to July, with runs on banks and failures; government relieves situation by issuing exchequer bills.
Moderate crop with low price.
War with France declared, February; France seizes all British goods, October, and England issues severe navigation restrictions; English army lands in Flanders, but is driven from Toulon; civil unrest causes suspension of Habeas Corpus Act.

1794 Depression.
Industry at a standstill; cotton trade most severely hit; further decline of commodity prices; revival in foreign trade.
Money easy.
Deficient crop and rising price.
English victories at sea and defeats on land; epidemic, Manchester.

1795 Revival.
Some improvement in industry; rapid rise in commodity prices; foreign trade dull.
Easy money tightens, last half-year; foreign exchange unfavorable.
Deficient crop and very high price.
Military impressment results in civil unrest, summer.

1796 Uneven prosperity.
Industrial activity; slow rise in commodity prices; foreign trade advances to new high record.
Continued tightening in money market; gold scarcity; security values decline.
Abundant harvest and lower price.
Severe distress, first half-year; extension of scope of poor relief; French invasion of Ireland fails, December.

1797 Recession; panic; depression.

Activity yields to stagnation, spring; unemployment; slight decline in commodity prices, summer; many failures; foreign trade reduced.

Monetary stringency; panic, February, with runs on banks; Bank of England suspends specie payments, February.

Poor crop, fair price.

Army and navy mutinies; British allies make separate peace with France.

1798 Depression.

Dullness in industry; revival in export trade.

Money eases; unfavorable foreign exchange and large imports of bullion.

Good crop, low price.

French invasion of England threatened, February; Irish rebellion, May; naval successes; Battle of the Nile, August, checks French attempt to win Egypt and India; Pitt presents income tax, December.

1799 Depression.

Inactivity continues; after feverish speculation, prices of imported goods collapse; decline in imports, active exports.

Money tightens, ascribed to continental stringency, especially Hamburg; improvement in security prices.

Harvest very deficient, especially wheat; prices very high.

Great distress and riots; military successes as new Coalition is formed; trade unionism checked by passing of Combination Act.

1800 Depression.

Continued stagnation of industry; further rise in commodity prices, especially foodstuffs; active foreign trade.

Money eases.

Harvest failure; very high prices; duties on grain suspended and active importation.

Distress and riots; Act of Union with Ireland, June; further extension of Combination Act.

1801 Depression; revival.

Improvement in industry late in year; commodity prices rise rapidly to peak, second quarter, and then decline; commerce prosperous.

Money easy; rapid depreciation of currency.

Moderate harvest, much lower price.

Embargo placed on Russian, Swedish, and Danish ships, January; battle of Copenhagen clears Baltic for British shipping; Pitt ministry succeeded by Addington, Whig, March; Peace of Amiens with France, October.

1802   Prosperity.
Rapid improvement and expansion in industry; building brisk; speculation; commodity price decline checked, last half-year; larger exports.
Money easy; large gold premium.
Good harvest, lower price.
Treaty of Amiens, March; income tax repealed.

1803   Prosperity; recession; depression.
With breaking of peace, industry slackens and commerce becomes stagnant; commodity prices rise to peak, third quarter; many failures.
Money tightens; gold premium greatly reduced.
Moderate harvest, lower price.
Peace broken, May, and troops mustered, June; embargo declared on all French and Dutch ships, May; Emmet's rebellion in Ireland, July; income tax reëstablished; Mahratta War in India.

1804   Mild depression.
Industry quiet, activity being concentrated on amassing of war forces; foreign trade dull.
Money eases.
Very deficient wheat and barley crops; sudden and great rise of prices following passing of new corn law with higher duties.
Addington gives way to Pitt, Tory, May; Spain declares war, December; French ports blockaded.

1805   Revival.
Improvement in industry and trade; slight rise in commodity prices.
Money easy.
Average crop, lower price.
Alliance with Russia formed, April; Austria, Sweden and Naples join coalition against France, September; French and Spanish fleets defeated at Trafalgar, October; severe defeats of Austrians and Russians, December.

1806   Prosperity.
General activity in industry; commodity prices decline; decreased imports and increased exports.
Money fairly easy.
Moderate harvests, lower prices.
Pitt dies and Grenville, Whig, becomes prime minister, February; Prussian ports closed to British shipping, March; Napoleon's Berlin Decree establishes "Continental System", November.

BUSINESS ANNALS

1807 Recession.
Activity continues, though slackening; commodity prices decline further; increased failures; many new companies and active speculation; marked reduction in foreign trade.
Money eases.
Poor harvest, lower price.
Orders of Council, January, forbid neutrals to trade with Napoleon; Grenville succeeded by Portland, Tory, March; slave trade abolished February; active war in Spain begun; expedition to Constantinople and Egypt fails; Treaty of Tilsit creates coalition of all European nations against England, July; American embargo declared, December; Napoleon extends blockade by Milan Decree, December.

1808 Mild depression.
Stagnation in manufacturing and further reduction in foreign trade; commodity prices rise rapidly; speculation; joint stock companies boom; enormous exports to South America.
Easy money tightens; security market very active.
Wheat crop deficient, barley and oats average; high prices.
Military successes in Portugal.

1809 Revival; prosperity.
Improvement in industry; prices high and speculation frenzied; extraordinary increase in foreign trade.
Money market tightens; increased gold premium.
Poor crop, very high price.
America passes Non-Intercourse Act; Portland succeeded by Perceval, Tory, October; disastrous expedition to the Scheldt.

1810 Prosperity; recession.
Activity and speculation continue to crisis, July; wild price fluctuations give way to general decline; many failures; manufacturing paralysis and unemployment, autumn; record imports with little increase in exports.
Money very tight; bank failures, summer; gold advances to large premium.
Good wheat and oats crops, fair barley; high prices.
Military successes in Portugal.

1811 Deep depression.
Complete stagnation of industry; many failures; unemployment; wage cuts; commodity prices decline; marked reduction in foreign trade.
Money eases; exchequer bills issued; currency improves.
Deficient crops, very high prices.
Universal distress; Luddite riots of frame-breaking; war successes after April; Regent appointed to displace George III, November.

1812   Revival.

Gradual improvement in industry despite unrest in manufacturing districts; distress and unemployment in cotton industry; revival of speculation, autumn; sharp rise in commodity prices; many failures; recovery of export trade.

Money easy; increased gold premium.

Fair crops; very high prices.

Severe distress, riots, and frame-breaking; Perceval assassinated, May, and Liverpool ministry formed, Tory; war with United States declared, June; victories in Spain; Napoleon's disastrous invasion of Russia.

1813   Prosperity.

Industry flourishes, except for severe cotton strike, Scotland; rapidly rising commodity prices; active speculation; increased foreign trade.

Money easy; large gold premium.

Abundant harvest, sharp fall in prices.

Military successes in Spain; coalition of Russia, Prussia, England and Austria against Napoleon; corn law eased.

1814   Uneven prosperity.

Great activity and full employment in manufacturing industries; rapid fall in commodity prices after first quarter causes much commercial distress and numerous failures; foreign trade booms.

Money tightens; record gold premium.

Deficient crop, low price.

Allies enter Paris, March; First Treaty of Paris, May; capture of Washington, August; American War ended by Treaty of Ghent, December.

1815   Boom; recession.

Great activity, temporarily checked by Napoleon's return; speculative boom after Waterloo; credit collapse and failures, autumn; unemployment; continued decline of commodity prices; foreign trade feverish, first half-year.

Money tight; many country bank failures; gold at very high premium during Hundred Days, followed by large importation.

Excellent harvest, very low price.

Napoleon returns from Elba, March; Waterloo, June.

1816   Deep depression.

Stagnation of industry and trade; iron and coal industries paralyzed; many failures; lower commodity prices; extensive unemployment; foreign trade greatly reduced.

Money tight and many small bank failures; foreign exchange returns to par.

Wheat crop failure, barley and oats under average; marked rise in prices.

Widespread distress leads to riots, May and June, and Spa Fields riots, December.

1817   Depression; revival.

Inactivity gradually gives way; improvement begins in spring, marked by autumn; some advance of commodity prices; strong revival in foreign trade.

Money very easy; marked improvement in currency.

Harvest below average, high price.

Derbyshire insurrection; Habeas Corpus Act suspended.

1818   Prosperity.

Great activity in industry; cotton spinners strike, Lancashire, July; active speculation, especially in imported commodities; foreign trade very active, especially imports.

Easy money tightens in autumn; currency depreciation.

Average wheat, deficient oats crops; wheat price drops, barley and oats rise.

Habeas Corpus Act reinstated.

1819   Recession; depression.

Relapse in early spring to stagnation of industry; commodity prices decline; many failures; cotton industry especially depressed; foreign trade greatly reduced, especially exports.

Money very tight, spring, and then eases; slight increase in gold premium.

Full average crops; high prices.

Increased civil unrest; reform movement culminates in Peterloo massacre, August.

1820   Depression; slight revival.

Continued depression in industry; partial revival, autumn, especially in cotton industry; declining commodity prices; some recovery in foreign trade.

Money eases; currency improves; banking crisis and suspension in Ireland, June.

Average harvest, low prices.

Civil unrest continues; George III dies, January, and George IV accedes to throne.

1821 Slow revival.
Considerable improvement in manufacturing, except iron industry; full employment; further decline in commodity prices; increased exports, decreased imports.
Money easy; resumption of specie payments, May.
Deep gloom in agriculture despite abundant harvest; poor quality wheat and very low price.
Coronation, July; death of Queen, August.

1822 Revival; prosperity.
Improvement in industry continues; slight further decline in commodity prices; increased export trade.
Money tightens; minor gold panic; rapid advance of security prices.
Abundant harvest; wheat price very low, but some improvement in oats and barley.
Severe Irish famine.

1823 Prosperity.
Quiet activity and expansion; manufacturing flourishes; large increase in imports, slight drop in export trade.
Money very easy and abundant.
Short crops with somewhat higher prices, especially wheat; agricultural distress relieved by lower costs.

1824 Prosperity.
Widespread activity and expansion; full employment at higher wages; rapid rise in commodity prices late in year; many new enterprises; some increase in foreign trade, especially exports.
Money easy; active speculation in securities, especially foreign stocks.
Good crops and prices.
Combination Acts repealed, followed by strikes in manufacturing districts.

1825 Prosperity; recession; panic.
Activity continues to spring, and then slackens; commodity prices reach peak, second quarter, and decline rapidly; stagnation with many failures late in year; large imports, smaller exports.
Money very tight; stock prices collapse, May; financial panic, November and December.
Excellent wheat, good barley and fair oats crops; wheat price lower, barley and oats higher.
New Combination Act.

1826   Depression.
Inactivity in industry and trade; further decline in commodity prices; many failures; small foreign trade.
Stringency and panic early in year; money gradually eases.
Excellent wheat, poor oats and barley crops; wheat price declines, oats and barley rise; corn laws temporarily relaxed.
Distress; machinery-wrecking prevalent.

1827   Revival.
Slow improvement in industrial activity; increased employment; gradual decline in commodity prices; recovery in foreign trade.
Money easy.
Good crops, lower prices.
Liverpool ministry supplanted by Canning, Tory, April; Goderich becomes prime minister upon Canning's death, August; alliance of England, Russia, and France endeavors to obtain self-government for Greece from Turkey; battle of Navarino destroys Turkish fleet, October.

1828   Prosperity.
Steady progress in industry; further decline in commodity prices; foreign trade quiet.
Easy money tightens late in year; Irish banking difficulties.
Poor harvests, especially wheat; marked advance in prices.
Wellington ministry, Tory, supplants Goderich, January.

1829   Recession; depression.
Sudden relapse in industry; stagnation in manufacturing by April; unemployment and lower wages; increased number of failures; some improvement in textile industries late in year; dullness in foreign trade, especially imports.
Money very tight.
Quantity and quality of crops deficient; lower prices.
Rioting and distress; Catholic Emancipation Bill for Ireland enacted, April; Corn Law rates lowered.

1830   Depression; revival.
Inactivity gradually yields to revival, spring; manufacturing active with full employment and rising wages; commodity prices at low level; foreign trade booms.
Money eases, then tightens sharply, summer.
Poor harvest; slightly higher price; Irish potato crop complete failure; *rot* destroys many sheep.
Wellington supplanted by Grey, with Whig ministry, November; King George IV dies, June, and William IV accedes to throne; Liverpool and Manchester Railway opened.

THE ANNALS OF ENGLAND

1831 Recession; depression.

Slackening of industrial activity; many failures; increased imports, smaller exports.

Money tight.

Good crops, low prices.

Continual agitation concerning Reform Bill; Bristol, London, and Nottingham riots; coronation, September.

1832 Depression.

Dullness in industry and trade; iron industry especially depressed; fewer failures; marked decline in imports, active exports.

Money eases; political conditions threaten panic.

Abundant crops, lower prices.

Continued agitation to passing of Reform Bill, June.

1833 Revival.

General improvement and healthy state of industry and trade; commodity prices rise; foreign trade expands.

Money easy; renewal of Bank Charter, bank notes being made legal tender.

Good crops; lower wheat and higher barley prices.

Abolition of colonial slavery, August; East Indian trade opened.

1834 Prosperity.

Calm activity and expansion; foreign trade booms.

Money easy, tightening somewhat in summer; active stock speculation.

Excellent harvest of wheat, fair barley and oats; wheat price depressed, barley and oats rise slightly.

Grey ministry replaced by Melbourne, Liberal, July; Poor Law reformed, August; Peel, Conservative, replaces Melbourne, November.

1835 Prosperity; stock exchange panic.

Continued activity and expansion; all branches of trade and manufacturing prosper; commodity prices rise; marked increase in exports.

Money slightly tighter; great stock exchange boom in foreign securities leads to panic, May.

Abundant harvest and very low prices increase agricultural distress.

Peel gives way to Melbourne, Liberal, April.

1836   Prosperity; financial panic.

Great activity and expansion; extreme speculation; commodity prices reach peak, second quarter; active formation of joint stock companies, especially banks; very active foreign trade.

Money tightens severely, precipitating panic, autumn; excited speculation in English railroad and bank stock.

Abundant yields in London district, but crop failures elsewhere; rapid rise in price.

1837   Recession; panic; depression.

Gradual recession of activity to stagnation, summer; many failures; commodity prices decline; foreign trade depressed.

Continued financial strain; panic, June; gradual easing of money market, last half-year.

Fair harvest, good price.

Victoria accedes to throne upon death of William IV, June; rebellion in Canada.

1838   Depression.

Inactivity and dullness in industry; slight rise in commodity prices; foreign trade expands rapidly.

Money very easy.

Very small harvest and high price of wheat.

Agitation for People's Charter begins; severe famine in India; Afghan War.

1839   Depression.

Deepening depression; many failures; smaller increase in foreign trade.

Money tightens severely; gold crisis, April.

Deficient harvests, high prices.

Melbourne resigns but is recalled, May; war with China, July, and Hong Kong captured, August.

1840   Depression.

Signs of improvement at beginning of year lead only to deeper depression; many failures; further increase in foreign trade.

Money tight.

Good yield but smaller acreage results in small crop; high price.

Chinese War truce after blockade of Canton and capture of Chusan; penny postage initiated, January; marriage of Queen Victoria and Prince Albert, February; French diplomatic strain.

1841 Depression.
Anticipated improvement in spring not realized; severe depression; many failures; widespread unemployment; foreign trade dull.
Money tight.
Crops under average, high price.
Activity by Quadruple Alliance against Turkey results in Treaty of London, July; Melbourne gives way to Peel, Conservative, September.

1842 Depression.
Continued stagnation with signs of recovery, last half-year; many failures; commodity prices decline sharply; improvement in foreign trade.
Money eases.
Abundant harvest; much lower price; Corn Law reduced.
Civil unrest; Chartist riots in manufacturing districts, summer; Ashburton-Webster Treaty with United States; Peel tariff policy of lower duties begun; income tax passed; peace with China.

1843 Depression; revival.
Gradual disappearance of dullness; active revival begins, March; beginning of rapid railroad construction; commodity prices reach low point, third quarter.
Money very easy.
Good harvest, slightly higher price.
Further tariff decreases; diplomatic crisis with France over Tahiti.

1844 Mild prosperity.
Increasing activity in manufacturing; full employment; increased foreign trade.
Money very easy; revival of speculation, especially in railroad securities; Bank Charter Act passed to regulate Bank of England issues.
Increased agricultural distress with very large harvest and very low prices.

1845 Prosperity.
Increased activity in manufactures; extensive railroad construction; foreign trade large.
Easy money gradually tightens; railroad speculation becomes feverish, and collapses, October.
Deficient harvest with somewhat higher price; potato disease causes great distress in Ireland.
Peel resigns but is returned to office, December; Sikh War.

1846   Prosperity.

Continued activity and expansion; commodity prices rise late in year, especially foodstuffs and cotton; foreign trade active.

Tight money early in year eases somewhat; speculation active.

Crop failures, especially potato yield; prices rise rapidly.

Continued Irish famine; Oregon boundary dispute with United States settled, June; Peel gives way to Russell, Liberal, July; Corn Law repealed.

1847   Prosperity; panic; recession.

Activity halted, autumn; many failures and paralysis of industry; unemployment; commodity prices reach peak, third quarter; foreign trade checked.

Tight money leads to financial panic, April; money market easier to autumn; stringency and panic, August; collapse of railroad speculation and colonial issues; restraints of Bank Charter Act removed.

Moderate harvest, price falls.

Continued Irish famine necessitates subsidies by government; ten-hour Act marks extension of factory legislation.

1848   Depression.

Severe inactivity in manufacturing; commodity prices decline; many failures; record completion of railway mileage; foreign trade dull.

Money eases rapidly; violent fluctuations in security prices, with continual decline in prices of railroad stock.

Small crop of poor quality, fair price.

Suppression of Chartists and Irish rebels.

1849   Depression; revival.

Gradual increase in industrial activity, last half-year; failures decrease in number; foreign trade revives.

Money easy; renewed panic and decline in railroad security market with exposures of fraud, February.

Abundant crop, low price.

Navigation Laws repealed; annexation of the Punjab.

1850   Prosperity.

General activity in industry; slight recovery in commodity prices; expansion in foreign trade.

Money easy; railroad security market steadies.

Agricultural distress with deficient crops and very low prices.

Greek dispute settled, April, after British fleet blockades the Piræus.

THE ANNALS OF ENGLAND

1851 Prosperity.

Continued activity in manufacturing; decline in prices of imported commodities results in distress in import trade; exports boom.

Money tightens, but eases late in year.

Fair harvest; prices very low, especially wheat.

Russell resigns but is returned to office, February; Hyde Park Exhibition, May to October; discovery of gold in Australia.

1852 Prosperity.

Activity and expansion in industry; employment abundant; considerable activity in forming new enterprises; expanding foreign trade.

Money very easy.

Crops below average; higher wheat, fair barley and low oats prices.

Derby, Conservative, replaces Russell, February; Aberdeen, Coalition, replaces Derby, December.

1853 Prosperity.

Continued activity and expansion; increasing speculation gradually slackens; commodity prices rise rapidly; marked increase in wages with full employment; marked expansion in export trade.

Easy money gradually tightens.

Wheat failure, average barley and oats crops; sharp rise in prices.

1854 Recession.

Gradual decline into dullness; factories on short time; unemployment and reduced wages; distress in shipping industry with many failures, autumn; commodity prices reach peak and decline; dullness and lower prices in import markets; export trade less active.

Money market tighter, spring.

Very large crops with high prices.

War against Russia declared, March; active campaign in the Crimea, last quarter.

1855 Mild depression.

Industry dull and quiet; unemployment; steady activity in war industries; marked reduction in imports, exports depressed.

Tight money eases somewhat, but tightens severely, autumn.

Crops average; very high prices.

Derby replaced by Palmerston, Liberal, February; military successes; capture of Sebastopol, September.

BUSINESS ANNALS

1856 Revival; prosperity.

Rapid improvement to state of general activity and industrial expansion; rapid rise in commodity prices other than foodstuffs; extraordinary boom in foreign trade.

Money tight, easing temporarily in summer.

Crops above average; very high prices, except oats.

Crimean War ended by Treaty of Paris, March; war with Persia, November.

1857 Prosperity; panic; recession.

Continued activity in manufactures and trade, slackening rapidly in autumn; many failures; commodity prices reach peak and decline; increase in foreign trade retarded late in year.

Money very tight; panic, failures, and bank suspension, November.

Abundant wheat harvest, average barley and poor oats; sharp decline in price of wheat, high barley and good oats prices.

Sepoy Mutiny in India; peace with Persia, March.

1858 Depression.

Dullness and inactivity in industry; many failures, especially first half-year; sharp drop in commodity prices; foreign trade reduced.

Money eases after February.

Abundant wheat and oats, fair barley harvest; further decline in prices.

Palmerston ministry supplanted by Derby, Conservative, February; pacification of India completed and government taken over by the Crown, November.

1859 Revival.

Gradual improvement in industry; unemployment disappears; commodity prices recover; marked improvement in foreign trade.

Money very easy, except summer; stock exchange panic, April.

Agricultural depression deepens; average wheat and barley, poor oats harvests; low wheat, good barley, and fair oats prices.

Palmerston replaces Derby, June; Limited Liability Act.

1860 Prosperity.

Widespread activity; full employment; cotton industry booms; commodity prices rise; large increase in foreign trade, especially exports.

Easy money tightens, last quarter.

Deficient wheat, average barley and oats crops; high prices, especially wheat and barley.

Commercial treaty with France, March; further Chinese difficulties lead to capture of Peking, August, and Treaty of Peking, October.

1861   Uneven prosperity.
Continued activity and expansion; cotton industry depressed as American Civil War causes value of raw material to boom late in year; commodity prices steady; increased exports, decreased imports.
Tight money gradually eases.
Small wheat, larger oats and barley crops; wheat price rises, oats and barley fall.
Diplomatic difficulty with United States over *Trent* affair, when two Confederate commissioners are seized; Prince Consort dies, December.

1862   Uneven prosperity.
Continued activity, little hampered by severe depression of cotton industry due to "cotton famine"; unemployment reaches peak in cotton industry, last quarter; active railroad construction; some increase in foreign trade.
Money very easy.
Continued agricultural prosperity; fair wheat, average barley and oats crops with good wheat and barley prices, low oats.
Joint Stock Company Act encourages incorporation.

1863   Uneven prosperity.
Increased activity and expansion in all lines except cotton; less unemployment; rise in commodity prices; appearance of speculation; large increase in foreign trade.
Money tightens with large exports of gold in payment for cotton, last quarter.
Abundant harvests, especially wheat; prices low.

1864   Uneven prosperity; financial strain.
Continued activity and expansion; some improvement in cotton industry; active speculation and promotion of new enterprises; numerous mercantile failures, October; commodity prices reach minor peak; big expansion of foreign trade.
Money very tight; stringency, January, April, and September; security market weak.
Good wheat and barley, poor oats crops; low prices, especially barley.

1865   Prosperity.
Continued expansion; revival in cotton industry; full employment and rising wages; foreign trade slackens.
Money eases, but tightens, last quarter.
Fair harvest, except poor oats; rising prices; cattle plague breaks out.
Palmerston dies, and Russell assumes prime ministership, November.

1866 Recession; panic; depression.

Slackening of industry to depression; many failures; cotton industry disorganized; increase in foreign trade.

Money very tight, easing late in year; security speculation collapses with Overend, Gurney & Company failure, April; panic; Bank Act suspended, May.

Poor wheat and oats, good barley yield; high wheat, very high barley, and good oats prices.

Russell displaced by Derby, Conservative, July; reform riots.

1867 Depression.

Retrenchment and lack of confidence; falling prices and wages; unemployment; many failures; marked decline in foreign trade.

Money very easy.

Deficient wheat and potato crop, barley and oats average; high prices, wheat very high.

Reform Bill passed, August, after much agitation; Dominion of Canada established.

1868 Depression.

Continued inactivity; cotton trade depressed severely; profits small; extensive unemployment; revival of imports.

Money very easy.

Bountiful wheat harvest, deficient barley and oats; wheat price declines, but barley and oats very high.

Disraeli displaces Derby, February, and Gladstone, Liberal, forms Cabinet, December; successful expedition against Abyssinia.

1869 Revival.

Gradual improvement and increase in industry; unemployment still extensive; some recovery in export trade.

Money very easy, with temporary tightening in summer.

Deficient wheat, excellent barley and good oats yields; lower prices with large importation.

Suez Canal opened; Corn Law completely abolished.

1870 Prosperity; panic.

Continued improvement and activity; iron industry especially prosperous; commodity prices reach low point and begin to rise; increase in foreign trade.

Easy money tightens sharply, July; brief financial panic; money easy by last quarter; security prices rise, first half-year, and then collapse.

Fair wheat, poor barley, oats and hay failures; good wheat, fair barley and oats prices.

1871   Prosperity.
General activity and expansion; rapid rise of commodity prices; many new companies formed; foreign trade booms.
Money very easy; temporary tightening in autumn ascribed to withdrawal of gold by German government; active speculation, especially in railroad securities.
Poor wheat, excellent barley and good oats crops; higher prices, except oats.
Alabama dispute with United States submitted to arbitration.

1872   Prosperity.
Industry and trade continue prosperous; commodity prices and wages rise; many strikes; large capital issues, especially first half-year; foreign trade boom continues.
Easy money tightens, autumn; advance in security prices arrested after first half-year.
Poor wheat and barley, average oats crops; good wheat, high barley and low oats prices; cattle plague.
Alabama claims settled, September.

1873   Prosperity; recession.
Continued activity, slackening late in year; full employment; expansion checked by high money rates; commodity prices tumble late in year; large imports, exports decline.
Money tight; stringency, last quarter.
Very poor wheat, average barley and oats crops; high prices.
Gladstone resigns but is returned to office, March.

1874   Depression.
Gradually increasing inactivity and dullness; marked decline in commodity prices; wage cuts; strikes in manufacturing districts, March; building boom in London; reduced foreign trade, especially exports.
Money eases; stock exchange dull.
Excellent wheat, average barley, and poor oats crops; wheat price declines, barley high and oats very high.
General election, February, won by Conservatives, and Gladstone gives way to Disraeli; difficulties in South Africa.

1875   Depression.
More pronounced depression in trade and industry; profits small and many failures; severe unemployment; commodity price decline continues; labor troubles; further marked reduction in exports.
Unsettled money market with many failures, May to June; stock exchange dull.
Small wheat, average barley, and fair oats crops; rising prices.
Suez Canal shares purchased, November.

1876   Depression.

Continued inactivity in industry; coal and iron trades most severely depressed; wool industry revives somewhat; increasing unemployment; further large reduction in exports.

Money very easy; speculation much curtailed; wide fluctuations in price of silver.

Poor wheat and barley crops, oats failure; higher prices.

1877   Depression.

Increased distress in industry and trade; increasing unemployment and labor troubles; larger imports, smaller exports.

Money easy; continued dullness in stock market.

Poor crops, especially wheat; high wheat and barley prices, good oats; cattle plague.

Severe famine in India; anxiety caused by Russian-Turkish War; annexation of Transvaal, March.

1878   Deepening depression.

Continued inactivity, increasing during year; unemployment becomes more widspread; labor disputes numerous; commodity prices fall rapidly, last half-year; many failures, especially last quarter; further reduction in foreign trade, especially imports.

Easy money tightens in summer; important bank failures cause much financial distress, October; revival of activity on stock exchange.

Fair wheat, poor barley, and average oats crops; decline in prices.

Military forces mobilized due to unsettled European conditions; Afghanistan War, September.

1879   Depression; revival.

Inactivity yields to improvement under stimulus of active American buying, last quarter; unemployment very severe; great activity in iron and steel industries begins, October; commodity prices reach bottom and then rise; smaller imports but revival in exports.

Money easy; quiet stock exchange becomes active, last quarter.

Extremely poor wheat and barley crops, fair oats yield; low prices with slight rise in wheat.

Distress; Afghan war ends, May; Zulu insurrection suppressed.

1880 Slow revival.

Rapid improvement, first quarter, checked by fall of commodity prices; general though slight improvement thereafter in manufacturing and employment; foreign trade booms.

Money easy; stock exchange active with steady rise in security prices.

Fair wheat, average barley and oats crops; fair wheat, low barley and oats prices.

Gladstone, Liberal, displaces Disraeli, April; Transvaal Republic proclaimed, December.

1881 Mild prosperity.

Growing activity and increased volume of trade; iron trade very prosperous; marked reduction in unemployment; commodity prices decline, but recover, last half-year; promotion of new companies; decreased imports and increased exports.

Easy money tightens in autumn; quiet stock exchange becomes very active, May, as prices rise rapidly; slump in security prices, August.

Fair wheat and oats, good barley crops; fair wheat, low barley and oats prices.

Independence of Transvaal recognized after Boer victories.

1882 Mild prosperity.

General activity and large volume of business, but small profits; iron boom ends; full employment; slowly declining commodity prices; increased activity in foreign trade.

Tight money eases; active year on stock exchange with sustained prices; marked fall in silver.

Excellent crops; prices fall except barley, which rises somewhat.

Egyptian troubles.

1883 Slow recession.

Activity continued with little unemployment; profits very small and lack of enterprise; iron industry depressed; failures, especially May; commodity prices decline; increased imports and smaller exports.

Money eases, summer; dull stock exchange with declining values.

Deficient wheat crop, barley and oats average; lower prices.

Egyptian occupation.

1884 Depression.

Inactivity and widespread unemployment; more rapid decline in commodity prices sets in; failures; slump in foreign trade.

Money tightens somewhat; stock exchange dull.

Excellent wheat, good barley and oats harvests; declining prices.

Continued difficulties in Egypt; Rand gold discoveries in South Africa.

1885 Depression.

Increased depression; extensive unemployment; many failures; continued fall in commodity prices; further reduction in foreign trade.

Money easy; stock exchange dull; great decline in price of silver.

Good wheat and oats crops, excellent barley; slight further decline in prices.

War with Russia threatened, spring; Gladstone replaced by Salisbury, Conservative, June.

1886 Depression; slight revival.

Continued inactivity and widespread unemployment; gradual improvement appears late in year; commodity price fall checked; foreign trade reaches low point.

Money easy; revival of activity on stock exchange; fall in price of silver halted, August.

Poor wheat, good barley and oats crops; price of wheat rises, barley and oats decline.

Gladstone, Liberal, replaces Salisbury, February; Salisbury returns to prime ministry, August; Transvaal gold rush.

1887 Revival.

Continued improvement despite temporary relapse, spring and summer; decreased unemployment; commodity prices rise late in year; recovery evident in foreign trade.

Money tighter; active speculation; security prices fall, first half-year, and then rise.

Excellent wheat, small barley and oats crops; wheat and oats prices low, barley higher.

1888 Moderate prosperity.

Well sustained activity; coal and shipbuilding industries very prosperous; iron revives strongly; commodity prices rise; unemployment disappears; foreign trade records marked increase.

Money market tight and disturbed; stock market active with rising prices, especially British railroads.

Good wheat, small barley and oats crops; wheat and oats prices sustained, lower barley.

1889 Prosperity.
Widespread activity and expansion; shipbuilding, iron, and coal industries boom; full employment and rising wages; dock-laborers strike; big increase in foreign trade.
Easy money tightens sharply, autumn; security prices advance; active gold mining speculation.
Excellent wheat, small barley, and good oats crops; lower wheat, higher oats and barley prices.

1890 Prosperity; panic, November; recession.
Record volume of home and foreign trade, slackening late in year; full employment with increased wages; numerous labor disputes; coal strike of short duration, March; profits less than previous year; commodity prices decline, temporary rise, summer; exports reach peak, July.
Money easier, first half-year; stringency and collapse of stock prices, November, culminate with failure of Baring Brothers in severe financial crisis.
Large crops and high prices.

1891 Industrial recession; financial prostration.
Home trade maintained, though diminished last half-year; increasing unemployment; slowly declining commodity prices; profits curtailed, especially in cotton industry; reduction in foreign trade.
Money eases; stock exchange dull.
Agricultural prosperity, except cattle farming, due to good crops and very high prices.

1892 Depression.
Dullness in home trade; cotton industry severely depressed, with strike at end of year; further increase in unemployment; commodity price fall checked, autumn; further reduction in foreign trade.
Money very easy; stock exchange dull.
Return to agricultural depression; poor crops, especially wheat, with low prices.
Fourth Liberal Gladstone ministry, August.

1893 Deep depression.
Severe curtailment of trade and industry; temporary improvement, early summer, checked by coal strike, July to November; gradual commodity price decline; widespread unemployment and extensive wage reduction, March; profits small; further slight decline in foreign trade.
Money generally easy, tightening and panicky, April, ascribed to Australian crisis, and October, ascribed to American troubles; further drop in stock exchange prices.
Drought causes crop failures; low prices, especially wheat.

1894 Depression.

Stagnation; little improvement in home trade; cotton industry revives; price decline greatly accelerated; very small margins of profit; decrease in unemployment; Scotch coal miners' strike, June to October; reduction in foreign trade checked.

Money very easy; gradual advance in first-class securities with speculative boom in South African shares late in year.

Large crops injured by excessive rainfall; unprecedentedly low prices increase agricultural depression.

Liberal Rosebery ministry formed, March.

1895 Depression; revival, last half-year.

Dullness gives way to marked improvement, summer; shipbuilding and woolen industries very active; employment improves; commodity price fall checked; increase in foreign trade, marked in exports.

Money very easy; stock exchange active to collapse of South African boom, September.

Poor crops, wheat failure; very low prices.

General election, June, returns large Unionist majority; Salisbury ministry formed, June; diplomatic difficulties with United States over Venezuela question, December.

1896 Revival; prosperity.

Improvement maintained; industry expanding; construction industries very active; bicycle boom; improved employment; commodity prices reach low point, summer; rapid expansion of foreign trade.

Money easy, tightening in autumn; rapid rise in security prices.

Good wheat and barley, fair oats crop; prices much improved.

Miltary campaigns in South Africa and Egypt.

1897 Prosperity.

Continued activity; some depression in textile industries; prolonged dispute in engineering trade, last half-year; widespread wage increases; little movement in prices; increased imports but smaller exports.

Money eases; stock prices rise to November, and then drop.

Wheat and barley yields smaller, oats larger; prices higher.

THE ANNALS OF ENGLAND

1898 Prosperity.

Further improvement in trade and industry; full employment; slow rise in commodity prices; further expansion of imports without increase in exports.

Money easy, especially summer; stock exchange cautious and dull.

Exceptional yields of wheat, barley, and oats; high prices; wheat falls after collapse of "Leiter" corner.

Relationship with France strained over spheres of influence in West Africa, and Fashoda in upper Egypt; naval mobilization; acquisition of Wei-hai-wei in China; Sudan reconquest, September.

1899 Prosperity.

Great activity and expansion; shipping, shipbuilding, and iron and steel especially prosperous; marked rise in commodity prices; increase in foreign trade, especially exports.

Easy money gradually tightens to stringency late in year; security prices reach peak, July.

Good crops, lower prices.

Boer War declared, October; British reverses, November and December.

1900 Prosperity; recession, summer.

Activity and progress, first half-year, yield to dullness and decline, summer; gradual increase in unemployment; commodity prices reach peak and then decline; coal prices extremely high; big increase in volume of foreign trade, slackening late in year.

Money tight, with large government loans floated; stock market unsteady with rapid rise in industrial stocks, first quarter, and boom in American railways.

Smaller crops, except oats; higher prices.

War continued with increasing demands for men and materials; British successes begin, March.

1901 Mild depression.

Continued recession; some shrinkage in volume of activity, but chiefly in prices; construction industry severely curtailed; decline in prices and wages; increased unemployment; volume of foreign trade unchanged, but value decline marked.

Money market firm, easing toward end of year; stock exchange quiet except for collapse of Northern Pacific corner and of American railways boom, May; industrial stocks reach peak, March, and decline rapidly.

Reduction in yields of all crops; prices unchanged.

War continues; death of Queen Victoria, January.

1902　Lessened depression.

Decline checked, but little improvement; some increase in volume of activity; increased unemployment; many wage decreases; commodity price fall halted; small increase in foreign trade.

Money fairly easy; stock market dull with falling prices.

Good crops, especially oats; prices low.

Boer War ended, May; coronation of Edward VII postponed from June to August; Unionist Balfour ministry formed, July.

1903　Depression deepens.

Dullness; cotton industry paralyzed by high prices; further increase in unemployment, especially last half-year; little change in commodity prices; revival in foreign trade.

Money tighter; stock exchange inactive, after temporary rise in prices.

Poor crops, wheat very small; low prices.

1904　Depression; revival.

Improvement to February checked by foreign difficulties; depression, summer; extensive unemployment and wage reductions; many failures; little change in commodity prices, except cotton; active revival sets in, last quarter; cotton industry recovers; expansion in foreign trade.

Money eases; stock exchange revives, last quarter.

Poor crops, wheat failure; low prices for oats and barley, wheat high.

Diplomatic difficulties with Russia over attacks on neutral shipping.

1905　Revival; prosperity.

Rapid improvement; unemployment declines; wages begin to rise, last half-year; upward movement in commodity prices begins, June; construction industry lags behind; big increase in exports.

Easy money tightens, last quarter; stock prices rise.

Average yields; wheat prices lower, barley and oats improve.

Formation of Liberal Campbell-Bannerman ministry, December.

1906　Prosperity.

Excellent year in both trade and commerce; industry active and expanding; full employment; continued rise of commodity prices; cotton industry booms; record expansion of foreign trade.

Money tight, stringency, autumn; stock market collapses early in year, but revives, last quarter.

Excellent harvest; good prices, lower wheat.

THE ANNALS OF ENGLAND

1907 Prosperity; recession.

Continued activity; gradual restriction of industry, autumn; rapid increase in unemployment sets in, August; commodity prices reach peak, May, and collapse, summer; copper speculation breaks, summer; very active foreign trade.

Money very tight; financial stringency, autumn; stock exchange slumps with failures, June.

Large crops, especially oats; high prices.

Railway dispute, September.

1908 Depression.

Marked and rapid decline in all branches of industry; stagnation; severe unemployment reaches peak, autumn; many wage reductions; severe engineering strike, summer, and general lockout in Lancashire cotton industry, autumn; many failures; large reduction in volume of foreign trade.

Money eases rapidly; stock exchange dull with declining stock prices; some revival, summer, in South American securities.

Smaller crops; wheat and oats prices low, barley good.

Distress among working classes; formation of Liberal Asquith ministry, April, upon death of Campbell-Bannerman; Old-Age Pensions Act.

1909 Revival.

Steady and continuous recovery; employment improves; strong commodity price rise after first quarter; cotton industry depressed; revival of foreign trade, second quarter.

Money easy to October, then tightens suddenly; revival of activity on stock exchange; Kaffir and rubber booms.

Large crops; higher wheat and oats prices, lower barley.

House of Commons and Lords deadlock in trial of strength over budget.

1910 Prosperity.

Great activity and expansion; woolen trade leader in prosperity, cotton depressed; shipbuilding lockout, summer and autumn; steady improvement in employment; slower rise in commodity prices; extensive creation of new capital issues; further expansion in foreign trade, especially exports.

Easy money tightens late in year; stock market collapses, summer.

Smaller crops; low prices except barley.

Two general elections; King Edward VII dies, May.

1911 Prosperity.

Continued activity, but rate of progress slackens; general rise of commodity prices, falling in summer; strikes of seamen, dock laborers, and transport workers; expansion of foreign trade retarded.

Money rates firm; revival on stock exchange with rubber boom gives way to dullness, summer.

Large wheat, fair oats and barley crops; marked rise in prices especially oats and barley.

Drought; coronation of George V, June; diplomatic crisis with Germany; Insurance Act against sickness and unemployment; Parliament Act limits power of House of Lords, August.

1912 Prosperity.

Record year with great activity and large profits; full employment and rising wage rates; national coal strike, spring; London dock workers strike; revival of construction industry; rapid rise of commodity prices; marked advance in foreign trade.

Money market tightens severely, autumn; active stock exchange slight panic, October; marked decline in bond values.

Poor crops with lower prices.

1913 Prosperity; recession, last quarter.

Great activity, large profits; full employment, rising wages; large volume of production but gradual reduction, last quarter; iron and steel industry decline marked; cotton depressed by end of year many strikes; commodity prices reach peak and decline; record foreign trade.

Money very high; stock exchange dull with declining prices, especially last quarter.

Poor wheat and oats crops, barley fair; further decline in oats and barley prices.

1914 Mild depression deepens with war.

Slow decline and dullness; severe paralysis with war; employment good to August, and then falls off sharply, recovering late in year; gradual decline of commodity prices changes to rapid rise, August; great activity in war industries late in year; slackening foreign trade restricted, especially exports.

Money eases, tightens sharply, autumn, and then gradually eases again; moratorium declared; stock exchange closed, last five months; with war, foreign exchange booms, and then becomes gradually unfavorable.

Average crops with rising prices.

Serious controversy over home rule for Ireland, first half-year; war with Germany declared, August; rapid enlistment of men; government takes over railways; North Sea closed by British Admiralty, November.

1915 War activity.

Industrial boom with shortage of labor, high wages, high prices, and few failures; textile industry depressed; war industries very active; rapid rise in commodity prices; increase in imports, decrease in exports.

Easy money tightens, summer; stock exchange reopened, January; steady decline in security values; foreign exchange becomes more unfavorable; New York loan floated, October.

Large wheat, good oats, poor barley crops; prices rising.

Continued enlistment of men; price control begins, summer; Germany adopts policy of submarine blockade; Dardanelles fiasco; first London air raid, May; formation of Coalition Asquith ministry, May.

1916 War activity.

Great activity in war industries; large profits; commodity prices rise rapidly; labor shortage and shipping difficulties; active foreign trade.

Money tighter; some revival in value of industrial shares; exchange pegged through J. P. Morgan and Co. loan.

Small wheat, fair barley and oats yields; prices rise, especially barley.

Limited conscription, January, made general, June; voluntary rationing adopted, February; Irish rebellion, May; Jutland naval victory, June; Coalition Lloyd George ministry formed, December.

1917 War activity.

Continued activity with increased government restrictions; raw material and labor shortage; commodity prices rise rapidly, except food; extensive government control of prices adopted, July; large increase in imports and decline in exports.

Money tight; some improvement in security prices; export of gold prohibited, May.

Excellent crops; wheat prices high, barley and oats lower.

Government control extended to coal and lighting; English victories in Belgium; submarine warfare severe, first half-year; Supreme War Council formed, November.

1918 War activity; recession.

Continued activity with greater government control; friction and confusion with Armistice, November; severe raw material shortage; many strikes; prices rise slowly to peak, October, and then fall; exports very small and imports enormous.

Money market dominated by government finance; money easier; rapid rise in industrial shares after May.

Record crops, due chiefly to increased acreage; steady prices.

Strict rationing of staples undertaken, February; severe German offensive, March; Allied successes begin, August; influenza epidemic, autumn; Armistice, November.

1919   Revival; prosperity.
Dullness gives way to boom; rapid industrial expansion; full employment; severe labor troubles, especially coal strike, July and August, and railway strike, September and October; commodity price decline gives way to rapid rise; increase in foreign trade, especially imports; tariff with Imperial preference effective, September.
Gradual tightening of money, marked in last quarter; rapid rise in value of industrial stocks; exchange unpegged, March, followed by rapid drop; bond values fall.
Good crops, high prices.
Rapid demobilization; gradual removal of government restrictions; Sinn Fein Republic declared, early in year; Versailles Treaty signed, June; war with Afghanistan, summer.

1920   Prosperity; recession; depression.
Feverish activity gradually gives way to steadily increasing depression, second half-year; unemployment becomes severe, autumn; coal strike, last quarter; commodity prices rise to peak, April, and fall; marked increase in value of foreign trade, especially exports.
Money very tight; industrial stocks reach peak, March, and fall rapidly; credit extension checked in spring by rise in bank rate; exchange improves slightly after February, and then falls off again; act controlling exports of specie passed, December.
Poor wheat, excellent barley, and fair oats yield; wheat and oats prices reach peak, barley declines.
Trouble in Ireland; Unemployment Insurance Act passed.

1921   Deep depression.
Widespread stagnation and severe unemployment; complete stoppage in coal industry, second quarter; many failures; rapid fall in prices; collapse of foreign trade, some recovery late in year.
Tight money eases somewhat; fall in security prices halted, autumn; stronger exchange except temporary relapse, summer.
Large wheat, small barley and oats crops; severe decline in prices.
Government control of coal removed, March; trade agreement with Russia signed, March; Irish Free State formed, December.

1922   Depression.
Depression deepens, first five months, with further contraction of trade and employment, except in wool industry which prospers; increased failures; signs of improvement late in year; unemployment severe though slightly improved; prices somewhat stabilized; slight revival in foreign trade, last half-year.
Money eases; stock exchange restrictions removed, May; rapid revival in industrial stocks; steady rise in sterling exchange.
Average crops with lower prices.
Conservatives returned to power, Bonar Law forming ministry, November; Stevenson rubber restriction scheme effective, November.

1923 Depression.

Continued dullness; slight improvement to May, checked, but resumed, September; increased production and employment; high costs restrict textile industries; commodity prices reach bottom, summer, and then rise; building improves; railroads consolidated; large increase in foreign trade, especially imports.

Easy money slightly tighter, second half-year; active stock exchange; industrial stocks reach peak, summer; exchange improves, first quarter, and then falls; United States debt funded.

Smaller wheat and barley crops, oats larger; low prices.

Breakdown of Paris Conference early in year; Conservative Baldwin ministry formed, May; general election, December.

1924 Lessening depression.

Dullness; improvement slackens in summer; unemployment reaches low point, June, and then increases; commodity prices rise, last half-year; marked improvement in shipbuilding and textile industries; imports increase more rapidly than exports.

Money tighter, last half-year; increased activity on the stock exchange, with rising prices; exchange improves, especially last half-year.

Crops larger except wheat; prices improve.

Labor MacDonald ministry formed, January; *De jure* recognition of Russia, February; Wembley Exposition opened, April; Experts' Committee on Reparations reports, April; report accepted at London Conference, August; Conservative Baldwin ministry formed, November; Egyptian difficulties, November.

1925 Depression.

Depression continues, worst in shipping, shipbuilding, coal, and iron and steel industries; increased dullness, summer, but signs of recovery late in year; coal labor crisis settled temporarily by government subsidy, August; extensive unemployment; shipping and wool industry strikes; commodity prices decline, especially textiles; larger imports and smaller exports cause record unfavorable balance of trade.

Money tight to May and after October; foreign exchange rises steadily to above export gold point, April, when specie payments are resumed; gold exports prohibition removed, November; active capital flotations and stock markets; home railroads and bond prices decline, but industrial stocks boom, April to November, especially rubber and tin.

Large wheat, good barley, and excellent oats crops; wheat price rises, barley falls, and oats steady.

Irish boundary dispute settled; import duties reimposed, July; provisional agreement reached on French debt, August; Locarno treaties signed, and British Mosul mandate established, December.

CHAPTER III.

THE ANNALS OF FRANCE.

The Republic of France assumed its present form on September 4, 1870, with the overthrow of Napoleon III. Previously, for two short periods, 1792-1804 and 1848-52, the people of France had overthrown monarchy, but, in both cases, the republican form had been of brief duration. The economic history of France during the nineteenth century was continually disturbed by political events.

France lies in the west of Europe, occupying the natural pathway between the Atlantic Ocean and the Mediterranean Sea. Except for its north-east boundary, it is naturally isolated from its neighbors by the Pyrenees, Alps, Jura, and Vosges mountains. In the west and northwest, its topography consists of fertile plains and low plateaus; in the center, east, and southeast, of mountains and high plateaus. There are large navigable rivers and excellent harbors.

The area of France in 1924 was 212,736 square miles.[1] Of this area, the 5,607 square miles of Alsace-Lorraine were not included in French territory during the period 1871-1919. The record of population at various census dates follows: [a]

Census Date	Population [b]	Persons per Square Mile [c]	Per Cent Urban [d]
August, 1821 [e]	30,461,875	144	... [f]
May-June, 1841 [e]	34,230,178	161	... [f]
May-June, 1851 [e]	35,783,170	168	25.5
May-June, 1861 [e]	37,386,313	173	28.9
April-May, 1872	36,102,921	174	31.1
Dec. 18, 1881	37,672,048	182	34.8
April 12, 1891	38,342,948	185	37.4
March 24, 1901	38,961,945	188	40.9
March 5, 1911	39,604,992	189	44.2
March 6, 1921 [e]	39,209,766	184	46.4

[a] France Statistique Générale, *Resultats statistiques du Recensement général de la Population, 1901, 1911* and *1921*. Paris.
[b] "Population légale ou de résidence habituelle."
[c] Computed by multiplying by 2.59, the data given originally in persons per square kilometer.
[d] Includes all persons living in places with more than 2,000 inhabitants.
[e] Includes Alsace and Lorraine.
[f] No data available.

[1] Computed by multiplying by .003861, data in hectares given in France Statistique Générale, *Annuaire statistique, 1923*. Paris, 1924. This area includes Corsica (3,367 square miles).

The population of France has increased more slowly than that of any other country keeping official population records except Ireland, where natural catastrophies and extensive emigration were notable in the nineteenth century. France is one of the few European countries in which immigration has probably exceeded emigration during the last century.

The extension and relative importance of various types of economic activity can be observed from the following percentage distributions of the working population at four census dates:

Industry	Percentage of Total Working Population [a]			
	1866	1881	1901	1911
Agriculture	49	49	42	41
Manufacturing, Mining, and Construction [b]	31	29	35	36
Commerce	7	10	9	10
Other [c]	13	12	14	13
Total	100	100	100	100

[a] France Statistique Générale, *Resultats statistiques du Recensement général de ..,* 5 Mars, 1911. Paris, 1916. Vol. I, part 3, p. 12.
[b] Includes transportation, which accounted for 2.7 per cent of the total in 1911.
[c] Includes persons engaged in professions, domestic service, public service, fishing, and other activities.

The loss of Alsace and Lorraine in 1871 accounts to a large degree for the decline in the proportion of population engaged in industry between the first two records. These provinces are centers for metallurgical and textile industries. Alsace has large potash fields and produces petroleum. Lorraine is rich in iron and coal.

Agriculture still remains the leading economic activity of France. Although wheat and wine are the two leading products, a distinguishing feature of French agriculture is its variety. Nearly one-tenth of the total area is devoted to the raising of wheat, chiefly in the northern departments. The vineyards, on the other hand, are located in the south. The wine industry has suffered from two severe plagues,— the *oidium* in the early fifties and *phylloxera* in the eighties greatly reducing the yield. Oats and potatoes are also important crops. Harvests come in the autumn.

The leading mineral products are coal and iron ore. Whereas the output of coal is not sufficient for domestic needs, with the addition of the iron ore fields in Lorraine, France will be surpassed only by the United States in iron output.

In manufacturing, France has made steady progress, though retarded by political difficulties prior to 1870. In the textile and clothing industry, the development has been particularly great. Some idea of the growth of factories can be gained from the following record of the number of establishments using steam power:

Year	Establishments Using Steam Power [a]
1852	6,543
1861	14,153
1871	22,192
1881	35,712
1891	46,828
1901	58,151
1911	62,901
1920 [b]	55,073

[a] France Statistique Générale, *Annuaire statistique, 1922.* Paris, 1923. p. 64.
[b] In the boundaries of 1918.

The rapid development of factories during the last half of the nineteenth century is made very evident by these figures. Since 1900, however, the increase has been slower, and the destruction during the war was extensive. Nevertheless, of 23,000 factories damaged or destroyed, more than 20,000 had been reconstructed by 1925, in most cases with improved facilities and equipment.

Transportation in France is aided by the presence of excellent rivers and numerous canals. The railroad system is highly developed and is composed of a state railroad and six private railroad companies. During the period of 1950 to 1960, all railways will revert to the State. The annual average mileage at various dates has been as follows:

Year	Miles of Railroad [a]
1841	317
1851	2,018
1861	5,981
1871	9,713
1881	15,068
1891	21,051
1901	23,782
1911	25,249
1921	24,566

[a] Computed by multiplying by 0.62137, the data in kilometers given in the *Annuaire statistique, 1922.*

French commerce has not grown steadily. After a period of rapid growth which began about 1850, there was little further increase during the last quarter of the nineteenth century. However, the expansion was renewed in the early years of the present century. France customarily has an unfavorable balance of trade, imports exceeding exports. The leading imports are cotton, coal, and wood; leading exports are clothing, millinery, silk fabrics, and cotton fabrics.

The Bank of France, though begun with the intention of becoming a state bank, became instead a bankers' bank. It completely dominates the French banking system. There have also developed four large credit companies with many agencies. In addition, there are numerous local banks. The Bank of France has had the monopoly of bank note issue since 1848.

At the beginning of the nineteenth century, France was at war with England. The brief peace of Amiens, 1802-1803, brought a burst of activity. The Bank of France was established in April, 1803. The resumption of hostilities and doubt as to the strength of the Bank of France led to a severe panic in 1805. Except for a brief period of activity about 1810, trade and industry were then depressed and in 1813 distress became severe, leading up to the panic of January, 1815. Activity was rapidly resumed after Waterloo. A monetary crisis came in 1818, due to the entanglement of the Bank of France with public finance. The Spanish War, in 1823, caused a slight recession, but a marked revival in 1824 ushered in a period of prosperity in 1825. The next recession came in 1829, and was accentuated by the revolution of 1830. France again revived in 1834, and another period of activity followed. The difficulties of other countries in 1836 did not involve French business. It was not until 1838 and 1839 that the turn came, and France was plunged into a depression, destined to be of very short duration.

1840 Revival.

  Gradual recovery of trade and industry; labor troubles; foreign trade active.

  Money eases.

  Very large wheat crop, fair price.

  Continued war in Algiers; Louis Napoleon *coup d'état* fails, August; war with alliance of England, Russia, Austria and Prussia threatened.

1841 Prosperity.
Continued improvement and general activity; further expansion of foreign trade.
Money easy.
Poor wheat crop, higher price.
Government offers to aid railroad construction.

1842 Prosperity.
Continued activity despite slump in export trade; railroad construction boom begins.
Money easy.
Poor crop, good price.
Vigorous campaign in Algiers.

1843 Prosperity.
Continued activity; commodity prices high; active promotion of new railroad companies; foreign trade dull but improving.
Money easy; rapid credit expansion.
Fair wheat crop, good price.
Diplomatic crisis with England over Tahiti.

1844 Prosperity.
Continued activity and expansion, especially railroads; commodity prices rising; marked increase in export trade.
Money plentiful.
Excellent wheat crop, low price.
Successful war with Morocco.

1845 Prosperity; bourse panic.
Continued activity in industry; extensive carpenters' strike, May; further expansion in foreign trade.
Money tightens; bourse activity leads to panic, November.
Poor wheat crop, high price.
United English and French expedition against Madagascar, June.

1846 Prosperity.
Industry continues active despite uneasiness late in year; expansion of foreign trade checked.
Money tight.
Harvest failure, extremely high price.
Widespread distress; floods.

1847 Recession; financial panic.

Gradual slackening of activity; many failures; commodity prices reach peak; increased imports, chiefly of grain; large reduction in exports.

Money very tight; financial panics, April and October; Bank of France raises discount rate for first time since 1820.

Very large wheat harvest, lower price.

Continued distress; civil disorder; pacification of Algiers completed, December.

1848 Depression; financial panic.

Complete paralysis of industrial activity; after Revolution, National Workshops opened, but closed again, June; commodity prices drop sharply; foreign trade greatly reduced.

Financial stringency; panic, February; Bank of France suspends specie payments, March.

Good wheat harvest, very low price.

Revolution, Louis Philippe abdicates, and Republic proclaimed, February; continued disorder and insurrection of Paris Commune, June; constitution promulgated, November, and Louis Napoleon elected president, December.

1849 Depression.

Disorder and uncertainty keep industry at standstill; widespread unemployment; commodity prices very low; revival in foreign trade.

Money tight.

Good wheat and wine yields, very low prices.

Cholera; insurrection, June; expedition to restore Pope captures Rome, July.

1850 Depression.

Business continues dull; unemployment; foreign trade very active.

Money eases; resumption of specie payments, August.

Good wheat and excellent wine yields; record low wheat and good wine prices.

Occupation of Rome continues; universal suffrage abolished, May.

1851 Depression.

Dullness and inactivity continue; confidence restored late in year; imports decline, but exports increase rapidly.

Money panic, December; gold replaces silver as monetary standard.

Good wheat and wine yields; low prices.

Struggle between President Napoleon and Chamber terminates with *coup d'état*, December.

1852 Revival.
Rapid increase in activity; foreign trade booms.
Money eases; Crédit Mobilier established, November, and Crédit Foncier, December.
Good wheat, poor grape harvests; prices considerably higher.
New constitution promulgated, January; empire restored by vote of large majority, November.

1853 Prosperity.
Great activity and expansion in industry; active speculation; many new schemes promoted; government encourages railroad construction; foreign trade extraordinary.
Money market very active, rates low.
Very poor harvests of wheat and grapes; prices rise, especially wheat.
Cholera; bread riots, September.

1854 Prosperity; temporary recession.
Hesitancy with war, March, gradually yields to increased activity; active speculation; railroad construction marked; increased imports and decline in exports.
Money tight.
Enormous wheat crop, grape failure; high wheat, very high grape prices.
War with England as ally declared against Russia, March; campaign in the Crimea, last quarter; cholera.

1855 Prosperity.
Activity continues; feverish speculation; some increase in foreign trade.
Money tighter; severe drain of specie.
Very small wheat and wine yields; high prices, especially wheat.
Military successes, culminating with fall of Sebastopol, September; exhibition; floods and cholera.

1856 Uneven prosperity.
Slackening of activity in internal trade; some improvement in autumn with rising prices and speculation; foreign trade booms after Peace.
Money very tight.
Very small wheat and wine yields; high prices.
Treaty of Paris, March; floods and cholera.

1857 Moderate prosperity; panic; recession.

Some increase in industrial activity, but improvement checked, autumn; unemployment severe late in year; commodity prices reach peak; very large railroad construction; foreign trade continues very active until last quarter.

Money very tight; panic, September.

Excellent wheat harvest, larger wine yield; wheat price declines, though still high.

1858 Depression.

Dullness in industry; unemployment; railroad construction continues large; commodity prices reach minimum; reduction of foreign trade, especially imports.

Money eases.

Excellent wheat and wine yields; prices low.

Strained relations with England.

1859 Revival.

Rapid recovery of industry; railroad construction halted; commodity prices low; foreign trade booms, especially exports.

Money easy.

Fair wheat, poor wine yields; low wheat price.

War supporting Italy, declared with Austria, May; rapid victories and peace declared, July.

1860 Prosperity; recession.

Activity continues to autumn, and then declines; commodity prices reach peak and decline; foreign trade continues unchecked.

Money tightens severely.

Good harvests and prices.

France obtains Savoy and Nice, January; free trade treaty with England completed.

1861 Recession.

Slow recession becomes more rapid, autumn; revival in railroad construction; marked increase in imports and reduction in exports.

Money very tight; financial crisis, autumn.

Wheat failure, very high price.

War scare; neutrality in American War declared.

1862 Mild depression.

General dullness, especially in cotton textile industries; active railroad construction; reduction of imports and recovery of exports.

Money eases.

Fair harvest and prices.

Invasion of Mexico, January; annexation of Cochin China, June.

1863	Uneven depression. Continued dullness and inactivity; foreign trade active. Money tightens. Record wheat harvest and excellent grape yield; fair prices. Mexico conquered, June.
1864	Depression; financial panic. Continued dullness except in foreign trade; commodity price decline sets in; cotton market collapses. Financial panic, January; money continues tight. Excellent yields; low wheat price, high wine. Agreement with Italy to evacuate Rome.
1865	Depression. Dullness continues; railroad construction halted; big drop in commodity prices; foreign trade continues active. Tight money eases, April. Fair wheat, record grape yields; low wheat price, very low wine.
1866	Revival. Slight improvement in industry; some improvement in commodity prices; foreign trade continues active. Money market unsettled. Agricultural depression with very small wheat crop and enormous grape yield; good wheat price, wine very low. Floods in South, September.
1867	Recession; mild depression; bourse panic. Industry dull; very active railroad construction; imports very large but exports decline. Financial difficulties culminate in final suspension of Crédit Mobilier and bourse panic, October. Very poor harvests; wheat price very high, wine fair. Withdrawal from Mexico; French troops defend Pope from Garibaldi attack, November.
1868	Depression; revival. Continued dullness gives way to improvement, last quarter; further increase of imports and decrease of exports. Money eases. Excellent wheat and good wine yields; good prices. Napoleon grants reforms, permitting greater freedom of speech, public assembly, and trade organization.

1869 Prosperity; bourse panic.

Great activity and full employment; imports decline and exports improve somewhat.

Money continues easy; panic on bourse, September, ascribed to illness of Emperor.

Good wheat, record grape yields; prices decline, especially wheat.

Parliamentary government established, September.

1870 Prosperity; recession; depression.

Activity continues to outbreak of war; cessation of business and paralysis of industry; commodity prices rise; foreign trade restricted.

Money tightens; Bank of France suspends specie payments, August.

Poor harvests; high prices.

Riots in Paris, February; constitutional reforms announced, March; plebiscite upholds Emperor Napoleon, May; outbreak of war with Prussia, July; defeats; Napoleon deposed and French Republic proclaimed, September.

1871 Depression; panic.

Continued inactivity and disorder; rise of commodity prices continues; some revival in imports, further reduction of exports.

Money very tight; high gold premium; gold panic, October.

Wheat crop utter failure, good wine yield; wheat price very high, wine fair.

Bombardment and fall of Paris, January; armistice, February, and Peace, March; widespread insurrection, second quarter; Alsace and Lorraine ceded to Prussia by Treaty of Frankfort, May.

1872 Revival.

Rapid recovery from war; activity increases; commodity prices reach maximum; foreign trade booms.

Money tight; heavy taxation and successful loan make indemnity payments possible.

Excellent wheat, fair wine yields; wheat price falls, wine rises slightly.

Compulsory military service established.

1873 Recession; depression.

Gradual slackening of industrial activity; decline in commodity prices; failures and unemployment; foreign trade very active, but slackens late in year.

Money tight; indemnity payments completed, September.

Wheat and grape failures; high prices, especially wine.

Political unrest; withdrawal of German troops completed, September.

1874 Mild depression.

Dullness in industry, except for prosperity in cotton manufacture; big decline in commodity prices; foreign trade restricted.

Money eases with large influx of gold; rapid rise in value of railroad shares.

Record wheat, large grape crops; lower prices, especially wine.

Political excitement.

1875 Revival.

Marked recovery in industry; decline in commodity prices halted; fewer failures; foreign trade records slight improvement.

Money easier.

Good wheat, record wine yields; very low prices.

Severe floods; restoration of Spanish monarchy, January; new Constitution adopted, February.

1876 Gradual recession.

Industry slowly relapses into dullness; slight increase in imports, exports decline.

Capital abundant and money very easy; bourse dull.

Poor crops; higher prices.

Civil unrest.

1877 Mild depression.

Stagnation in industry and trade; unemployment; distress among small railroad companies; foreign trade restricted.

Money easy.

Good crops; higher prices.

Distress; political difficulties.

1878 Depression.

Continued inactivity with signs of improvement late in year; commodity prices fall tremendously; large imports but smaller exports.

Money easy; resumption of specie payment, January.

Poor wheat, good wine yield; higher prices.

Successful Paris Exposition.

1879 Revival; bourse panic.

General improvement; many strikes, May; commodity prices reach minimum; activity in foreign trade, especially imports.

Money easy; speculation leads to bourse panic, September.

Very deficient wheat and grape yields; lower wheat price, big rise in wine.

1880 Prosperity.
Widespread activity; commodity prices rise; promotion active, including floating of company for making Panama Canal; renewed speculation; revival in railroad construction; foreign trade improves.
Money easy.
Fair wheat crop; grape yield enters series of poor returns due to *phylloxera;* higher prices, especially wine.
Dispute with Italy regarding Tunis.

1881 Moderate prosperity.
Continued activity under increasing strain; reduction of imports and increased exports.
Money tighter; stringency and near-panic, October; speculation feverish with rapidly advancing security prices.
Poor wheat and wine yields; fair wheat, high wine prices.
French occupation of Tunis, November; tariff system adopted.

1882 Recession; panic.
Slackening activity; fall in commodity prices; foreign trade dull.
Money tight; severe financial crisis, September and October; security speculation collapses with bourse panic, January.
Excellent wheat, poor wine yield; prices unchanged.
Political disturbances follow Gambetta's death, December.

1883 Depression.
General dullness in industry; railroad construction halted; continued decline of commodity prices; further reduction in foreign trade.
Money market unsteady with continual panics and scares; security prices very low.
Fair wheat crop, larger wine yield; lower prices.

1884 Depression.
Continued stagnation of industry and trade; many failures; rapid decline of commodity prices; activity in railroad construction resumed; further reduction of foreign trade.
Money eases; further decline of security prices.
Good crops; lower wheat, higher wine prices.
Revision of Constitution, August; program of social insurance begins with Sickness Insurance, December.

1885 Depression.
Continued dullness; further decline of commodity prices; smaller foreign trade.
Money easy; revival begins on bourse.
Good wheat, small wine yields; lower prices, especially wheat.

1886   Depression.
Industrial depression deepens; many failures; railroad construction checked; further decline in commodity prices; some revival in foreign trade.
Money easier and abundant; security prices rise.
Fair wheat, poor wine yields; slightly higher prices.

1887   Revival.
Rapid improvement; increasing activity and employment; commodity prices reach minimum and then rise; foreign trade dull.
Money easy; speculation active despite bourse difficulties, first half-year.
Good wheat, very small wine yields; wheat price rises, wine falls.
Political and foreign troubles.

1888   Moderate prosperity.
Activity continues though hampered by many forces; commodity prices rise; slight improvement in foreign trade.
Money tightens; active speculation.
Agricultural distress severe; small wheat and poor wine yields; wheat price low, wine very low.

1889   Moderate prosperity; financial strain.
Continued activity in trade and industry; strikes; commodity prices rise; marked revival in foreign trade.
Money tight; bourse collapses with Panama Canal failure, January; breakdown of copper corner and failure of Comptoir d'Escompte, March; money eases late in year.
Fair wheat, worst wine yield on record; lower wheat, high wine prices.

1890   Recession; mild depression.
Gradual decline of activity; commodity prices steady; little advance in foreign trade.
Money becomes strained, March, and continues tight.
Very good wheat and wine yields; good prices.

1891   Mild depression.
Dullness; commodity prices decline despite higher food prices; imports reach peak, exports smaller.
Money tight; banking difficulties, March.
Very small wheat crop with high price; good wine yield, lower price.
Alliance formed with Russia.

1892 Depression.
Stagnation of commerce and industry; further decline in commodity prices; marked reduction in foreign trade.
Money eases.
Fair wheat harvest and wine yield; prices lower.
Tariff extended.

1893 Depression.
Continued inactivity; further decline in general price level; decreased foreign trade.
Money tightens.
Poor wheat harvest with low price; excellent wine yield, price declines.
Anarchistic uprisings.

1894 Depression.
Continued dullness; more rapid decline of commodity prices; increased failures; foreign trade reaches low point.
Money very easy; revival on bourse.
Excellent wheat, fair wine yield; prices slightly lower.
President Carnot assassinated, June; Dreyfus case, October.

1895 Depression; revival.
Dullness gives way to increased activity, summer; severe fall in food prices, rise in prices of industrial commodities; foreign trade revives, especially exports.
Money very easy; speculative boom in gold mining shares leads to minor panic, last quarter.
Excellent wheat crop with low price; very small wine yield, price rises.
Madagascar protectorate established.

1896 Revival.
Continued improvement; commodity prices decline to low point; foreign trade improves slowly.
Money very easy; dull bourse.
Excellent wheat crop with low price; larger wine yield, lower price.
Madagascar made French colony after revolt.

1897 Moderate prosperity.
Increased activity; mining industry extremely prosperous; slight rise in commodity prices; foreign trade more active.
Money easy; more active bourse.
Very poor wheat crop with high price; poor wine yield, lower price.

1898 Prosperity.
Activity and expansion somewhat hampered by foreign and political unrest; commodity prices rise; increase in number of failures; imports boom but exports decline.
Money easy, but tightens, last quarter; stock exchange troubled by foreign disturbances.
Excellent wheat crop with high price; poor wine yield, higher price.
Kwangchow-Wan in China occupied; Dreyfus affair re-opened, August; Fashoda difficulty with Great Britain.

1899 Prosperity.
Activity and expansion; rapid rise in commodity prices; foreign trade booms.
Money tightens; stringency late in year; security prices decline.
Excellent wheat crop, price declines; large wine yield with low price.
Relations with England strained.

1900 Prosperity; recession.
Continued activity; decline sets in, summer; commodity prices reach peak; foreign trade reaches high point, especially imports.
Money gradually eases.
Fair wheat crop, very low price; record wine yield, extremely low price.
Paris Exposition, spring.

1901 Depression.
Increasing dullness in commerce and industry; commodity prices decline; foreign trade restricted.
Money easy.
Poor wheat, large wine yield; very low prices.

1902 Depression.
Continued inactivity, increased by severe coal strike, last quarter; decline of commodity prices continues; some revival in foreign trade, especially exports.
Money easy, tightening late in year.
Fair wheat and wine yields, higher prices.

1903 Revival.
Distinct improvement, spring; manufacturing active, except cotton; commodity prices rise; some further expansion in import trade.
Money easy.
Excellent wheat, very poor wine yield; higher prices.

1904 Moderate prosperity.
Continued improvement; decline in imports and increased exports create favorable balance.
Money easy; stock market improves after slight panic, February.
Poor wheat, excellent wine yields; prices decline.
Entente with England formed.

1905 Prosperity.
Continued activity and expansion; rapid rise of commodity prices; improvement in foreign trade.
Easy money tightens late in year.
Good wheat crop with higher price; large wine yield, extremely low price.
Relations with Germany strained over Morocco; separation of Church and State, December.

1906 Prosperity.
Great activity and expansion; commodity prices rise rapidly; foreign trade booms, especially imports, returning to unfavorable balance.
Money fairly easy; bourse very active.
Fair wheat crop, large wine yield; higher prices.
Dispute with Germany settled; beginning of period of syndicalist troubles.

1907 Prosperity.
Continued activity and expansion; commodity prices very high; foreign trade increases rapidly.
Money tightens; stringency late in year but no severe shock; security prices decline.
Excellent wheat crop, good price; large wine yield, price lower.
Floods; wine growers riot in southern France, beginning May; trouble in Morocco, last half-year.

1908 Recession; mild depression.
Slight check to domestic trade and industry; commodity prices fall; few failures; foreign trade declines.
Money easy, summer; security prices revive somewhat.
Fair wheat crop, large wine yield; lower prices.

1909 Revival.
Improvement hampered by labor troubles, April; energetic revival, last half-year; commodity prices reach bottom, summer; foreign trade very active.
Money easy; bourse active with rising values.
Good wheat crop and wine yield; slight improvement in prices.

1910 Prosperity.
Continued growth in production and volume of business; severe railroad strike, summer; extensive issue of new securities; marked rise in commodity prices; foreign trade very active.

Easy money tightens, autumn; security prices decline, especially bonds.

Very poor wheat harvest and vintage; high prices, especially wine.

Floods in Paris district, January; tariff increased, March; severe agricultural distress.

1911 Prosperity.
Continued activity, hampered somewhat by agricultural conditions and foreign affairs; further rise in commodity prices; railway strike, August, stopped by military force; imports increase, exports decline.

Easy money tightens, September; stock exchange revives, first half-year, and then slumps.

Fair crops, high prices.

War with Germany threatened, late summer; Morocco crisis, autumn.

1912 Prosperity.
Vigorous activity and expansion; further rise of commodity prices; foreign trade very active.

Money tightens; bourse activity leads to panic, October.

Good yields, high prices.

Protectorate established over Morocco, March.

1913 Prosperity; recession.
Continued activity, first half-year; gradual recession to dullness, last half-year; commodity prices reach peak, first quarter; record foreign trade.

Money tight, especially last half-year; bourse dull.

Fair crops, higher prices.

War in northern Africa.

1914 Depression.
Growing depression becomes complete suspension with war; unemployment; government gradually revives activity; some decline in commodity prices; foreign trade completely checked.

Money market collapses with war; Bank of France suspends specie payments; moratorium; rapid expansion of currency; bourse collapse, July; foreign exchange very high, July, but gradually declines.

Poor wheat crop, high price; excellent wine yield, low price; severe shortage of agricultural labor.

War with Germany, August; immediate mobilization; rapid German advance halted, September.

1915 War activity.

Gradual and uneven revival under government regulation and restriction; unemployment declines; commodity prices rise very rapidly; big increase in imports, exports decline.

Continued currency expansion; moratorium ended; bourse reopened; large public loans floated; rapid decline in foreign exchange.

Very small wheat crop and vintage; prices high.

Trench warfare on western front, largely in French territory; extensive mobilization of men.

1916 War activity.

War industries very active; labor shortage; commodity prices rise rapidly, increasing import trade.

Foreign exchange stabilized, September; slow increase in currency circulation.

Smaller wheat crop, larger vintage; prices higher.

Continued trench warfare; price control undertaken early in year; gradual driving back of German lines.

1917 War activity.

Maximum activity; severe shortage of labor and raw materials; further extraordinary rise in commodity prices; active import trade.

Government loans dominate money market; slight improvement in exchange; accelerating currency expansion.

Very small wheat crop, fair vintage; big rise in prices.

Germans forced back to Hindenburg line, spring; United States enters war, April.

1918 War activity; stagnation.

Continued activity increasingly hampered by scarcity of coal and raw materials, the blockade, use of ships as American transports, railway difficulties, and the German advance; business and industry paralyzed, last two months; commodity prices rise but decline late in year; decline in both imports and exports.

Exchange stronger; continued currency expansion.

Larger crops, very high prices.

German advances, first half-year; tide turns in favor of French, summer; Armistice, November.

1919 Depression; revival; boom.

Severe though short depression; slow but accelerating revival sets in as reconstruction work is extended, summer; wholesale prices decline to May and then rise rapidly; strong recovery in imports, no exports.

Support withdrawn from exchange, March, followed by severe decline; continued currency expansion checked, November.

Very small wheat, large wine yields; wheat price lower, wine at peak.

Demobilization; Versailles Treaty signed, June; higher tariff decrees, June and July; Alsace-Lorraine ceded to France.

1920 Prosperity; recession; depression.

Activity and reconstruction; slump, summer, to depression; iron production reaches peak, October; employment reaches peak, April, and declines sharply late in year; railroad labor troubles; wholesale prices reach peak, April, and fall off rapidly; general strike attempted, May; active imports, some revival in exports.

Severe financial depression; stock prices reach peak, April; foreign exchange falls except for temporary improvement, second quarter; resumption of inflation policy, August.

Larger crops still far below pre-war level; wheat prices at peak, wine lower.

1921 Depression; revival.

Depression most severe, first half-year; some resumption of activity, summer; production reaches low point, third quarter, and then revives rapidly; unemployment most severe, spring, and rapidly diminishes; wholesale prices decline, first half-year, and then improve; small foreign trade.

Money very tight, ascribed to extensive government borrowings; money eases somewhat, last half-year; exchange improves, spring, but declines again, summer; currency expansion checked.

Larger wheat, smaller wine yields; wheat price declines, wine remains high.

Tariff revised upwards, March and June.

1922 Revival.

Improvement in commerce and industry, especially last half-year; recovery marked in textile industries, notably woolen; full employment; wholesale prices decline, first half-year, and then rise; foreign trade revives.

Money tight; further improvement in exchange to April, when decline sets in; stock prices reach bottom, second quarter, and rise.

Poor crops.

France breaks with Allies on reparations problems.

1923 Prosperity.
Continually improving conditions; marked increase in production; absence of unemployment and strikes; rapid rise of prices, first and fourth quarters; exports increase vigorously.
Money easy; steady fall in foreign exchange; security prices rise; slight increase in circulation.
Larger wheat, smaller wine yields.
Occupation of Ruhr, January; passive resistance overcome, September; German coke and coal stocks confiscated, March.

1924 Prosperity.
Continued improvement in trade and industry; full employment; wholesale prices very high, declining, February to April, and then rising; active export trade creates favorable balance.
Money tighter; stock prices reach peak, March, and then slump; foreign exchange fluctuates violently, falling, first two months, and then rising rapidly; large foreign loans floated; gradual increase in currency circulation.
Agricultural conditions improve; fair wheat, good wine; excellent beet sugar and potato yields; higher prices.
Russia recognized *de jure*, October; Ruhr evacuated, October.

1925 Prosperity.
Continued high level of industrial production; commodity prices steady to May, rise to July, and soar, last quarter; severe labor shortage despite immigration of many factory workers; restoration work halted; active foreign trade, balance becoming unfavorable, August.
Money very tight, especially first half-year; violent foreign exchange fluctuations, with gradual decline to summer, and collapse, October; public finances chaotic with unsuccessful attempts by seven finance ministers to balance budget; domestic gold loan and funding of American debt fail; active stock speculation with declining prices.
Exceptionally large wheat crop, good beet sugar and very poor wine yields; lower cereal prices, higher wine.
Continual political crisis; Riff troubles, spring and summer; Syrian revolt, August; provisional agreement reached concerning Anglo-French debt, August; Locarno treaties signed, December.

CHAPTER IV.

THE ANNALS OF GERMANY.

The German Republic was established on November 9, 1918, after the abdication of the Emperor. The German Empire had been formed in 1871 by treaties between the North German Confederation and the South German states, including Alsace and Lorraine which had just been won from France by Prussia. In 1890, the island of Heligoland was purchased from Great Britain.

Germany is the third largest country in Europe, and ranks second in population. The boundaries of the Empire were: on the east, Russia, on the southeast, Austria and Switzerland, on the southwest, France, on the west, Luxemburg, Belgium, and the Netherlands, and on the north, the North Sea, Denmark, and the Baltic Sea. The most important changes made by the war were the creation of the buffer states, Lithuania, Poland, and Czecho-Slovakia between Germany and Russia. The free state of Danzig and the "Polish corridor" now separate East Prussia from the rest of Germany. The larger part of Germany to the north is plain, but to the south, the topography is varied with large plateaus, fertile low plains, mountain chains and isolated peaks. Germany has about 7,000 miles of natural waterways, but few good harbors. Navigation in the Baltic Sea is closed several months each year by ice.

The present area of Germany is 182,252 square miles [1] which represents a decrease of 26,573 square miles from the pre-war area. The records of population growth are given in the following page.

Not only was there the rapid population growth shown by these data, but in addition it is estimated that during the eighty years from 1821-1900, the United States received over four and one-half million immigrants from Germany. German emigration increased during the first part of the century to the decade ending with 1860, when nearly one million persons left for the United States. However, the great boom in migration came in the decade of the eighties, the peak being

---

[1] Computed by multiplying by 0.3861, the data given in square kilometers in Germany. Statistisches Amt, *Statistiches Jahrbuch für das deutsche Reich, 1923*. Berlin, 1923.

THE ANNALS OF GERMANY

December 1,—	Population [a]	Persons per Square Mile [b]	Per Cent Urban [c]
1840 [d]	32,787,150	157	... [e]
1852 [d]	35,931,691	172	... [e]
1861 [d]	38,139,410	183	... [e]
1871	41,058,792	197	36.1
1880	45,234,061	217	41.4
1890	49,428,470	237	47.0
1900	56,367,178	270	54.3
1910	64,925,993	311	60.0
1919 [f]	59,852,682	328	62.5

[a] Germany Statistisches Amt, *Statistisches Handbuch*. 2 vol. Berlin, 1907, and *Statistisches Jahrbuch, 1923*. Berlin, 1923.
[b] Computed by multiplying original data in persons per square kilometer by 2.59.
[c] Computed from data given in *Wirtschaft und Statistik*, October 28, 1924, vol. I, p. 493. Berlin. Includes all persons living in communities with more than 2,000 inhabitants.
[d] Official estimates.
[e] No data available.
[f] Census taken October 8, 1919.

reached in 1882, when 250,630 German immigrants reached the United States. Since that time, the movement has been on a much smaller scale.

The relative importance of different types of economic activity may be observed from the following table:

Industry	Percentage Distribution of Gainfully Employed [a]			
	June 5, 1882	June 14, 1895	June 12, 1907	Dec. 31 1920 [b]
Agriculture	47	40	37	36
Manufacturing, Mining and Construction	36	40	42	43
Commerce and Transportation	9	11	13	13
Other [c]	8	9	8	8
Total	100	100	100	100

[a] Computed from data in *Statistik des Deutschen Reich*. Berlin, vols. 102, 202, 211.
[b] Official estimate in *Wirtschaft und Statistik*, vol. 1, p. 46. However, in the report presented to the Committee of Experts of the Reparations Commission, *Germany's Economy, Currency and Finance*, the following statement is made:
"The present number of workers in agriculture and forestry may be regarded as identical with that of 1907. Mining and industry have, as may be assumed from other statistics increased by about 20%; trade and traffic have increased in at least the same proportion. . . . A decrease has taken place through the abolishment of compulsory military service (decrease of the army from about 800,000 to 100,000 men), as well as through professional persons taking up other means of earning a livelihood." p. 8.
[c] Includes persons engaged in personal service, professions, public service, and other occupations.

At the time of the founding of the Empire, Germany was chiefly an agricultural country and it was only in the latter part of the nineteenth century that Germany became an important factor in the world of industry and trade.

About five-eighths of the territory of Germany is cultivated and an additional quarter is covered with forests. The leading crops by acreage, are rye, oats, potatoes, and wheat. In the north and east, rye, oats and barley predominate, in the south and west, wheat is the principal crop. The harvest is in the autumn. In the annals, statements are given concerning production and prices for the wheat, rye, and potato crops.

The rapid development of Germany since 1870 has been due in a large measure to abundant mineral wealth. Before the War, its coal fields represented one-half the total resources of Europe, and it controlled one-fourth the iron supply. The rapidity with which the output of coal has increased is notable, and to some extent reflects the growth of industry.

Year	Coal Output [a] (millions of metric tons)
1871	29.4
1881	48.7
1891	73.7
1901	108.5
1911	160.7
1921 [b]	136.2

[a] *Statistisches Jahrbuch.*
[b] New area.

A further indication of the rapid growth of German manufacturing industry can be obtained from the census records of industrial establishments employing six or more workers: [a]

Date	Establishments	Employees
1882	94,482	2,653,252
1895	157,400	4,809,371
1907	216,107	7,652,591

[a] Germany Statistisches Amt, *Statistisches Jahrbuch, 1910* and *Statistisches Handbuch.* Berlin.

The iron and steel industries are perhaps the leaders in Germany's economic development, but textiles, glass, chemicals, instruments, and toys are all important. The loss of Alsace and Lorraine, Upper Silesia and the Saar Basin have resulted in the reduction by 26 per cent of Germany's coal and 74 per cent of her iron ore resources. Though this

THE ANNALS OF GERMANY

may retard further advance, it must be noted that, since the formation of the Empire, German industry has advanced with very rapid strides.

Railroad facilities are well developed in Germany. Ninety-three per cent of the railways are state roads. The statistical record of railway growth follows:

Year	Miles of Railway [a]
1851	3,761
1871	12,253
1881	21,026
1891	26,638
1901	31,715
1911	37,135
1921	34,583

[a] Computed by multiplying by 0.62137, data in kilometers published originally in *Statistisches Jahrbuch*.

There are also excellent inland water transportation facilities, and many state canals.

In recent years, German exports have obtained prominence in international trade. However, the trade balance of Germany is customarily unfavorable, imports exceeding exports, imports being chiefly indispensable foodstuffs or raw materials. The leading imports are cotton, wool, and wheat; leading exports are iron and steel, chemicals and dyes, and machinery.

Prior to the formation of the Empire, the banking and currency systems of the German States were very confused. There were seven different currency systems and many issuing banks. In 1876, the Reichsbank replaced the Bank of Prussia, under the superintendence and management of the government. It dominates the banking system of Germany, fixing the discount rate below which the private banks do not go.

The German Zollverein became active on January 1, 1834, and was gradually extended to include greater areas. This was the first step towards creating an economic unit out of the many German states. Steady development was checked somewhat in 1848 by the French revolution and its echoes in the German states. Depression continued to 1853, when the revival which was general throughout Europe, became apparent in Prussia. Prior to the formation of the Empire, the annals refer chiefly to Prussia or the states included in the Zollverein.

1853   Revival.

Improvement and expansion; speculative boom begins; big rise in commodity prices.

Money tightens slightly; new banks opened.

Crop failures.

Commercial treaty signed with Austria; neutrality declared in Russo-Turkish War.

1854   Prosperity.

Activity and expansion; many new companies formed, especially railroads; active speculation; further rapid rise in commodity prices.

Money eases, May.

Poor crops.

1855   Prosperity.

Activity continues; speculation increases despite promotion scandals; rise in commodity prices checked.

Money tightens, August.

Poor crops.

1856   Prosperity; bourse panic.

Great activity; marked increase in quantity of production; commodity speculation increases with collapse of security prices; feverish activity in promotion of new companies.

Money tight, especially autumn; security prices rise rapidly, first half-year, and collapse, September, with bourse panic.

Excellent crops.

1857   Prosperity; panic; recession.

Continued activity in industry; commodity prices reach peak, summer; severe check to foreign trade late in year.

Tight money market leads to financial panic, November, with many failures, especially in Hamburg; bourse depressed, with falling prices.

Good crops.

Prussia obtains Neufchâtel from Switzerland.

1858   Recession; depression.

Continued activity in industry, slackening but slowly; commodity prices fall sharply; foreign commerce deeply depressed.

Money tight.

Average crops.

William made Regent of Prussia, replacing Frederick William IV.

1859 Depression.

    General inactivity, most severe in mining and metal industries; widespread unemployment; fall in commodity prices halted.

    Money eases, second half-year; stock market panic at outbreak of war, May.

    Fair crops.

    Feeling against France strong, especially after her entrance into Austro-Italian war, May; neutrality maintained although troops mobilized along Rhine.

1860 Revival.

    Gradual improvement; moderate activity with little profit; large coal output; recovery in construction and manufacturing industries most evident; foreign trade dull.

    Money easy; bourse dull.

    Good crops.

    Protest against French annexation of Savoy.

1861 Mild prosperity.

    Slow general improvement, hampered somewhat by foreign conditions; marked increase in coal output.

    Money easy.

    Crops fail.

    Frederick William IV dies and William I becomes King of Prussia, January.

1862 Uneven prosperity.

    Continued improvement in iron and coal industries; manufactures active except for paralysis of cotton industry; construction boom; commodity prices rise.

    Money easy; revival in bourse activity with higher prices.

    Good crops.

    Prussia signs commercial treaty with France, excluding Austria, March; Bismarck becomes Chancellor, September.

1863 Moderate prosperity.

    Continued activity; cotton industry depressed but progress made in other industries; commodity prices rise.

    Money easy; political uncertainty ends bourse boom.

    Excellent crops.

    Revolution in Poland.

1864 Moderate prosperity.
Activity continues, little disturbed by war; cotton market crisis, autumn; further rise in commodity prices.
Money tightens; heavy demand for silver for export causes scarcity and minor panic, August; bourse dull.
Good crops, very low grain prices.
War with Austria as ally against Denmark; invasion of Schleswig-Holstein, January; victories and peace, August.

1865 Prosperity.
Greater activity and expansion of industry; cotton price falls.
Money tight after September; marked increase in activity on bourse.
Average crops.

1866 Prosperity; recession; depression.
Continued activity in basic industries completely interrupted during war months, and severely depressed after peace; small coal output; higher commodity prices.
Very tight money market gradually eases, last half-year; temporary bourse boom, autumn.
Fair crops.
War with Austria declared, June; rapid victories and armistice, July; peace, August; Germanic Confederation ended and North German Confederation formed.

1867 Depression; revival.
Dullness and inactivity, especially in coal and iron industries; marked improvement, last quarter; commodity prices higher; foreign trade dull.
Money very easy; bourse quiet.
Deficient grain crops and very high prices.
Distress in East Prussia due to crop shortage; first meeting of North German Confederation Parliament, February.

1868 Revival.
General improvement; active railroad construction; steady commodity prices.
Money tightens; extensive speculation in securities with rising prices.
Good crops, but cattle disease prevalent.

1869 Prosperity.
Activity in manufactures; construction industry booms; railroad construction notable; steady commodity prices.
Money fairly tight with great demand for capital; bourse active.
Crops below average.

1870 Prosperity; brief recession.
Continued prosperity until war; short period of stagnation; rapid revival, especially war industries; reduction in coal output; commodity prices decline sharply.
Money tightens, and then eases.
Fair crops.
War with France, July; invasion of France and victories.

1871 Prosperity.
Great activity and expansion of industry; widespread speculation and promotion of stock companies; commodity prices rise rapidly; building boom.
Money very easy; bourse exceedingly active; currency reformed, adopting gold mark standard, October.
Fair crops.
German Empire established, January; capture of Paris, January; armistice, February; treaty, May, wins Alsace-Lorraine; cholera, August.

1872 Prosperity.
Industry active and expanding, especially iron; commodity prices rise rapidly; continued excited promotion of new companies.
Money tightens; bourse very active.
Good crops.
Large indemnity payments received from France.

1873 Prosperity; panic; recession; depression.
Continued activity rapidly dwindles to stagnation, last half-year; commodity prices reach peak and collapse; many failures; foreign trade severely restricted after period of great expansion.
Money very tight; panic, April, May, and November; security prices decline extremely.
Poor crops.
Prussian Bank becomes the Reichsbank; May laws extend State control over church.

1874 Depression.

Gradual decline in industrial production; many failures; lower commodity prices; unemployment; serious railroad crisis, end of year, ascribed to small receipts; small coal output.

Money very tight; dull bourse with falling prices.

Average crops.

1875 Depression.

Stagnation in industry; widespread unemployment; commodity prices fall; larger coal output; further decline in foreign trade.

Money very tight; gold standard attained; temporary improvement on bourse, spring.

Poor crops.

Bank Act passed regulating banking system, March; Prussia adopts elaborate public works program to relieve unemployment.

1876 Depression.

Depth of depression; many failures; declining wages and prices; some revival in foreign trade.

Money eases; security prices reach minimum.

Very poor crops.

1877 Slow revival.

General industrial improvement; small coal output; commodity price fall checked; marked increase in export trade.

Money easy; bank failures and fiscal difficulties from gold speculation; stock exchange disturbed by Russian-Turkish War.

Good crops.

1878 Recession; depression.

Industry slackens to depression as commodity prices fall rapidly; reduced imports but larger exports.

Money easy.

Large wheat and rye crops, good potato yield; fair wheat price, low rye.

Severe legislative measures taken against Socialists.

THE ANNALS OF GERMANY

1879 Depression; revival.

Gradual improvement, especially iron and textile industries; commodity prices decline rapidly to low point, and then rise; increased imports, exports decline slightly.

Money very easy; security markets revive, stock prices having reached low point in summer; failure of Hamburg bankers threatens colonial industries.

Fair wheat, good rye, and poor potato crops; high prices, especially wheat.

Purchase of railways by state; tariff imposed on imports, July, ending long period of free trade.

1880 Recession; mild depression.

Industry hampered by dullness of markets; active coal mining; unemployment; rising commodity prices; big reduction in imports, some increase in exports.

Money easy.

Fair wheat, poor rye and potato crops; high prices, especially rye.

1881 Renewed revival.

General industrial improvement; active railroad construction; increased foreign trade.

Money tightens; bourse booms.

Poor wheat, good rye, and excellent potato crops; high prices, especially wheat.

Active anti-Semite agitation and riots.

1882 Prosperity; recession.

Short period of activity and increased production turns to dullness; commodity prices decline; exports reach peak, and imports advance.

Money tight; quiet bourse booms in spring, dull last half-year.

Good wheat, excellent rye, and very poor potato crops; much lower prices, except that of potatoes.

1883 Mild depression.

Continued slackening of industrial activity; falling prices; increase in foreign trade checked.

Money eases; declining stock prices.

Fair wheat and rye crops, good potato; good prices, except rye.

Social insurance program adopted.

1884 Depression.

Dullness and inactivity; declining commodity prices; growing dullness in foreign trade.

Money easy; declining stock prices.

Fair harvests; low prices.

South-West Africa and other territories acquired.

1885 Depression.
Depth of depression; stagnation severe in coal and iron industries; decline in commodity prices continues; reduction in foreign trade.
Money easy.
Good crops, especially potatoes; low prices.
Policy of ship subsidies adopted.

1886 Depression; revival.
Continued inactivity, lessening in last quarter; commodity prices reach bottom and rise; smaller coal output; imports decline and exports increase.
Money very easy; revival in stock prices.
Good wheat and potato crops, excellent rye; low prices.
Agricultural and labor distress.

1887 Revival.
Steady improvement, especially in metal and mining industries; extensive construction; commodity prices rise; active foreign trade.
Money very easy; increasing speculation in stocks.
Excellent harvests of wheat and rye, good potato crop; low wheat, very low rye, and fair potato prices.
Kiel Canal commenced.

1888 Moderate prosperity.
General activity in industry; rising commodity prices; active promotion of kartels and joint stock companies; growing foreign trade.
Money very easy; intense speculation with temporary relapse, autumn.
Fair wheat and rye, poor potato crop; good prices.
Death of William I, March, and Frederick, June, brings William II to throne.

1889 Prosperity.
Widespread activity and expansion; further rise in commodity prices; feverish speculation; imports boom while exports decline.
Money tighter, last half-year; bourse booms.
Poor wheat and rye, good potato crops; high wheat and rye, low potato prices.

1890 Recession.
Gradual decline in industry accelerated, autumn; coal and iron prices fall; some increase in foreign trade.
Money very tight; security market depressed.
Excellent wheat, good rye, fair potato crops; prices high.
Fall of Bismarck, March; Heligoland acquired from Great Britain July.

THE ANNALS OF GERMANY

1891 Depression.

Dullness and inactivity; year of liquidation, falling profits, and lack of confidence; commodity prices higher, exports decline, imports increase.

Money eases late in year; stock prices decline; Berlin bank panic and failures, November.

Crop failures and very high prices.

Distress; exportation of grain prohibited, August; severe uprising in East Africa.

1892 Depression.

Increased inactivity; severe unemployment; reduction in coal output; commodity prices decline; reduction of foreign trade.

Money very easy; dull bourse with declining values.

Large wheat and rye crops, good potato yield; lower prices, especially wheat.

Distress; riots in Berlin, February; uprisings in East Africa suppressed; policy of lower tariffs adopted; outbreak of cholera, Hamburg; legislation facilitates construction of local railways.

1893 Depression.

Continued pessimism and dullness; further decline in commodity prices; decrease in foreign trade.

Money tightens, summer; bourse revives, first quarter, and then returns to dullness.

Very large crops, low prices.

Tariff war with Russia, last half-year.

1894 Depression; revival.

Inactivity gives way to upward movement, autumn; revival of speculation; commodity price decline continues; revival in imports, exports decrease.

Money very easy; bourse revives.

Large wheat and rye, good potato crops; very low wheat and rye, good potato prices.

Russian treaty completed.

1895 Revival.

Steady improvement; rapid expansion in electrical industries; commodity prices reach bottom, February; marked revival in exports.

Easy money tightens late in year; great activity on bourse; gold mining stock boom; stock prices collapse, November.

Poor wheat and rye, large potato crops; improved wheat price, very low rye and potato prices.

Kiel Canal opened, June.

1896 Moderate prosperity.

General prosperity and expansion; commodity prices rise, last half-year; period of marked increase in foreign trade begins.

Easy money tightens late in year; bourse weak and unsteady.

Good wheat and rye, poor potato crops; fair prices.

1897 Prosperity.

Steady progress, especially coal, iron and machine industries; commodity price rise halts, first half-year, and then resumes; marked increase in foreign trade.

Money eases somewhat; slow improvement in security market.

Poor crops, especially rye; good prices, except rye.

Occupation of Kiaochow.

1898 Prosperity.

Brilliant year, with great activity and rapid expansion; shortage of labor and raw materials; extensive formation of new companies; price rise halts, summer; further increase in foreign trade.

Money tightens, especially late in year; bourse dull with declining values, last half-year.

Good harvest, especially rye; fair prices, rye good.

1899 Prosperity.

Unprecedented prosperity; severe raw material shortage; construction restricted; some unemployment late in year; many new companies; rapid price rise; marked increase in foreign trade.

Money very tight late in year; revival of speculation on bourse.

Excellent wheat and potato, good rye crops; low wheat, fair rye, good potato prices.

1900 Prosperity; recession; depression.

Continued activity, first quarter; gradual decline to depression late in year; severe coal famine, spring; construction severely depressed; commodity prices reach peak, autumn, and then decline; very large foreign trade.

Gradual reduction of monetary stringency; great collapse in stock prices after April; many bank failures and minor panic, December.

Good crops, especially wheat; low wheat, fair rye, good potato prices.

Adoption of gold standard; active participation in Peking expedition against Boxers.

1901 Depression.

Dullness and inactivity; slow decline in commodity prices; many failures; reduction in foreign trade.

Tight money eases; stock market depressed with declining prices; financial difficulties and bank failures, summer.

Wheat and rye crop failures, very large potato yield; fair wheat, good rye, and low potato prices.

1902 Depression.

Continued inactivity; further increase in unemployment, first eight months, followed by slight improvement; home market restricted but some revival in foreign trade.

Money very easy; slight revival of stock prices, first quarter, followed by slow decline.

Good crops, especially wheat; low wheat, fair rye, good potato prices.

Higher tariff passed, December.

1903 Revival.

Steady improvement with active production; unemployment diminished; commodity prices low; marked increase in foreign trade.

Money rates firm; rising stock prices.

Poor wheat, excellent rye, and good potato crops; fair wheat, low rye, and high potato prices.

Revolt of Hereros in South-West Africa begins, lasting for several years.

1904 Mild prosperity; recession; depression.

Further improvement, first half-year, yields to stagnation, autumn; unemployment; commodity prices reach bottom and begin to rise; increase in imports, reduction in exports.

Money tightens late in year; stock prices rise after panic, February, with several important failures.

Good wheat, very good rye, and potato failure; wheat price good, rye fair, and potato very high.

1905 Revival; prosperity.

Rapid revival after Ruhr coal strike, first quarter; full employment; notable activity; speculation; rise in commodity prices; active foreign trade.

Money eases, and tightens severely late in year; great bourse activity with rapidly rising prices.

Poor wheat and rye crops, excellent potato yield; high wheat and rye, low potato prices.

Strained relations with France, last nine months.

1906 Prosperity.

Great activity, especially in coal and iron industries; full employment and rising wages; continued price rise; extensive formation of new companies; further marked increase of foreign trade.

Money very tight; moderate bourse activity with some price decline.

Excellent wheat, poor rye and potato crops; good prices.

Dispute with France over Morocco settled.

1907 Prosperity; recession; depression.

Continued activity to summer, when decline sets in; marked relapse in construction; increased unemployment and many failures, last quarter; commodity prices boom to third quarter; great activity in foreign trade.

Monetary stringency, especially late in year; declining stock prices.

Very poor wheat, fair rye, and good potato yields; high prices.

Food riots in several large cities.

1908 Depression.

Stagnation in industry and trade deepens throughout year; many failures; increasing unemployment; mining industry maintains activity until autumn and then declines; steady price decline; many new security issues; reduction in foreign trade, especially exports.

Money eases slowly; bourse inactive; security prices advance, last half-year.

Good crops; high wheat and potato prices, average rye.

1909 Depression; revival.

Continued stagnation gives way to revival, autumn; speculation; price decline halted, summer; foreign trade revives.

Monetary stringency; bourse boom sets in, September.

Good crops; good prices, high wheat.

1910 Revival; prosperity.

Gradual improvement in industry except cement; diminishing unemployment; commodity prices rise; labor troubles; marked increase in foreign trade.

Money eases, but tightens later; quiet bourse revives, summer.

Fair crops, good wheat; high wheat, poor rye, and fair potato prices.

1911 Prosperity.

Activity and expansion; full employment and large volume of production; commodity prices rise; further advance in foreign trade.

Money easier, advancing sharply in fall; active speculation, especially first half-year; stock prices decline, autumn.

Excellent wheat, good rye, and very poor potato crops; high prices, especially potato.

Morocco difficulties threaten war with France, autumn, but are settled by treaty, November.

1912 Prosperity.

Great activity and marked expansion of industry and trade; coal, metal and manufacturing industries flourishing; construction depressed; labor difficulties; increased number of failures; rapid rise in commodity prices to peak, summer; foreign trade expands.

Money fairly tight, becoming stringent, November; vigorous rise in security prices to bourse panic, October.

Excellent crops; good prices, wheat high.

1913 Prosperity; recession.

Continued activity and progress to turning point, summer; coal and iron industries slacken advance; textile and construction industries severely depressed; increased unemployment; declining commodity prices; foreign trade increases, chiefly in exports.

Money very tight; diminished bourse activity with declining prices, last half-year.

Excellent crops; good wheat, fair rye, and very low potato prices.

Political disturbances.

1914 Mild depression; revival.

Continued dullness and increased unemployment but with signs of improvement to War; severe industrial disturbance gives way to great activity, October; enormous increase in unemployment; rapid rise of commodity prices; foreign trade halted.

Money easy except for temporary rise in rates, August; stocks decline and bourses are closed, last five months; marked increase in currency circulation, third quarter.

Fair crops, good potato yield; high prices.

War declared on Russia, France, and Great Britain, August; rapid advance of German armies toward Paris checked at Marne, September.

1915   War activity.
Great activity and readjustment to war demands; diminishing unemployment; commodity prices rise rapidly.

Money easy; decline in foreign exchange; gradual expansion of circulation.

Fair crops, excellent potato yield; prices controlled by government.

Increased submarine warfare; blockade pronounced, February; trench warfare on Western front; on Eastern front, Russians capture Przemysl, March, but lose it June, with further defeats; Warsaw captured, August; consumption regulated by government.

1916   War activity.
Continued feverish activity with increasing government control; further reduction in unemployment; raw material and labor scarcity; price rise halted after temporary boom, summer.

Government controls money market; further decline in exchange, with temporary revival, summer; slow increase in circulation.

Small crops, potato failure.

German advance at Verdun, spring, driven back later in year; fleet defeated by British at Jutland, June.

1917   War activity.
Further extension of government control; increasing scarcity of raw materials; commodity price rise resumed at faster rate, summer.

Money easy; rapid fall in exchange, first half-year, with recovery last quarter; more rapid expansion of currency.

Very small crops, good potato yield.

Retreat to Hindenburg line, spring, followed by trench warfare; victories on Eastern front; Riga occupied, autumn; extension of submarine warfare; United States enters war, April; Russian armistice, November.

1918   War activity; disorganization, November.
Continued organization of industry for war purposes; labor troubles and raw material shortage; commodity prices steady except for summer boom; disorganization with Armistice; eight hour maximum working day established, November.

Rapid fall in exchange, second half-year; currency expansion, especially last half-year.

Very small crops.

Great offensive, March, fails to gain objectives; severe defeats begin, August; naval mutiny, October, becomes revolution, November; Kaiser abdicates; Armistice signed; Workers' and Soldiers' Councils formed; widespread disorder and unrest.

THE ANNALS OF GERMANY

1919 Depression.

Little activity, due to lack of raw materials, depreciation of machinery, and shortage of coal; widespread unemployment; transportation disorganized; labor troubles; rapid rise of commodity prices.

Money market freed from control at beginning of year; money easy; steady and rapid fall in exchange; gradual expansion of currency.

Very small crops; serious food shortage.

Allied blockade of imports lifted, June; repeated disturbances and bloodshed; Liebknecht killed, January; Ebert elected President, February; Treaty signed, June; Weimar Constitution adopted, July.

1920 Depression.

Continued disorganization and inactivity; unemployment; great shortage of raw materials; commodity prices rise, first quarter, and then decline.

Money easy; stock exchange boom; exchange decline checked with some recovery in summer; active foreign speculation in mark; gradual expansion of currency.

Small wheat, record small rye, and improved potato crops.

Continued unrest and riots; Kapp revolution suppressed, March; federal income tax law enacted, March.

1921 Revival, spring.

Some improvement; rapid diminution of unemployment; transportation and labor difficulties; commodity prices decline to May, but rapid rise sets in, August; revival of construction, summer.

Exchange fairly stable to July, when rapid decline sets in; speculative boom in exchange late in year; inactive stock market booms, autumn; more rapid expansion of currency.

Improved wheat and rye crops, potato smaller.

Continual unrest; Rhine sanction, reparations claims, and loss of Upper Silesia severe blows; revolt in Poland and numerous communist uprisings.

1922 Revival checked, summer; disorganization.

Continued improvement of industry to summer, when rapid fall of mark makes ordinary business impossible; little unemployment until late in year; railroad strike, February; continual commodity price rise.

Money rates very high; extensive speculation in stocks and foreign exchange; foreign exchange depreciates rapidly, last half-year; terrific increase in circulation, especially last half-year.

Wheat failure, poor rye, and good potato crops.

Rathenau assassinated, June; reparations problem still unsettled

1923   Depression.

Disorganization becomes more severe, last half-year; stagnation; unemployment extreme; commodity prices rise to high point, November; paralysis, last two months; maximum eight hour work day breaks down, December; smaller foreign trade.

Currency stable to April, and then rapid decline in exchange; stabilized on gold basis, November; continuous rise in security prices with severe collapse, end of year; money very tight; even greater currency expansion.

Improved crops.

Ruhr occupation by French, January; passive resistance given up, September; Reparations Commission determines to appoint Committee of Experts, November.

1924   Revival; temporary check, summer.

Early improvement checked, late spring; paralysis and many failures, summer; further revival sets in, autumn; marked decrease in unemployment; decided improvement in mining and manufacturing; commodity prices relatively stable; many failures; imports increase more than exports.

Sharp restriction of credit, spring; money gradually eases, last quarter; exchange stabilized; large foreign loans floated and Reichsbank divorced from Government, October; Reichsmark introduced, October; stock prices collapse, first half-year, followed by partial recovery; slackening currency expansion.

Poor wheat, fair rye and potato crops.

Dawes plan published, April, adopted, August, and put into operation, November; economic barriers in the Ruhr removed, October.

1925   Halting revival; recession.

Continued improvement, except iron and steel industry, to relapse, last quarter; steady reduction of unemployment, first half-year, but enormous increase, last quarter; railroad strike, March; many failures after August; commodity prices reach peak, January, decline to April, rise to July, and then decline rapidly; increased foreign trade; very large unfavorable balance early in year, becomes favorable as imports shrink, December.

Money very tight; some increase in circulation; drastic decline in security prices from February peak.

Much larger harvest, especially rye.

Von Hindenburg elected President, April, after March election yields no majority; new and higher tariff, September; Ruhr evacuation completed, October; Locarno treaties ratified, November.

CHAPTER V.

THE ANNALS OF AUSTRIA.

Prior to 1918, the Empire of Austria-Hungary occupied a large part of central Europe. Austria and Hungary maintained much of their individuality, acting in concert on matters of foreign affairs, finance and defense, and being ruled by one monarch. Bosnia and Herzegovina were annexed in 1908. Austria proper, about which the pre-war annals are chiefly written, included 44 per cent of the area and 55 per cent of the population of the Empire.

On November 12, 1918, the Republic of Austria was proclaimed. The boundaries of the new republic were fixed by the Treaty of St. Germain, and the new Austria represents 28 per cent of the area of pre-war Austria-Hungary and includes 23 per cent of the pre-war population. Austria was never a geographical unit. The area now remaining is chiefly part of the Alps and Danube valley. In addition pre-war Austria included Galicia, part of the Russian plain, Bohemia, extending into Germany, and Dalmatia, belonging geographically with the Balkan peninsula. Pre-war Austria had very little coast, post-war Austria has none. There are several large rivers, most important of which is the Danube.

The area of pre-war Austria, not including Hungary, was 115,832 square miles.[1] This area was reduced by post-war treaties to 32,368 square miles,[2] the present area of Austria. The population records, giving the total for the post-war as well as the pre-war area for 1910, are shown in the following page.

In 1880, 70 per cent of the population were rural, i.e., lived in places with less than 2,000 inhabitants. By 1910, the rural population was reduced to 39.8 per cent. In 1920, 51 per cent of the population of the Austrian Republic was rural. Emigration became an im-

---

[1] Computed by multiplying by 0.003861, data in hectares given in Austria Statistische Zentralkommission, *Österreichisches statistisches Handbuch, 1916-17*. Vienna, 1918.
[2] Computed by multiplying by 0.3861, data in square kilometers given in Austria Bundesamt für Statistik, *Statistisches Jahrbuch für die Republic Österreich*. Vienna, 1924.

December 31,—	Population [a]	Persons per Square Mile [b]
1850	17,534,950	150
1869	20,217,531	174
1880	21,981,821	189
1890	23,707,906	205
1900	25,921,671	223
1910 pre-war	28,324,940	243
post-war	6,646,537	205
1921 [c]	6,426,294	199
1923 [d]	6,535,759	202

[a] Pre-war data, *Handbuch* above; post-war data, *Jahrbuch* above.
[b] Computed by multiplying by 2.59, data given originally in persons per square kilometer.
[c] Census of January 31, 1920.
[d] Census of March 7, 1923.

portant factor in Austrian population records at the beginning of the twentieth century, when large numbers departed for America. This movement was checked by the war and subsequent restriction by the United States Government.

Although data for the occupational distribution of the population of the Austrian Republic are not available, the records of pre-war Austria show definitely the trends in economic activity.

Industry	Per Cent of Total Gainfully Employed [a]			
	1867	1890	1900	1910
Agriculture	64	62	58	53
Manufacturing, Mining and Construction	20	20	21	23
Trade and Transportation	4	8	9	10
Other [b]	12	10	12	14
Total	100	100	100	100

[a] Data for 1867 based on Austria Statistischen Central-Commission, *Statistisches Handbüchlein, 1871.* Vienna, 1873. Other data from *Handbuch,* see above.
[b] Includes persons engaged in military and public service, professions, persons with independent incomes, and others.

The dominating importance of agriculture is made evident by the above data for occupations. Although the Austrian Empire included much excellent farm land, it never became self-supporting. In general, Hungary was agricultural and Austria industrial in interest. The most important crops are rye, oats, wheat, and barley. Rye and wheat have gradually declined in acreage, and barley and oats have advanced. The harvests come in the autumn.

The mineral resources of the Austrian Empire were rich and

varied. Coal was the chief product, but many other minerals were produced in considerable amounts. The reconstruction of central Europe took from Austria much of this as yet little-developed wealth. Less than one per cent of her former coal resources remain, and many other former products lie wholly outside the new boundaries.

Manufacturing industry in Austria developed slowly. According to Drage, until 1850, it was stifled by the guild system and an antiquated industrial code. The industrial expansion was just getting under way when the crash of 1873 brought this development to a complete halt. Even by 1910, manufacturing employed less than one-half as many workers as agriculture. Development has been most notable in the textile, metallurgical, glass, and wood-products industries. About Vienna, the production of art products and luxuries has been highly developed. The establishment of new boundaries has occasioned a reorganization of industrial activity.

Prior to 1860, imports customarily exceeded exports, but since that time, the balance has been generally favorable. Chief imports at present are coal, cotton goods, and grain; exports are iron and steel, cotton goods, and non-ferrous metals.

The development of railroads was slow to begin, but progressed rapidly thereafter.

Year	Railway Mileage [a]
1850	843
1860	1,819
1870	3,798
1880	7,102
1890	9,490
1900	11,948
1910	15,299
1920 [b]	3,939

[a] Austria Statistischen Zentralkommission, *Österreichisches Statistisches Handbuch, 1911*. Vienna, 1912, p. 212. Data in kilometers converted to miles by multiplying by 0.62137. Data for 1920 from *Jahrbuch*, see above.
[b] New boundaries.

Over two-thirds of the railways are government owned. There is also some development of canals, and inland waterways.

The Austro-Hungarian Bank has had exclusive right to issue banknotes. It was liquidated in 1923, the National Bank of Austria, a private institution, replacing it. Specie payments were suspended in 1848, and it was not until 1892 that an attempt was seriously made to reëstablish the currency on a sound basis.

The history of Austria has been dominated by political and racial antagonisms. In 1848, the French Revolution upset the equilibrium, and the revolution in Austria caused the abdication of the Emperor and the granting of a constitution by his nephew, Francis Joseph. In 1855, in a war against Italy supported by France, the Austrians were severely defeated. A further short period of peace, which included much political disagreement and, in 1862, a severe flood of the Danube, was broken in 1864 by a war with Prussia against Denmark. In 1866, Prussia overwhelmed Austria in a brief campaign, and the annals begin with Austria slowly recovering from the confusion which immediately followed the war.

1867   Revival.

Recovery after stagnation resulting from defeat by Prussia in previous year; commodity prices very high; rapid improvement in foreign trade.

Money eases.

Excellent crops.

Dual monarchy established, December.

1868   Moderate prosperity.

Further improvement in industry and trade; railroad and joint stock company promotion; commodity prices decline; large increase in foreign trade.

Money easy; rising stock prices; speculation excesses in Budapest.

Poor crops.

1869   Prosperity; panic; recession.

Continued activity slackens late in year; promotion active; failures in autumn; foreign trade restricted.

Money tightens and security prices boom to panic, September; banking failures.

Very poor crops.

1870   Slow recession.

Industrial activity gradually reduced; small rise in commodity prices; exports decline and imports increase, causing unfavorable balance.

Money tight; some revival of stock speculation, autumn.

Fair crops.

Foreign difficulties and political unrest.

1871 Mild depression.
Further slackening of industry to dullness, except railroad construction; commodity prices rise; foreign trade booms, increased unfavorable balance.
Money tight; speculation active.
Fair crops.

1872 Revival; prosperity.
Rapid improvement in industry; enormous stock flotations; rapid extension of railroads; commodity prices high; exports decline and imports increase.
Money eases, autumn, and bourse booms; slight bourse panic, December, and money tightens severely.
Average crops.

1873 Prosperity; panic; recession.
Continued activity slackens, summer; commodity price decline sets in; many failures; smaller imports and larger exports.
Money very tight; bourse panic, suspension of Bank Act, and moratorium, May; continued distress to financial panic, October; collapse in security prices.
Poor wheat and large rye crop.
Epidemic of cholera in Hungary; National Representative Assembly replaces Reichsrath, March.

1874 Deep depression.
Industrial stagnation; widespread unemployment, railroad construction halted; rapid fall of commodity prices; imports decline and exports increase slightly.
Money eases.
Excellent wheat and rye crops, poor oats.
Distress and famine.

1875 Depression.
Continued inactivity; signs of improvement noted in several industries; further marked fall in commodity prices; increased exports and smaller imports create favorable balance of trade.
Money eases gradually.
Very small crops, especially wheat and oats.

1876 Depression.
Increased stagnation; some recovery of commodity prices, especially foodstuffs; expansion of exports with decreasing imports.
Money easy.
Poor wheat and rye, good oats crop.

1877 Depression.
Depth of depression; production at minimum; further increase in foreign trade.
Money easy.
Good crops, especially rye.
Russian-Turkish War results in giving Austria mandate over certain Balkan states; higher tariff.

1878 Depression.
Some increase in volume of production but marked decline in commodity prices; reduction in foreign trade.
Money easy.
Excellent crops.
Occupation of Bosnia, July; storming of Sarajevo, August; amnesty, November.

1879 Depression.
Continued dullness; fall in commodity prices halted; slight recovery in foreign trade.
Money very easy; resumption of activity in security markets with rising prices, especially of bonds; free coinage of silver suspended, and paper standard adopted.
Very small crops, especially rye.
Alliance with Germany formed.

1880 Revival.
Distinct improvement in industry; commodity prices reach low point and then rise; marked increase in imports, smaller exports.
Money very easy; security prices rise.
Fair wheat and oats, poor rye crops.

1881 Mild prosperity.
Increasing activity in industry; commodity prices rise; marked improvement in foreign trade.
Money very easy.
Fair wheat, good rye and oats crops.
Disturbances in Herzogovina require military force to restore order.

1882 Moderate prosperity; bourse panic.
General activity in industry; revival of railroad construction; rise in commodity prices ceases; big increase in exports.
Money tightens; bourse panic, January; further tightening of money market, autumn.
Excellent wheat, good rye and oats crops.
Insurrection finally quelled, October.

1883 Prosperity.
Continued activity and quiet expansion of industry; foreign trade declines.
Money eases somewhat late in year.
Poor wheat and rye, good oats crops.
Legislation establishing factory inspection introduces period of rapid increase of industrial regulation.

1884 Recession.
Gradual slackening of industrial activity; further decline of commodity prices sets in; marked reduction in foreign trade.
Money easy; large agricultural bank in Bohemia fails.
Good wheat and rye, record oats crops.

1885 Mild depression.
Continued slackening of activity to dullness; commodity prices decline rapidly; further reduction in foreign trade.
Money very easy.
Excellent wheat, good rye, and fair oats crops.
Political apprehension, after intervention in Bulgarian-Servian War.

1886 Depression; revival.
Dullness gives way to revival, summer; commodity price decline checked; decline of imports continues but exports recover.
Money easy.
Fair wheat, poor rye, and record oats crops.
War with Russia threatened.

1887 Revival.
Irregular improvement; railroad construction more active; increased imports and smaller exports.
Money tightens gradually.
Record wheat and rye crops, fair oats yield.

1888 Prosperity.
Rapidly increasing activity in industry; speculation appears; reduced imports but greatly increased exports.
Money tightens, stringency late in year.
Excellent wheat and rye, fair oats yield.

1889 Prosperity.
Industry active; foreign trade booms.
Money eases; increased activity on bourse late in year.
Crops very small, especially wheat and oats.

BUSINESS ANNALS

1890   Uneven prosperity.
        Some lines of industry very prosperous, others inactive; severe strikes in textile and metal industries; increase in foreign trade.
        Money tightens late in year.
        Good rye and wheat, fair oats crops.

1891   Prosperity.
        Increased activity and profits; slight rise in commodity prices; exports expand more rapidly than imports.
        Money tight, but easing.
        Very poor rye and wheat crops, good oats; prices very high.

1892   Recession.
        Industry and trade slackening; profits less; marked decline in commodity prices; sharp restriction of exports.
        Money easy; scheme for establishing gold standard adopted, August; stock market boom, summer.
        Fair rye, good oats and wheat crops; prices lower.
        Serious internal political crisis; cholera.

1893   Revival.
        Marked improvement in industrial activity; slight rise in commodity prices; foreign trade booms.
        Money gradually tightens; increasing premium for gold; bourse revives, March.
        Excellent rye, very poor oats, fair wheat crops; prices fall due to extensive American sales.

1894   Recession; mild depression.
        Inactivity and dullness appear; further decline in commodity prices; imports increase but exports decline.
        Money eases; active speculation with rapidly rising stock prices.
        Very good crops, record wheat yield; low prices.

1895   Mild depression.
        Industrial and commercial conditions improve slowly; higher food, lower industrial commodity prices; many failures; slight increase in imports, sharp decline in exports.
        Easy money tightens late in year; wild speculation in gold mining shares begins, February; bourse panics, November and December.
        Poor rye, record oats, and fair wheat crops; prices very low.
        Civil unrest.

1896 Mild depression.

Some improvement in industrial activity; commodity prices reach bottom; foreign trade sluggish, imports declining and exports increasing.

Money eases; bourse depressed.

Severe agricultural depression with low prices; good wheat and rye, poor oats yields.

Disorder among agricultural classes.

1897 Mild depression.

Dullness and inactivity; commodity prices very low; increase in imports, smaller exports.

Money easy.

Severe distress with crop failures.

Nationalist difficulties between Czech and German groups result from Badeni Language Ordinances.

1898 Mild depression; revival.

Continued dullness yields to revival, last half-year; commodity prices rise; foreign trade booms, unfavorable balance.

Money fairly tight.

Good crops.

Empress assassinated, September.

1899 Mild prosperity.

Good progress in trade and industry, especially first half-year; improvement marked in mining and metal industries; commodity price rise continues; enormous increase in exports returns foreign trade to favorable balance.

Money tight late in year; bourse active.

Good rye, record oats and wheat crops.

1900 Recession; depression.

Decline to depression, especially iron and textile industries; severe coal strike sends price of coal very high, February; commodity prices reach peak; further expansion of both imports and exports.

Money easy somewhat; bourse becomes dull; Austro-Hungarian Bank begins gold redemption.

Poor crops.

Continued political difficulties between nationalities.

BUSINESS ANNALS

1901 Depression.

Further decline of industry, particularly mining and construction; unemployment; commodity prices decline; restriction in foreign trade.

Money very easy; bourse dead, with declining prices.

Poor oats, fair wheat and rye crops.

Continued dissension; elaborate public works program adopted, June.

1902 Depression.

Increased dullness and inactivity; few failures; further decline in commodity prices; some revival in foreign trade.

Money very easy; bourse inactive.

Good crops, especially wheat.

1903 Depression; revival.

Inactivity and widespread unemployment early in year; improvement begins, last quarter; depression most severe in iron and machine industries; commodity prices rise slightly; foreign trade booms.

Money easy; dull stock market revives, last quarter.

Fair crops, good oats.

Protective tariff raises rates; period of political unrest begins; record emigration; political crisis between Austrians and Hungarians threatens dual system.

1904 Revival.

Continued improvement; textile industries hampered by important failures; further rise in commodity prices; imports increase but exports decline.

Easy money grows firmer; bourse more active.

Large rye and wheat, very poor oats yields.

Reduction in emigration; political unrest.

1905 Mild prosperity.

Continued improvement and expansion hampered by railway dispute in which workers use passive resistance; further rise in commodity prices; expansion in foreign trade.

Money rates gradually tighten; some slackening on bourse.

Large rye and wheat, poor oats yields.

Revival of emigration; political deadlock between Austria and Hungary.

THE ANNALS OF AUSTRIA

1906 Prosperity.

Great activity; prosperity particularly in mining and transportation; building trades strike, Vienna; more rapid advance of commodity prices; foreign trade very active.

Money tight; bourse sluggish.

Excellent crops.

Political difficulties finally adjusted, April; universal suffrage established; new tariff with very high rates.

1907 Prosperity.

Continued activity; expansion somewhat hindered by state of money market; labor shortage; plants at capacity; commodity prices reach peak; increased imports and decline in exports create unfavorable balance of trade.

Money very tight; strong decline in stock prices late in year.

Poor rye and wheat, excellent oats crops.

Socialists win election, May; very large emigration.

1908 Recession; depression.

Dullness spreads through industry and commerce; commodity prices decline; some restriction of foreign trade.

Tight money eases slowly; bourse quiet.

Record rye and wheat crops, very poor oats yield.

Bosnia and Herzogovina annexed, October; marked reduction of emigration.

1909 Depression.

Little activity, basic industries most depressed; some increase in commodity prices; foreign trade revives.

Money easier; fiscal difficulties; some improvement in stock market late in year.

Excellent rye and oats, good wheat crops.

Acute diplomatic crisis with Servia, February; big increase in emigration.

1910 Depression.

Continued dullness in industrial activity; revival in construction; marked increase in foreign trade.

Easy money tightens, November; speculative boom with rising prices of industrial stocks.

Fair rye and wheat, very poor oats yields.

1911   Revival.

Uneven improvement, marked in construction, iron and steel, and textile industries; slight decline in exports, imports increase rapidly.

Money eases, and then becomes very tight; active bourse speculation.

Poor rye, fair oats and wheat crops; food prices very high.

Reduction in emigration; riots and martial law, September.

1912   Prosperity; recession; depression.

Increasing activity and progress; Balkan War, autumn, plunges industry into deep depression; numerous failures; foreign trade very active.

Severe monetary strain; active speculation, especially first half-year; bourse severely depressed, last quarter; Balkan moratoria cause difficulties.

Excellent crops.

Revival of emigration; uncertainty due to Balkan War, October.

1913   Depression; panic.

Widespread inactivity; much unemployment; foreign trade declines sharply.

Money tight; financial panic necessitates moratorium; bourse dull.

Fair rye and wheat, excellent oats crops.

Internal and external political troubles; record emigration; army mobilized for several months fearing Russian aggression.

1914   Depression.

Dullness gives way to stagnation with war; widespread unemployment; foreign trade halted.

Money tight; bourse closed after panic, July; moratorium; foreign exchange declines severely, last quarter.

Very small crops.

War, July, with immediate mobilization.

1915   War activity.

Gradual reorganization of industry for war purposes; full employment; foreign trade completely restricted.

Money eases; currency expansion begins; foreign exchange declines, with temporary recovery in autumn.

Further decrease in crops.

After spring, campaign against Russians very successful; Italy declares war, May; Serbian campaign ends with complete victory, November.

1916 War activity.
Further extension of government control of industry; raw material scarcity; prices rise rapidly.

Money remains easy; reopened bourse shows moderate activity; wild fluctuations in exchange, with general tendency, after February, downward; bank control of foreign exchange, February, gives way to government control, December.

Smaller crops, except oats.

Further victories over Russians; victories in Italy, spring, and reverses, autumn; death of Emperor Franz Joseph, November, brings Charles I to throne.

1917 War activity.
Government dominates all industrial activity, regulating practically all industries; raw materials very scarce; prices rise rapidly.

Steady decline of foreign exchange; some recovery, December.

Further reduction in crops.

Distress; Russians driven back and Riga occupied, autumn; Italians severely defeated, October.

1918 War activity; chaos.
Continued domination of industry by government; raw material scarcity relieved somewhat by separate peace; after October, industry completely disorganized; prices rise rapidly.

Recovery of exchange to February, followed by sharp decline, which becomes severe late in year; government control more strict, June.

Slight improvement in rye and oats crops, poorer wheat.

Reduction of daily rations causes hunger riots, January; separate peace signed with Russia and Roumania; internal disintegration, autumn; Czech revolution, October; Emperor Charles forced to abdicate and Republic proclaimed, November; Armistice, November.

1919 Depression.
Industry paralyzed by political and economic separation of empire into separate states; coal shortage; raw material scarcity; unemployment reaches maximum, May; labor troubles; some improvement in production of industries for export, last half-year.

Rapid fall in exchange; stock exchange boom.

Crops smallest.

Demobilization; Relief Missions preserve Vienna from starvation, February; Treaty of St. Germain, September; continual internal difficulties; trade restrictions imposed by neighboring states.

1920   Slow revival.

Improvement in manufacturing, especially industries producing for export; unemployment diminishes, except for temporary relapse in summer; coal shortage; commodity prices boom.

Money tight; increasing speculation in securities and foreign exchange; exchange falls to February, improves to August, and then falls again when restrictions are removed, October.

Small but larger crops, especially wheat and oats.

Intense feeling between new countries; universal works councils established; Unemployment Insurance Law passed, May.

1921   Revival.

Revival continued to December; full employment and industrial activity; great speculation; commodity prices soar late in year; exports boom, last half-year.

Continued currency depreciation; foreign exchange recovers from low point, January, but falls rapidly, summer to December; bourse very active.

Small crops; food shortage.

Gradual removal of price regulation; riots, December, Vienna; food subsidies abolished and purchase of foreign money forbidden, December.

1922   Uneven recession; depression.

Dullness, first quarter; feverish activity, with full employment and active foreign trade, summer; depression last four months with industry at a standstill; commodity prices rise rapidly, May to September; severe failures, end of year; foreign trade declines, last half-year.

Money very tight; exchange decline halted, February to May, and then resumed at rapid rate; continual currency inflation; exchange stabilized, September; bourse boom, August, and crisis, December.

Small but larger crops.

American Relief Administration active, spring; government closes foreign exchange market, July; League of Nations plan adopted, October.

1923   Depression.

Severe depression, first six months, lightening somewhat thereafter; unemployment, worst in March, diminishes slightly; manufacturing industries which depend on export trade severely depressed; commodity prices reach peak, May; many new issues of securities; active imports, large unfavorable balance.

Money very tight; National Bank of Austria opened, January; bourse boom and active speculation; American Loan floated, June. which strengthens government finance.

Larger crops, though still much below pre-war level.

1924 Depression; financial strain.

Some increase in production; slump in iron and steel industries; severe unemployment; many failures; commodity prices gradually rise; foreign trade increases.

Money extremely tight, especially autumn; stock exchange and franc speculation collapse, spring; many bank failures; bourse boom reaches peak, January, and prices fall precipitately to October; foreign exchange stable.

Larger crops of beets, potatoes, rye, and corn; smaller oats, barley, and wheat crops.

1925 Depression.

Slow increase in volume of production except iron and steel industries; severe unemployment, worst in spring; many failures; wholesale prices reach peak, January, and fall, declining most rapidly in third quarter; imports much smaller, larger exports greatly restricted, last quarter.

Stringent money eases slightly with foreign loans; bourse dull with declining prices; foreign exchange continues steady even after government support is removed, August.

Much larger harvests of rye, barley, wheat, and oats.

League of Nations relaxes financial supervision, end of year; tariff revisions remove many restrictions.

CHAPTER VI.
THE ANNALS OF RUSSIA.

The Russian Empire, which included the northern part of both Europe and Asia, constituted one-sixth of the total land surface of the globe and one-twelfth of its population. Russia in Europe, with which the annals are chiefly concerned, covered more than one-half the area of that continent, but included only thirty per cent of the total population. The revolution of March 12, 1917, ushered in a period of rapid political and economic change. Finally, in 1923, the Union of Soviet Socialist Republics was formed. The area and population under the new government are somewhat smaller than those under the Empire.

European Russia includes the eastern half of Europe. It extends from the Black and Caspian Seas to the Arctic Ocean. Near its southern boundaries, it is mountainous or highland, but the bulk of the country is plateau, plain and flat land. There are large rivers and lakes. Much of Russia lies in the frigid zone where economic activity is restricted during the winter.

The area of the Russian Empire before the war was 8,291,438 [1] square miles, not including Finland. In 1920, the area was 8,078,193 [1] square miles, and on January 1, 1925, it totaled 8,170,108 [1] square miles. The census records for Russia follow:

Census Date	Population [a]	Persons per Square Mile [b]
1860	74,120,100 [c]	9
1880	97,705,100 [c]	12
1897	125,640,021 [d]	15
1915	182,182,600 [c]	22
1920	131,546,045 [e]	16

[a] Russian Empire, not including Finland.
[b] Based on area data given above.
[c] Official estimate. Russia Tzentral'nyi Statisticheski Komitet, *Ezhegodnik Rossii, 1912*. Petersburg, 1913. p. 1, 121.
[d] Census of 1897. Russia Tzentral'nyi Statisticheski Komitet, *Pervaya vseobshchaya perepis' naseleniya Rossiiskoi imperii*. (Bulletin no. 4) Petersburg, 1905.
[e] See source for area in 1920.

[1] Data for 1912 computed by dividing by 2,275,787, data given in versts in Russia Tzentral'nyi Statisticheski Komitet, *Ezhegodnik Rossii, 1912*, p. 1, 25. Petersburg, 1913. For 1920, computed from Russia Tzentral'noe Statisticheskoe Upravlenie, *Statisticheskii Ezhegodnik, 1918-1920*, p. 3. Moscow. For 1925, from United States Bureau of Foreign and Domestic Commerce, *Commerce Yearbook, 1924*. Washington, 1925.

In 1860, 10 per cent of the population was urban; in 1897, 13 per cent; in 1924, 16 per cent. Emigration became a factor of considerable importance early in the twentieth century. In 1906 and 1907, the 200,000 per year mark was passed. The peak was reached in 1913, but emigration has been much smaller since that time.

The distribution of the working population by occupation as recorded in the Census of 1897 follows:

Industry	Per Cent of Total [a]
Agriculture	74.6
Manufacturing, Mining and Construction	9.6
Trade and Transportation	5.4
Other [b]	10.4
Total	100.0

[a] Russia Tzentral'nyi Statisticheski Komitet, *Ezhegodnik Rossii, 1912.* Petersburg, 1913. p. 1, 87.
[b] Includes those engaged in public service, professions, military and domestic service, persons with independent incomes, and others.

The proportion engaged in manufacturing has presumably increased somewhat since 1897, but agriculture still dominates economic activity.

The area of Russia is so great that a wide diversity of agricultural products is possible. In order of acreage, the most important are rye, wheat, oats, barley, and potatoes. Russia is large enough to permit plenty to exist in certain states simultaneously with famine in others, although this condition has been somewhat relieved by the development of railroads. The land area of European Russia is divided into cultivated, 26 per cent; meadow and pasture, 16 per cent; forests, 39 per cent; and uncultivated land, 19 per cent. The annals report the results each year of the wheat, rye, and oats harvests.

Russia possesses vast wealth in minerals and metals. Despite various attempts on the part of the government to develop these resources, progress has been slight. The mining of iron is perhaps most highly developed, coal mines are being opened, and the petroleum industry is expanding rapidly.

Manufacturing has extended slowly into Russia. Since 1860, some real advance has been made, especially in the textile, food, and metal industries. On January 1, 1913, there were 17,356 industrial establishments, employing 2,151,191 workers. Industrial activity was greatly checked by the war, the revolution, and consequent economic reorganization. The gradual recovery is shown by the following table:

Year	Total Value of Industrial Output [a] (1913 roubles = 100)
1913	100.0
1920	14.6
1921-22	21.6
1922-23	32.3
1923-24	42.0

[a] Segal, Louis and A. A. Santilov, *Commercial Year-book of the Soviet Union, 1925.* New York, 1925. p. 142.

Recovery has been most rapid in the oil, rubber, chemical, and paper industries, which have all reached 60 per cent of the pre-war output.

Russian foreign trade grew rapidly from 1855 to 1875, then went through a period of slow expansion until 1900, when development was resumed. In general, exports have exceeded imports. Leading exports are wheat, barley, lumber, and petroleum; leading imports are machinery and cotton.

Much of Russia's transportation is done by means of inland waterways. There are 153,782 miles of rivers, canals, and lakes in European Russia, of which 20,670 miles are navigable by steam vessels, and 7,482 miles by sailing vessels. In comparison with Russia's area, the development of railroads has been slight.

Year	Miles of Railroad [a]
1851	310
1871	6,690
1891	18,939
1901	32,595
1911	39,489
1921	40,328

[a] France Statistique Générale, *Annuaire Statistique, 1922.* Paris, 1923. p. 299. Original data in kilometers multiplied by 0.62137.

The Bank of Russia, established in 1860, acted both as a state bank and as a private bank. It had more than one hundred branches. In addition, there were two state agricultural banks, formed prior to 1890. The state banking system dominates the private banks. In 1894, the Bank of Russia assumed the functions of a modern central bank of issue, and in 1897 paper money was given a gold exchange value. During the years 1918-21, there was no normal banking activity, but with the adoption of the new economic policy in 1921, a new state bank was founded which now controls currency and credit conditions.

Russian economic conditions have always been dominated by two factors, political and agricultural conditions. In 1858, the crisis which had developed in the United States and England in 1857, reached Russia. Banks and joint stock companies were closed and there was a consequent paralysis of industry. The emancipation of the peasants with the abolition of serfdom in February, 1861, made possible the rapid development of industry. The textile industry, however, was severely strained by the cotton famine of the early sixties. Rapid railroad construction between 1868 and 1871, coupled with the closing of the French source of capital by the Franco-Prussian War, caused a recession in 1871. Revival came in 1873, although the Austro-German crisis of that year retarded foreign trade and the activity of the Nijni-Novgorod fair somewhat. After the Russian-Turkish War, 1877-78, Russian industry entered into a period of rapid expansion and enormous profits. A recession ensued in 1880, and the depression was long and severe. Recovery in 1887 had gradually developed into prosperity by the time the annals begin.

1890 Mild prosperity.
Activity continues; increased employment and wages advance; decline in foreign trade.
Money easy; extensive speculation in exchange.
Normal harvest.

1891 Recession; depression.
Decline to depression; further decline in imports.
Money tightens late in year; security prices fall.
Crop failures.
Severe famine; high protective tariff, July; construction of Trans-Siberian Railroad begins; French Alliance formed.

1892 Depression.
Dullness prevails; business failures, February; revival of imports, stagnation in foreign trade, especially exports.
Tight money eases; slight financial panic, February.
Poor crops; grain export prohibited.
Continued famine; severe outbreak of cholera.

1893 Revival.
Industrial activity; period of industrial expansion begins; railroad building and speculation; marked increase in foreign trade, favorable balance.
Money easy.
Large harvests.
Government establishes monopoly of spirituous liquor industry.

1894 Prosperity.
Manufacturers flourish; greater expansion in foreign trade.
Money tightens; St. Petersburg bourse boom begins.
Large crops, low prices.
Death of Czar Alexander III, November.

1895 Prosperity.
Industrial progress and activity; industry and trade vigorous; rise in commodity prices begins; expansion in foreign trade halted.
Money firm; continued bourse boom.
Smaller crops; higher prices.

1896 Prosperity.
Continued industrial progress and activity; commodity prices rise; marked increase in imports.
Tighter money eases; crisis on bourse.
Fair harvests; higher prices.
National Exposition at Nijni-Novgorod; coronation of Nicholas II, May.

1897 Prosperity.
Great activity; period of rapid expansion begins; commodity prices rise; very large exports and favorable balance.
Money rates firm; gold standard established, January; calm year on bourse.
Crop failures.

1898 Prosperity.
Continued activity and expansion of industry and trade; imports increase.
Money easy; security market calm.
Good wheat and rye crops, oats failure.
Port Arthur concession obtained in China, March.

THE ANNALS OF RUSSIA

1899 Prosperity; panic; recession.

Activity gradually slackens; cotton industry stagnant, autumn; many failures late in year; marked decline in exports creates unfavorable balance.

Money tight; bourse panic, September; financial panic, Baku, November.

Very large crops, except wheat.

1900 Recession; depression.

Gradual decline to depression; sharp fall in price of iron; decline in imports and increase in exports cause return to favorable balance of trade.

Severe financial stringency and many failures; security market depressed.

Average crops, record rye.

1901 Depression.

Dullness widespread; general level of prices declines; further improvement in balance of trade.

Tight money eases; bourse depressed.

Very poor rye and oats crops, fair wheat.

Famine and civil unrest.

1902 Depression.

Continued inactivity; further decline in commodity prices; rapid expansion in exports.

Money eases; bourse revives.

Excellent harvests.

1903 Depression; revival.

Inactivity yields to slow improvement late in year; commodity prices low; boom in foreign trade.

Money easy; bourse revival accelerated.

Good crops.

Labor troubles; civil unrest.

1904 Recession; depression.

Continued revival checked, February; rapid decline to depression; commodity prices rise; foreign trade boom halted.

Money tight; bourse panic, February.

Record crops.

War with Japan, February; internal disorder; difficulties with Britain over attacks on neutral shipping.

1905 Depression.
Industry and trade paralyzed; severe railroad troubles; strikes; record favorable balance of trade.
Money very tight; government finances embarrassed.
Average crops.
Port Arthur surrendered to Japanese, January; fleet decisively defeated, June; peace treaty signed, September; internal turmoil and revolution; constitution granting representative Parliament signed, October.

1906 Depression; slight revival.
Continued paralysis; prolonged strikes; revival begins in textile and sugar industries; commodity prices rise; marked increase in imports.
Continued financial stringency; security prices fall.
Very poor crops.
Civil disorder continues.

1907 Revival.
Gradual improvement in industries other than iron and steel; commodity prices fall; decline in exports.
Money very tight; bourse depressed.
Wheat failure, fair rye and oats crops.

1908 Recession; depression.
Slackening of industry and commerce; further decline in commodity prices; exports reach low point.
Money eases; some revival on bourse.
Poor wheat, fair rye and oats crops.
Internal unrest.

1909 Depression; revival.
General improvement sets in, last half-year; commodity prices rise; revival in export trade, very large favorable balance.
Money easy; active revival on bourse.
Record crops; high prices.
Political calm.

1910 Prosperity.
General activity and increased production; further advance in commodity prices; further improvement in foreign trade.
Money easy; vigorous rise in security prices.
Excellent harvests; high prices.
Cholera severe.

THE ANNALS OF RUSSIA

1911 Prosperity.

Brilliant year in manufacturing and mining; commodity prices rise; exports reach peak.

Money easy; upward movement in security prices.

Very poor crops, especially wheat.

Expedition to Persia.

1912 Prosperity.

Great industrial activity; some scarcity of raw materials; energetic railway construction; general rise in price level; wide speculation; foreign trade falls off.

Money tightens; continued rise on bourse to Balkan crisis, September.

Large crops, record rye.

Russian army mobilized.

1913 Prosperity, except bourse.

Continued activity and progress in industry; raw material shortage; increase in imports.

Money tightens; severe credit strain develops; bourse panicky.

Excellent harvest, record wheat.

1914 Recession; panic; depression.

Gradual slackening to war, then stagnation; labor troubles; transportation shortage; foreign trade paralyzed; unfavorable balance.

Money tight and exchange unfavorable; panic with war; moratorium; gold payments suspended, August, and inflation of currency begins.

Poor harvests, much unmarketed; lower prices.

War declared, August; consumption of alcoholic liquors forbidden, August; Russian successes, occupying Galicia.

1915 War activity.

Government assumes control of transportation, industry, and prices; decline in private activity; severe transportation congestion; commodity prices rise; small exports, extensive imports.

Money tight; steadily falling exchange.

Excellent crops; higher prices.

Russsian victories, spring, but defeats and retreat thereafter; bread riots, Moscow and Petrograd, first quarter.

1916   War activity.

Government control extended to include market distribution; commodity prices fixed; transportation shortage severe; some industrial expansion, last half-year; foreign trade declines, while value of imports advances.

Money tight; rapid currency expansion; exchange steady.

Fair crops.

Some military success against Austria.

1917   Recession; depression.

Decline in activity and industrial production; temporary improvement in spring; rapid advance of commodity prices.

Money very tight; banks nationalized, December; rapid fall of exchange begins, May.

Average crops.

Wide distress; Czar overthrown, March; Korniloff attempt, August; Bolsheviki overthrow Kerensky, November; armistice with Germany, November; continual unrest.

1918   Depression.

Communistic economic policy, with nationalization of bonds, trade, and industry; disorder in transportation.

No money or credit market.

Average crops.

Civil war; blockade; Brest-Litovsk treaty signed, March; famine in towns and cities.

1919   Depression.

Policy of national operation continues; government control of production and distribution; distress due to imperfect coördination of different branches of industry.

Intensive currency deflation.

Policy of confiscation of peasant's products adopted.

Famine in towns and cities; civil war; blockade; Kolchak, Denikin, and Yudenich all defeated.

1920   Depression.

Continued communistic policy; small production.

Continued attempt to abandon use of currency.

Policy of confiscation of peasant's products continued.

Famine in towns and cities; war with Poland; Wrangel attempt successfully defeated; peasants uprise; blockade raised, January.

1921 Depression.

New economic policy adopted, March; gradual reorganization of industry and markets; rapid increase of prices; foreign trade monopoly modified; imports increased, last half-year.

Severe depreciation of currency; money again permitted full circulation, June; state bank established, November.

Unprecedented crop failure; very high prices; government ends policy of confiscation and taxes on commodities of peasants.

Famine and severe distress; trade agreement with Great Britain, March.

1922 Depression; slight revival.

Some increase in manufacturing and mining; foreign trade revives, especially imports; state foreign trade monopoly abolished, October.

Bourse and credit organization reëstablished; continued inflation of currency; issue of bank notes, or chervonetzi, authorized.

Very good crops.

Severe famine necessitates American relief.[1]

1923 Revival; recession, October.

Increase in industrial production and trade; depression, April and May, and end of year; unemployment; favorable balance of trade due to large decrease in imports and doubling of exports.

Continued monetary inflation; severe credit restriction, August, culminating in crisis, October; government opens additional banks.

Average crops; relative value of agricultural commodities continues to fall.

New constitution, July, changing government to union of four republics; various trade agreements made.

1924 Mild depression; revival.

Some increase in production; severe depression, spring, lessens in summer; steady growth of foreign trade, though still far below prewar totals.

Very rapid depreciation of rouble, and rise in chervonetz exchange; currency stabilized, March, on the basis of chervonetz; currency shortage, March and April; currency restriction, spring.

Poor crops, improved prices.

Lenin dies, January; *de jure* recognition by Great Britain, February, followed by eleven other countries.

---

[1] The famine resulted from the failure of the 1921 crop, the very good crop of 1922 not becoming available for relief until late in the year.

1925 Uneven prosperity; recession.

Further increase in volume of production; unemployment; commodity prices advance to peak, May, decline to September, and then advance somewhat; recession to dullness, last quarter; increased foreign trade, state restricting imports.

Money tight; increased currency circulation.

Large wheat crop, lower price; large increase in barley, some in rye yield.

Diplomatic relations with Japan resumed, January; partial prohibition of liquor consumption abolished, October.

CHAPTER VII.

THE ANNALS OF SWEDEN.

The kingdom of Sweden consists of the eastern and larger section of the Scandinavian peninsula. It is divided from Norway by a natural boundary of mountains at the north, but at the south, the boundary line often has been shifted. Sweden has a backbone of rugged mountain ranges. Deep river valleys run to the sea, with intervening highlands. The southern end of the peninsula is lowlands and plains. Although the latitude of Sweden is that of Hudson Bay, its climate is much more favorable, due to the salubrious effect of the Gulf Stream.

The total area of Sweden on January 1, 1925, was 173,151 square miles.[1] The census records of population growth have been as follows:

December 31,—	Population [a]	Persons per Square Mile [b]
1750	1,780,678	10.3
1850	3,482,541	20.1
1880	4,565,668	26.4
1890	4,784,981	27.6
1900	5,136,441	29.6
1910	5,522,403	31.9
1920	5,904,489	34.1

[a] Sweden Statistiska Centralbyrån, *Statistisk Årsbok, 1925*. Stockholm, 1925. p. 5. "Population de droit."
[b] Computed by means of area given above.

The periods of greatest Swedish emigration were 1867-73 and 1879-93. Since then the numbers have been smaller, though rushes occurred in certain years such as 1902 and 1903. There is a marked tendency towards urban development. In 1850, 10 per cent of the population was urban, in 1900, 21.5 per cent, and in 1920, 29.5 per cent.

Perhaps the best picture of the economic nature of Sweden and its development is obtained from the following table, in which the

[1] Computed by multiplying by 0.3861, data in square kilometers given in Sweden Statistiska Centralbyrån, *Statistisk Årsbok, 1925*. Stockholm, 1925. p. 2.

population is divided according to the industries upon which it depends. The percentages are as follows:

Industry	Percentage of Total Population [a]				
	1880	1890	1900	1910	1920
Agriculture	50	50	46	42	39
Manufacturing, Mining and Construction	11	16	22	28	31
Commerce and Communication	4	6	7	10	13
Other [b]	35	28	25	20	17
Total	100	100	100	100	100

[a] Sweden Statistiska Centralbyrån, *Statistisk Årsbok, 1925*. Stockholm, 1925. p. 36.
[b] Includes public officials, professional workers, domestic workers, store-keepers, retired persons, and others.

Agriculture still holds its position of primacy, but the notable development during the period has been the steady increase in the proportion of the population engaged in manufacturing, commerce and communication.

Although the acreage of land under cultivation is slowly increasing in Sweden, it has not yet included one-tenth of the total area, and nearly sixty per cent of the total area is occupied by forests. The most important crops are oats, rye, and barley, in the order named. In addition to noting the results of these three crops, the annals give a general statement for all crops, based upon the "index of harvest" computed each year by the Swedish Central Bureau of Statistics. Annual records of the total agricultural income, compiled by the same Bureau, form the basis for statements concerning the return to farmers.

Mining is one of the oldest economic activities of Sweden. Prior to the development of modern methods of smelting, Sweden was the leading iron producer in Europe. The mining of iron ore is still important.

The growth of manufacturing in Sweden has already been noted in the discussion of the occupations of the workers. This activity is not concentrated in a few industrial centers, but factories are spread fairly well over the entire country. In 1923, there were 10,990 manufacturing establishments employing 358,083 workers. Of special importance is the production of lumber, wood products, and paper, and the manufacture of complex machinery.

The foreign trade of Sweden has grown steadily. Since 1855, imports have exceeded exports except for the war years, and 1922.

The leading imports are coal, iron and steel, and wheat; the more important exports are lumber, wood pulp, and machinery.

Railway building began late in Sweden, but once begun, it progressed rapidly. Official records are as follows:

December 31,—	Miles of Railroad [a]
1880	3,651
1890	4,982
1900	7,023
1910	8,593
1920	9,420

[a] Computed by multiplying by 0.62137, data given in kilometers in Sweden Statistiska Centralbyrån, *Statistisk Årsbok, 1925*. Stockholm, 1925. p. 169.

In 1924, the government owned 37 per cent of the total railway mileage. It should be remembered that Sweden has always been able to carry on a large part of her domestic trade by water.

The Riksbank, or Bank of Sweden, is the bank of issue, and is a government owned central bank. In addition to being a bank for rediscount, it does a general banking business. There were ten private banks and 23 joint-stock banks, on January 1, 1925, performing the regular banking functions, except the issuing of banknotes, which is done by the Riksbank.

Beginning about 1860, Sweden entered upon years of vigorous development. Since that time, there have been periods of slackened growth, but the tendency has been continually one of expansion. Bad harvests in 1866, 1867, and 1868 brought with them a state of depression which lasted to 1870. A period of extremely rapid expansion set in, and continued until 1878, when a recession of activity occurred. The period from 1879 to 1887 was, except for short intervals, a period of stagnation and severe agricultural depression. A gradual improvement was evident late in the decade and 1890 can be considered a prosperous year.

1890 Prosperity.

    Increasing activity and expansion; commodity prices rise; slight increase in foreign trade.

    Money tightens.

    Excellent harvest, especially barley and oats; some decline in prices.

1891 Prosperity.
Continued activity; expansion of merchant marine; commodity prices reach peak; decline in imports but large increase in exports.
Money tight.
Fair harvests, rye improving but oats and barley smaller; larger return to farmers.
Political crisis, July.

1892 Recession; mild depression.
Gradual decline to dullness; sharp decrease in commodity prices; smaller imports; rate of increase of exports slackens.
Money easier.
Record harvests; excellent return to farmers.
Political disturbances; large emigration.

1893 Depression.
Some improvement in volume of domestic business but marked decline in foreign trade; commodity prices lower.
Money easy.
Poor crops except for record rye yield; decline in farmers' return.

1894 Mild depression.
Dullness continued; home trade inactive; further decline in commodity prices; some revival in imports but diminished exports.
Money easy.
Good crops, rye failure; marked reduction in farmers' return.

1895 Revival.
Decided improvement and increase in industrial activity; commodity prices reach bottom; revival in export trade.
Money easy.
Crops fair; oats and barley excellent, rye very poor; return to farmers still low.
Controversy with Norway over flag and consular service.

1896 Prosperity.
Improvement in trade and industry; slight rise in commodity prices; foreign trade booms.
Money extremely easy.
Good crops except oats; some improvement in return to farmers.

THE ANNALS OF SWEDEN

1897   Prosperity.
        Continued activity and expansion; further rise in commodity prices; increase in foreign trade marked.
        Money tightens rapidly.
        Good harvest; further improvement in position of farmer.

1898   Prosperity.
        Activity and expansion with full employment; speculation; commodity price rise accelerated; large increase in imports, exports decline.
        Money tight.
        Excellent crops, except rye only fair; further increase in return to farmer.

1899   Prosperity.
        Great activity and industrial development; real estate boom; rapid rise in commodity prices; very active foreign trade.
        Money tight, with occasional stringency.
        Very poor crops, oats and barley failures; marked reduction in return to farmers.
        Prince Gustavus acts as regent for Oscar II, January to May; difficulties with Norway finally adjusted.

1900   Prosperity.
        Continued activity and progress, but signs of uneasiness; wild speculation leads to crisis in wool industry; less activity in promotion of new enterprises; commodity prices reach peak; big expansion in foreign trade.
        Money very tight.
        Excellent crops with very large return to farmers.

1901   Recession; depression.
        Gradual decline to stagnation; marked decline in manufacturing; commodity prices fall; foreign trade severely restricted.
        Money tight, easing somewhat.
        Poor harvest and reduction of return to farmers.
        Drought.

1902   Depression.
        Dullness in home industry; slight further decline in commodity prices; many failures; foreign trade revives.
        Money eases.
        Poor harvest, especially barley; crop failures in northern territory; poor return to farmers.
        Famine in northern districts.

1903　Revival.

Steady and slow progress; rapid revival and expansion in iron industry; fall in commodity prices halted; foreign trade very active.
Money easy.
Good crops; improved income to farmers.
Emigration reaches peak.

1904　Mild prosperity.

Very slow improvement; little unemployment and a few labor difficulties; commodity prices slowly rise; increase in imports, but decline in exports.
Money easy.
Very poor harvest, especially oats; decrease in return to farmers.

1905　Prosperity.

Marked improvement in trade and industry; further rise in commodity prices; big increase in exports.
Money easy.
Fair harvest with larger return to farmers.
Diplomatic crisis with Norway, April, and union dissolved, June.

1906　Prosperity.

Continued upswing of industry, except coal; speculation; rapid rise of commodity prices; foreign trade boom.
Money tightens.
Large harvests, especially rye; very favorable return to farmers.

1907　Prosperity; recession; panic.

Continued activity to autumn, when decline sets in; prices rise, first half-year, and then decline rapidly; many failures late in year; very active foreign trade.
Money very tight; financial panic, December.
Fair harvest, rye and barley poor; good return to farmer.
Gustavus V accedes to throne upon death of his father, December.

1908　Depression.

Continued decline to stagnation; increased unemployment; sharp fall in commodity prices; foreign trade severely restricted.
Money tight.
Record harvests; increased return to farmers.
Distress among working classes.

1909   Depression.

Dullness continued, first half-year; strikes, May; slight improvement checked by general strike, August, lasting several months; further decline in volume of production; fall in commodity prices checked; increased import but decline in export trade.

Money eases.

Good crops, but some decline in return to farmers.

1910   Revival.

Improvement in trade and industry; rise in commodity prices; marked revival in foreign trade.

Money easy; private bank difficulties; stock prices begin to rise.

Good harvest, especially oats; improvement in position of farmer.

1911   Prosperity.

Calm and healthy advance in home trade; commodity prices rise; foreign trade booms.

Money easy, with financial retrenchment; gradual rise in stock prices.

Fair crops; very large return to farmers.

1912   Prosperity.

Great activity and expansion; accelerated rise in commodity prices; great expansion of foreign trade.

Money easy; stock prices reach peak, summer.

Good harvest, especially rye; very large income to farmers.

1913   Prosperity; slight recession.

Continued activity; with autumn, slow and gradual decline sets in; little unemployment; slower rise of commodity prices; foreign trade expansion continues.

Money tightens; gradual decline in security prices.

Good harvest, record oats and barley; marked reduction in return to farmers.

1914   Recession; depression.

Gradually increasing dullness turns to stagnation with war; marked increase in unemployment; many failures; rapid rise in commodity prices; foreign trade checked with war, favorable balance.

Easy money quickly tightens; moratorium declared; Bank suspends gold payments, August; stock exchange closed, and reopened, November; foreign exchange declines rapidly.

Very poor crops, record rye but barley and oats failures; prices very high.

Swedish neutrality declared.

1915 Revival; prosperity.

Stagnation gradually yields to industrial boom; unemployment disappears; rapid commodity price rise; foreign trade very active.

Money market eases; gradual revival on stock exchange; foreign exchange declines, first quarter, and then gradually improves, going to a premium, November.

Fair crops, higher prices.

1916 Prosperity.

Great activity in industry, hampered somewhat by increasing scarcity of raw materials; much speculation; commodity prices rise rapidly; very active foreign trade.

Money market easy; National Bank of Sweden resumes payments in gold, January; security prices boom; further advance in foreign exchange to May followed by gradual decline.

Good crops; larger return to farmers.

Food rationing begins, October.

1917 Recession.

Decrease in volume of production due to scarcity of raw materials; unemployment appears; extensive speculation; continued price rise, accelerated late in year; reduction of foreign trade, especially imports.

Easy money tightens rapidly late in year; stock prices reach peak, and long period of decline sets in; rapid appreciation of exchange, June to November, followed by sharp decline.

Crop failures; very high prices increase farmers' return.

Food riots, spring.

1918 Depression.

Industry paralyzed by shortage of raw materials; severe unemployment; commodity prices rise to peak, end of year; foreign trade restricted by blockade; depression deepened by Armistice.

Money very tight; great activity on stock exchange, falling prices; foreign exchange remains at high level, first half-year, and then declines.

Crop failures; some improvement in rye; prices at peak; return to farmers at maximum.

1919 Depression; revival.

Severe depression gradually lightens, summer; fuel shortage; labor troubles, with severe unemployment early in year; commodity prices decline to October; marked revival of foreign trade, especially imports, creating unfavorable balance once more.

Money eases somewhat, summer; stock prices decline; exchange falls, passing par in March.

Good crops, but smaller return to farmers.

Government regulations gradually removed; food rationing ends, August.

1920 Boom; recession; depression.

Rapid and feverish activity; employment reaches peak, April, and severe unemployment appears, November; commodity prices reach peak, June, and fall rapidly, last quarter; production reaches peak, autumn; strikes; severe depression by end of year; great increase in failures, last quarter; after feverish activity, foreign trade declines, last half-year.

Money very tight; slight revival of stock prices, spring, and then further fall; gold payments suspended; foreign exchange reaches low point, February, improves in spring, and again declines in autumn.

Good harvests, but smaller return to farmer.

1921 Depression.

Continued contraction of trade and industry to summer; many failures; severe unemployment; commodity prices fall; foreign trade greatly restricted, imports showing some revival last half-year.

Money market eases; dull stock exchange with falling prices to November; gradual improvement in exchange with severe setback, summer.

Fair crops, excellent rye; low prices greatly reduce return to farmers.

1922 Depression; revival.

Continued liquidation, but gradual revival becomes evident by summer; some improvement in employment; commodity price fall halted, spring; increased exports create favorable balance.

Money easy; temporary stock speculation boom, spring; foreign exchange rises gradually to par.

Fair crops; further reduction in farmers' income to very low point.

1923 Revival.

Gradual improvement, hampered by serious labor disputes; lessening of unemployment; fewer failures; further decline of commodity prices; increase in imports returns foreign trade to unfavorable balance.

Money very easy, tightening slightly late in year; decline of stock prices resumed, to November; exchange fluctuates about par.

Fair crops, good rye and poor barley; prices and farmers' income higher.

1924 Mild prosperity.

Continued improvement; few failures; full employment; commodity prices reach minimum, July; further increase in foreign trade.

Money fairly easy; return to gold redemption and export of gold permitted, April; some improvement in stock prices.

Poor harvests; severe failure of rye crop; marked increase in return to farmers; outbreak of hoof-and-mouth disease.

1925 Mild prosperity.

After slackening business activity, first six months, manufacturing improves, especially last quarter; iron and steel industries somewhat depressed; little unemployment; commodity prices decline from peak, early in year, to October; increased foreign trade, smaller unfavorable balance.

Money easier; rising security prices slump, spring and October.

Record wheat, rye, and potato crops; lower prices; much higher return to farmers.

CHAPTER VIII.

THE ANNALS OF THE NETHERLANDS.

The Netherlands, sometimes called Holland, is one of the smallest European nations. It lies in the northwest of Europe, bounded on the south by Belgium and on the east by Germany, otherwise by the sea. Much of its territory is flat and lies below the sea-level, protected by dikes. The area is partially land once under water, redeemed from the sea by extraordinary effort. The coast is relatively long and much indented. The Zuider Zee is a large inland sea covering nearly 2,000 square miles. The Rhine, Meuse, and Scheldt empty into the ocean from Dutch territory.

The area of the Netherlands is continually changing due to the action of the sea. On January 1, 1924, it was 13,208 square miles.[1] The census records of population in recent times are as follows:

December 31,—	Population [a]	Persons per Square Mile [b]
1879	4,012,693	315
1889	4,511,415	359
1899	5,104,137	400
1909	5,858,175	465
1920	6,865,314	545

[a] Source same as for area. Figures for "population customarily resident".
[b] Computed by multiplying by 2.59, data given originally in persons per square kilometer. Based on land area, not including inland waterways.

In 1921, the rural population and that of the smaller towns amounted to 54.3 per cent of the total, while 45.7 per cent lived in cities and towns of more than 20,000 inhabitants. There has been very little emigration from the Netherlands in recent years.

The importance of different types of economic activity, and the trend of development, can be seen in the following table of the distribution of male and female workers:

[1] Computed by multiplying by 0.3861, data in square kilometers given in Netherlands Centraal Bureau voor Statistiek, *Jaarcijfers voor Nederland, 1923-24*. 's-Gravenhage, 1925. Area is for land plus inland waterways.

Industry	Per Cent of Total Workers [a]	
	Dec. 31, 1899	Dec. 31, 1920
Agriculture	30.0	22.9
Manufacturing, Mining and Construction	34.2	37.8
Commerce and Transportation [b]	17.5	21.3
Other [c]	18.3	18.0
Total	100.0	100.0

[a] Netherlands Centraal Bureau voor Statistiek, *Jaarcijfers voor Nederland, 1905* and *1923-24.* 's-Gravenhage.

[b] Includes persons engaged in commerce, communications, credit and banking, and insurance.

[c] Includes persons engaged in hunting and fishing, professions, public and domestic service, and other activities.

Although agriculture has apparently declined in importance during the period covered by the above figures, this decline is purely a relative matter. Agriculture has actually increased in the number of its workers, but not as rapidly as the other types of economic activity. Approximately three-fourths of the land area is under cultivation, and the increase in recent years has been slight. Although there has been practically no change in the forty to sixty distribution of land used for pasture and for crops in the last fifty years, there has been a definite change in the type of crops cultivated. The production of cereals has been steadily decreasing and specialized products such as bulbs, seeds, vegetables, fruits, and flowers are increasing. Leading crops according to acreage are rye, potatoes, oats, sugar beets, and wheat. Cattle and dairy products are also of considerable importance.

The manufacturing industries of the Netherlands work under the peculiar disadvantage of having neither coal nor iron supplies of adequate size in the country. During the war, some coal mining was undertaken, but the supply is chiefly anthracite and found in narrow seams, making the mining expensive. The leading manufactured products are ships, cotton textiles, machinery, and margarine. In cutting diamonds, the Dutch have long been leaders of the world.

The Netherlands is a very active maritime nation and conducts an extensive carrying trade among other nations. In foreign trade, its imports have for many years exceeded its exports. At present, the leading imports are oil seeds, coal, and wheat; leading exports are vegetables, sugar, and vegetable oils.

Transportation in the Netherlands is by no means confined to railroads. There were about 2,000 miles of canals, 3,000 miles of roads, 1,810 miles of tramways, and 2,400 miles of railroad in 1924. Some indication of the importance of the inland waterways is obtained from the following table, indicating the per cent distribution of freight according to the routes taken in foreign trade:

Routes	Per Cent Distribution of Foreign Trade Movements [a]			
	1913		1923	
	Imports	Exports	Imports	Exports
By Sea	43	22	56	32
By River or Canal	39	65	25	29
By Land	18	13	19 [b]	39 [b]
Total	100	100	100	100

[a] *Jaarcijfers,* noted above.
[b] Includes small entries by air.

It may be that the elaborate system of canals explains somewhat the tardy development of railroads in the Netherlands. The following table gives the length of railroad within the limits of the kingdom at various dates:

December 31,—	Miles of Railroad [a]
1860	208
1880	1,147
1890	1,636
1900	1,725
1910	2,054
1920	2,116

[a] Netherlands Centraal Bureau voor Statistiek, *Statistiek van het vervoes op de spoorwegen, . . . 1920.* (Bijdragen no. 341) 's-Gravenhage, 1922. Computed by multiplying by 0.000,621,37 data in meters.

The Bank of the Netherlands is a private bank with many agencies. It is the only bank given the right to issue bank notes in the Netherlands. There are also joint stock banks, which have formed special groups for concerted action.

The early years of the nineteenth century were years of extreme depression for the Netherlands, due to the maritime restrictions of Napoleon. In 1813, independence was recovered and union with Belgium established. This union was violently broken by Belgium in 1830. Interference by the large powers in 1831 brought apparent peace, but final settlement was not reached until 1839. Unrest and expensive armament during this period caused a long depression. About 1850, a period of prolonged prosperity, especially in agriculture, set in. The end of the Franco-Prussian War, the improving of ports, and the opening of canals in the seventies proved a further aid to commerce. However, the rapid development of American competition in providing foodstuffs for Europe and a costly war with the Sultan of Acheen over the occupation of Sumatra, made themselves felt in the eighties. And the late years of the decade, which produced full prosperity in so many countries, developed it but mildly in the Netherlands.

1890 Mild prosperity.
Continued activity; increase in foreign trade.
Money tightens; severe financial strain, autumn.
Fair rye and oats, poor potato crop.
King William III dies, and Queen Emma becomes Regent, November.

1891 Recession.
Gradual decline in activity; much speculation; extension of merchant marine and further increase in foreign trade.
Money eases somewhat, first quarter.
Rye and potato crop failures, record oats yield.

1892 Depression.
Dullness and inactivity; severe depression in shipping and diamond industries; reduction in foreign trade.
Money eases.
Excellent crops.

1893 Depression.
Continued dullness; commodity speculation with sharp drop in prices of foodstuffs; some revival in foreign trade.
Money tightens severely to November.
Excellent potato, good rye, and poor oats crops.

1894 Depression.
Continued inactivity; further decline in price of foodstuffs; some increase in imports.
Money eases.
Good rye and oats, very poor potato crops; severe agricultural distress.

1895 Depression.
Dullness continued; labor troubles; further reduction in price of foodstuffs; decrease in imports, increase in exports.
Money very easy; South African gold mining speculation causes bourse crisis, November.
Good crops.

1896   Revival.
    General improvement, especially in shipping; prices of foodstuffs reach lowest point; marked improvement in foreign trade.
    Money tightens.
    Excellent rye and oats, good potato crop.

1897   Mild prosperity.
    Increased activity; commodity prices rise; foreign trade booms.
    Tight money eases gradually.
    Fair crops, good oats.

1898   Prosperity.
    Continued activity and expansion; further slight rise in prices; some increase in foreign trade.
    Money eases.
    Excellent rye and oats, fair potato crop.
    Queen Wilhelmina accedes to throne, August.

1899   Prosperity.
    Continued activity, but lessened expansion; some advance in price of foodstuffs; further expansion of foreign trade.
    Money very tight, especially late in year.
    Good crops, record potato yield.
    Peace Conference at the Hague, July; much excitement over the Boer War, autumn.

1900   Prosperity.
    Continued activity; manufacturing progresses despite high costs; severe railroad strike, April; further increase in foreign trade.
    Tight money eases slowly.
    Excellent rye and oats, poor potato crop.

1901   Recession; mild depression.
    Gradual decline to depression, especially shipping; raw material prices high; increase of foreign trade checked.
    Money fairly easy.
    Record crops.

1902   Depression.
    Continued inactivity and dullness; prices of foodstuffs decline; revival in foreign trade.
    Money easy.
    Excellent crops, low prices.

1903 Depression.
Continued dullness in home trade; severe strikes early in year; further increase in foreign trade, especially exports.
Money tightens; wild speculation in American securities causes panic.
Excellent rye and oats, very poor potato crops.

1904 Revival; prosperity.
Marked improvement except shipping industry; sharp rise in price of foodstuffs; slight increase in imports.
Money eases.
Fair rye and oats crops, excellent potato yield.

1905 Prosperity.
Activity and expansion; shipping industry revives; marked increase in imports.
Money very easy and abundant.
Poor crops, especially oats.

1906 Prosperity.
Activity; industries flourish; commodity prices rise; increased failures; decreased imports, increased exports; merchant marine at peak registration.
Money tightens, autumn.
Excellent crops.

1907 Prosperity; recession.
Activity and expansion of commerce and industry yields in autumn to inactivity and dullness; many failures, spring and late in year; commodity prices rise; very active foreign trade.
Money tight, especially autumn; tremendous fall in security prices.
Excellent crops.

1908 Depression; revival.
Inactivity and dullness give way to rapid revival, autumn; continued rise in commodity prices; rapid recovery of foreign trade after slight check.
Money eases.
Excellent crops, especially rye.
Punitive expedition sent to Venezuela.

1909 Revival; prosperity.
Continued improvement to prosperity; building boom; commodity prices rise; marked increase in foreign trade.
Money easy.
Excellent rye, good potato, and fair oats crops.

1910   Prosperity.
Continued activity, stimulated by rubber and oil booms; more rapid rise in prices; further increase in foreign trade.
Easy money tightens, spring; financial strain.
Fair crops.

1911   Prosperity.
Continued activity and expansion; further rise in prices; lessened increase in foreign trade.
Money tight, with ease in summer.
Excellent crops.

1912   Prosperity.
Continued activity; rapid rise in commodity prices; foreign trade booms.
Money tight.
Fair crops; record potato yield and oats failure.

1913   Prosperity; recession.
Continued activity with signs of slackening; severe decline in commodity prices; increased imports, but exports unchanged.
Money tighter, July.
Good crops except poor potato yield.

1914   Recession; panic; depression.
Continued decline to war; complete interruption of business; rapid rise of commodity prices; severe restriction of foreign trade.
Money tight; panic with war; foreign exchange goes to a slight premium; stock exchange closed; export of gold prohibited.
Good crops, except complete failure of rye; prices fair.
Neutrality declared.

1915   Revival; uneven prosperity.
Gradual readjustment; prosperity and extreme activity in war industries and necessities; severe unemployment relieved somewhat, last quarter; commodity prices boom; further decline in foreign trade, due to navigation difficulties.
Money easy; exchange depreciates to below par, February, but improves rapidly, last four months; stock exchange reopened, February.
Excellent crops, especially oats and potatoes.
Diplomatic difficulties concerning sinking of Dutch ships by submarines.

1916 Moderate prosperity.

Continued activity, curtailed by shortage of raw materials and restriction of foreign trade; fuller employment; large war profits; continued boom in commodity prices.

Money easy; foreign exchange at premium, but gradually declining.

Very poor crops.

Flood with breaking of Zuider Zee dike, January; war scare, March; government given full power for intervention in industry and trade, August; food rationing adopted, October.

1917 Recession.

Activity severely hampered by coal shortage, lack of raw materials, and blockade; England prohibits coal export to Holland, March; extensive unemployment; further rise in prices; very small foreign trade.

Money fairly easy; exchange falls nearly to par, first quarter, and then advances gradually.

Poor crops, except fair potato yield.

Distress.

1918 Depression.

Industry and trade inactive; commodity prices rise to peak; many failures; foreign trade completely stopped, some revival with Armistice.

Money rates steady; exchange rises to record premium, but falls rapidly after August.

Some improvement in crops, except rye.

Riots and much distress; war scare, April; Allies seize Dutch ships.

1919 Revival; prosperity.

Boom in trade and industry; severe labor troubles; commodity prices lower; very active foreign trade.

Money rates steady; gradual decline in exchange, passing par, June.

Good rye and potato crops, fair oats yield.

1920 Prosperity; recession; depression.

Continued activity gives way to depression in autumn; severe strikes, May; some improvement in commodity prices to July, with sharp decline, last quarter; unemployment late in year; very active foreign trade.

Money easy and abundant; rapid depreciation of exchange to minimum point, November.

Fair rye and potato crops, excellent oats yield.

1921 Depression.

Trade and industry at a standstill; continued rapid decline of prices checked, May; labor troubles, especially strike in metal industries, last quarter; unemployment; foreign trade activity continues.

Money tight; after period of recovery, foreign exchange depreciates further, summer, but improves late in year.

Excellent rye, good oats, and very poor potato yields.

1922 Depression.

Severe depression; acute unemployment and many failures; further decline in commodity prices; increased volume of foreign trade, decreased value.

Money eases; exchange gradually rises, nearly reaching par at end of year; two serious bank failures.

Good rye, poor oats, and enormous potato crops.

1923 Depression.

Continued dullness; shipping and industry inactive; extensive unemployment; further decline in prices to low point, August; fishing improves; larger foreign trade, especially exports.

Easy money tightens severely; Hanze Bank failure; stock market dull with slight revival, end of year; slight decline in foreign exchange, especially last quarter.

Good oats, poor rye and potato crops.

1924 Revival.

Steady improvement becomes marked, autumn; diminished unemployment; labor troubles; increased number of failures; sharp rise in commodity prices, late autumn; improvement in foreign trade, with marked expansion of import trade.

Money market eases somewhat, with temporary tightness, summer; stock market dull except at the beginning and end of year; foreign exchange gradually improves, exceeding parity at end of year.

Fair rye and potato crops, poor oats.

Import duties increased.

1925　　Mild prosperity.

Quiet activity; continued though declining unemployment; marked improvement in textile industries; fewer failures; commodity prices decline rapidly, first quarter, but then stabilize; increased foreign trade, profiting from tin and rubber booms.

Money easy, official discount rate being twice reduced; gold standard resumed, April, and gold currency put into circulation, November; marked rise in security prices, last half-year, bonds reaching peak, October, and stocks, December.

Good crops, lower prices.

Internal political difficulties.

CHAPTER IX.

THE ANNALS OF ITALY.

The Kingdom of Italy was established in 1861, although Rome continued as a separate state until 1872. Italy occupies a peninsula extending from central Europe south into the Mediterranean Sea. Surrounded on three sides by water, its north territory is separated from the rest of Europe by the barrier of the Alps. The topography is dominated by the Apennines mountain chain, which enters the peninsula from the northwest, and runs its entire length. The section between the Apennines and the Alps is called northern Italy, while the remainder of the peninsula is central and southern Italy. There is a decided difference not only in the economic activities of these sections, but also in the racial characteristics of the population.

The area of Italy before the war, including Sicily and Sardinia, was 110,660 square miles.[1] The additional territory obtained by the war treaties has increased this area to 119,728 square miles.[1] The population of Italy has shown a steady increase, despite the large emigration and high density. The census records follow:

Census Date	Population [a]	Persons per Square Mile [b]
Jan. 1, 1872	26,801,154	242
Jan. 1, 1882	28,459,628	257
Feb. 10, 1901	32,475,253	293
June 10, 1911	34,671,377	313
Dec. 1, 1921 { old area	37,142,886	336
{ new area	38,710,576	323

[a] Subject to continuous revision, the figures here given are the latest official totals available. The source is that given above for area.
[b] Computed from data given originally in persons per square kilometer by multiplying by 2.59.

The outstanding feature of the population records of Italy has been the enormous emigration to North and South America. The

[1] Computed by multiplying by 0.3861, data in square kilometers given in Italy Direzione Generale della Statistica, *Annuario Statistico Italiano, 1919-1921*. Rome, 1925.

movement was most active in the decade prior to the war, reaching a total of 872,598 departures in 1913.

The relative importance of different types of economic activity can be judged from the following percentage distributions of the population according to industry.

Industry	Per Cent of Population over 9 Years of Age [a]	
	1901	1911
Agriculture	55.7	55.8
Manufacturing and Mining	25.9	29.8
Commerce and Transportation	5.7	5.6
Other [b]	12.7	8.7
Total	100.0	100.0

[a] Italy Direzione Generale Statistica e del Lavoro, *Censimento della Populazion, al 10 febbraro 1901,* and *al 10 giugno 1911.* Rome.

[b] Includes persons engaged in domestic service, professions, government offices, defense, religion and other occupations.

The figures for occupations demonstrate the prime importance of agriculture in Italy. In spite of its mountains, 92 per cent of the land area is productive, and 43 per cent was planted with crops in 1923. The three most important agricultural products are very unlike in nature,—wheat, grapes, and olives. Wheat is harvested beginning August, the grape yield is gathered from September to November, and the olive harvest is gathered during the winter months. The growing of silk is one of the early industries of Italy. All four of the crops enter extensively into foreign trade.

Mining is not of great importance, the leading products being sulphur and marble. The lack of coal resources is met in a large degree by elaborate hydro-electric developments.

The latest census of manufactures, that of 1911, reported 243,926 industrial establishments employing 2,304,438 workers. Similar records for 1876 reported 9,177 establishments with 382,131 employees. The largest group of workers was connected with the textile industry. Records for individual industries indicate in general very rapid growth in the first decade of the twentieth century, but little expansion in more recent years.

Foreign trade plays a very important part in the economic life of Italy. The principal imports are cotton, wheat, and coal; the principal exports are silk, cotton fabrics, fruit, and nuts, the last two groups having displaced wine, sulphur and olive oil in recent years. Total imports always exceed total exports.

The following table pictures the development of railway facilities in Italy:

December 31,—	Miles of Railroad [a]
1881	5,479
1891	8,252
1901	9,738
1911	10,619
1923	12,991

[a] Computed by multiplying by 0.62137, original data published in Italy Ufficio Centrale di Statistica, *Annuario Statistico Italiano, 1917-21.* Rome, 1925. p. 507.

In 1906, the government began to take over the railroads, and by 1923 nearly four-fifths of the railways were state owned.

Prior to 1893, the banking and currency systems of Italy were quite unorganized. Banks were not adequately supervised, and were often seriously involved in public finance. In 1893, the right of issue was limited to three banks, and a stricter banking code was enacted.

The Kingdom of Italy was formally established in February, 1861. The period from 1866 to 1873 was one of activity and prosperity. In common with the rest of Europe, Italy suffered a depression, though mild, from 1873 to 1878. After a period of rapid expansion, accompanied by active speculation, building booms, and undue banking expansion, lasting nearly ten years, a quiet recession occurred in 1887 or 1888, and the beginning of the record of the *Annals* finds Italy in a state of depression.

1890   Depression.
       Commercial and industrial inactivity; some reduction in volume of foreign trade.
       Money tight; strained financial situation.
       Good wheat and wine, excellent olive yield; very high wheat and silk prices.
       Influenza epidemic.

1891   Depression; panic.
       Increased dullness in industry; many failures, autumn; marked reduction in foreign trade.
       Financial embarrassment; panic, October.
       Record grain and excellent wine yields, good olive crop; price of wheat reaches high point and then declines; sharp decline in silk price.

1892 Depression.
Inactivity in commerce and industry; slight revival in foreign trade.
Money very easy; stock exchange dull; foreign exchange unfavorable.
Poor wheat and olive yields, fair wine output; higher silk price, poor yield.

1893 Depression; financial panic.
Stagnation; depression more severe; many failures; some further increase in exports.
Money tightens severely; banking scandals early in year; panic and important bank failures, last quarter; suspension of specie payments; rapid decline in foreign exchange; stock exchange dull; stricter banking code enacted.
Good wheat, fair wine, and large olive yields; very large silk yield reduces silk price from high level, spring.
Insurrections and riots.

1894 Depression.
Continued dullness and inactivity; many failures, especially in construction industry; foreign trade quiet.
Continued financial uncertainty; bank failures and runs on local banks; wide foreign exchange fluctuations on unfavorable level, with temporary improvement, spring, and permanent improvement late in year; government finance put on sound basis.
Poor crops; large silk yield; wheat price reaches record low point; silk price very much depressed.
War with Abyssinia, winter, in an attempt to extend colonial enterprise; riots in Sicily; trade relations with France uncertain.

1895 Depression.
Continued dullness; little expansion in foreign trade.
Money easy; steadily improving exchange.
Very poor wheat and wine yields; excellent olive output; wheat price very low; average silk yield, higher price.
After early victories, severe defeat in Abyssinia, December; marked increase in emigration.

1896 Depression; slight revival.
Continued inactivity, with some signs of improvement; revival in foreign trade.
Money easy, further depreciation in exchange.
Good wheat, poor wine and olive yields; low wheat price; distress in silk industry, small yield and low price.
Famine and internal disorder; disaster of Adua, March.

1897   Revival.
Slow and gradual improvement; increase in foreign trade.
Exchange recovers somewhat.
Wheat crop failure, strong rise in price; poor wine and olive yields; poor silk yield, very low price.
Famine and distress.

1898   Uneven prosperity.
More rapid improvement and expansion, except agriculture; foreign trade booms.
Money easy; currency depreciation with premium for gold.
Severe agricultural distress early in year; good wheat and olive yields, fair wine return; wheat price reaches high point; average silk yield, higher price.
Political crisis; bread riots, Milan; tariff war with France finally settled, November.

1899   Moderate prosperity.
Increased industrial activity; formation of numerous new stock companies; active speculation; foreign trade boom continues.
Money tightens; further depreciation of currency.
Good wheat, fair wine yields; olive crop destroyed by *mosca olearia*; excellent silk yield, much higher price.

1900   Prosperity; brief recession.
Continued activity and expansion somewhat retarded, especially in iron and coal industries; imports continue to increase though exports fall off sharply.
Money very easy; currency improves rapidly; stock exchange dull.
Poor wheat, fair wine and olive yields; large silk yield, collapse of silk market.
Marked increase in emigration; King Umberto assassinated, July; Victor Emanuel III succeeds to throne.

1901   Prosperity.
Continued activity, especially in foreign trade; labor difficulties.
Marked improvement in foreign exchange.
Excellent crops; fair silk yield, low price.
Large emigration.

1902   Moderate prosperity.
Continued activity, but less eager expansion; some dullness in foreign trade.
Money tightens; gold premium disappears; further improvement in foreign exchange.
Fair wheat, good wine, and poor olive yields; very large yield, slight improvement in silk price.

1903 Prosperity.
Continued activity; silk industry depressed; big increase in imports.
Further improvement in exchange.
Excellent wheat and olive, very poor wine yields; very small silk yield, high price.
Agricultural depression, especially in southern Italy; some decline in emigration.

1904 Prosperity.
Continued activity, especially in cotton industry; general strike, September; increased activity in exports.
Money easy; exchange temporarily upset by war in Far East.
Fair wheat, good wine, and poor olive yields; abundant silk yield, much lower price.
Dispute with Austria.

1905 Prosperity.
Great economic progress; much speculation; active formation of new companies; foreign trade increases rapidly.
Great activity on stock exchange.
Poor wheat yield, wine failure, and record olive crop; smaller silk yield, higher price.
Enormous emigration.

1906 Prosperity.
Continued activity and expansion; volume of production increased; foreign trade booms.
Money tight; stock exchange dull with declining prices.
Good wheat crop; wine and olive failures; good silk yield, high price.
Further increase in emigration.

1907 Prosperity; recession.
Activity and expansion gradually yield to dullness, last quarter; decline most severe in automobile and textile industries; very active foreign trade.
Money tight; wild stock speculation to stock exchange panic, June, followed by rapid decline; severe financial strain.
Abundant crops; excellent silk yield, very high price collapses, last quarter.
Slackening emigration, and considerable return of migrants from America.

1908 Depression.
Dullness, most severe in cotton, silk, and automobile industries; other activities quiet; marked reduction in exports.
Money eases; stock exchange dull.
Very poor wheat crop, sharp rise in price; good wine yield; olive crop absolute failure; small silk yield, and very low price.
Violent anti-Austrian feeling, autumn; earthquake, December.

1909 Depression.
Stagnation in industries; severe distress in silk manufacture; some revival in foreign trade.
Money easy, tightening slightly in fall; stock exchange inactive.
Large wheat and record wine yields, excellent olive crop; very high wheat price; small silk yield, fair price.
Renewal of emigration.

1910 Mild depression.
Continued inactivity despite occasional signs of improvement; foreign trade active.
Money tightens severely; stock exchange boom, first five months, checked with rapid decline in values, autumn; some revival of speculation late in year.
Crop failures; very poor silk yield and low price.
Increased emigration.

1911 Revival halted, autumn.
Slow improvement checked by Turkish War; further increase in foreign trade.
Money tight; stock exchange dull with panic at outbreak of war.
Excellent wheat, poor wine and olive yields; severe distress in silk industry, small yield and low price.
War with Turkey over Tripoli declared, September; Italian successes.

1912 Uneven prosperity.
Increased activity in war industries; economic conditions dominated by war; big expansion in foreign trade; activity with peace halted by Balkan War.
Money tight; small premium on gold temporarily; stock exchange revives with peace, but is again depressed by Balkan War.
Poor wheat and wine crops, olive failure; good silk yield, very low price.
Peace declared with Turkey, October.

1913 Mild prosperity; recession.

Moderate activity; labor troubles; commodity prices reach peak; very extensive foreign trade.

Money tight; stock exchange dull.

Record wheat and wine crops, fair olive yield; revival in silk industry, small yield, higher price.

Record emigration.

1914 Recession; panic; depression.

Continual decline accentuated by war; industry disorganized; unemployment; commodity prices decline to July, and then rise; foreign trade restricted.

Easy money tightens with war; panic; moratorium; stock exchange closed; wild foreign exchange fluctuations.

Fair crops; very small silk yield, fair price.

Civil unrest; political difficulties due to activities of Socialist Party; riots and bloodshed, March; neutrality declared, August.

1915 Uneven depression.

Industrial stagnation due to severe shortage of raw materials, especially coal; some activity resulting from increased government expenditures and foreign purchases; very rapid rise in commodity prices; big increase in imports, exports slightly larger.

Money easy; exchange depreciates.

Fair wheat and olive yields, wine failure; small silk yield, low price.

Treaty of London, containing Allied promises, signed, April; political uproar and Italy declares war against Austria, May.

1916 War activity.

War industries prosper, others depressed; commodity price rise checked, but is resumed, last quarter; further large increase in imports.

Money easy; reopened stock exchanges begin with great activity and then decline; foreign exchange steady with temporary improvement.

Good wheat, fair wine, excellent olive yields; poor silk yield, rising price.

Severe defeats, spring, and some victories, autumn; general price control authorized, April; war against Germany declared, August.

1917 War activity.

Continued prosperity in war industries, and deeper depression in others; coal shortage severe; full employment; active promotion of new companies; rapidly rising commodity prices; further large increase in value of imports, slight increase in exports.

Money abundant, except during October and November panic; rapid decline in foreign exchange sets in, August; stock exchange dull.

Very poor wheat, excellent wine and olive crops; poor silk yield, very high price in summer.

Further successes, spring; autumn offensive fails; overwhelming Austrian victories, October; food shortage developing; riots, August, Turin; Allies send support late in year.

1918 War activity; slight recession.

Continued activity in war industries; commodity prices rise to peak, October, and then decline; continued activity in promotion of stock companies; balance of trade becomes even more unfavorable, with government requisitioning all imports, August.

Money easy; government attempt to stabilize exchange by monopoly fails, spring; arrangement with foreign nations, August, stabilizes exchange on much improved level.

Good wheat, fair wine, and record olive yields; high silk price with speculation, poor yield.

Austrian offensive checked, spring; Italian armies drive out Austrians in brilliant campaign, October; Armistice signed November.

1919 Mild depression; revival.

Dullness gradually yields to revival of activity; labor troubles; extensive unemployment early in year; commodity prices rise rapidly after first quarter; balance of trade improves with active export.

Money easy; rapid fall of exchange after removal of support, March; stock exchange booms, second and fourth quarters.

Fair crops; record small silk yield, price very high; very poor olive yield.

Fiume controversy; D'Annunzio seizes Fiume, September; capital levy adopted, November; civil unrest.

1920 Recession; depression.

Production limited by civil disturbances and coal famine; depression prevails, last quarter; continued labor disputes; commodity prices rise rapidly to April, peak in November; metal-workers seize factories, September; smaller imports and markedly increased exports.

Money rates higher; further decline in foreign exchange, temporary revival, summer; stock prices rise, first two months, and collapse, May.

Very poor wheat, good wine and olive crops; good silk yield, price collapses late in year.

Civil unrest; Fiume question still bothers; extensive emigration; severe earthquake, September.

1921 Depression; panic.

Severe recession leads to complete interruption of business and industry, summer; great increase in unemployment; commodity prices fall rapidly to June, ascribed to a "change in the 'bread policy' of the Government" and then recover somewhat; decrease in foreign trade.

Money rates high; important banking difficulties lead to failures and panic, December; stock prices decline to July, rise to October, and then fall sharply; foreign exchange improves, first half-year, and then declines.

Excellent wheat, fair wine and olive yields; large silk yield, much lower price.

D'Annunzio driven out of Fiume by force, January; higher tariff, July; emigration checked, summer.

1922 Depression.

Continued inactivity; slight improvement, mid-year, checked by political and civil disturbances; extensive unemployment; commodity prices fall to May, and then rise; imports decline, exports increase slightly.

Money eases; banking troubles continue early in year; stock exchange revives with advancing prices; foreign exchange improves, summer, and end of year.

Poor wheat, fair wine, and good olive yields; poor silk yield, rising price.

Fascisti march on Rome and Mussolini ministry formed, October.

1923 Depression; revival.

Gradual adjustment to new conditions; improvement becomes marked, last half-year; unemployment diminished; commodity prices steady; foreign trade more active.

Money rates firm; advance in stock prices, last half-year; continued decline in foreign exchange.

Excellent wheat and grape yields, poor olive return; excellent silk yield, good price.

Corfu occupied, August.

1924 Moderate prosperity.

Steady improvement with little unemployment and increased production, especially last half-year; rapid rise of commodity prices late in year; further increase in foreign trade, declining unfavorable balance.

Money tighter; rapid rise in stock prices; inflation of currency resumed at mid-year; slow and steady decline in exchange rate, especially late in year.

Poor wheat, fair olive and wine yields; silk price falls sharply with very large yield.

1925 Prosperity.

Activity and industrial progress; less unemployment; engineering trades strike, March; commodity prices advance rapidly, May to August, and then gradually decline; much larger foreign trade, very large unfavorable balance, especially first half-year.

Money market very tight, official discount rate being raised twice; stock prices reach peak, February, and decline severely to October; foreign exchange steady except for temporary slump, third quarter.

Excellent crops, especially wheat and rice; poor silk and olive yields; fair grape harvest; high prices, especially silk; wheat duty reëstablished, July.

United States debt funded, November.

CHAPTER X.

THE ANNALS OF ARGENTINA.

The Argentine Republic is a wedge-shaped country, occupying the greater part of southern South America. Its territory may be divided into three regions, the mountainous zone and tablelands in the west, the great plains or pampas in the east, and the desolate, arid steppes of Patagonia in the south.

The area of Argentina has varied from time to time as boundary disputes with other South American nations have been settled. On January 1, 1924, its area was 1,153,419 square miles.[1] The record of population growth of Argentina is as follows:

Date	Population [a]	Persons per Square Mile
Sept. 15, 1869 [b]	1,737,076	1.6 [c]
May 10, 1895 [b]	3,954,911	3.6 [c]
June 1, 1914 [d]	7,885,237	7.3 [c]
Jan. 1, 1924 [e]	9,556,072	8.3 [f]

[a] Data for "population counted". This figure is sometimes slightly increased by adding estimates for Indians, Argentines in foreign countries, and persons not counted.

[b] Argentine Republic Comisión directiva del Censo, *Segundo Censo de la República Argentina*. Buenos Aires, 1898. vol. ii, pp. XVII, CXXV.

[c] Computed from original data given in square kilometers by multiplying by 2.59.

[d] Argentine Republic Comisión directiva del Censo, *Tercer Censo Nacional*. Buenos Aires, 1916. vol. ii, pp. XII, 109.

[e] Official estimate in *Revista de Economía Argentina*, June, 1925. Buenos Aires. p. 441.

[f] Computed by means of the area stated above.

The period of largest immigration was the decade between 1880 and 1890. It is estimated that approximately 60 per cent of the population is rural, but that only 9 per cent of the total land area is under cultivation.

Argentina is chiefly an agricultural country. Alfalfa is the chief crop, but is used entirely for fodder. Three crops—wheat, corn, and linseed—dominate the agricultural situation. They are harvested in the early months of the year. The records of wheat and

[1] *Statesman's Year-book, 1925.* London, 1923. p. 672.

THE ANNALS OF ARGENTINA

corn are given through the entire annals of Argentina. The linseed crop is first noted in 1903, when there was a large expansion in its acreage. During the twenty years from 1892 to 1912, the area in all crops under cultivation increased seven-fold. The cereal crop area is in the central part, the cattle and sheep are in the south. The wool clip has decreased in importance in recent years, while the meat industry has increased rapidly. No direct record of production is available for either of these industries. However, since wool is clipped in the fall, and the bulk of the clip is exported, the export of the following year has been used as indicating the success of the clip.

Mining is of little importance in Argentina. The discovery of large fields of petroleum, however, has led to rapid development in that industry in the last few years.

Because of the shortage of coal, metals, and water power resources, Argentina is severely hampered in becoming an industrial nation. Manufacturing is not extensive, except in those industries which prepare raw material for shipment, such as meat packing, flour milling, wool scouring, sugar refining, and the like. During the war, the check to imports increased the activity of other home industries, but this force was somewhat offset by the poor agricultural yields during these same years.

The importance of Argentina's foreign trade is indicated by an estimate published in the *Revista de Economía Argentina*, April, 1925, p. 287. This estimate demonstrates that for the ten years 1910-1919, 59.7 per cent of Argentina's total national production was consumed in the country and 40.3 per cent was exported. Ordinarily, these exports consist of agricultural products, 55 to 60 per cent; animal products, 35 to 40 per cent; all others, less than 5 per cent. The chief articles of import are textiles, and iron and steel products; the more important exports are wheat, corn, linseed, wool, and frozen meat. Prior to 1890, the balance of trade was continually unfavorable, but, in more recent years, exports have generally exceeded imports.

The currency of Argentina was placed on a gold basis in 1899. Much of the banking business is carried on through branches of foreign banks. In 1922, there were 32 principal banks in Buenos Aires having over 300 branches and agencies. There are two state banks, the Banco de la Nacion and the Banco de la Provincia de Buenos Aires. References made in the annals to foreign exchange are based on exchange on London prior to 1915 and on New York City thereafter.

There has been little increase in the railroad mileage of Argentina since 1914. The rapidity of development prior to that time is indicated by the following table:

Year	Miles of Railways [a]
1890	5,861 [b]
1900	10,292 [b]
1910	17,495 [b]
1920	22,490 [c]

[a] Computed from original data given in kilometers by multiplying by 0.62137.
[b] Argentine Republic Dirección General de Ferrocarriles, *Estadística de los Ferrocarriles in Explotación, 1911*. Buenos Aires, 1915. pp. 305, 306.
[c] *Revista de Economía Argentina*, April, 1925. Buenos Aires. p. 292.

The development of Argentina has involved the use of enormous quantities of foreign capital. In 1913, over 90 per cent of the capital employed in railways was British.

In 1810, Argentina freed herself from Spanish dominion. A long period of anarchy and civil disturbance followed, and it was not until 1853 that stability was attained and a constitution declared. The war with Paraguay, 1865 to 1868, interrupted a period of steady development. After severe disturbances arising out of the election of 1880, practically a civil war, a period of rapid development and expansion set in. This boom period lasted through the decade and with its speculation and extravagant government expenditures, led up to the political, financial, industrial and commercial collapse of the early nineties.

1890   Recession; depression.

Sharp decline in industrial activity to stagnation; many failures; railroad construction boom checked; exports continue large, but imports decrease severely.

Marked financial stringency; much speculation; acute financial crisis begins, March; constant fluctuation in value of currency; depreciation increased by further issue of inconvertible notes; government finance collapses with failure of financial agents, Baring Brothers, November; many bank failures.

Good wheat and maize crops, and fair wool clip realize high prices.

Revolution, July, results in overthrow of President; great drop in immigration.

1891 Depression; panic.

Stagnation general, especially in construction; unemployment; maintenance of exports, with further decline in imports yields first favorable balance of trade in ten years.

Financial chaos; wide currency fluctuations with gradual fall in gold premium; bank failures and panic, June; moratorium for six months; feverish speculation.

Cereal crops small with fair prices; good wool clip, lower price.

Political unrest with riots and siege of capital, February, and revolts, May and July; low point in immigration.

1892 Revival; recession.

Improvement in all branches of industry, first half-year; relapse, autumn; revival in imports, and further increase in exports.

Money tight; currency steadier.

Wheat crop fair, maize good, wool clip small; prices decline.

High tariff established; slight increase in immigration; emigration begins.

1893 Mild depression.

Monetary and political difficulties cause dullness and inactivity; foreign trade declines, slight unfavorable balance.

Wide fluctuations in currency; record gold premium; point of greatest paper circulation reached; government finances unsettled.

Large wheat crop, poor maize crop, wool clip fair; prices decline further, except wool.

Civil war, January, and revolt, July, soon collapse; boundary treaty with Chile successfully negotiated.

1894 Depression.

Continued inactivity with many failures; dullness in foreign trade.

Tight money eases, end of year; continued monetary instability.

Large wheat crop, low price; maize crop small with good price; wool clip large with lower price; drought causes great loss to pastoral interests.

Severe drought; political difficulties between President and Congress cause President's resignation.

1895 Lessening depression.

Home industries continue severely depressed; slight revival in foreign trade.

Exchange slightly improved and more stable; government aids banks.

Smaller wheat crop, higher price; larger maize crop with lower price; good wool clip, very low price.

War scare with Chile.

1896 Revival.

Gradual improvement in trade and industry; sporadic failures; foreign trade improves, particularly imports.

Rapid appreciation in exchange; large gold imports; public finances embarrassed.

Further reduction in wheat crop with higher price; record maize with low price; large wool clip, price improved.

Dispute with Chile submitted to arbitration; influx of immigrants.

1897 Revival retarded.

Dullness; many failures early in year; foreign trade falls off.

Money tight to spring; rising exchange with wide fluctuations.

Cereal crops reduced by locusts, prices high; large wool clip with high price.

Cash payments on foreign debt resumed.

1898 Mild prosperity.

Steady improvement and expansion; return of confidence; foreign trade increases rapidly with large favorable balance.

Continued appreciation of currency; speculation.

Small wheat and good maize crops, sharply declining prices; record wool clip, high price.

Large reduction in immigration.

1899 Prosperity.

Continued increase in production and export; expansion in home industries.

Rapid appreciation of currency; currency stabilized, 44 gold pesos equaling 100 paper pesos.

Large harvests with low prices; wool clip small, high price.

1900 Recession; depression.

General decline into dullness; decrease in volume of foreign trade, especially exports.

Currency stable; government finance improves.

Large wheat crop and poor maize crop with rising prices; large wool clip with high price.

Export duties established.

1901 Depression.

Internal trade stagnant; many failures; commodity prices rise; foreign trade improves slightly.

Money market and exchange firm.

Poor wheat and excellent maize crops with rising prices; good wool clip, price falls sharply.

Floods; drought; political troubles; Chile war scare; large immigration.

1902 Depression; revival.

Continued inactivity, first half-year; general insecurity and uncertainty; sporadic failures; revival, autumn; large increase in exports and decline in imports.

Money easier.

Poor cereal crops with rising prices; wool clip good with high price.

Decline in immigration and increased emigration.

1903 Prosperity.

General activity and expansion; foreign trade records enormous increase.

Money abundant.

Cereal crops large with fair prices; increase in linseed crop with low price; wool clip fair, higher price; live-stock industries expand rapidly.

Beginning of period of large immigration.

1904 Prosperity.

No interruption to activity and expansion; foreign trade much increased.

Money abundant.

Very large crops with rising prices; wool clip fair, high price.

Strikes; tariff lowered; period of railroad expansion begins.

1905 Prosperity.

Activity and expansion continue; record favorable balance in foreign trade.

Money easy; extensive stock speculation.

Enormous wheat crop with slightly lower price; smaller maize crop, higher price; large linseed crop, price very high; wool clip poor, high price; meat export increases.

Emigration extensive; martial law due to threatened railroad strike, October.

1906 Prosperity.

Continued activity and growth; commodity prices rise to peak.

Money tightens, checking speculation.

Poor wheat and linseed crops, large maize and wool; prices rise, especially wool; export of live-stock prohibited because of hoof-and-mouth disease.

1907 Prosperity.

No check to widespread activity and expansion; slight increase in failures; commodity prices high; foreign trade increase continued.

Money tight.

Wheat crop abundant with high price; failure of maize due to drought, very high price; linseed crop good, price fair; good wool clip with high price; meat exports small.

Railroad strike, July; revolution, autumn.

1908 Mild recession.

Expansion less general; dullness in summer; prices high; foreign trade increases.

Money tight.

Large wheat and linseed crops; small maize crop; good wool clip; large meat exports; prices high.

Political unrest.

1909 Revival; prosperity.

Widespread prosperity in agriculture extends to other lines of activity; labor troubles, May; further increase in foreign trade.

Money eases.

Fair crops of wheat and maize, large linseed harvest; wool clip fair; meat exports increase; prices very high.

Drought and locusts; political unrest leads to declaration of martial law for sixty days, November.

1910 Prosperity.

Domestic trade and industry active and expanding; general strike, May, causes temporary confusion; land speculation; commodity prices lower; volume of foreign trade increases, especially imports.

Money tightens.

Poor wheat and linseed crops with high prices; good maize crop, lower price; poor wool clip, price high; meat exports show large increase.

Severe drought late in year.

1911 Recession; mild depression.

Gradual recession to dullness; many important failures; volume of exports falls off sharply, resulting in unfavorable balance.

Money tight; exchange weak.

Crops very poor; prices low, except linseed which reaches high point; good wool clip at lower price; meat exports continue to increase.

Difficulties with Italy check immigration; emigration increases.

THE ANNALS OF ARGENTINA

1912 Depression; revival, autumn.

General improvement, especially in foreign trade; large favorable balance; commodity prices advance; many strikes.

Money continues tight.

Excellent wheat and maize crops, linseed poor; wheat price rises, maize and linseed prices very low; period of smaller wool clips begins; meat export increases.

Drought; immigration revives.

1913 Recession.

Slackening industrial activity; promotion of new companies; much speculation; commodity prices rise sharply; many failures; unusually large imports.

Money very tight.

Large wheat and maize crops with good prices, excellent linseed crop, very low price; crisis in meat export due to low prices.

1914 Depression; panic.

Period of liquidation with many failures gives way to general paralysis at outbreak of war; decrease in volume of foreign trade, especially imports; scarcity of shipping facilities late in year.

Collapse of real estate speculation, March; financial stringency with panic and moratorium, August; foreign exchange rises, spring, but collapses, autumn; stock exchange dull.

Very small wheat crop with high prices; good maize and linseed crops, prices low; export of meat increases slightly.

Peace treaty signed with Brazil and Chile; immigration falls below emigration.

1915 Uneven depression.

Boom in industries receiving war orders, stagnation in others; many failures; rapid rise in commodity prices; foreign trade records further decrease in imports and large increase in exports.

Exchange rises to April, then drops to low point, September.

Excellent crops with high prices; wool clip increases; meat exports small.

Bitter political campaign; further decrease in immigration.

1916 Depression; slow revival.

Business continues slack; slow improvement evident, summer; lack of confidence; commodity price rise continues; volume of foreign trade reduced but value increased, particularly imports.

Financial condition sound; exchange fluctuates slightly above par.

Poor crops, especially maize; prices high; marked increase in meat exports.

Droughts and locusts.

1917 Revival.
Gradual improvement; agricultural depression retards expansion of home industries; revival of activity accelerated, autumn; railroad strike, autumn; foreign trade volume reduced.
Money abundant; exchange very favorable.
General crop failures; prices high; meat exports continue large.
Export of food-stuffs prohibited.

1918 Moderate prosperity.
General activity with improvement in agricultural conditions; very low imports, exports increase largely with favorable balance.
Money easy; exchange reaches peak, May.
Large wheat, fair maize and poor linseed crops bring high prices; wool clip large; meat exports reach peak.
Serious labor disturbances threatened late in year.

1919 Prosperity.
Uncertainty in spring gives way to general boom; slight drop in commodity prices early in year, followed by gradual rise; serious labor troubles; great increase in foreign trade with record favorable balance.
Exchange falls; slight improvement, October.
Fair crops with good prices; wool clip small; meat exports continue large.
End of period of excess of emigration over immigration, and beginning of period of rapidly increasing immigration.

1920 Prosperity; recession.
General activity and prosperity; commodity prices continue to rise; wages advance; boom ends and prices fall near end of year; strikes, November; foreign trade large, with great increase in imports.
Money continues easy; exchange rises to peak, spring, and then falls, passing par in June, to low point in November.
Very large crops bring excellent prices; meat industry severely depressed.
Earthquake, December.

1921 Depression.
Severe depression; many failures; railroads in financial difficulties; labor troubles; commodity prices continue decline; foreign trade decreases; unfavorable balance.
Money tight; exchange rises to February, falls sharply to July, and then rises again.
Abundant corn and linseed crops, low prices; meat industry continues depressed.
Riots, May.

THE ANNALS OF ARGENTINA

1922 Depression.
Liquidation with little activity and many failures; commodity prices decline; temporary revival, summer; further decline in foreign trade.
Money eases; foreign exchange steady after improving, first quarter.
Fair crops with higher prices; livestock industry continues severely depressed.
Uncertainty precedes Presidential election, April.

1923 Lessening depression.
Uneven improvement; building construction boom; decrease in number of failures; commodity price decline slackens; large increase in imports creates unfavorable balance of trade.
Money tightens; exchange improves to March, falls sharply to November.
Good wheat, very poor maize, and fair linseed crops; prices improve; meat export large.
Large immigration.

1924 Revival.
General revival of activity; continued commodity price decline; building continues brisk; many failures early in year; increase in exports enormous, decrease in imports, favorable balance.
Foreign exchange rises rapidly with temporary halt in late summer.
Large crops with higher prices; small wool clip, price very high; large meat exports.
Reorganization of State Railways; smaller migration.

1925 Prosperity.
Domestic trade active; construction slackens; increased failures in textile industry, last quarter; much smaller exports, slightly larger imports.
Money fairly tight; exchange declines to April, and then recovers nearly to parity; export of gold permitted, May; stock exchange quiet, prices firm.
Smaller crops of wheat and oats, good linseed yield; small wool clip; higher wheat, lower linseed, oats, and wool prices; marked increase in sugar production.
Declining immigration.

CHAPTER XI.

THE ANNALS OF BRAZIL.

The Brazilian Empire, an absolute monarchy, was overthrown in 1889. The United States of Brazil, according to the Constitution adopted in 1891, comprises twenty states, one Federal District, and the Territory of Acre, acquired in 1903 by treaty with Bolivia. The United States of Brazil includes 43 per cent of the continent of South America, and 48 per cent of its population. The bulk of the country lies in the basin of the Amazon River and is tropical in character, but there are also extensive plateaus along the coast and in the southern districts.

The area of Brazil is 3,286,170 square miles,[1] ranking as the fourth largest country in the world. The total population in recent years is given in the following table:

Census Date	Population	Persons per Square Mile
August 1, 1872	10,112,061 [a]	3.1 [d]
Dec. 31, 1890	14,333,915 [a]	4.4 [b]
Dec. 31, 1900	17,318,556 [a]	5.3 [b]
Dec. 31, 1910	23,414,177 [c]	7.1 [b]
Sept. 1, 1920	30,635,605 [a]	9.3 [d]

[a] Official census record. Brazil Directoria Geral de Estatistica, *Synopse do Recenseamento em 1 de Setembro de 1920*. Rio de Janeiro, 1924. p. 67 and vol. i, p. 412 of the *Report*.
[b] Brazil Directoria Geral de Estatistica, *Annuaire Statistique du Bresil*, 1908-1912. Rio de Janeiro, 1916. Vol. i. p. 254. Computed from original data given in square kilometers by multiplying by 2.59.
[c] *Ibid.*, p. 252. Official estimate.
[d] Computed from area given above.

The increase in population is chiefly due to natural growth, the total immigration for the 100 years prior to 1922 totaling only 3,774,450 persons. Only 15.6 per cent of the population is urban, the remainder living in small towns or rural districts.

Brazil is essentially an agricultural country, although, even in-

[1] Brazil Directoria Geral de Estatistica, *Summary of Some Financial and Economic Statistics*. Rio de Janeiro, 1924. p. 7. Computed from original data in square kilometers by multiplying by 0.3861.

cluding rubber and cocoa forests, but one-fifth of its area is under cultivation. By far the most important commodity produced is coffee. The coffee region in southern Brazil supplies four-fifths of the world's requirements. The coffee crop is harvested in the fall, but often does not reach the market until the following year. Because of this interval, a crop is named according to these two years. In these annals, the crop is discussed as of the year in which it is harvested. Since 1897, when the coffee crop was unusually large, the government, particularly that of the state of São Paulo, has entered the coffee market during periods when the industry was near collapse, and has purchased and withdrawn large quantities of coffee from the market. This process is known as valorization. The cultivation of rubber in northern Brazil, chiefly in the Amazon basin, became important in the nineties, but since the development of enormous plantations in the East Indies, the Brazilian industry has suffered. During the war, agriculture developed rapidly along other lines, sugar, cotton, cocoa, rice, and cattle-raising becoming increasingly important. The production of wheat, rye, and barley is small and insufficient for home demands.

Manufacturing industries have developed slowly in Brazil. In 1920, there were 13,423 factories with 356,615 employees. Before the war, the textile industry was the only one of note, but the war gave impetus to many others. The mineral resources are very rich, especially iron and manganese, but they are chiefly undeveloped.

Construction of the first railway was begun in 1852. The following table gives the length of railroads in operation:

December 31,—	Miles of Railways [a]
1880	2,112
1890	6,198
1900	9,519
1910	13,342
1920	17,747

[a] Brazil Directoria de Estatistica Commercial, *Economical Data about Brazil*. Rio de Janeiro, 1924.

Approximately 57 per cent of the railway mileage is owned by the Federal Government, and an additional 10 per cent by the various States.

For the first fifteen years covered by the annals, there was little increase in the total value of goods entering into foreign trade. Since 1905, however, there has been gradual expansion. During the entire period, only five years reported an unfavorable balance of trade. Coffee constitutes about two-thirds of the total exports. Rubber, which was second in importance, has been displaced since the war by sugar, cotton, and hides and skins. Important imports are wheat, metal products, and cotton goods.

The leading bank is the semi-official Banco do Brasil, organized in 1905. Acting at first as a purely commercial bank and as fiscal agent of the Government, in 1923 it was made a central bank of issue, and began issuing notes in July, 1923. There are a number of other large domestic banks, with little government supervision. Banks controlled by foreign capital are also prominent. References made in the annals to foreign exchange are based on rates on London prior to 1914, and New York City thereafter.

The history of Brazil has been dominated by political and monetary uncertainties. Extensive foreign borrowing and a costly government resulted in a depreciated currency and continual fiscal difficulties. In 1822, Brazil separated from Portugal. After a period of unsteadiness, Dom Pedro II ascended the throne in 1840, and reigned until 1889. The war with Paraguay, 1865-1872, exhausted the country and was followed by a long and severe depression. The decade 1880-1889 was prosperous, but the revolution of November, 1889, whereby Dom Pedro II was dethroned and a republic formed, although very quiet, nevertheless introduced a period of depression.

1890   Depression.

Little industrial activity; speculative promotion of new companies; falling off in foreign trade.

Great increase in note issues with establishment of banks of issue, January; speculation; money tight with Baring crisis, November; marked fall in foreign exchange.

Small coffee crop, good price.

Revolution continues; decline in immigration.

1891   Depression.

General paralysis of home trade; commodity prices rise rapidly; reduction in foreign trade.

Currency inflation fosters speculation; further sharp drop in exchange; banking and government finance in unsound condition.

Coffee crop fair, falling price; good rubber yield.

Constitution promulgated, February; civil war, November, with settling up and overthrow of Fonseca's dictatorship; record immigration.

1892 Depression.

Little industrial activity; home trade stagnant; foreign trade improves with large favorable balance.

Further currency inflation; continued decline in exchange.

Agricultural depression lessened by excellent coffee crop with rising price and good rubber yield.

Political situation unsettled with continual riots and revolts; decided falling off in immigration.

1893 Depression.

Home trade continues inactive; large increase in imports but greater decline in exports.

Financial situation grows worse; foreign exchange fall slackens.

Small coffee crop, high price; fair rubber yield.

Unrest, February, requires martial law; serious insurrections, September, with naval bombardment of Rio de Janeiro.

1894 Revival.

Improvement in industry and domestic trade; great excess of imports.

Exchange decline checked by sharp rise, August.

Coffee crop very large; good rubber yield; good prices.

Election of President, March; insurrections quelled, April; further decline in immigration.

1895 Mild prosperity.

Increased activity and expansion hampered by transportation shortage; large foreign trade with favorable balance.

Rising but fluctuating exchange.

Excellent crops with higher prices.

Political calm except for brief rebellion, spring; great increase in immigration.

1896 Recession; panic; depression.

Industrial activity slackens; crisis, October; general paralysis; many failures, particularly railroads; decline in foreign trade, excess of imports.

Increasing financial strain leads to panic, October; exchange depressed; government finances embarrassed.

Good coffee crop with very low price; merchants combine to suspend coffee exports, July; small rubber yield with slightly higher price.

Yellow fever epidemic, summer; anti-Italian demonstrations with internal riots; Italian immigration restricted.

1897 Depression; panic, October.

Inactivity in home trade; failures decrease; foreign trade shows large favorable balance.

Money tight; currency depreciates; financial panic, October, precipitated by agricultural situation; public finance very unsatisfactory; sharp drop in foreign exchange to low level.

Enormous coffee crop with very low price causes São Paulo government to undertake valorization; good rubber yield with slightly higher price.

Rebellion and martial law, November.

1898 Depression deepens.

Increased depression in home trade; many failures; foreign trade maintained.

Financial distress; wild fluctuations in exchange; suspension of specie payments; government's creditors agree to moratorium, June, when Rothschild's loan stabilizes government finance; period of currency inflation ends.

Large coffee crop further depresses price; fair rubber yield, high price.

Improved political conditions with suppression of rebellion, February; period of lessened immigration begins.

1899 Depression; revival.

Home trade shows improvement, autumn; foreign trade declines.

Exchange falls sharply, reviving late in year; speculation; improvement in public finance.

Large coffee crop with higher price; large rubber yield, price very high.

Plague.

1900 Revival; panic; recession.

Increase in activity checked by financial situation, autumn; bank failures, September, cause general disorganization; further decline in foreign trade.

Widespread speculation; sharp financial and monetary panic, September, with collapse of Bank of Brazil; after gradual rise, foreign exchange drops, last quarter.

Large coffee crop with fair price; rubber yield very poor, price extremely high; government assists rubber industry by subsidies.

1901   Mild depression.
        Home trade quiet; foreign trade increases with large favorable balance.
        Money very tight; exchange recovers and rises gradually; government resumes gold payments on debt, June.
        Enormous coffee crop with rising price; fair rubber yield, lower price.

1902   Mild depression.
        Home trade recovery checked by agricultural depression; sporadic failures; foreign trade declines.
        Foreign exchange firm.
        Excellent coffee crop with low price depresses coffee industry; poor rubber yield, low price.
        Government begins extensive railroad construction.

1903   Depression deepens.
        Decline in home and foreign trade; many banks and planters fail.
        Money very tight; financial panic; fall in exchange.
        Good coffee crop, fair rubber yield; prices low; São Paulo prohibits new coffee plantations.
        Settlement of Bolivia boundary dispute increases area 60,000 square miles.

1904   Depression.
        Gradual liquidation; many failures; slight improvement in foreign trade.
        Money tight; foreign exchange steady.
        Small coffee crop and fair rubber yield with higher prices.
        Distress and revolt.

1905   Depression.
        Inactivity in home trade; many failures; decided decline in foreign trade.
        Money tight; rising exchange; Bank of Brazil organized.
        Poor coffee crop at low price causes great distress; rubber yield good with slightly higher price.

1906   Slow revival.
        Home trade quiet but improving; increase in foreign trade with large favorable balance.
        Money easier; exchange steadies and is put on gold basis, December.
        Record coffee crop with very low price; government enters market; average rubber yield with lower price.

BUSINESS ANNALS

1907 Revival; recession.
Reviving home trade relapses, autumn, with many failures; foreign trade improves.
Money tight and credit restricted; exchange steady.
Large coffee crop with low price; increased rubber yield, lower price.
Japanese agreement stimulates Japanese immigration.

1908 Depression.
Domestic trade sluggish; rubber boom begins; marked decline in foreign trade with slight improvement late in year.
Money tight; foreign exchange steady.
Fair coffee crop; large rubber yield; prices low, improving late in year.
Tariff reduction, January; large immigration.

1909 Revival.
Home trade improves with rubber boom; record volume and favorable balance in foreign trade.
Paper currency fluctuation; exchange steady.
Good coffee crop with improved prices revives coffee industry; large rubber yield with high price.

1910 Prosperity.
Decided improvement in home trade; rubber boom continues; foreign trade maintained.
Money abundant; exchange rises, summer, but suddenly drops, December.
Record low coffee crop with higher price; excellent rubber yield, record price.
Brief naval mutinies, November and December.

1911 Prosperity.
Active home trade and improved foreign trade.
Exchange firm on higher level.
Small coffee crop with high price brings prosperity to coffee trade; good rubber yield, price drops sharply late in year; tobacco and sugar crops fail.
Increase in immigration.

1912 Prosperity; recession.
Continued activity retarded late in year; commodity prices very high but profits curtailed; speculative land boom; volume of foreign trade increases.
Exchange steady.
Poor coffee crop and falling price; record rubber yield with lower price.
Further increase in immigration.

1913 Depression.

Gradually declining industrial activity accelerated by agricultural difficulties; land boom terminates; many failures; large but unfavorable foreign trade.

Money very tight; financial strain severe, autumn; government finances unsound.

Small coffee crop and fair rubber yield; sharp decline in prices; "plantation" rubber exceeds Brazilian yield for first time; government adjusts taxation to aid rubber industry.

Immigration peak.

1914 Depression deepens.

Home trade paralyzed; many important failures; severe decline in foreign trade.

Continued financial strain; foreign debt defaulted, August, and Rothschild organizes funding scheme; falling foreign exchange collapses, October, when low is reached for war period; moratorium.

Poor crops; coffee prices falling; rubber prices very low.

Rebellion, February.

1915 Depression; revival.

General inactivity; improvement late in year; exports maintained, imports very small.

Money tight; exchange recovers; moratorium extended.

Large coffee crop with fair price; fair rubber yield, sharp rise in price, November.

England restricts coffee imports.

1916 Revival; prosperity.

Trade brisk and expanding along new lines; commodity prices rise; foreign trade improves.

Money eases; exchange more favorable; public finances improve.

Coffee crop good with falling price; poor rubber yield, price rises gradually after collapse at beginning of year.

Revolt suppressed, April.

1917 Prosperity.

Trade sound and active; expansion; commodity price rise continues.

Money plentiful; exchange improves strongly.

Coffee crop poor with low price; rubber yield excellent, price high; government undertakes coffee valorization.

Coffee consumption restricted in United States; Brazil enters war, October.

1918 Prosperity; brief recession.

Expansion in home industry continues; confusion, Armistice, gives way to gradual readjustment; great activity in foreign trade retarded by shipping shortage.

Active security speculation; falling foreign exchange rises rapidly after Armistice; export of specie prohibited.

Record low crops, frost killing one-half coffee-bearing trees, June; prices rise.

1919 Prosperity.

Domestic expansion continues unchecked; commodity prices high; large volume of foreign trade.

Exchange rises rapidly to peak, December; speculation.

Good coffee crop, price peak, July; excellent rubber yield with declining price.

1920 Prosperity; recession; depression.

Continued activity; general strike, March; commodity prices rise, then fall rapidly, summer; commodity speculation; industrial activity checked, autumn; peak year in foreign trade, particularly imports.

Exchange falls slowly to June, then very rapidly.

Poor crops; sharp fall in coffee and rubber prices causes distress.

Heavy immigration.

1921 Severe depression.

Little activity; many commercial and financial failures; commodity prices decline; exports maintained, imports fall off severely.

Financial strain; exchange declines to July, then recovers slightly.

Good coffee crop and very low prices cause government to undertake valorization; rubber yield very small and price low.

1922 Lessening depression.

Gradual improvement hampered by political and monetary conditions; imports continue small, exports revive.

Further decline in exchange late in year.

Good coffee crop, but continued low prices require further government aid; rubber yield increases with slightly improved price.

Political disturbances, June and July.

1923 Revival.
Decided improvement in domestic trade; local industries flourish; foreign trade increases.

Money tight; brief panic with bank failures, June; further decline in exchange to low point in November; Treasury transfers authority to issue currency to Bank of Brazil.

Good coffee crops and price; coffee panic, July, when government leaves market; rubber yield very small, good price.

Widespread civil unrest.

1924 Mild prosperity; recession.

Increased activity and expansion in domestic industry, first half-year; dislocation of trade and commerce, second half-year; severe transportation shortage; commodity prices rise; increase in volume of foreign trade in spite of serious port congestion; favorable balance maintained.

Money tight, especially last half-year; exchange improves to February, falls to August, then rises; revolt, November, causes thirty days' moratorium.

Fair coffee crop with sharply rising price; coffee plague appears; rubber yield high, price low.

Political difficulties and revolutions, July and November.

1925 Depression.

Continued dullness; transportation troubles and water shortage with consequent lack of power hamper manufacturing; urban unemployment and rural labor shortage; commodity prices rise; increased foreign trade with large unfavorable balance early in year.

Money very tight, especially autumn; foreign exchange declines, first half-year, and then recovers strongly; marked reduction in currency in circulation and restriction of bank credit.

Increased rubber output, very high prices; good coffee yield, prices high under government regulation of export.

Gradual suppression of revolt; continuance of martial law; Colombia boundary dispute settled, February.

CHAPTER XII.

THE ANNALS OF CANADA.

The Dominion of Canada includes the entire northern half of North America, with the exception of Alaska, which belongs to the United States, and Newfoundland and Labrador, which constitute a separate British colony. Canada is shaped like a huge trough, mountains to the east and west, and plains in the center, sloping gently to the shallow basin of Hudson Bay. There are excellent harbors on both coasts, and the Great Lakes and St. Lawrence River form an important waterway to the Atlantic Ocean. Activity along many lines is necessarily seasonal because of the severity of the winter climate.

The land area of Canada is 3,603,909 square miles,[1] nearly equaling the total area of Europe, or that of the continental United States. The census records of population are as follows:

Census Date	Population [a]	Persons per Square Mile [b]
April 2, 1871	3,689,257	1.0
April 4, 1881	4,324,810	1.2
April 6, 1891	4,833,239	1.3
April 1, 1901	5,371,315	1.5
June 1, 1911	7,206,643	2.0
June 1, 1921	8,788,483	2.4

[a] Canada Dominion Bureau of Statistics, *Sixth Census of Canada, 1921*. Ottawa, 1924. vol. i, p. 3.

[b] Computed by means of the area given above. No boundary changes made during the period were of sufficient importance to affect the results materially.

A large part of the increase in recent years is due to immigration. In 1897, the first year of official record, the number of immigrants totaled 21,716. It had increased to 402,432 persons in the record year, which ended March 31, 1913. Of the total population enumerated in 1891, 31.80 per cent were in cities, towns and incorporated villages. In 1921, 49.52 per cent were classed as urban.

[1] Canada Dominion Bureau of Statistics, *The Canada Year Book, 1924*. Ottawa, 1925. p. 90.

The following table gives the value of products for each industry in 1922. Since these figures do not include the values produced by the transportation, trade, public service, personal service, and professional groups, they cannot be taken to indicate the "national income". The figures for net value represent the gross value minus the value of materials consumed in the process.

Industry	Value of Products, 1922 [a] (millions of dollars)	
	Gross	Net
Agriculture	1,499	1,149
Forestry	362	266
Fishing	53	42
Mining	184	177
Construction	339	220
Manufacturing [b]	2,420	1,131
Other [c]	190	157
Total [d]	4,661	2,951

[a] Canada Dominion Bureau of Statistics, *The Canada Year Book, 1924*. Ottawa, 1925. p. 184.
[b] Includes dairy factories, saw mills, pulp mills, fish-canning and curing, shipbuilding and certain mineral industries also included under other headings.
[c] Includes trapping, electric power, and custom and repair industries.
[d] Because of duplication among the various items, the total does not equal the sum of the individual industries.

Manufacturing has reached its present position of importance in Canadian industry only since the War. In 1921, when agricultural depression was most severe, the net product of manufacturing actually exceeded that of farming. However, agriculture has always been the dominating activity in Canadian economic life. Wheat, oats, potatoes, barley, rye, and flax are the most important crops. The first two crops account for nearly two-thirds of the entire acreage planted. That the acreage under cultivation has increased very rapidly is shown by the fact that in 1901 there were 30 million acres of improved land, and by 1921, such area had increased to nearly 71 million acres. Wheat is harvested chiefly in the autumn, although fall wheat, harvested in the spring, is important in the province of Ontario.

Canada is very rich in forests and has profited in recent years to a marked degree as an indirect result of the early stripping of forests in the United States. In addition to the production of lumber, lathe, and shingles, the manufacture of wood pulp and paper has developed rapidly since 1911, and these products are of considerable importance as exports to the United States. The mineral products of Canada are varied, but for the period of the annals coal has been the most important. In 1924, the mining products ranked as follows, according to the value of the output: coal, gold, nickel, silver, lead, cement, and copper. In earlier years, copper and asbestos were relatively more important. The Klondike gold discoveries resulted in a rapid increase of gold output to 1900, since which year it has slowly declined.

Manufacturing has developed to a marked degree despite the ease with which products can be obtained from the industrial centers of the United States and Great Britain. In 1922, there were 22,184 manufacturing establishments in Canada, with 462,573 employees. The wood and paper industries employ the largest number of workers.

The foreign trade of Canada has shown remarkable growth, particularly since 1896. Prior to the War, the balance was continuously unfavorable, except for the years 1894 to 1903, and 1920. Wheat and wheat flour dominate the export trade, followed by newsprint and raw lumber. The most important imports are coal and coke, iron and steel, and machinery. For the year ending March 31, 1923, which may be compared with the data given in the table Value of Production above, the exports of Canadian products totaled 931 million dollars, and the imports 803 million dollars.

The shifting importance of Canadian industries can best be shown by the proportions of the working population engaged in the various industries. Unfortunately, no figures are available, which might record the increase in manufacturing during the War.

Industry	Persons Engaged in Gainful Occupations [a] (per cent of total)		
	1891	1901	1911
Agriculture	45.8	40.2	34.3
Manufacturing	14.1	15.4	18.0
Building Trades	11.6	12.0	9.0
Trade and Merchandising	6.8	9.0	10.0
Transportation	4.3	4.5	8.0
Mining	1.0	1.6	2.3
Other [b]	16.4	17.3	18.0
Total	100.0	100.0	100.0

[a] Canada Dominion Bureau of Statistics, *The Canada Year Book, 1924*. Ottawa, 1925. p. 661.

[b] Includes persons engaged in domestic and personal service, civil and municipal government, fishing and hunting, forestry, professions, and miscellaneous activities.

Perhaps the most important single aid in the rapid development of Canada of recent years, has been the opening of new railroad lines. The first transcontinental railroad, the Canadian Pacific, was completed in 1885. Railroad construction has employed many thousands of workers. Much valuable territory has been made available for settlement. The mileage operated during the years under consideration has been as follows: [a]

Date	Miles of Railroad in Operation	
	Steam	Electric
June 30, 1881.................	7,331	....[b]
June 30, 1891.................	13,838	....[b]
June 30, 1901.................	18,140	553
June 30, 1911.................	25,400	1,224
Dec. 31, 1921.................	39,771	1,687

[a] Canada Dominion Bureau of Statistics, *The Canada Year Book, 1924.* Ottawa, 1925. pp. 588, 601.
[b] No records reported.

There has been a definite tendency toward government operation of the railways in recent years. In 1923, 55 per cent of all lines were government owned.

The banking system of Canada is based upon a small number of chartered banks with many branches. At the close of 1924, there were 12 chartered banks with 4,422 branches throughout the country. That the tendency is toward amalgamation is shown by the fact that there were 24 banks in 1914. These banks coöperate informally in the Canadian Bankers Association. The various government Bank Acts restrict the activity of banks, but there is no direct government control.

The record of business in Canada prior to 1890, is very similar to that of the United States and England. In general, it can be said that agricultural conditions played a more important part and that crises were not as sharp and severe as in other countries. Canada has had very few panics. After a long period of prosperity, Canadian business suffered a collapse in 1837, followed by depression. Business revived in 1844 and was moderately prosperous until the next recession in 1848. The ensuing depression was very short, the period from 1850 to 1856 recording a tremendous expansion in trade and industry. The collapse in 1857 was also followed by a short depression. After a period of moderate expansion, checked temporarily in 1866, Canadian business entered upon years of active prosperity and expansion.

This continued to 1873, when the severe disturbances in other countries were gradually felt. By 1875, Canada was in a state of depression, which was unbroken until the fall of 1879. Activity and speculation in the next three years led to a severe crisis in 1882 with the completion of the Canadian Pacific construction work, and the collapse of the Manitoba land boom. The ensuing depression gave way to some revival in 1885, but several important bank failures in 1887 and 1888, and very poor crops in 1888 and 1889, prevented further advance. The annals begin, therefore, with Canada in a state of mild depression.

1890   Mild depression.

General dullness and inactivity; many failures; foreign trade active with large unfavorable balance.

Money easier; important banking legislation.

Large crops with high prices.

Northwest Territories granted responsible government.

1891   Depression; revival.

Continued dullness gives way to increased activity, autumn; commodity prices decline; some increase in exports.

Money fairly easy.

Large crops with high wheat and lower oats prices.

1892   Mild prosperity.

Moderate activity in domestic trade; commodity price decline continues; period of rapid expansion in foreign trade begins with large increase in exports.

Money easy.

Fair crops with lower prices.

Active immigration; Behring Sea Seal Fisheries dispute with United States submitted to arbitration.

1893   Recession; depression.

Slowly decreasing business activity seriously restricted, autumn; commodity price decline slackens; many failures late in year; further large increase in exports.

Easy money tightens.

Good harvests; very low wheat price; higher oats.

THE ANNALS OF CANADA 301

1894 Acute depression.
Severe industrial depression; sharp decline in commodity prices; many failures; restriction of foreign trade, especially imports, favorable balance.
Money eases.
Poor crops, very low prices.
Tariff reduced.

1895 Depression.
Continued stagnation in domestic industry; slight decline in commodity prices; foreign trade reaches low point.
Money easy.
Large crops; some recovery in wheat price, further decline in oats.
New Sault Ste. Marie Canal opened, September.

1896 Lessening depression.
Continued dullness in domestic trade; further decline in commodity prices; increased number of failures; foreign trade revives, especially exports.
Money easy.
Fair crops; wheat price higher but oats very low.
Immigration at low point; Klondike gold discoveries, August; excited election puts Liberals in office.

1897 Revival.
Marked improvement appears; rapid expansion in mining industry; commodity price decline checked; further expansion of foreign trade.
Money easy.
Good crops and higher prices.
Gold stampede, May; period of rapid increase in immigration begins; Behring Sea arbitration award favors United States.

1898 Prosperity.
General activity; commodity prices rise; very active foreign trade.
Money abundant.
Large harvests; wheat price declines, oats rises.
Further gold discoveries in British Columbia; tariff with British preference goes into force, August.

1899 Prosperity.
Marked activity and expansion; further rise in commodity prices; increase in imports and decrease in exports.
Money tightens slightly.
Good crops; further decline in wheat price and rise in oats.
Canada enters Boer War, sending troops, October.

1900　　Prosperity; slight recession.

Continued activity, with decline in autumn; commodity price rise checked late in year; gold production reaches maximum; boom in foreign trade.

Money fairly tight.

Failure of wheat crop, oats fair; prices high.

Ottawa fire, April; drought, autumn.

1901　　Revival; prosperity.

Enormous expansion in domestic industries; extensive construction; commodity prices lower; small increase in foreign trade.

Money eases with introduction of much foreign capital.

Very large wheat crop, good oats; high prices.

1902　　Prosperity, with financial distress.

Great activity and expansion; full employment and many new enterprises organized; commodity price rise resumed; speculation; large increase in foreign trade.

Money tightens, autumn; rapidly rising security prices collapse, October; slight panic with some bank failures.

Agriculture prosperous with exceptional crops and good prices.

Increased immigration.

1903　　Prosperity.

Continued activity and progress; very few failures; commodity prices steady; coal shortage early in year; large increase in foreign trade.

Money tight; stock market depressed with falling security prices.

Small wheat, larger oats crop; good prices.

Immigration boom; Alaskan boundary dispute settled in favor of United States, October.

1904　　Uneven prosperity.

Continued prosperity in trade and manufacturing; fishing and lumbering depressed; construction boom; increase in business failures; commodity prices continue steady; imports increase and exports decline, creating unfavorable balance.

Money eases; continued stock market depression.

Poor wheat, good oats crop; favorable prices.

1905　　Full prosperity.

Great activity and expansion; prices steady; further increase in unfavorable balance of trade.

Money easy; security prices rise.

Excellent crops, good prices.

Provinces of Alberta and Saskatchewan created, September.

1906 Prosperity.

Continued activity and expansion; industrial boom; commodity prices advance rapidly; labor shortage; severe coal dispute causes coal famine; extensive railroad construction; enormous increase in foreign trade.

Money tightens; stock prices steady.

Large crops, high prices.

Cobalt mining rush.

1907 Prosperity; panic; recession.

Continued activity and expansion slackens, autumn; land speculation collapses; commodity prices reach unprecedented levels; foreign trade very large, especially imports.

Money tightens; financial stringency, autumn, leads to panic, October; gradual decline in security prices.

Crop failures, high prices.

Industrial Disputes Investigation Act, March; immigration reaches peak; active anti-Japanese agitation.

1908 Depression; revival.

Curtailment of activity gives way to improvement, last quarter; severe depression in manufacturing; many failures; sharp decline in commodity prices; relapse in foreign trade, especially imports.

Tight money eases late in year; inactive stock market.

Bountiful crops; excellent prices.

Land Act encouraging homesteading creates great rush to Northwest Territory, September.

1909 Revival.

Gradual improvement becomes pronounced, summer; manufacturing active; failures continue numerous; commodity price rise resumed; period of rapid expansion of imports begins.

Money easy; revival of security markets.

Excellent crops; high prices.

1910 Prosperity.

General activity and expansion; active railroad and building construction; commodity prices rise; fewer failures; exports decline, large increase in imports.

Money tight, autumn; stock exchange activity halts temporarily, summer.

Poor yields; prices decline.

Record immigration.

1911 Prosperity.
Increased volume of domestic and foreign trade; building activity continued; active land speculation; many new enterprises organized; large unfavorable balance of trade.
Money eases; stocks boom.
Excellent crops; wheat price falls, oats rises.
Drought; active immigration; Conservative party returned to power.

1912 Prosperity.
Record activity in many lines; active building and exceptional mining and manufacturing outputs; active speculation; commodity prices rise; further large expansion in foreign trade.
Money tightens severely late in year; security prices reach peak and then decline.
Excellent harvests, low prices.
Record immigration.

1913 Prosperity; recession.
Activity continues, first half-year, and then gradually slackens; speculation checked; many failures; price rise halted; unemployment appears late in year; large exports, imports decline.
Money very tight; stock markets depressed.
Excellent harvests, better prices.
Bank Act establishes central gold reserve.

1914 Depression, deepening with war.
Increasing dullness becomes stagnation with war, August; extensive unemployment; slow rise in commodity prices; many failures; great reduction in foreign trade, favorable balance.
Money tight, stringent with war; stock exchanges closed, July to October.
Poor crops, good prices.
War declared, August; troops landed in England, October.

1915 Depression; revival.
Paralysis gives way to war activity; manufacturing industries stimulated by war material demands; rapid rise of commodity prices; many failures; foreign trade recovers.
Money very tight; security prices rise, spring.
Magnificent crops; good but lower prices.
Extensive enlistment; government initiates "production and thrift campaigns."

1916 War activity.
Great activity, especially in manufacturing industries; commodity prices boom, with temporary relapse, summer; labor shortage and transportation congestion late in year; very large exports.
Money easy; considerable increase in currency in circulation; war loans; real estate crisis, Vancouver.
Partial failure of crops; higher prices.
Business profits tax imposed.

1917 War activity.
Continued activity, hampered by labor and supply shortage; rapid price rise slackens, May; exports reach peak.
War loans dominate money market; security values decline.
Poor crops, very high prices; government control of wheat crop.
Food controller appointed, June; fuel controller appointed, July.

1918 War activity; recession.
Continued activity, slackening with Armistice; prices rise to peak, November; decline in foreign trade late in year.
Financial strain.
Very poor wheat crop, large oats; government control with very high prices.
Influenza epidemic, October; Armistice, November.

1919 Revival; prosperity.
Dullness gradually gives way to great activity; production low to last quarter; prices decline to April and then rise; severe labor difficulties, especially Winnipeg, second quarter; revival in foreign trade.
Money tight; great stock exchange activity; gradual decline in foreign exchange accelerates, November.
Poor wheat, fair oats crop; prices rise to peak.
Fuel and food control ended, March; Canadian National Railways formed, December; demobilization.

1920 Prosperity, recession.
Activity continues; boom reaches peak, summer, and then decline sets in; commodity prices reach peak, May; production continues high to end of year; unemployment appears, October; imports reach peak, exports decline, unfavorable balance.
Money tightens, especially last half-year; severe decline in security values.
Larger wheat, record oats crop; prices slump sharply.
Large immigration.

1921 Depression.

General stagnation; widespread unemployment and many failures; production at very low level; falling commodity prices; decline in foreign trade, balance favorable.

Money eases; foreign exchange improves; temporary banking strain, December.

Agricultural depression severe; large wheat, smaller oats crops; prices very low.

Immigration declines; Liberal party comes into power, December.

1922 Depression; revival.

Continued dullness gradually disappears; construction boom; manufacturing improves, autumn; commodity prices reach bottom, September; many failures early in year; employment improves; revival in foreign trade, marked increase in exports.

Money easy; exchange returns to parity, August.

Record wheat crop, large oats; prices slightly improved.

1923 Moderate prosperity.

Generally improved and sound business conditions; production reaches very high peak, summer; prices steady; failures continue numerous; further improvement in employment; fishing industry severely depressed; further revival in foreign trade.

Money abundant; exchange falls, first quarter; banking troubles and scandals.

Record crops with low prices; agricultural distress lessens.

Revisions of tariff encourage British and American trade, May; extensive emigration to the United States; revival of immigration.

1924 Recession; mild depression.

Slump in manufacturing and other industries, especially last half-year; many failures; unemployment; prices decline to May and then recover; increased exports but smaller imports; signs of improvement late in year.

Money fairly easy; stock market active in spring and last quarter; exchange returns to par.

Good crops, much higher prices.

Slackening immigration.

1925   Revival; prosperity.

Marked improvement, particularly in mining, and paper and pulp industries; manufacturing active, except iron and steel industries; Nova Scotia coal strike, March to August; construction active after first quarter; commodity prices reach peak early in year, decline to April, and rise late in year; large increase in foreign trade, especially exports.

Money plentiful and easy; stock market very active with rising prices, especially last half-year.

Very large wheat and oats, record barley crops; good wheat and oats, high barley prices.

Immigration much smaller; Conservatives win general election, October.

CHAPTER XIII.

THE ANNALS OF SOUTH AFRICA.

In 1910, the Union of South Africa was formed from the four British colonies, Cape of Good Hope, Natal, Transvaal, and Orange Free State. The Cape of Good Hope formally became a British colony in 1814, Natal was annexed in 1844, and Transvaal and Orange Free State, after annexation and later restoration of freedom, were again annexed to the British Crown in 1900 as a consequence of the Boer War. These four colonies occupy the southern extremity of the continent of Africa. They form an extensive interior plateau, with a diversified tract of country between it and the ocean on the east, south, and west.

The area of the Union of South Africa is 472,347 square miles.[1] The population as recorded by the various censuses has increased as follows: [a]

Census Date	Population	Persons per Square Mile
April 5, 1891 [b]	3,400,000	7.2
April 17, 1904	5,175,824	10.9
May 7, 1911	5,973,394	12.6
May 3, 1921	6,928,580	14.7

[a] Union of South Africa Office of Census and Statistics, *Census of the Population, 3 May, 1921.* Part I. Pretoria, 1922. pp. vii, 1, 3.
[b] Estimated for Transvaal and Orange Free State. See *Official Year Book, 1924.* p. ix.

Of the population in 1921, 21.9 per cent were Europeans. Nearly 56 per cent of this European population live in cities, while one-sixth of the natives are classed as urban.

Some indication of the importance of different types of economic activity in South Africa can be gained from the following table of occupations, taken from the data given in the Census of 1921:

[1] Union of South Africa Office of Census and Statistics, *Official Year Book, 1924.* Pretoria, 1925. p. 39.

THE ANNALS OF SOUTH AFRICA

Industry	Thousands of Persons [a]	
	White [b]	Bantu (native) [c]
Agriculture and Fishing	169	2,750 [d]
Mining	20	236
Manufacturing	102	9 [e]
Commerce	104	15 [f]

[a] Exclusive of colored and Asiatic population, who amount to 10 per cent of the total, chiefly engaged in agricultural occupations and personal service.
[b] *Statesman's Yearbook, 1925.* London, 1925. p. 223.
[c] Union of South Africa Office of Census and Statistics, *Census of the Population, 3 May, 1921.* Part VIII. Pretoria, 1924. p. 143.
[d] "Peasants" plus "farm labourers".
[e] "Artisans" plus "skilled labourers". A group entitled "other labourers", totaling 146,534, not included in this table, may possibly include many which should be in this group.
[f] "Shop assistants" plus "petty traders and hawkers" plus "interpreters, clerks, etc."

The above table of occupations indicates that agriculture is much the most important industry. The Union of South Africa has shown steady development in the area under cultivation. Maize is the leading crop, wheat coming second. Maize is the staple food of the native population, and is harvested in July and August. When a crop is recorded by a two-year title, as the crop of 1910-11, it has been included in the year in which it was harvested, in this case, 1910. The raising of wool is one of South Africa's oldest activities, and is its most important pastoral occupation. The maximum number of sheep was reached in 1913. Cattle raising expanded tremendously during the War, but has since declined somewhat. Prior to the War, there was a boom in ostrich farming, but the decline which began in 1913 was accelerated by the outbreak of hostilities.

South Africa is best known for its two mineral products, gold and diamonds. It is by far the most important source of diamonds in the world, and is the leading gold field. The Witwatersrand gold fields in the Transvaal were opened in 1884, a period of rapid expansion following. According to the U. S. Director of the Mint, this district produced more than one-half of the world's gold output in 1923. Diamonds were discovered in 1870. The industry developed very quickly, the maximum output being won in 1887. The value has increased greatly since that time in the face of a diminishing output. In recent years, large deposits of coal have been discovered which provide cheap fuel for the gold and diamond mines and the developing manufacturing industries.

Manufacturing has not extended rapidly in South Africa in spite of its distance from other manufacturing centers. In 1915-16, there were 3,998 factories in the Union, including as factories all establishments employing 4 or more workers, or using mechanical power. Because of the restriction on imports occasioned by the War, manufacturing has been accelerated in recent years, the number of factories by 1922-23 having increased to 7,029. Some of the increase is due, however, to the extension of the term "factory" to include establishments employing 3 workers. Nearly one-fourth of the establishments are engaged in producing articles of food and drink.

Foreign trade plays a very important part in the life of South Africa. According to Professor Lehfeldt, "The goods exported have a value equal to more than half that of the total output of the country."[1] The volume of foreign trade has increased steadily, exports expanding especially since the Boer War. The volume of both exports and imports reached its maximum in 1913, although, in 1919, the value exceeded that of 1913 by 60 per cent, and, in 1920, was nearly double. The balance of trade is customarily favorable. Before the World War, the leading exports were gold, diamonds, wool, and ostrich feathers. In recent years, ostrich feathers have been supplanted by hides and skins, and coal. The leading imports are cotton goods, apparel, and machinery.

Further comparison of the importance of the great industrial fields is made possible by the following table:

Industry	Total Value of Product 1922-1923 [a]	Contribution to National Income 1918 [b]
	Millions of Pounds Sterling	
Agriculture and Pastoral	81.6	40.3
Minerals	54.6	22.0
Manufacturing	37.3 [c]	22.2
Other	...	52.7
Total		137.2
Exports	81.4	...
Imports	57.8	...

[a] Union of South Africa Office of Census and Statistics, *Official Year Book, 1924.* Pretoria, 1925. pp. 456, 487, 543, 606.
[b] Lehfeldt, R. A., *The National Resources of South Africa.* Johannesburg, 1922. p. 77.
[c] Value added by manufacture.

[1] Lehfeldt, R. A., *The National Resources of South Africa.* Johannesburg, 1922. p. 43.

The development of railroads in South Africa showed greatest rapidity during the decade from 1900 to 1910. The statistics for mileage operated are as follows:

Date	Miles of Railway [a]	
	Government Owned	Total
Dec. 31, 1880...............	1,007	.....
Dec. 31, 1890...............	2,240	.....
Dec. 31, 1900...............	3,990	.....
Dec. 31, 1910...............	7,041	7,586
Mar. 31, 1920...............	9,600	10,107

[a] Union of South Africa Office of Census and Statistics, *Official Year Book, 1922.* Pretoria, 1924. pp. 791, 792. All railways and harbors are, with few exceptions, the property of the government.

Banking in South Africa has undergone a period of amalgamation so that, in 1924, there were six joint stock banks with many branches trading in the Union. Of these six, three carry on business in all the provinces. The government exercises supervision over these banks, and requires periodical reports. The South African Reserve Bank was opened in June, 1921, and took over complete control of note issue on June 30, 1922.

The period of rapid growth of South Africa has been within the last fifty years. In 1861 and 1862, two large banking corporations were established, which brought much new capital to South Africa. A speculative boom followed, resulting in a serious crisis in 1865 and 1866. Then, after a period of quiescence, came the diamond rush which began in 1870. Rapid expansion continued to the Transvaal secession and Basuto War in 1880, a severe crisis occurring in 1881. The ensuing depression reached its acutest point in 1883 but continued until 1885. The announcing of the discovery of the Witwatersrand gold field and the founding of Johannesburg in 1886 led to a mining boom. In 1889, activity was transferred to the stock market, and there was mad speculation in shares. The annals begin with South Africa in a state of rapid and excited expansion.

1890   Prosperity; recession; depression.

General activity and prosperity; extensive railroad construction; gold speculation precedes crisis, September; diamond trade prosperous, but output reduced; foreign trade small, unfavorable balance.

Rapid expansion of credit and currency; banking crisis with many failures, September; stock market collapses.

Agriculture depressed; fair maize, poor wheat crop.

Important railroads opened.

1891 Depression.
Domestic trade inactive; commodity prices advance; gold output increases; diamond industry depressed in spite of increased output; foreign trade continues small, favorable balance.
Wool exports reach peak.
British assume control of Central Africa, heretofore claimed by the Portuguese.

1892 Rapid revival.
Great activity in mining districts; extensive railroad construction; real estate and building boom; rapid increase in gold output; diamond trade prospers; exports increase slightly.
Decline in wool exports begins; poor maize crop, excellent wheat.

1893 Prosperity.
Great activity and expansion; increase in production checked, first half-year, then resumed; slight decline in diamond output, increased value; slow expansion of foreign trade.
Banks prosperous.
Crops excellent, especially wheat.
Responsible government granted Natal; first Matabele War, July to October.

1894 Prosperity.
Continued progress and expansion; large increase in gold output; diamond prices fall, some reduction in output; slight increase in exports.
British-Boer antagonism, Johannesburg.

1895 Prosperity; recession.
Continued activity with gradual recession in autumn; speculation; gold production declines after August; diamond industry improves with rising price; further increase in exports.
Influx of foreign capital.
Crops reduced by drought and locusts; cattle disease; wool exports increase.
Jameson raid fails to gain Transvaal for British, December.

1896 Depression.
Conditions generally unsettled; rise in cost of living; gold industry depressed by mine riots; diamond production large, price low; enormous increase in imports creates unfavorable balance of trade.
Banks in sound condition.
Fair maize, very poor wheat crop; heavy loss of cattle due to *rinderpest*.
Racial feeling high; second Matabele Revolt, March to August; large immigration.

THE ANNALS OF SOUTH AFRICA

1897 Depression.

Internal trade continues dull; gold production expands rapidly; diamond industry depressed; further expansion in foreign trade with unfavorable balance.

Severe agricultural depression, very poor crops.

Disorder continues.

1898 Depression.

Internal trade stagnant; marked increase in gold production; diamond production reaches peak; imports decline, exports increase, balance favorable.

Money tight.

Continued agricultural depression; small crops.

Tariff lowered.

1899 Revival; recession.

General revival, except Rhodesia; improvement checked by war, October; gold output continues large to September; diamond output restricted, price rises; foreign trade checked, last quarter.

Agriculture severely restricted by war.

War with Boers declared, October; Boer victories, December.

1900 Depression.

Internal trade disrupted; commodity price rise accelerated; gold mining at a standstill; diamond mining output very small, price high; increased imports, exports collapse.

Small crops.

British successes, March; occupation of Transvaal and Orange Free State.

1901 Revival.

General revival and war expansion; rapid rise in commodity prices; speculation; resumption of gold mining on very small scale, May; diamond mining revives, high price; further increase in imports, continued restriction of exports.

Small crops.

Bubonic plague, Cape of Good Hope; guerilla warfare.

1902 Prosperity.

Great activity with end of war, May; trade and land boom; commodity prices very high; speculation; gradual revival in gold mining hampered by labor shortage; diamond mining depressed; great increase in imports, some revival in exports.

Small crops.

Peace declared, May.

1903   Recession.

Gradual decline into inactivity; commodity prices decline; gold production still restricted; diamond depression continues; imports reach peak, exports reach pre-war level.

Money tight.

Cattle and horse disease; drought causes failure of crops.

Chinese labor imported to gold mines; General Customs Union formed by colonies.

1904   Depression.

Continued inactivity; unemployment severe in cities; commodity prices decline; some improvement in gold production; diamond trade revives with high prices; import decline marked, export expansion continues.

Money eases, and tightens, September.

Reduction in immigration.

1905   Depression.

Continued inactivity; unemployment; gold reaches pre-war level of output; diamond industry relapses; further decline in imports and increase in exports cause return to favorable balance of trade.

Money eases, August.

Agriculture improves.

Record mileage of new railroad opened.

1906   Depression.

Continued dullness with many small failures; beginning of period of expansion in ostrich feather industry; increase in gold production continues; diamond industry revives; foreign trade increases.

Money tight.

Cattle disease; poor crops, but higher prices.

Drought; rebellion of natives.

1907   Depression deepens.

Inactivity; commodity price decline continues; gold miners' strike, production severely restricted; great diamond prosperity; imports decline, exports increase.

Money tight.

Agriculture improves, except cattle farming.

Responsible government given to Transvaal and Orange Free State.

1908 Depression lessens.
Continued dullness; commodity prices reach bottom; gold production revives; diamond output and price decline; foreign trade relapses.
Money very tight.
Good agriculture.
Immigration reaches lowest point.

1909 Revival.
General and steady revival, marked during last three months; commodity prices rise; gold production maintained with little increase; gradual recovery in diamond trade; foreign trade improves.
Agriculture prosperous.
South African Union Act passed.

1910 Prosperity.
Activity and expansion; many new enterprises developed; commodity prices rise rapidly; slight increase in gold output; record diamond production with good price; expansion in foreign trade, especially imports.
Good crops.
Union of South Africa established, May; marked increase in immigration.

1911 Prosperity.
Activity and expansion; period of gradual rise in commodity prices begins; gold and diamond mining prosperous; diamond values rise strongly; foreign trade maintained.
Great agricultural expansion.
Immigration reaches high point.

1912 Prosperity.
General activity hampered temporarily by coal crisis, spring; railroad rates materially reduced; gold production continues to increase; diamond industry very prosperous; increase in foreign trade, especially exports.
Drought hinders agricultural expansion.

1913 Uneven recession.
Continued activity with marked increase in failures; decline in gold production due to miners' strike, June; diamond industry very prosperous; ostrich feather industry reaches peak, collapsing toward end of year; record volume of foreign trade.
Agricultural prosperity.
Riots and civil unrest in gold centers.

1914 Recession; depression.
Dullness gives way to paralysis with outbreak of war; failures; wholesale prices fall; gold production curtailed after temporary revival, summer; diamond mining suspended; marked decrease in foreign trade, especially exports.
Money tight, but no financial crisis.
Drought reduces good crops.
Semi-protective tariff passed; September rebellion suppressed, December; martial law required on the Rand; Bank of England arranges to take entire gold output at standard rate.

1915 Slow revival.
Gradual increase in activity; wholesale price boom begins; revival in gold production; diamond mines closed; further reduction of foreign trade.
Money easy.
Poor maize and wheat crops.
Drought; conquest of German South-West Africa completed, July.

1916 Rapid revival.
Rapid recovery of trade and industry; expansion of manufacturing; record gold production; diamond mining resumed, high prices; recovery in foreign trade.
Money tightens.
Agricultural expansion; good maize, very poor wheat crop.
Drought in Cape Midlands necessitates government aid; tariff raised several times; expeditionary force sent to German East Africa.

1917 Prosperity.
Activity and expansion; shipping shortage stimulates local industry; excellent gold production; improvement in diamond industry; volume of foreign trade declines, though total value of exports increases notably.
Money tight; banks prosperous.
Agricultural expansion; excellent maize and record wheat harvests; Imperial government agrees to purchase entire wool clip.
Floods.

1918 Prosperity; recession.
Activity slackens late in year; rapid commodity price rise reaches peak in autumn; shipping curtailment results in further expansion of home industry; gold production declines; slump in diamonds; imports increase, exports decline.
Money tight.
Great agricultural prosperity with high prices for products; poor maize, good wheat crops; wool boom.
Drought; influenza epidemic severe, September and October; labor unrest.

1919 Revival; prosperity.

Great activity after temporary decline; much speculation as prices soar, last half-year; gold production slightly restricted; agreement for gold purchase terminates, July, and gold goes to premium; diamond prices high; exports increase, imports decrease.

Money plentiful; foreign exchange fluctuates widely.

Fair maize crop, wheat failure; wool boom continues; high prices.

Drought; influenza continues severe, spring; industrial unrest and native disturbances.

1920 Prosperity; recession; depression.

Great activity continues, first half-year, followed by rapid decline to deep depression; commodity prices reach peak, summer; many failures; gold premium at maximum, February, gold production restricted; diamond prices very high; extraordinary increase in imports, doubling those of previous year, with decline in exports, creates unfavorable balance.

Money tightens; exchange becomes unfavorable.

Excellent maize crop, fair wheat; prices decline; wool boom collapses.

Floods followed by drought.

1921 Deep depression.

Stagnation; industrial unrest and unemployment; commodity prices fall; many failures; high gold premium declines, last quarter, gold production restricted; diamond industry dead; foreign trade declines, especially imports, favorable balance.

Money somewhat easier; exchange rises above sterling par, March, but falls very rapidly, summer, becoming unfavorable; South African Reserve Bank opened, June.

Fair maize and good wheat crops; many agricultural bankruptcies; government aids wool industry.

Civil unrest; political difficulties.

1922 Depression.

Continued stagnation; price fall continues; many failures; severe strike in gold mines, March; gold premium falls, gold industry revival begins, summer; diamond depression deeper; increased volume of foreign trade but diminished values.

Money tight; exchange with London becomes favorable.

Poor maize, good wheat crop.

"Red Revolution" and martial law, spring.

1923   Revival.

Gradual improvement; commodity prices reach minimum, summer; many failures; building industry active; large gold output; resumption of activity in diamond industry; large increase in foreign trade.

Exchange continues above sterling par.

Good crops; wool prices recover.

Severe drought.

1924   Mild prosperity.

Business conditions improve, relapsing March to October; decreased unemployment; reduction in number of failures; prices rise slightly; building brisk; record gold output; diamond industry improves; increased foreign trade, especially imports.

Further advance in sterling exchange.

Poor maize crop.

Severe drought and locusts.

1925   Prosperity.

Steady industrial improvement although seamen's strike hampers expansion; little unemployment; declining commodity prices; record gold output; increased production and high price of diamonds under government control; slight increase in volume of foreign trade.

Foreign exchange rises to par and gold standard restored, May; stock prices advance after slump, July.

Wool industry prospers; record maize crop.

CHAPTER XIV.

THE ANNALS OF AUSTRALIA.

The Commonwealth of Australia includes the entire continent of Australia proper, and the island of Tasmania. It is the only inhabited continent wholly in the Southern Hemisphere, and two-fifths of its area lie in the tropic zone. The continent has a low-lying, well-watered coast, with mountain systems parallel to and not far from the coast-line. The interior is a low plateau, consisting chiefly of desert and arid grass land. The population is concentrated along the southeastern coast.

Prior to 1901, this area was governed as seven separate British colonies: New South Wales, Northern Territory, Queensland, South Australia, Tasmania, Victoria, and Western Australia. On January 1, 1901, these states were federated into the Commonwealth of Australia.

The area of the Commonwealth is 2,974,581 square miles. Its population has been as follows: [a]

Census Date	Population	Persons per Square Mile
April 3, 1881	2,250,194	0.8
April 5, 1891	3,174,392	1.1
March 31, 1901	3,773,801	1.3
April 3, 1911	4,455,005	1.5
April 4, 1921	5,435,734	1.9

[a] Australia Bureau of Census and Statistics, *Official Year Book, 1924*. Melbourne, 1925. Exclusive of full-blood Australian aboriginals, estimated at 60,000.

Immigration to Australia was greatest during the decade 1881-1890. After years of quiet, it was resumed in 1907 and the years 1909-1913 recorded a net immigration of 281,193 persons. This source of increase was stopped by the War. Australia is not only one of the least densely populated countries in the world, but the little population which it has is largely urban in nature. The *Census of 1921* reported that 62.1 per cent of the population lived in incorporated cities and towns.

The following table indicates the relative importance of the various branches of activity in Australia:

Industry	Estimated Value of Production [a] (millions of pounds sterling)	
	1911	1923-24
Agriculture	39	81
Pastoral	51	103
Dairy, Poultry and Bee-Farming	19	42
Forestry and Fisheries	6	12
Mining	23	22
Manufacturing [b]	51	132
Total	188	393
Imports	67	141
Exports	79	119

[a] Australia Bureau of Census and Statistics, *Official Year Book of the Commonwealth of Australia, 1924.* Melbourne, 1924. pp. 223 and 1,040, and *Quarterly Summary of Australian Statistics,* September, 1925. Melbourne.

[b] Value added by manufacture, excluding items included under other headings, especially dairy products and forestry. Census refers to Queensland, Western Australia, and Tasmania for year ending December 31; New South Wales, Victoria, and South Australia for year ending June 30, six months later.

In Australia, the pastoral and agricultural interests are each dominated by one product. The number of cattle and sheep reached a peak soon after 1890, and then fell off to 1902, since which time the number of sheep has slowly increased, and cattle herds have grown extensively. However, wool remains the chief factor in pastoral wealth. The bulk of the wool is exported. Because it is clipped in November, the clip generally known as that of 1890-91, for example, is discussed in the following annals as the clip of 1890.

Agriculture has shown rapid development, the acreage under crops having increased during the thirty years between 1890 and 1920 from 5.4 million to 15.1 million acres. Nearly two-thirds of this area is given over to wheat, which is by far the most important agricultural commodity. Since wheat is harvested in January, the crop generally known as the 1890-91 crop, for example, is discussed in these annals as the crop of 1891.

Although it was mineral wealth which first gave Australia prominence in the eyes of the world, the value of its mineral production is today much less than that of either the pastoral or agricultural industries. Coal mining has become the most important mining industry and its annual output accounts for nearly one-half the total value of mineral products, though gold, copper, lead, zinc, and iron are mined in appreciable amounts. Maximum gold production was reached in 1903.

Largely due to the nature of its population, and its distance from other industrial centers, Australia has developed manufacturing facilities more rapidly than most newly settled countries. In 1921, the Census reported for the first time a larger proportion of the breadwinners engaged in industrial employment than in agricultural, pastoral, and mining activities combined. In 1923-24, there were 20,189 factories, each employing four or more employees, or using power. The industries employing the largest number of wage-earners are the manufacture of textiles and clothing, and metal works and machinery.

The foreign trade of Australia is of great importance. This is shown by the fact that the sum of the exports and imports equals about two-thirds of the total value of domestic products in any year. Up to 1892, the annual returns generally indicated imports larger than exports, but since that time, with few exceptions, the balance of trade has remained favorable. Great Britain is gradually losing the quasi-monopoly on Australian trade which it has held for many years. The chief articles of export are wheat and wool, and of import are apparel and textiles, machinery, and metal products.

The following table shows the distribution of breadwinners by occupations at decennial periods, 1881 to 1921. The arrest of industrial progress by the financial crisis of the nineties is clearly shown, breaking the advance of the industrial group into two sections, that prior to 1891, and the resumption of advance after 1901.

Industry	Per Cent of Total Breadwinners [a]				
	1881	1891	1901	1911	1921
Primary Producers	38	31	32	30	26
Manufacturing	30	31	26	28	31
Commerce	9	12	14	15	15
Transport and Communication	5	7	8	8	9
Others [b]	19	20	20	19	19
Total	100	100	100	100	100

[a] Percentages computed from original data given in *Official Year Book, 1924.* p. 938.
[b] Includes professional, domestic, and independent groups.

The industrial development of the Commonwealth has been paralleled by improvement in the means of transportation. The following table demonstrates the growth of railroads during the last thirty years:

Date	Railway Mileage [a]
June 30, 1891 [b]	10,123
June 30, 1901 [c]	13,551
June 30, 1911	18,012
June 30, 1921 [d]	26,202

[a] Australia Bureau of Census and Statistics, *Official Year Book of the Commonwealth of Australia, 1922.* Melbourne, 1923. p. 537. Excluding sidings and cross-overs.
[b] Including Tasmania as of December 31, 1891.
[c] Including Tasmania as of December 31, 1901.
[d] Including Western Australia as of December 31, 1921.

On June 30, 1921, 89 per cent of the railways were government owned, only small and relatively unimportant railways remaining in private hands.

The banking facilities in Australia have developed in the hands of a small number of banks. In 1911, the various State banks were consolidated into the Commonwealth Bank. In December, 1920, the control of the Australian note issue was handed over to the Commonwealth Bank. The various private banks have undergone a gradual process of amalgamation, and on June 30, 1922, there were eighteen private commercial banks trading in Australia.

Australian history prior to 1890 is one of sporadic spurts of development coupled with increasing fiscal difficulties. The first notable crisis came in 1839 with the failure of the Bank of Australia. Depression was severe in the early forties, and was not completely dispelled until the discoveries of gold in 1851. The next decade was one of rapid growth. The excitement gradually waned, and the following decade, from 1861-1872, was one of quiet and pause, broken by a severe financial crisis in Queensland in 1866. From the early seventies until 1884, the Australian colonies were generally prosperous, interrupted only in 1879-1880 by a severe drought. Much new mineral wealth was discovered, public land was sold extensively, and large sums were expended on public works. From 1886 on, expansion was at a slower rate, and prosperity became strained as it approached the crises of 1890 and 1893.

1890 Recession; depression.

Activity retarded by maritime strike, August to November; industrial crisis in Queensland; many failures; silver mania of 1888 subsides; foreign trade depressed, especially exports.

Money easy, but banks cautious.

Agricultural prosperity; record wheat harvest; small wool clip; good prices; sheep shearers' strike temporarily disorganizes wool trade.

THE ANNALS OF AUSTRALIA 323

1891 Depression.

Severe depression somewhat relieved late in year; home trade restricted; many failures; foreign trade active with unfavorable balance.

Easy money gradually tightens; failures of banks and building societies, beginning July; financial panic in Melbourne, December; large governmental borrowing.

Small wheat crop, large wool clip; good prices.

Drought; much distress in Victoria; gold discoveries in Western Australia.

1892 Depression.

General stagnation in industry; widespread unemployment; Broken Hill silver mines closed for three months by strike; land boom collapses late in year; beginning of period of large increases in gold production; fall in commodity prices; foreign trade declines.

Financial stringency; run on Savings Bank of New South Wales, February; general panic averted, March, by concerted action of banks; continued failures of building and land societies.

Small wheat crop with high price; large wool clip with depressed price.

Agricultural distress becomes widespread; higher tariff, March; gold rush.

1893 Depression; panic.

Continued inactivity with sharp fall in commodity prices; many failures; period of wage reduction begins; foreign trade slack.

Money very tight; financial panic causes many bank failures, April and May; fiscal difficulties.

Large harvest and wool clip, very low prices.

Droughts and floods.

1894 Depression.

General sluggishness; failures continue numerous; wage fall checked, increased unemployment; greater activity in local manufacturing; complete cessation of construction; commodity price fall continues; low point in foreign trade.

Money market recovers slowly.

Small wheat crop and large wool clip; prices very low; wool shearers' strike.

1895 Depression; slight revival.
Gradual increase in activity; marked decline in business failures; commodity prices very low; foreign trade revives, particularly exports.
Money eases; signs of recuperation on stock exchange; influx of British capital for gold mining.
Large wheat crop, but smaller wool clip; low prices.
Drought.

1896 Strong revival.
Great increase in activity; sharp decrease in unemployment; Western Australia gold boom; marked increase in imports.
Money easy, with temporary tightness in autumn.
Very small wheat crop and wool clip; wheat price rises sharply; slight improvement in wool price.
Severe drought; tariff reduced, January.

1897 Mild prosperity; agricultural depression.
Continued activity in home trade; railroad construction revives; many new enterprises formed; foreign trade active.
Money very easy; large bullion shipments.
New South Wales wheat crop very large, but Southern and Western Australian crops complete failures, high wheat price; small wool clip, good price.
Continued drought; colonies adopt Commonwealth Bill, March.

1898 Prosperity.
Rapid expansion; great activity in building construction; commodity price rise begins; continued growth in foreign trade.
Money tightens gradually.
Large wheat crop with fair price; small wool clip, high price.
Drought breaks; tariff increase, December.

1899 Prosperity.
Activity and expansion; slight depression in Western Australia; foreign trade very active.
Money easy; rapid extension of credit causes tightening; stock exchange active.
Good wheat crop, low price; small wool clip, high price.
Contingent of troops sent to South Africa.

1900 Prosperity.
Further activity and expansion; gold production falls off; increase in imports and slight decline in exports.
Money market active.
Good wheat crop with low price; small wool clip, price collapse.

1901 Recession.
Activity continues though somewhat retarded; revival in gold production; foreign trade reaches peak.
Money fairly easy with occasional tendencies to tighten.
Larger wheat crop and wool clip; low prices.
Severe drought begins; Commonwealth inaugurated, January; Immigration Restriction and Industrial Arbitration Bills passed; troops sent to South Africa.

1902 Mild depression.
General dullness; unemployment; wages fall sharply; falling off in foreign trade.
Money tightens; stock exchange dull.
Very poor wheat crop and wool clip; good prices.
Continued drought; federal protective tariff adopted; additional troops sent to South Africa.

1903 Depression.
Inactivity; peak in gold production; some revival in exports, but imports fall off severely.
Money tight; bank deposits decline.
Failure of wheat crop; wool clip slightly larger; low prices.
Continued drought.

1904 Revival.
Increased activity with lower commodity prices; decline in gold production sets in; considerable increase in exports with further decline in imports.
Money continues tight; stock exchange inactive.
Very large wheat crop with low price; larger wool clip with good price.

1905 Mild prosperity.
Industry quiet and sound; slow rise in commodity prices; foreign trade steady.
Money eases.
Wheat crop small with higher price; large wool clip with high price.

1906 Prosperity.
Gradual improvement and expansion in home industry; many wage increases; declining output of gold causes stagnation in Western Australia; foreign trade increases rapidly, especially exports.
Money easy with rapid extension of credit; mild boom in mining securities late in year.
Good wheat crop brings good price; very large wool clip with high price.
Period of increased immigration begins.

1907 Prosperity.
Activity maintained in domestic trade except in Western Australia; rising commodity prices; further expansion of foreign trade.
Credit restriction evident; security prices decline late in year.
Good wheat crop with low price; larger wool clip, lower price.
Drought; higher tariff "to regulate wages" passed; marked increase in immigration.

1908 Recession; mild depression.
Expansion checked and general activity somewhat retarded; coal strike, March; commodity prices reach peak; foreign trade declines.
Further tightening in money market, August.
Very poor wheat crop and small wool clip; prices low.
Drought; tariff of 1907 declared unconstitutional.

1909 Rapid revival; prosperity.
Strong increase in business and industry; many new enterprises; coal miners' strike late in year; commodity prices low; foreign trade continues somewhat depressed.
Money eases, May; security prices rise.
Good harvest and wool clip; fair wool price and sharply rising wheat price.

1910 Prosperity.
Great activity and expansion; extensive construction; wage rates advance; long coal strike; foreign trade very active.
Money easy.
Excellent harvest and clip; high wheat, low wool price.
Excitement in Western Australia over Bullfinch gold boom, October.

1911 Prosperity.
Internal activity retarded slightly by labor troubles; further increase in foreign trade.
Excellent wheat crop with high price; good wool clip and price.
Large increase in immigration.

1912 Prosperity.
Increased activity and expansion; rapid extension of frozen meat industry; commodity prices rise; imports increase while exports remain stationary.
Money tight, second quarter; Commonwealth Bank opened.
Deficient harvest with sharp decline in price; small wool clip with high price.
Trans-Australian Railway begun; immigration reaches peak.

1913 Mild recession.
Dullness gradually extends through industry; foreign trade reports first unfavorable balance since 1891.
Banks cautious; reform in banking organization.
Large wheat crop and wool clip with high prices.
Decline in immigration.

1914 Revival; recession; depression.
Revival and expansion evident, first half-year; after August, home industry inactive; shipping shortage; much employment; foreign trade checked.
Increased caution in money market.
Excellent harvest with high price; small clip with sharp fall in price.
Export of wheat prohibited except to Great Britain, September; immigration checked.

1915 Mild depression; revival.
Dullness and inactivity at beginning of year gradually disappear; unemployment severe to spring, then rapid decline; commodity prices rise rapidly first half-year; foreign trade severely depressed.
Money market tightens.
Wheat failure, good price; small wool clip, price recovering.
Severe drought; government undertakes control of wheat; embargo placed on wool export; widespread enlistment of men.

1916 War activity.
War boom; commodity prices gradually decline; full employment; rapid increase in foreign trade.
Money eases.
Enormous wheat crop with high price; very small wool clip and high price; government assumes control of both markets; price-fixing policy adopted.

1917 War activity.
Rapid expansion of home industry; labor troubles, with railroad strike lasting three months; ship shortage; commodity prices rise; severe unemployment; increase in exports and decline in imports cause return to favorable balance.
Money fairly easy, in spite of floating of War Loans.
Excellent harvest, lower price; small wool clip with very high price; government control continues.
Trans-Australian Railway completed, October; referendum returns majority against conscription; importation of luxuries prohibited.

1918   War activity.

Continued activity; flurry after Armistice followed by increased activity; full employment; commodity price rise accelerated; foreign trade continues expanding with large increase in imports.

Money continues abundant.

Small wheat harvest and large wool clip; wheat price high, but wool declines.

1919   Prosperity.

Continued activity disturbed by severe maritime and coal strikes; wages rise rapidly; full employment; commodity price rise continues; foreign trade very active with great increase in volume of exports.

Gold goes to premium, February; money tightens.

Large wool clip with peak price; very poor wheat crop, price slightly lower.

Severe drought; civil unrest, April; extensive immigration; epidemic of influenza; Australian Army returns.

1920   Prosperity; recession.

Continued activity; rapid recession, last quarter, with increase in unemployment; commodity prices reach peak, August; foreign trade boom continues, large increase in imports creating an unfavorable balance.

Money tightens, July; severe financial strain late in year; control of note issue transferred from Treasury to Commonwealth Bank.

Crop failure with high price; small wool clip with falling price; British government contract to purchase wool clip expires, June.

New protective tariff; sharp drop in immigration.

1921   Depression.

General dullness and depression; maximum unemployment reached, second quarter; many failures; wage rates reach peak, end of year; imports continue large but gradually decline, balance favorable.

Money tight and banks very cautious.

Large wheat crop with good price; good wool clip, low price; British-Australian Wool Realization Association formed to dispose of heavy stocks of wool.

Little immigration, but increase in emigration; higher tariff instituted.

1922 Slow revival.

Gradual increase in activity retarded by numerous labor difficulties, especially in mining where government intervention is necessary; failures continue numerous; commodity prices reach bottom, March, and then gradually rise; increased imports and small exports cause return to unfavorable balance.

Money eases; security prices rise; foreign exchange strengthens.

Good harvest, but sharp decline in price; good wool clip with much higher price.

1923 Revival; mild prosperity.

Recovery continues; employment fair, with wage rates at lowest point, first half-year; construction active; commodity prices rise to peak, July, and then fall; increase in imports with drop in exports.

Money tightens toward end of year.

Very small wool clip and harvest; higher wool price, but lower wheat price.

Police strike, Melbourne, October, with accompanying riots.

1924 Mild recession.

General activity in home trade; unemployment increases steadily; commodity prices fall to August and then rise; foreign trade shows large increase with favorable balance, last half-year.

Tight money eases and then tightens in autumn; foreign exchange difficulties.

Good wheat crop and excellent wool clip; high wheat price, wool collapses.

1925 Revival; prosperity.

Production at high level; commodity prices decline slightly to April, and then rise to peak, November; record volume of foreign trade despite seamen's strike, August to October; return to favorable balance.

Money easy; gold standard restored, April; stock market very active with rising prices.

Tremendous wheat crop, good prices; large wool clip, some recovery of wool price.

Labour Party wins general election, May, but is defeated, November; severe flood, New South Wales, May; new tariff increases rates, September.

CHAPTER XV.

THE ANNALS OF INDIA.

India is shaped like a huge triangle, having its base in the Himalaya Mountains, and running south to the ocean. In the north, it is mountainous country, in the center are extensive river plains, and the southern portion of the peninsula is table land. Of the 1,805,332 square miles which constitute this area, 1,094,300 square miles are under British dominion, i.e., subject to British law.[1] The remaining Native States, about 700 in number, are autonomous, except for certain restrictions such as inability to make war or peace, limitation of armament, and need for special sanction to employ Europeans.

The rate of population growth in India is not rapid. The records of the last four censuses are as follows:

Census Date	Population [a]	Persons per Square Mile
Feb. 26, 1891	287,314,671	159 [c]
Mar. 1, 1901	294,361,056 [d]	163 [b]
Mar. 10, 1911	315,156,396 [e]	175 [b]
Mar. 18, 1921	318,942,480 [f]	177 [b]

[a] India Census Commission, *Census of India, 1921*. vol. I, part II. Calcutta, 1924. p. 6.
[b] *Ibid.*, vol. I, part I. p. 5.
[c] India Census Commission, *Census of India, 1911*. vol. I, part I. Calcutta, 1913. p. 84. In the *Census of 1901*, the density for 1891 is given as 163 and for 1901 as 167 persons per square mile.
[d] Including 2,672,077 due to new areas enumerated.
[e] Including 1,793,365 due to new areas enumerated.
[f] Including 86,633 due to new areas enumerated.

In 1921, the population of British India was 247,003,293. The British Provinces are much more populous than the Native States, their density being 226 persons per square mile, the Native States but 101. In 1921, the urban population, i.e., those living in communities of

[1] India Census Commission, *Census of India, 1921*. vol. I, part II. Calcutta, 1924. p. 3.

more than 5,000, and 690 places of smaller population, constituted 10.2 per cent of the population.

The importance of agriculture in India is indicated by the following table of the industrial distribution of the working class in 1921:

Industry	Per Cent Distribution of Workers [a]
Pasture and Agriculture	73.0
Manufacturing and Mining	10.7
Trade and Transportation	7.1
Other [b]	9.2
Total	100.0

[a] India Census Commission, *Census of India, 1921*, vol. I, part I, Calcutta, 1924. p. 242.
[b] Includes persons engaged in public service, professions, domestic service, unclassified, unproductive occupations, and persons with independent incomes.

Approximately one-third of the area of the British India is sown with crops, and more than six per cent yields two or more crops per year. The acreage employed in the cultivation of rice is more than three times that of any other crop, and ten times that of any other country producing rice. Wheat and native grains are next in importance. Cotton is the leading non-food crop. In these annals, the returns are noted yearly for rice, wheat, and cotton. Rice is harvested in April, wheat in March, and cotton in November. Consequently, in these annals, the rice and wheat crops discussed in the annals for 1890, for example, were harvested in April and March, 1890, and are commonly known as the crops of 1889-90, while the cotton crop was harvested in November, 1890, being commonly called the crop of 1890-91. Although statements of crop yields are given in the annals, they are based at best on estimates which, before 1897-98, were highly unreliable.

The most important mineral product of India is coal. The maximum production was attained in 1919, and amounted to 22.6 million tons.

Although the industrial distribution of the working class indicates that 10.5 per cent are employed in manufacturing, the bulk of these are engaged in unorganized, or "cottage" industries connected with the supply of personal and household necessities and the simple implements of labor. Organized industries occupy only 1 per cent of the people. Factory production has made but gradual headway in India. In 1921, there were 6,570 "large industrial establishments" in British India, and 944 in the Native States.[1] The greatest progress has been made in the textile industries, particularly in the spinning and weaving of cotton.

The development of railways has been very important in opening up the interior states of India, and especially in dealing with the severe famines to which India is subject. The mileage open for traffic has increased as follows:

Date	Miles Open for Traffic [a]
Dec. 31, 1890	16,404
Dec. 31, 1900	24,752
Dec. 31, 1910	32,099
June 30, 1920	36,735

[a] India Department of Commercial Intelligence, *Statistical Abstract for British India, 1885-95*, p. 159; *1895-05*, p. 140; *1904-14*, p. 138A; *1912-22*, p. 372. Calcutta.

India's foreign trade has grown rapidly since 1900. With the exception of the years 1856-1862, and a short period since the close of the war, Indian foreign trade has recorded a large excess of exports over imports. In India, this is called the "economic drain". The leading articles of import are cotton goods, iron and steel, machinery, and sugar; of export, raw cotton, grains, tea, and jute. The opium trade to China, which was extensive in the early years of the annals, has been of little consequence since 1913, due to an international agreement.

Silver was the basis for Indian currency until 1899, when the sovereign was made legal tender. The financing of Indian foreign trade is done chiefly by European banks having branches in India. Banking development in India itself has been very slow. The Imperial Bank of India, formed in 1921 by the amalgamation of the Presidency Banks of Bengal, Bombay, and Madras, has recently established many branches through the country. It acts as fiscal agent for the Government, and is a private joint stock company under government control. In addition, there were in 1922 18 exchange banks, having their head offices abroad, engaged chiefly in financing foreign trade. A new development of the last two decades has been the 68 joint stock native banks having over 300 branches and agencies, and a rapidly expanding system of coöperative societies. The bulk of the internal trade, however, is financed through native bankers or money-

[1] India Department of Commercial Intelligence, *Statistical Abstract for British India, 1912-13 to 1921-22.* Calcutta, 1924. p. 599.

lenders. The right of note issue is held only by the Treasury. All references to foreign exchange are based on rates on London.

India was for many years under the control of the East India Company. Under its commercial policy, the old hand industries had declined, and agriculture remained the only national industry. Even after the Crown assumed the administration of India in 1858, little was done to aid the development of new industries, and, at the time of the beginning of the annals, India was an agricultural country with an active foreign trade, but with little factory development or commercial organization. Points of importance in the early history are the Sepoy mutiny of 1857, the cotton boom during the American Civil War, which proved largely temporary, the speculation in tea, which collapsed in 1866, the Afghan War of 1878-1880, the minor famines of 1860, 1866, 1869, and 1874, and the extremely severe famine of 1877 and 1878.

The period after 1870, with the exception of 1879-1885, was one of slowly declining value of the rupee. The annals begin in 1890 with India in a state of mild depression, following a recession in 1889, when money was very tight, commodity prices reached a peak, exchange was unsteady, and a famine threatened.

1890 Mild depression.

General dullness in industry and trade; imports increase slightly, exports fall off.

Money easy after first quarter; wide foreign exchange fluctuations with declining trend; embarrassed government finances require increase in taxation.

Rice crop fair, wheat poor, average cotton; low rice and wheat, good cotton prices.

Local famine, Bombay.

1891 Depression.

Deepening depression with numerous failures, last half-year; foreign trade hampered by exchange fluctuations.

Money abundant; wide exchange fluctuations continue with more rapid fall of exchange.

Crops average; rice and wheat prices good, cotton low.

Floods.

1892 Uneven depression.

Business conditions unsettled; commodity prices rise; imports decline as foreign trade continues dull.

Money very easy; further fall in foreign exchange.

Crops poor; rice and wheat prices high, but cotton continues low.

New factory regulations go into effect, January; cholera severe.

1893 Depression.

Industry disorganized by mint closing; gradual readjustment; commodity prices decline; speculation; foreign trade falls off.

Mints closed to free coinage of silver, June; money tightens; great fall in value of silver, especially third quarter.

Fair rice crop, good wheat and cotton crops; rice and wheat prices fall, cotton rises rapidly.

1894 Uneven revival.

Internal trade revives with large increase in imports; further commodity price decline.

Money very tight, February to June; further fall in the value of silver.

Good crops with fair prices.

Import duties imposed after twelve years of free trade, March; cholera severe.

1895 Mild prosperity.

Widespread activity; manufacturing flourishes; commodity price decline checked; record exports with slight reduction in imports create very large favorable balance.

Money easy; exchange reaches low point and then rises.

Excellent rice crop, fair wheat and cotton; slightly higher prices.

Chitrāl expedition; cholera severe.

1896 Prosperity; recession; depression.

Activity gives way to stagnation, autumn; rapid rise in commodity prices, notably foods; large decline in exports.

Money tightens rapidly late in year; exchange rises.

Very poor rice and wheat crops, excellent cotton; rice and wheat prices rise sharply, cotton unchanged.

Severe drought; famine late in year; extensive relief work by Government; bubonic plague breaks out in Bombay, September.

THE ANNALS OF INDIA

1897 Depression.

"Year of calamities" causes general disorganization; food prices very high, other prices lower; further decrease in foreign trade.

Monetary stringency; exchange rises rapidly, almost to par; Government remits taxes; sale of Council Bills suspended.

Rice crop failure, poor wheat and cotton crops; rice and wheat prices very high, cotton falls.

Famine continues severe, slightly relieved at end of year; earthquake, June; widespread disturbance on northwest border, last half-year; cyclone, October; bubonic plague spreads.

1898 Slow revival.

Gradual increase in activity; food prices fall rapidly; activity in railroad construction; foreign trade revives.

Extremely tight money eases rapidly, July; exchange steady.

Good rice, excellent wheat, and good cotton crops; prices fall, especially cotton.

Plague continues and spreads in spite of quarantine restriction.

1899 Moderate prosperity.

Continued expansion and increase in activity; foreign trade improves.

Money somewhat easier; sovereign made legal tender and gold reserve established, September.

Record rice and cotton crops, excellent wheat; fair prices, except cotton still very low.

1900 Recession.

Prosperity greatly restricted by famine; cotton industries severely depressed; coal scarcity; sharp rise in commodity prices; increase in imports.

Money tight, first half-year; exchange steady.

Poor rice and wheat crops, cotton failure; prices high, especially cotton.

Extensive famine; cholera severe.

1901 Depression.

Continued dullness; manufacturing industries severely depressed; commodity prices decline; marked revival in foreign trade late in year.

Money eases.

Poor rice, excellent wheat, and good cotton crops; prices decline.

Famine relieved in some districts; recurrence of bubonic plague.

1902 Revival.
Increased activity in internal trade; manufacturing industries revive, especially cotton; foreign trade revival continues.
Money easy.
Rice failure, good wheat and cotton crops; further decline in prices.
Plague spreads.

1903 Prosperity.
General activity and expansion; extensive development of new manufacturing enterprises; large increase in foreign trade.
Money easy.
Excellent crops; rice and cotton prices high, wheat low.
Tibetan expedition; Delhi Durbar in honor of the King's coronation, January; plague very severe.

1904 Prosperity.
Continued activity and expansion; cotton industry depressed, but revives strongly late in year; commodity price rise begins; increased foreign trade, large favorable balance.
Money easy.
Fair rice, excellent wheat, and good cotton crops; rice and wheat prices fair, cotton very high declining late in year.
Further extension of bubonic plague.

1905 Prosperity.
Industrial boom; manufacturing industries very prosperous, particularly cotton; commodity prices rise rapidly, especially foodstuffs; rapid expansion of foreign trade.
Money easy, tightening late in year.
Fair rice and wheat crops, good cotton; rice and wheat prices rise, but cotton falls.
Plague begins to subside; earthquake, April.

1906 Prosperity.
Continued activity and expansion under increasing difficulties; manufacturing profits smaller; further increase in foreign trade.
Money very tight, except summer.
Poor rice, good wheat and cotton crops; good prices; great prosperity in jute industry.
Cholera severe; *Swadeshi* or anti-foreign movement hampers import trade.

1907 Prosperity; recession.

Boom continues; formation of many new companies; speculation; manufacturing industries lessen activity; commodity prices continue to rise; foreign trade reaches peak.

Money very tight; Government closes mint; exchange falls suddenly, November.

Poor rice, good wheat and excellent cotton crop; further price rise.

Minor famine; worst year of plague; period of civil unrest begins with riots, lawlessness, and assassinations.

1908 Depression.

Deep depression; cotton industry severely depressed; food prices very high; other commodity prices fall; marked decline in foreign trade.

Financial stringency; exchange weak, with some improvement late in year; Government sells sterling drafts; many taxes remitted.

Very small crops, high prices.

Famine continues; cholera severe; reduction of opium shipments begins according to Anglo-Chinese agreement, January.

1909 Depression; slight revival.

Continued dullness; signs of increased activity late in year; commodity prices fall; imports decline, exports increase.

Money market eases.

Poor rice, good wheat and cotton crops; rice and wheat prices fall, cotton booms.

Governmental reform grants more authority to native states.

1910 Revival.

General increase in activity; commodity prices reach low point; marked revival in foreign trade.

Money easy.

Excellent crops; further decline in rice and wheat prices, high cotton price.

Plague breaks out again.

1911 Prosperity.

Expansion and activity, except in cotton industry.

Money easy.

Excellent rice, wheat, and good cotton crops; high rice, fair wheat, and very high cotton prices.

Further extension of plague; great Delhi Durbar with King present, December.

1912 Prosperity.

Continued activity and expansion; improvement in cotton manufacturing industry; rapid growth of foreign trade continues.

Money continues abundant; free coinage of silver resumed; minor banking difficulties.

Excellent rice and wheat, fair cotton crops; very high rice, good wheat, and high cotton prices.

New Factory Bill enacted regulating hours of labor in certain factories, July.

1913 Uneven prosperity.

Continued activity and expansion; cotton industry depressed late in year; foreign trade very active.

Banking difficulties, last quarter; many bank failures; general money market little affected.

Fair rice, excellent wheat and cotton crops; rice price falls decidedly, wheat good and cotton high.

1914 Prosperity; recession.

Continued activity to declaration of war; dullness; deep depression in cotton industry; active foreign trade becomes stagnant.

Money tighter, banking difficulties continue; exchange falls with war; run on Postal Savings Bank late in year.

Fair rice, poor wheat, bumper cotton crops; good rice and high wheat prices; cotton market collapses.

Indian contingent lands in France, September.

1915 Depression.

Continued unsettled business conditions; crisis in cotton industry with failures, September, requires government credit extension; prices of foodstuffs rise rapidly; foreign trade greatly restricted.

Money tight; exchange satisfactory after January.

Poor rice crop, excellent wheat and cotton; good rice, very high wheat, and poor cotton prices.

Drought.

1916 Revival.

Increased activity; cotton industry recovers; imports continue to decline, exports increase rapidly.

Money very tight, ascribed to curtailment of Council Bills.

Excellent rice and cotton crops, poor wheat; rice and wheat prices decline, but cotton rises.

Tariff rates increased; troops supplied for Mesopotamia, Egypt, and other campaigns.

1917 Prosperity.

Rapid improvement and expansion of home industry hampered by transportation difficulties, shipping shortage, and coal scarcity; commodity price rise checked; foreign trade active.

Money market eases; exchange rises steadily; Government requisitions all imports of gold and silver.

Excellent rice, record wheat and cotton crops; rice price very low, wheat good, and cotton booms.

Government takes over factories, regulating such industries as salt, cotton, tea, and rice; Britain announces intent to confer responsible government on India; Home Rule Movement violent; northwest border trouble.

1918 Prosperity; recession.

Activity continues; recession with Armistice; prices rise, but tumble, last two months; much speculation; shipping shortage; cotton industry very active to slump; foreign trade retarded.

Silver crisis and rise of exchange, April; paper currency circulation increases rapidly; foreign exchange unsteady, November.

Record rice, good wheat, and fair cotton crops; fair rice, very high wheat, peak in cotton prices.

Severe influenza epidemic beginning September; drought; famine, end of year; Government controls food rigorously.

1919 Revival; prosperity.

Boom in trade and industry; rapid extension of new companies; commodity prices rise rapidly; foreign trade very active.

Exchange rises, accelerating late in year.

Crop failures; rice price high, wheat very high, and cotton falling.

Famine relieved by government organization; civil outbreaks, April; war with Afghanistan, summer; Gandhi revives *Swadeshi* movement.

1920 Prosperity; recession; depression.

Boom reaches height early in year; collapse of prices and industrial activity, autumn; exports reach peak, spring, but imports continue large.

Money tight; exchange rises sharply to peak, April, rapid fall after October.

Good rice, excellent wheat and cotton crops; rice price high, wheat and cotton prices drop.

Minor famine begins late in year; Gandhi wins control of National Congress, December.

1921   Depression.

Stagnation of internal trade; price fall continues, despite temporary boom in summer; cancellation of orders rife; coal miners' strike; restricted exports and large imports create unfavorable balance of trade.

Money eases slightly; exchange fall continues to March, with temporary improvement, autumn; three Presidency Banks amalgamated forming Imperial Bank of India.

Wheat failure, poor rice and cotton crops; peak prices for wheat and rice, cotton very low; Government places embargo on export of foodstuffs and encourages import.

Famine relieved; tariff raised, March; severe civil outbreak, August; rebellion in Malabar suppressed by end of year.

1922   Depression.

Continued liquidation; gradual recovery from paralysis; cotton industry revives; price decline continues; further reduction in foreign trade.

Financial stringency.

Excellent rice, wheat, and record cotton crop; high prices for rice and wheat, fair for cotton.

Tariff raised; floods in Bengal, June; civil disturbances lessen; Gandhi imprisoned, March.

1923   Slow revival.

Dullness gradually yields to activity; prices continue to decline; cotton strike, March and April; slight increase in imports, large gain in exports.

Money very tight late in year; banking difficulties, April; foreign exchange rises gradually.

Excellent crops, lower prices.

1924   Revival; mild prosperity.

Rapid improvement; price fall halted, mid-year; foreign trade improves with large favorable balance.

Money eases, spring; steady improvement in exchange.

Excellent crops with improved prices.

Serious labor troubles, Bombay, February and March; Gandhi released from prison, February.

1925   Moderate prosperity.

General improvement, especially in mining; cotton mills strike, last four months; commodity price decline continues to summer; larger exports and smaller imports cause favorable balance of trade.

Easy money; Government stabilizes exchange; stock prices decline, bonds little changed.

Good crops, except wheat and cotton; food prices much lower.

Political calm.

CHAPTER XVI.

THE ANNALS OF JAPAN.

The Empire of Japan consists of a chain of islands lying off the east coast of Asia. Korea, on the mainland, was annexed in 1910. Formosa and the Pescadores, toward the south, were ceded by China after the War of 1894-1895, and the southern half of Sakhalin, called Karafuto by the Japanese, was ceded by Russia in 1905. There are several thousand islands in all, of which 432 have a coast-line of at least 1 *ri* (2.44 miles) or serve as sea-marks. The islands are transversed north and south by ranges of mountains, and the country is extremely rugged. The larger islands are covered by elaborate networks of small streams.

The census of the entire Japanese Empire, taken October 1, 1920, reported a total population of 76,988,379 persons, and an area of approximately 262,842 square miles, a density of 293 persons per square mile.[1] The following table gives some indication of the rate of growth of the population of Japan proper:

December 31,—	Persons Having Legal Residence in Japan Proper [a]	
	Thousands of Persons [b]	Persons per Square Mile [c]
1880	36,359	243
1890	40,453	270
1900	44,826	299
1910	50,985	340
1920	57,919	387

[a] Published in original source under the heading, "Population ayant le domicile légal dans l'Interieur. (Population de droit.)" The data are based on censuses made by district authorities, and estimates from births, deaths, etc. Koreans, Formosans, and natives of Karafuto are not included.

[b] Japan Bureau de la Statistique Générale, *Résumé Statistique de l'Empire du Japon, 1924.* Tokio, 1924. pp. 4, 5.

[c] Computed from original data given in square kilometers by multiplying by 2.59.

[1] Japan Bureau de la Statistique Générale, *Résumé Statistique de l'Empire du Japon, 1924.* Tokio, 1924. pp. 1, 4. Area figures computed from original data given in square kilometers by multiplying by 0.3861. Small islands with a coast-line of less than one ri, unless inhabited or serving as sea-marks, are not included.

About 45 per cent of the population live in towns of 2,000 inhabitants or less.

Japan is not naturally suited to agriculture, due to the irregularity of its topography. Nevertheless, one-sixth of its area is under cultivation. During recent years, there has been little increase in the farm area, and, in addition, such area has already reached a high degree of intensive cultivation. By far the most important agricultural product is rice. The rice crop is harvested in November. The next largest crops are those of barley, rye, and wheat, but the area occupied by these three together is but half as large as that of the paddy-fields. Next to the rice industry in importance is silk culture. Contrasted to the rice industry, which has shown little growth during the last twenty years, sericulture has expanded steadily and rapidly, the number of cocoons produced annually more than doubling in the last twenty years.

The manufacturing industries of Japan have rapidly adopted the methods of Western civilization. That the rate of growth has been extraordinary is evidenced by the following table of persons employed in factories:

Year	Factory Workers [a] (thousands)
1900 [b]	422
1910 [c]	865
1920 [d]	1,580

[a] Japan Bureau de la Statistique Générale, *Résumé Statistique de l'Empire du Japon, 1917, 1920* and *1924*. Tokio. For the year 1900, data are given under the head of "ouvriers"; for 1910 and 1920, as "ouvriers" and "ouvriers inferieurs", which have here been summed.

[b] Establishments included which employ more than 10 workers or apprentices.

[c] Establishments included which employ an average of 10 workers or apprentices per day.

[d] Establishments included which employ an average of 5 workers per day.

The bulk of the workers are employed in the textile or affiliated industries.

Coincident with the rapid industrial development, has been the expansion of Japan's foreign trade. At present, the United States is its chief customer. The most important articles of export are silk and cotton textiles; those of import are raw cotton, iron and steel, and machinery. With the exception of a few years in the early nineties, and those during the War, Japan's foreign trade returns regularly show an excess of imports over exports.

A further indicator of the industrialization of Japan is the rapid extension of railroads. The first railroad was built in 1872. The following table shows the later development:

March 31,—	Railroads in Japan Proper [a] (miles)
1880	73
1890	1,213
1900	3,637
1910	5,130
1920	8,208 [b]

[a] Japan Bureau de la Statistique Générale, *Résumé Statistique de l'Empire du Japon, 1917* and *1924*. Tokio. Data are for lines in use, including those government owned, privately controlled, and *Kéibentétsudô* (defined as "Tramway à petit nombre de voitures"). The privately owned roads disappear after 1916, and the last group appears first in 1910.
[b] Computed from original data given in kilometers, by multiplying by 0.62137.

Nearly 80 per cent of the total railway mileage is government owned.

Japanese currency was based on a silver standard until 1897, when a gold standard was established. In 1921, there were 2,016 banks in Japan. These include 7 special banks, the most important of which is the Bank of Japan, the central bank. In addition, there are 42 agricultural and industrial banks, 1,331 ordinary banks and 636 savings banks. The banking system is loosely organized, the vast majority of banks being private, local in character, and possessing only small resources.

In April, 1881, a sharp drop in the value of the yen ushered in a period of severe depression. The Bank of Japan was established in 1882, following a period of rapid depreciation of the currency. By 1886, gradual recovery had begun, and the years 1887 to 1889 were years of expansion and active speculation. In 1889, the good influence of the granting of the Constitution was offset by complete failure of the rice crop, and 1890 was ushered in amid uncertainty and distress.

1890   Recession; depression.

    Activity culminates in crisis with many failures; commodity prices rise suddenly; great reduction in exports, but imports continue large.

    Money very tight; stock exchange panic; violent foreign exchange fluctuations; bank failures.

    Exceptional rice yield; price falls from very high point.

    Food scarcity due to failure of 1889 rice crop; beginning of operation of new constitution.

1891   Depression.
Increased dullness and stagnation; large fall in imports creates favorable balance of trade.
Money continues tight.
Fair rice crop with higher price.

1892   Depression.
Dullness continues with little activity in industry; slight increase in volume of foreign trade.
Money eases; security prices rise; rapid decline in rate of exchange.
Good rice crop, low price.

1893   Mild depression.
Internal trade continues dull; some revival in imports.
Money very easy.
Poor rice crop, low price.

1894   Revival; recession.
Industry and trade show definite improvement, first half-year; with Chinese war, unsettled conditions, shipping difficulties, and military requirements cause recession; large increase in foreign trade with unfavorable balance.
Money market tightens sharply, July; violent exchange fluctuations.
Excellent rice crop with low price; small silk yield.
War with China declared, July; victories and capture of Port Arthur, November.

1895   Depression; revival.
Temporary depression with end of war, April, quickly yields to boom; many new enterprises organized; commodity prices rise; foreign trade very active, small favorable balance.
Tight money eases, summer.
Good rice crop, low price; large silk yield and high price.
War ends, April, Japan receiving large indemnity; Formosa acquired; foreign powers force return of Liaotung Peninsula.

1896   Prosperity.
Widespread activity and expansion, especially manufacturing; commodity prices rise; speculation; imports increase, creating large unfavorable balance.
Money easy.
Very poor crops; rice price high, but silk low.
Tidal wave on northeast coast.

THE ANNALS OF JAPAN   345

1897   Prosperity; recession.

Continued activity and expansion, slackening in autumn; commodity price rise accelerated; continued activity in foreign trade, with exports retarded late in year.

Gold standard established; new currency in force, October; easy money tightens.

Rice crop failure, very high price; good silk yield with good price.

Tariff revised.

1898   Depression.

Dullness in internal trade; manufacturing depressed; many failures; government aid prevents severe crisis; imports continue to expand.

Money very tight, spring; silver ceases to be legal tender, March.

Large rice crop lowers price; fair silk yield with good price.

Payment of Chinese indemnity aids government finances.

1899   Depression.

Inactivity continues, especially in manufacturing industries; commodity price rise halted; exports revive, but imports fall sharply.

Slight financial panic; money eases, summer, but tightens late in year.

Poor rice yield with high price; good silk yield, price high.

Tariff increased, January; export duty abolished, July; new treaties make Japan "wide open" to foreign commerce.

1900   Deeper depression.

Increased dullness; many failures; manufacturing severely depressed; commodity prices fall after February; some revival in imports, exports decline.

Money very tight; many bank failures, December.

Good rice crop with good price; silk yield excellent with high price.

Japan joins Western nations in quelling Chinese Boxer uprisings.

1901   Depression; panic.

Depression continues; commodity prices fall; small increase in exports, decrease in imports.

Money very tight, easing late in year; financial panic, spring, with further bank failures.

Large rice crop with good price; poor silk yield price falls.

1902　Slow revival.

Gradual recovery; marked improvement in manufacturing; commodity prices reach bottom, May; slow revival in foreign trade.

Money eases.

Very poor rice crop, with high price; poor silk yield, low price.

Anglo-Japanese Alliance formed.

1903　Revival.

Increased activity in internal trade and manufacturing; foreign trade begins period of rapid expansion.

Money easy.

Good crops; rice price falls and silk price recovers.

1904　Prosperity.

Great activity; temporary setback with Russian War gives way to increased industry and commerce; commodity prices rise.

Money tightens.

Very large crops diminish prices.

War with Russia declared, February.

1905　Prosperity; recession; depression.

War activity continues; depression sets in with peace, September; enormous increase in imports.

Money tight.

Very poor rice crop, high price; poor silk yield with good price.

Port Arthur surrenders, January; Russian fleet decisively defeated, June; peace treaty signed, September.

1906　Revival; prosperity.

Steady increase in activity; boom appears, summer; many new companies formed; commodity prices rise; speculation very extensive; foreign trade expands rapidly, small favorable balance.

Money eases; stock exchange active.

Good crops with higher prices.

1907　Prosperity; panic; recession; depression.

Boom continues to recession, spring; industry slackens gradually; many failures late in year; imports continue to pour in at record rate.

Money tight; financial panic with bank failures, spring; severe stock market liquidation, beginning March.

Good rice crop and price; silk yield small, very high price.

Government purchases important railroads; emigration to United States checked by agreement; Korea made a protectorate, July.

THE ANNALS OF JAPAN

1908 Depression.

General inactivity and dullness; commodity prices fall at accelerating rate; decline in foreign trade.

Tight money eases late in year.

Very good crops, low prices.

1909 Depression; revival.

Continued dullness gives way to gradual recovery, fourth quarter; manufacturing activity increases; imports continue to decline, but exports revive, creating favorable balance.

Money easy.

Enormous rice crop, following attempt to corner market, causes sharp fall in price; good silk yield with low price.

1910 Revival; prosperity.

Steady progress in trade and industry; commodity prices rise slowly; marked increase in foreign trade, balance unfavorable.

Money abundant; government finances reorganized; stock exchange revives.

Poor rice crop, improved price; expansion in silk yield with low price.

Korea annexed, August; serious floods, autumn.

1911 Prosperity.

Continued development and expansion; extensive railroad construction; further marked increase in volume of foreign trade.

Money gradually tightens.

Good crops; rice price very high, silk fair.

Tariff raised, July.

1912 Prosperity.

Continued development and expansion; temporary halt in autumn, ascribed to Emperor's death; industrial promotion active; prices rise rapidly, first five months; foreign trade expansion continues.

Money very tight, after September.

Fair rice crop with very high price; revival in silk industry with good yield.

Emperor dies, July; first notable strike, occurring on Tokio tramways.

1913   Prosperity.

Continued activity; domestic expansion somewhat limited by money market; foreign trade expansion continues with large profits. Money tight.

Good rice crop, but local failure in northeast causes much distress; good silk yield with low price.

Strong anti-American feeling due to Californian legislation; political difficulties lead to riots, February.

1914   Recession; depression.

Slump in internal trade increased by war; foreign trade active to war, then unsettled.

Money tight, first half-year and end of year; exchange unfavorable, last half-year.

Enormous rice crop; low prices necessitate government aid; silk industry desperate with no markets.

Japan declares war on Germany, August; Tsingtau seized, August; Kiaochow seized, November.

1915   Revival; prosperity.

Depression slowly gives way to activity; prosperity, last half-year; export boom and further decline in imports result in favorable balance.

Money easy; rapid increase in note circulation; further drop in foreign exchange, recovering late in year.

Large rice crop with low prices forces Government to enter market to assuage agricultural distress; silk industry booms late in year.

"Twenty-one Demands" submitted to China, January, and modified form accepted, May.

1916   Prosperity.

Activity and expansion with formation of many new enterprises; foreign trade active.

Money easy; stock exchange boom; foreign exchange rises above par.

Excellent rice and good silk harvest with rising prices.

1917   Uneven prosperity.

War boom continues, but many strains develop; severe panics in stock, cotton, and silk exchanges; commodity prices rise rapidly to August and then drop; foreign trade activity continues with much speculation.

Tight money, beginning of year, eases somewhat; foreign exchange above par; export of specie prohibited, September.

Poor rice crop and further expansion in silk yield; higher prices.

Great Britain limits imports, February; France limits imports, March.

THE ANNALS OF JAPAN 349

1918 Uneven prosperity; recession.

Some improvement in internal trade; boom in war industries continues to Armistice; severe depression sets in, November, with many failures; commodity prices fall; foreign trade continues large.

Easy money tightens, autumn; foreign exchange continues above par.

Poor rice crop, further expansion in silk; high prices.

Japanese troops invade Siberia; serious rice riots, August.

1919 Depression; revival; prosperity.

Dullness continues to May, when revival sets in, followed by period of great activity; commodity prices fall to April and then rise rapidly; speculation; labor troubles arise; value of exports reaches peak, imports large, unfavorable balance.

Money eases to July and then tightens; stock exchange very active, prices reaching peak in October; foreign exchange continues above par.

Agricultural prosperity; excellent rice crop with record price; record silk yield with high price.

Korean revolt, March, suppressed by summer.

1920 Prosperity; recession; depression.

Continued acceleration to crisis, March, with collapse of silk market; rapid decline to severe depression and stagnation by August; failures; commodity prices reach peak, March, and then fall; exports and imports reach peak, spring, and then fall off rapidly, large unfavorable balance.

Money very tight; stock exchange panic, March; financial panic, April, with many bank failures; foreign exchange dips below par but recovers, May.

Record rice crop with extremely low price; smaller silk yield with very low price.

1921 Depression.

Dullness and inactivity; commodity prices reach bottom, March; temporary revival, late summer; further decline in prices and deeper depression, autumn; foreign trade small.

Money eases and tightens, autumn; foreign exchange below par, slowly falling.

Poor rice crop with improved price; good silk yield, price booms, November.

Typhoon and flood; Crown Prince constituted Regent owing to ill health of Emperor, November.

1922 Depression.

Depression in internal trade deepens; further curtailment in mining and manufacturing; unemployment; commodity prices fall to minimum, end of year; some revival in foreign trade, especially silk exports.

Money tight, temporary ease in summer; many runs on banks and failures, especially March and November; stock prices tend downwards; foreign exchange steady.

Excellent rice and fair silk yields, rising prices.

Troops withdrawn from Siberia, October.

1923 Depression.

Continued dullness and stagnation; beginning of revival checked, September; much distress with earthquake, September, and thirty days' moratorium declared; unemployment; commodity prices reach peak, October; exports decline, imports increase, enormous unfavorable balance.

Improved financial conditions hard hit by earthquake; money very tight late in year; exchange drops, end of year; dull stock market.

Poor rice, but good silk yield.

Earthquake and fire, September; Government takes emergency measures, including requisitioning of supplies, and suspending import duties.

1924 Depression.

Temporary activity in restoration work; depression deepens late in year; many failures; commodity prices fall, but rise after July; foreign trade active, especially imports.

Tight money market eases; marked fall in foreign exchange; embargo placed on export of gold.

Fair rice and poor silk yields.

Anti-American feeling aroused by Immigration Bill excluding Japanese from the United States on racial grounds; very high tariff on importation of luxuries established, July.

1925 Depression; revival.

Continued depression gives way to improvement, summer; decreasing unemployment; commodity prices decline, first four months and last quarter; fewer failures; very active and expanding foreign trade, improving balance.

Money market easing; exchange improves to April, slumps to September, and then recovers; stock speculation very active late in year; silver embargo removed, December.

Agriculture prosperous; good rice crop, record silk yield, and large wheat crop; rice and silk prices high, wheat declines.

Diplomatic relations with Russia resumed, January; earthquake, May; influenza epidemic, Tokio.

CHAPTER XVII.

THE ANNALS OF CHINA.

The Chinese Empire became the Chinese Republic on February 12, 1912. Nearly one-fourth of the population of the globe is concentrated in this one nation. China occupies the east and central part of Asia. Its western area is mountainous highland, and sparsely populated. The eastern area is densely populated lowland. This eastern section is divided into three large river basins, the Hwang Ho or Yellow River in the north, the Yangtze in the center, and the Si Kiang or West River in the south.

Accurate statistics concerning the area and population of China have never been compiled. The following estimates have been made for China proper, which does not include Mongolia, Chinese Turkestan, and Tibet. In 1922, the population was estimated to be 444,973,829 persons.[1] The corresponding area in 1924 was estimated to be 1,896,500 square miles,[2] which would be more than doubled, were the outlying territories included. Consequently the density of population within the area of China proper is 234 persons per square mile. Of this population, 80 per cent is rural and two-thirds live along the coast or in the river valleys, in one-third of the area.

China is essentially an agricultural country. An estimate is offered by the *China Year Book* that 85 per cent of the population is engaged in agriculture. In the northern provinces, wheat, barley, and maize are the chief crops. In the south, rice predominates. The growth of cotton is being rapidly developed, and tea and silk culture have always been important industries.

It is probable that China has rich mineral resources. At present, coal is its most important mineral product, and has been the basis for active competition for concessions among foreign nations.

---

[1] China Maritime Customs, Statistical Series: Nos. 3 to 5, *Foreign Trade of China, 1924*, part I, pp. 156, 157. Shanghai, 1925. This figure is the sum of the "Chinese population" and the "foreign population in China". It is presumably highly inaccurate.

[2] Same figure given in United States Department of Commerce, *Commerce Yearbook, 1923*. Washington, 1924, and *China Year Book, 1924-25*. London, 1925.

There has been little development along the lines of modern industry. A small number of factories, especially in the textile industry, have been established. In 1922, there were 7,700 miles of railroad capable of operation, of which 60 per cent were government owned. Though China is as yet an agricultural rather than a manufacturing country, the possibilities for an extensive industrial development are there. Almost every form of raw material known to commerce is produced in China, and labor is plentiful and cheap.

Chinese foreign trade has been hampered by the slow opening of ports to foreign commerce. Even after the opening of ports, the markets have been restricted to the coast districts by the limitations of transportation. Consequently, the growth of foreign trade has been slow. The chief articles of export are silk and food products; of import, cotton goods, metal products, rice, and kerosene.

The currency of China is on a silver basis. It is by no means standardized, various units of value being used among the different provinces. There has been little development along lines of modern banking until very recently, the facilities necessary for foreign trade being provided by branches of foreign banks. References in the annals to the rate of foreign exchange are based on London rates before 1914 and New York rates thereafter.

The annals here given for China are based chiefly on conditions in provinces which are active in international commerce, particularly those along the coast. Conditions in interior provinces are noted only when their isolation is broken by famine or disaster, necessitating external assistance. Because of the size and wide difference between the conditions of its various provinces, it is probably true that any year will offer prosperous conditions in certain districts of China and depression in others.

The Chinese annals begin in 1890 with trade and industry in a state of mild depression. The boom which had followed the war with France, ending in 1885, came to an end in 1888 because of declining exchange rates, severe floods, and two years of crop failures.

1890   Mild depression.

         Marked decline in tea, opium, and cotton industries; foreign trade depressed.

         Money very tight; improvement in foreign exchange to September, then rapid decline.

         Excellent cotton, poor silk yields.

         Severe floods, Chihli; opium growing legalized.

1891 Mild depression.
Internal trade disorganized; improvement in foreign trade, but very small profits.
Money continues tight, easing late in year; bank failures; prolonged fall in exchange begins.
Good tea, silk, and cotton crops.
Various anti-missionary riots and attacks on foreigners require intervention by foreign Governments.

1892 Depression deepens.
Stagnation; foreign trade severely depressed.
Financial crisis in spring; bank failures; rapid drop in exchange.
Cereal crop failures; silk and tea yields small.
Yellow River floods; severe famines, Mongolia and Shantung.

1893 Depression.
Dullness continues; foreign trade depressed.
Exchange fall continues.
Internal disturbances; Yellow River floods and famine, Shantung.

1894 Depression.
War causes some activity in internal trade; volume of foreign trade reaches low point, restricted by blockade and uncertainty.
Exchange fall continues at accelerated pace.
Crop failures, except silk.
Korea rebellion, March; war with Japan, July; continued defeats and fall of Port Arthur, November; outbreak of plague, Hongkong; famines, Mongolia and Shantung.

1895 Depression; revival.
Activity with peace, April; foreign trade increases rapidly.
Money very easy; fall in exchange checked.
Peace restored, April, with large indemnity required; Japan forced to return Liaotung by foreign powers; right to import machinery granted.

1896 Prosperity.
General activity and evidences of boom; many manufacturing enterprises organized; silk speculation; large increase in imports.
Exchange steady; internal trade hampered by scarcity of minor copper coins.
Poor silk yield with high price.
Imperial Post Office opened.

1897   Gradual recession.

Continued activity and expansion hampered by monetary conditions; many failures late in year; decline in imports with expansion of exports.

Money tight; exchange declines rapidly, July to September.

Small silk yield with high price.

Political unrest; Germans occupy Kiaochow; West River opened to foreign trade.

1898   Mild depression.

Internal trade dull despite influx of foreign capital; extensive railroad construction undertaken and active promotion of mining enterprises; foreign trade quiet.

Money very tight; severe scarcity of copper and minor coins; exchange decline continues.

Rapid succession of reform edicts, June to September, checked by *coup d'état* returning Empress Dowager to power; foreign governments strive for concessions, Russia obtaining Port Arthur, England obtaining Wei-hai-wei and Hongkong, and France obtaining Kwangchow-wan; internal disorder; Yellow River floods.

1899   Revival; prosperity.

General activity and expansion; new railroads open up large districts; record year in volume of foreign trade with large profits.

Exchange steady and higher.

Poor wheat crop, abundant rice; prosperous year for silk industry.

Increased brigandage and piracy; United States Secretary of State Hay announces the "Open Door Policy", September.

1900   Prosperity; recession; depression.

Continued activity and foreign trade brisk to Boxer uprising, May; depression, last half-year; active foreign trade suspended with uprising.

Foreign exchange steady.

Good silk crop, low price.

Boxer uprising, May; legations attacked, June; Allies occupy Peking, August; southern rebellion suppressed; severe famine in Shensi.

1901   Depression; revival.

Gradual return to normal conditions; rapid recovery in foreign trade, especially imports.

Exchange collapses, July.

Improvement in silk industry.

Famine; foreign occupation continues; gradual withdrawal of troops; large indemnity; serious floods in Yangtze Valley; tariff increased.

1902 Mild prosperity.
Conditions quiet; slow expansion in foreign trade.
Heavy fall in exchange.
Deficient crops; small silk yield.
Droughts followed by floods; severe outbreak of cholera.

1903 Mild prosperity.
Continued quietness; small expansion in foreign trade.
Money very tight; price of silver reaches low point in January and then rises rapidly.
Abundant harvests; silk yield failure; excellent tea year.
Tariff increased.

1904 Mild prosperity.
Increasing activity hampered by tight money market and Russian-Japanese War; large increase in volume of foreign trade.
Severe monetary stringency.
Silk industry prosperous, tea depressed.
Treaty regulating entrance of Chinese into the United States terminates.

1905 Mild prosperity.
Rapid expansion in activity retarded by boycott on American goods; manufacturing prosperous; speculation; large increase in imports.
Foreign exchange erratic, but rising; Imperial Bank opened, September.
Excellent crops; poor silk yield.
United States passes exclusion law; floods; typhoon, September.

1906 Recession.
Many natural calamities check internal trade; active speculation; foreign trade continues active, especially imports.
Money tight; gradually rising exchange.
Crop failures; fair silk yield.
Drought; floods; famine; political difficulties in North; Imperial edict provides for complete elimination of poppy-growing, November.

1907 Depression.
Internal trade dull; food prices very high; rapid decline in foreign trade late in year.
Exchange steady, but drops severely, last quarter; financial panic.
Crops fair or excellent.
Many local uprisings; severe famine in interior provinces.

1908 Depression.

Continued dullness; progress made in formation of new manufacturing companies; great reduction in volume of foreign trade.

Continuous fall in exchange to December.

Excellent harvests; rice price falls from high level; small silk yield, price advances.

Deaths of Emperor and Empress Dowager; United States remits Boxer indemnity payment.

1909 Revival.

Gradual increase in activity; beginning of period of development of industry; some activity in foreign trade, especially exports.

Low and steady exchange.

Poor wheat crop, tea and silk exceptionally abundant; bumper rice crop.

First meeting of Provincial Assemblies, October.

1910 Recession.

Internal trade hampered by financial stringency; rubber boom ends disastrously, June; widespread speculation in opium; foreign trade very active.

Financial stringency, summer, causes many bank failures; money very tight; exchange steady, rising in October.

Poor crops and high prices; rice exports prohibited; good silk and tea yields with low prices.

Famine; widespread civil unrest; National Assembly meets, October; pneumonic plague breaks out, October.

1911 Depression.

Dullness continues; railroad construction halted; foreign trade active until late in year.

Bank failures continue; exchange declines, but rises, end of year.

Poor crops.

Severe famines; plague spreads rapidly, spring; Yangtze flood, autumn; serious riotings, August; revolution, October; Emperor abdicates, December.

1912 Depression.

Internal trade dull; large increase in volume of foreign trade.

Money market disorganized with suspension of credit and banking facilities; extensive issue of paper money by provinces; exchange rate rises; Bank of China formed, February.

Excellent harvests; large tea crop; good silk yield; resumption of poppy planting in many districts.

Chinese Republic established; continual civil unrest throughout year; troops mutiny, Peking, February.

1913 Depression.

Poor internal trade; conditions unsettled; record foreign trade.

Money very tight; exchange slowly falls with slight temporary recovery, spring; financial distress late in year.

Good harvests, except tea.

First Presidential election held; United States recognizes the Republic, May; unrest continues.

1914 Depression.

Internal trade continues unsettled; foreign trade falls off, April.

Financial stringency with moratorium at outbreak of war; exchange drops to lower level, July.

Fair crops; silk yield small, price collapses with war.

Brigandage rife; severe floods in Kwangtung; Japan seizes Kiaochow, November.

1915 Depression.

Continued dullness with temporary improvement, summer; shipping shortage; imports greatly restricted, revival in exports.

Steadily rising foreign exchange.

Good crops, except silk.

Japan submits "Twenty-one Demands", January; China yields to modified demands, May; extensive anti-Japanese agitation; attempt to reëstablish monarchy fails, summer.

1916 Revival; prosperity.

Gradual revival in internal trade; marked rise in commodity prices; foreign trade active.

Exchange rises sharply, despite brief setback, July; specie payments suspended by both national banks, May.

Good crops.

Anarchy in provinces; insurrection in South.

1917 Uneven prosperity.

General activity, hampered in certain areas by political strife; foreign trade boom.

Rising exchange.

Poor crops.

Disorder and revolts; flood in Chihli; unsuccessful attempt to replace Emperor on throne, July; war declared against Germany, August; opium smoking prohibited.

1918 Uneven prosperity.

Increased internal strife hampers internal trade in large areas; foreign trade continues to expand.

Exchange rises to September, and then falls.

Crops abundant.

Continued disorder; Southern provinces secede and set up own government; tariff revised; plague.

1919 Prosperity.

General improvement in internal conditions; foreign trade boom continues.

Exchange falls to March and then rises rapidly.

Excellent crops; embargo on export of cereals lifted.

Relative calm in political and military activity; decreased brigandage; boycott of Japanese goods; tariff revised, August.

1920 Prosperity; recession; depression.

Great activity, speculation, and commodity price rise; decline sets in, mid-year; stagnation; many failures; foreign trade very active, first half-year, declining in autumn, especially exports.

Money very tight; exchange reaches peak, February; rapid fall, autumn.

Poor crops; disastrous silk and tea year.

Severe drought and famine in five provinces; earthquake; political strife renewed between Northern and Southern Governments.

1921 Depression.

Internal stagnation; commodity prices very high; seamen's strike for two months, Hongkong; foreign trade volume greatly reduced.

Money eases, summer; foreign exchange reaches low point, March, and slowly recovers; government finances desperate.

Improved crops; higher silk and tea prices.

Political chaos with continued civil war and inter-provincial difficulties; organized brigandage; Yangtze flood; famine.

1922 Depression.

Continued inactivity; commodity prices fall sharply, spring, but rise, fourth quarter; shipping strike, Hongkong; slight revival in exports, further decline in imports.

Exchange falls after temporary rise in spring.

Good crops.

Continued internal disquiet; nine-power treaty relating to Chinese territorial integrity and independence signed, February; Shantung controversy with Japan settled, December; tariff increased.

1923   Depression.

Continued dullness; wide commodity price fluctuations; failures; temporary activity arising from Japanese earthquake; further decline in imports and increase in exports.

Money plentiful; exchange steady except for temporary boom, spring.

Good crops, except wheat; revival of tea industry.

Continued warfare with combination of North and South against Central Government; President driven out of Peking, June; new constitution promulgated, October; Linching bandit outrage against foreigners, summer.

1924   Depression.

Deepening depression; commodity prices reach highest point in February, and fall sharply; increased foreign trade, especially imports.

Money tightens; exchange improves, autumn.

Poor crops; severe famine in northern provinces; very poor tea yield.

Outbreak of civil war, August; capture of Peking, October, by Northern Government; overthrow of President and establishment of Provisional Government; heavy floods, summer.

1925   Depression.

Domestic trade dull; commodity prices steady on high level; disorganized railroads threaten defaults; strikes, especially that of Shanghai cotton mill workers, first quarter; increased foreign trade.

Money very tight; foreign exchange steady, declining to April, rising to September, and then declining again.

Drought reduces crops; rice yield large, Kwantung, and failure, Kiangsi.

Severe earthquake, Yunan, March; after period of lessened hostilities, civil war resumed, last half-year; progressive disintegration of centralized authority; anti-British boycott; student riots, April and June, Shanghai; tariff autonomy gained, November.

CHAPTER XVIII.

BIBLIOGRAPHY.

The annals are no more correct than their sources. However, they should be more correct than any one source, since they represent a consensus of data. As far as possible, every statement represents the view of at least two independent sources. Special care has been given to instances in which disagreement appears.

The chief materials used have been government reports, commercial, financial, and trade papers, consular reports, bank reports, and year books. These materials have been supplemented by many historical, political, and descriptive books and pamphlets. Since many of these latter are avowedly controversial in nature, they have been used as sources only for data not pertaining to the subject of the controversy.

This study has been carried out chiefly in the New York Public Library. Consequently, the sources used are, in the main, those available there. Fortunately, the materials in the Reference Department are abundant, and the value of expert assistance and rapid service cannot be adequately acknowledged.

The titles listed below represent those which were actually used, either as sources providing information not found elsewhere, or as confirming some doubtful point. If all materials were included which were examined but which did not prove to be helpful, the list would be much longer.

The sources used in compiling the annals for several countries, are given in group (a). Other titles are listed according to the specific country for which they were used.

(a) General.

Annals of the American Academy of Political and Social Science, 1910–1926. Philadelphia.
Annual Statistician, 1876–1904. San Francisco.
Appleton's Annual Cyclopædia, 1890–1902. New York.
Bankers' Magazine, The, 1846–1926. New York.
Bankers' Magazine, The, 1844–1926. London.
Board of Trade Journal and Commercial Gazette, The, 1924–1926. London.

BIBLIOGRAPHY

Calwer, Richard, ed., *Jahrbuch der Weltwirtschaft*, 1911–1912. Jena.
Calwer, Richard, ed., *Das Wirtschaftsjahr*, 1902-1904, 1910. Jena.
Chamber of Commerce Journal, The, 1925-1926. London.
Economic Review, The, 1925-1926. London.
Economist, The, "Review Section," 1895–1926. Chicago.
Economist, The, 1843–1926. London.
Économiste Européen, L', 1925–1926. Paris.
Économiste Français, L', 1873–1926. Paris.
Encyclopædia Britannica, The. 11th and 12th ed. Cambridge (Eng.), 1910, 1922.
European Economic and Political Survey, 1925–1926. Paris.
Foreign Affairs, 1922–1926. New York.
France. Affaires Commerciales et Industrielles, Direction des, *Rapports Commerciaux des Agents Diplomatiques et Consulaires de France*, 1890–1911. Paris.
France. Statistique Générale, Bureau de la, *Annuaire Statistique*, 1885–1922. Paris.
Great Britain. Commercial, Labour, and Statistical Department, *Statistical Abstract for the Principal and Other Foreign Countries in Each Year*, 1879–1914. London.
Great Britain. Foreign Office, *Diplomatic and Consular Reports. Annual Series and Miscellaneous Series*, 1890–1914. London.
Great Britain. Foreign Office. Historical Section, *Peace Handbooks*. London, 1920.
Great Britain. Industry and Trade Committee, *Survey of Overseas Markets*. London, 1925.
Great Britain. Overseas Trade Department, *Economic Survey of Certain Countries Specially Affected by the War at the Close of the Year 1919*. London, 1920.
Hansard's Parliamentary Debates, 1803–1838. London.
Hassall, Arthur, *European History Chronologically Arranged, 476–1920*. London, 1920.
Haydn's Dictionary of Dates. 18th ed. New York, 1891.
Hazen, Charles D., *Modern European History*. New York, 1917.
Hyndman, Henry M., *Commercial Crises of the Nineteenth Century*. London, 1892.
Institut International de Statistique, *Aperçu de la Démographie des Divers Pays du Monde*. The Hague, 1925.
Institut International de Statistique, *Bulletin Mensuel*, 1925. The Hague.
International Institute of Agriculture. Statistics Bureau, *Annuaire International de Statistique Agricole*, 1910, 1915 et 1916. Rome.
International Institute of Agriculture. Statistics Bureau, *Monthly Statistical Bulletin*, 1924–1926. Rome.
International Labour Office, *Enquête sur la Production*. 4 vols. Paris, 1923.
International Labour Office, *International Labour Review*, 1921–1926. Geneva.
International Labour Office, *Statistics of Unemployment in Various Countries*, 1910–1922. (Studies and Reports, Series c. No. 6) Geneva, 1922.
International Labour Office, *Unemployment, 1920–1923*. (Studies and Reports, Series c. No. 8) Geneva, 1924.
International Year Book, 1907–1923. New York.
Investors' Monthly Manual, 1865–1926. London.
Juglar, Clément, *Des Crises Commerciales*. 2d ed. Paris, 1889.
Juglar, Clément, "Des Crises Commerciales et Monétaires de 1800 à 1857." *Journal des Économistes*, April, 1857. Second series, vol. xiv, pp. 35, 225. Paris.
Kral, J. J., *International Trade in 1924*. (United States Bureau of Foreign and Domestic Commerce, no. 373.) Washington, 1925.
Laveleye, Emile L. V. de, *Le Marché Monétaire et ses Crises Depuis Cinquante Ans*. Paris, 1865.
League of Nations, *Memorandum on Central Banks, 1913 and 1918–1923*. Geneva, 1924.
League of Nations, *Memorandum on Currency, 1913–1924*. Geneva, 1925.
Lloyds Bank, Limited, *Lloyds Bank Monthly*, 1920–1926. London.
London and Cambridge Economic Service, *Calendar of Chief Economic Events, 1919-25*. London, 1926.
London and Cambridge Economic Service, *Monthly Bulletin* and *Special Memoranda*, 1923–1926. London.

Manchester Guardian Commercial, The, "Annual Review," 1920–1926. Manchester (Eng.)
Mitchell, Wesley C., *Business Cycles.* (University of California Memoirs, vol. iii) Berkeley, 1913.
Mitchell, Wesley C., *Index Numbers of Wholesale Prices in the United States and Foreign Countries.* (United States. Bureau of Labor Statistics, Bulletin 284) Washington, 1921.
New York Evening Post, "Annual Financial Review," 1902–1926. New York.
New York Times Current History, 1911–1926. New York.
New York Times Financial Review, "Annual Financial Review," 1899–1913. New York.
New York Times Index, The, 1913–1925. New York.
Ogg, Frederic A., *Economic Development of Modern Europe.* New York, 1917.
Palgrave, R. H. Inglis, *Bank Rate in England, France, and Germany, 1844–1878.* London, 1880.
Raffalovich, Arthur, *Le Marché Financier,* 1894–1914. Paris.
Review of Economic Statistics, The, 1919–1926. Cambridge.
Robertson, Dennis H., *A Study of Industrial Fluctuation.* London, 1915.
Statesman's Year-Book, The, 1925. London.
Statist, The, 1882–1926. London.
Swiss Bank Corporation, *Bulletin mensuel,* 1925-1926. London.
Swiss Bank Corporation, *Financial and Commercial Review,* 1905-1924. London.
Times, The, Trade and Engineering Supplements, 1924-1926. London.
United States. Federal Reserve Board, *Federal Reserve Bulletin,* 1915–1926. Washington.
United States. Foreign and Domestic Commerce Bureau, *Commerce Reports,* 1914–1926. Washington.
United States. Foreign and Domestic Commerce Bureau, *Commerce Reports, Supplements,* 1914–1925. Washington.
United States. Foreign and Domestic Commerce Bureau, *Commerce Yearbook,* 1922–1924. Washington.
United States. Foreign and Domestic Commerce Bureau, *Commercial Relations of the United States with Foreign Countries,* 1911–1912. Washington.
United States. Foreign and Domestic Commerce Bureau, *Trade Information Bulletin,* 1922–1926. Washington.
United States. Foreign and Domestic Commerce Bureau, *Trade Promotion Bulletin,* 1925–1926. Washington.
United States. Gold and Silver Inquiry Commission, *European Currency and Finance.* 2 vols. Washington, 1925.
United States. Labor Department, *Annual Report of the Commissioner, 1886.* Washington, 1886.
United States. Manufactures Bureau, *Commercial Relations of the United States with Foreign Countries,* 1903–1910. Washington.
United States. Statistics Bureau (State Department), *Commercial Relations of the United States with Foreign Countries,* 1890–1902. Washington.
Volkswirtschaftliche Chronik. (Abdruck aus den *Jahrbüchern für Nationalökonomie und Statistik*), 1882-1925. Jena.
Wirth, Max, *Geschichte der Handelskrisen.* 2d ed. Frankfurt a. M., 1874.
World Almanac, 1920–1925. New York.

(b) *Argentina.*

Argentine Republic. Censo, Comision Directiva del, *Secundo Censo, 1895.* Buenos Aires, 1898.
Argentine Republic. Censo, Comision Directiva del, *Tercer Censo Nacional, 1914.* Buenos Aires, 1916.
Argentine Republic. Estadistica, Direccion General de, *Annuario del Comercio Exterior,* 1912, 1918–1920. Buenos Aires.

Argentine Republic. National Commission to the Panama-Pacific Exposition, *The Argentine Republic.* New York, 1915.
Argentine Yearbook, The, 1915–1916. Buenos Aires.
Great Britain. Overseas Trade Department, *Report on the Financial and Economic Condition of the Argentine Republic,* 1919–1924. London.
Hirst, William A., *Argentina.* New York, 1910.
Koebel, William H., *Modern Argentina.* London, 1907.
Martinez, Alberta B., and Lewandowski, Maurice, *The Argentine in the Twentieth Century.* 3d ed. Boston, 1912.
Revista de Economia Argentina, 1920–1926. Buenos Aires.
South American Journal, The, "Annual Review Issue," 1922–1926. London.
Tornquist, Ernesto & Cía., *Argentina.* (tr. by Peter H. Goldsmith. Interamerican Digests. Economic Series: no. 1) New York, 1924.
Tornquist, Ernesto & Cía., *Business Conditions in the Argentine.* (Bulletins no. 140-169) 1918–1926. Buenos Aires.
Tornquist, Ernesto & Cía., *The Economic Development of the Argentine Republic in the Last Fifty Years.* Buenos Aires, 1919.
United States. Foreign and Domestic Commerce Bureau, *The Economic Position of Argentina During the War.* (Miscellaneous Series, no. 88) Washington, 1920.

(c) *Australia.*

Annual Review of Australian Manufactures, The, 1920–1921. Sydney.
Atkinson, Meredith, ed., *Australia.* Melbourne, 1920.
Australasian Insurance and Banking Record, 1923–1926. Melbourne and Sydney.
Australia. Census and Statistics Bureau, *Quarterly Summary of Australian Statistics,* 1918–1925. Melbourne.
Australia. Census and Statistics Bureau, *Official Year Book,* 1908–1924. Melbourne.
Australia. Census and Statistics Bureau, *Quarterly Summary of Australian Statistics,* 1918–1925. Melbourne.
Australia. Central Wool Committee, *Report of the Central Wool Committee for the Season 1919–1920.* Melbourne, 1920.
Australia To-Day, 1925. Melbourne.
British Australian and New Zealander, The, 1925. London.
Chapman, Emmett A., *Australia.* (United States Bureau of Foreign and Domestic Commerce, Trade Information Bulletin, no. 390.) Washington, 1926.
Coghlan, Timothy A., *Labour and Industry in Australia.* 4 vols. London, 1918.
Copeland, D. B., "The Economic Situation in Australia, 1918–1923." *The Economic Journal,* March, 1924. vol. xxxiv, p. 32. London.
Great Britain. Overseas Trade Department, *Report on the Economic and Commercial Situation of Australia,* 1921–1923. London.
Great Britain. Trade Commissioner for the Commonwealth of Australia, *Report to the Board of Trade,* 1911–1919. London.
Heaton, Herbert, *Modern Economic History with Special Reference to Australia.* 2d ed. Adelaide, 1922.
New South Wales. Statistician, Office of, *Official Year Book,* 1904–1909. Sydney.
New South Wales. Statistician, Office of, *A Statistical Account of Australia and New Zealand,* 1902–1904. Sydney.
New South Wales. Statistician, Office of, *A Statistical Account of the Seven Colonies of Australia,* 1896–1900. Sydney.
New South Wales. Statistician, Office of, *The Wealth and Progress of New South Wales,* 1890–1901. Sydney.
Roberts, Stephen H., *History of Australian Land Settlement (1788–1920).* Melbourne, 1924.
Rusden, George W., *History of Australia.* 3 vols. 2nd ed. Melbourne, 1897.
Wise, Bernard R., *The Commonwealth of Australia.* Boston, 1909.
Year-Book of Australia, The, 1891, 1897, 1901, 1916. Sydney.

(d) Austria.

Austria. Bundesamt für Statistik, *Statistische Nachrichten,* 1923–1926. Vienna.
Austria. Bundesamt für Statistik, *Statistisches Handbuch,* 1920–1924. Vienna.
Austria. Central-Commission, *Statistisches Jahrbuch, 1881.* Vienna, 1884.
Austria. Haus-, Hof-, und Staatsarchiv, *Volkswirtschaftliche Chronik,* 1912–1916. Vienna.
Brezigar, Emil, "Die wirtschaftlichen Konjunktur- und Depressionswellen in Österreich seit dem Jahre 1896." *Zeitschrift für Volkswirtschaft, Sozialpolitik und Verwaltung,* 1914. vol. xxiii, p. 39. Vienna and Leipzig.
Drage, Geoffrey, *Austria-Hungary.* London, 1909.
German, Peter, *Die Geschichte der Börsenkrisen.* Vienna, 1921.
Great Britain. Overseas Trade Department, *Report on the Industrial and Commercial Situation of Austria,* 1919–1925. London.
Jankovich, Béla von, "Die Fluktuation der Waarenpreise im Grosshandel und die Schwankungen der Wechselkurse der Österreich-Ungarischen Papiervaluta in den Jahren 1867–1897." *Kozgazdasagi Szemle,* 1899.
Kilborne, R. D., "The Rejuvenation of Austria." *Harvard Business Review,* April, 1924. vol. ii, p. 334. Chicago.
Kralik, Richard von, *Österreichische Geschichte.* Vienna, 1914.
League of Nations. Layton, W. T., and Charles Rist, *The Economic Situation of Austria.* Geneva, 1925.
Leonhardt, Gustav, *Die Verwaltung der Österreichisch-Ungarischen Bank,* 1878–1885. Vienna, 1886.
Łopuszánski, Eugen, *Die Volkwirtschaft Österreich in den Jahren, 1900 bis 1904.*
Mayer, Franz M., *Geschichte Österreichs.* 2 vols. Vienna, 1909.
Mecenseffy, Emil, *Die Verwaltung der Österreichisch-Ungarischen Bank,* 1886–1895. Vienna, 1896.
Mises, Ludwig von, "Die Störungen im Wirtschaftsleben der Österreichisch-Ungarischen Monarchie während der Jahre 1912–1913." *Archiv für Sozialwissenschaft und Sozialpolitik,* 1915. vol. xxxix, p. 174. Tübingen.
Oesterreichische Credit-Anstalt für Handel und Gewerbe, *Economic Review,* 1925–1926. Vienna.
Oesterreichische Volkswirt, Der, 1909–1926. Vienna.
Schäffle, Albert E. F., "Der Grosse Börsenkrach des Jahres 1873." *Zeitschrift für die Gesammte Staatswissenschaft,* 1874. vol. xxx, p. 1. Tübingen.
Steed, Henry W., *The Hapsburg Monarchy.* 4th ed. London, 1919.
Walré de Bordes, J. van, *The Austrian Crown.* London, 1924.
Wirth, Max, "The Crisis of 1890." *Journal of Political Economy,* March, 1893. vol. i, p. 214. Chicago.

(e) Brazil.

Brazil. Agricultura, Industria e Commercio, Ministerio da, *Exposição Nacional de Borracha de 1913* (Monographia no. 23) Rio de Janeiro, 1913.
Brazil. Delegation to the Third International Rubber Exhibition, *Brazil the Land of Rubber.* Rio de Janeiro, 1912.
Brazil. Estadistica Commercial, Directoria de, *Economical Data About Brazil.* Rio de Janeiro, 1924.
Brazil. Estadistica, Directoria Geral de, *Annuaire Statistique du Brésil, 1908–1912.* Rio de Janeiro, 1916.
Brazil. Estadistica, Directoria Geral de, *Resumo de Varias Estadisticas Economico-Financeiras.* Rio de Janeiro, 1924.
Brazilian Business, 1921–1926. Rio de Janeiro.
Brazilian Year Book, The, 1909. Rio de Janeiro.
Buley, Ernest C., *North Brazil.* New York, 1914.
Buley, Ernest C., *South Brazil.* London, 1914.
Centro Industrial do Brazil, *Brazil; Its Natural Riches and Industries.* 2 vols. Rio de Janeiro, 1910.
Denis, Pierre, *Brazil.* London, 1911.

BIBLIOGRAPHY 365

Dettman, Eduard, *Das Moderne Brasilien.* Berlin, 1912.
Great Britain. Overseas Trade Department, *Report on the Economic and Financial Conditions in Brazil,* 1919–1924. London.
James, Herman G., *Brazil After a Century of Independence.* New York, 1925.
Oakenfull, J. C., ed., *"Brazil" Past, Present and Future.* London, 1919.
South American Journal, The, "Annual Review Issue," 1922–1926. London.
Ukers, William H., *Coffee Merchandising.* New York, 1924.
United States. American Republics Bureau, *United States of Brazil.* Washington, 1901.
United States. Foreign and Domestic Commerce Bureau, *Brazil; A Study of Economic Conditions Since 1913.* (Miscellaneous Series, no. 86) Washington, 1920.
Woodroffe, Joseph F., *The Rubber Industry of the Amazon.* London, 1915.

(f) Canada.

Boam, Henry J., *Twentieth Century Impressions of Canada.* London, 1914.
Bradstreet's, 1879–1926. New York.
Breckenridge, Roeliff M., *The History of Banking in Canada.* (United States. National Monetary Commission. 61st Congress, 2d Session, Senate Documents, vol. vii) Washington, 1910.
Canada. Census and Statistics Office, *The Canada Yearbook,* 1904–1918. Ottawa.
Canada. Commercial Intelligence Service, *Canada as a Field for British Branch Industries.* Ottawa, 1922.
Canada. Cost of Living, Board of Inquiry Into, *Report of the Board.* 2 vols. Ottawa, 1915.
Canada. Labour Department. *The Labour Gazette,* 1900–1926. Ottawa.
Canada. Labour Department, *Wholesale Prices, Canada,* 1890–1916. Ottawa.
Canada. Statistics Branch, *Statistical Yearbook of Canada,* 1890–1904. Ottawa.
Canada. Statistics Bureau, *The Canada Year Book,* 1918–1924. Ottawa.
Canada. Statistics Bureau. Internal Trade Division, *Prices and Price Indexes, 1913–1923.* Ottawa, 1924.
Canada To-Day, 1911–1924. London.
Canadian Annual Review of Public Affairs, 1902–1923. Toronto.
Canadian Bank of Commerce, *Annual Report,* 1882–1925. Toronto.
Canadian Bank of Commerce Year Book, 1920–1924. Toronto.
Canadian Pacific Railway, *Agricultural and Industrial Progress in Canada,* 1920–1926. Montreal.
Canadian Year Book, 1900–1913. Toronto.
Chronicle, The, 1925–1926. Montreal.
Commercial Intelligence Journal, 1925–1926. Ottawa.
Dominion Bank, The, *Fifty Years of Banking Service, 1871–1921.* Toronto, 1922.
Donald, William J. A., *The Canadian Iron and Steel Industry.* Boston, 1915.
Financial Post of Canada, "Annual Review Number," 1916–1925. Toronto.
Financial Post Survey, 1925–1926. Winnipeg.
Fisk, Harvey E., *The Dominion of Canada.* New York, 1920.
Fleck, Anton A., *Kanada.* (Schriften des Instituts für Seeverkehr und Weltwirtschaft an der Universität Kiel. vol. x) Jena, 1912.
Gazette, The, "Annual Commercial Review," 1911–1916, Montreal.
Gleichen, Edward, comp., *British America.* (In the Nations of To-Day) London, 1923.
Great Britain. Overseas Trade Department, *Report on the Financial, Industrial, and Commercial Conditions in Canada,* 1921–1923. London.
Great Britain. Trade Commissioner for the Dominion of Canada and Newfoundland, *Report to the Board of Trade,* 1912–1919. London.
Johnson, Joseph F., *The Canadian Banking System.* (United States. National Monetary Commission. 61st Congress, 2d Session, Senate Documents, vol. xxxvi) Washington, 1910.
Mavor, James, *Report on the North West of Canada, with Special Reference to Wheat Production for Export.* (Great Britain. Parliamentary Papers, 1905, liv, cd. 2628) London, 1905.

Michell, H., "Physical Volume of Production in Canada." *Industrial Canada*, Nov., 1925. vol. xxvi, p. 47. Toronto.
Monetary Times, The, 1919–1926. Toronto.
Rew, Henry, *Economic Resources of Canada*. (Great Britain. Agriculture and Fisheries Ministry, Economic Series no. 3) London, 1925.
Royal Bank of Canada, *Annual Report*, 1916–1925. Montreal.
Royal Bank of Canada, *Monthly Bulletin*, 1925–1926. Montreal.
Shortt, Adam, ed., *Canada and Its Provinces*. 23 vols., especially vols. ix and x. Toronto, 1914–1917.
Shortt, Adam, *Early Economic Effects of the European War Upon Canada*. New York, 1918.
Skelton, O. D., *General Economic History, 1867–1912*. (In Canada and Its Provinces, vol. ix) Toronto, 1914.
Times, The London, *The Times Book of Canada*. London, 1920.
Viner, Jacob, *Canada's Balance of International Indebtedness, 1900–1913*. Cambridge, 1924.

(g) China.

American Bankers' Association. Commerce and Marine Commission, *China, An Economic Survey, 1923*. New York, 1923.
Arnold, Julean, *Commercial Handbook of China*. (United States Bureau of Foreign and Domestic Commerce, Miscellaneous Series, no. 84) 2 vols. Washington, 1919.
Bau, Mingchien J., *The Foreign Relations of China*. New York, 1921.
Bell, H. T., Montague, and Woodhead, H. G. W., *China Year Book*, 1912–1922. London.
China. Economic Information Bureau, *The Chinese Economic Bulletin*, 1923–1926. Shanghai.
China. Economic Information Bureau, *The Chinese Economic Monthly*, 1925–1926. Peking.
China. *The Chino-Japanese Negotiations*. (Chinese Official Statement Reprinted from *Peking Gazette*, May 14, 1915) Peking, 1915.
China. Imperial Maritime Customs, *Statistical Series: nos. 3–4. Returns of Trade and Trade Reports. Part I*. 1889–1900. Shanghai.
China. Imperial Maritime Customs, *Statistical Series: no. 6. Decennial Reports*, 1882–1892, 1892–1901. Shanghai.
China. Maritime Customs, The, *Statistical Series: nos. 3 and 4. Returns of Trade and Trade Reports. Part I*, 1911–1915. Shanghai.
China. Maritime Customs, The, *Statistical Series: nos. 2 and 5. Foreign Trade of China. Part I*, 1920–1923. Shanghai.
China and Far East Finance and Commerce Year Book, 1921–1923. Shanghai.
Chu, Chin, *The Tariff Problem in China*. New York, 1916.
Clements, Paul H., *The Boxer Rebellion*. New York, 1915.
Couling, Samuel, *The Encyclopædia Sinica*. London, 1917.
Donovan, John P., *Yesterday and To-Day in China*. London, 1923.
Eastern Commerce, 1916–1923. Yokohama.
Great Britain. Overseas Trade Department, *Report on the Commercial, Industrial, and Economic Situation of China*, 1920-1924. London.
Hall, Ray O., *Chapters and Documents on Chinese National Banking*. Shanghai, 1920.
Lee, Frederic E., *Currency, Banking and Finance in China*. (United States Department of Commerce, Trade Promotion Series, no. 27) Washington, 1926.
MacNair, Harley F., *Modern Chinese History. Selected Readings*. Shanghai, 1923.
Morse, Hosea B., *The Trade and Administration of China*. 3d ed. London, 1921.
Overlach, T. W., *Foreign Financial Control in China*. New York, 1919.
Pan, Shu-lun, *The Trade of the United States with China*. New York, 1924.
See, Chong Su, *The Foreign Trade of China*. New York, 1919.
United States. Statistics Bureau, "Commercial China in 1900." *Monthly Summary of Commerce and Finance*, June, 1901. p. 2823. Washington.
Wagel, Srinivas R., *Finance in China*. Shanghai, 1914.

BIBLIOGRAPHY

Wei, Wen Pin, *The Currency Problem in China.* New York, 1914.
Williams, Samuel W., *A History of China.* New York, 1897.
Willoughby, Westel W., *Constitutional Government in China.* (Pamphlet Series of the Carnegie Endowment for International Peace. Division of International Law. no. 47) Washington, 1922.
Willoughby, Westel W., *Foreign Rights and Interests in China.* Baltimore, 1920.
Woodhead, H. G. W., *The Truth about the Chinese Republic.* London, 1926.

(h) *France.*

Aftalion, Albert, *Les Crises Périodiques de Surproduction.* 2 vols. Paris, 1913.
Annuaire Général de la France et de l'Étranger, 1920-1925. Paris.
Banque de France, Conseil Général de la, *Compte Rendu des Operations de la Banque de France,* 1891-1926. Paris.
Bourgeois, Emile, *Modern France.* Cambridge (Eng.), 1919.
Bulletin de la Statistique Générale de la France et du Service d'Observation des Prix, 1920-1926. Paris.
Clapham, J. H., *The Economic Development of France and Germany, 1815-1914.* Cambridge (Eng.), 1921.
Davis, Joseph S., "Recent Economic and Financial Progress in France." *Review of Economic Statistics,* July, 1921. Prelim. vol. iii, p. 219. Cambridge.
Deville, Louis, *Les Crises de la Bourse de Paris, 1870-1910.* Paris, 1911.
Droppers, Garrett, *Economic History in the Nineteenth Century.* New York, 1923.
Fontaine, Arthur, *L'Industrie Française Pendant la Guerre.* Paris, 1924.
Forrester, R. B., *The Cotton Industry in France.* Manchester (Eng.), 1921.
Fournière, Eugene, *Le Règne de Louis-Philippe.* (Histoire Socialiste, 1789-1900. vol. viii) Paris, 1906.
France. Agriculture, Ministère de l', *Statistique Agricole Annuelle,* 1910-1922. Paris.
France. Commission des Crises Économiques (Cahan, Georges J. E. and Laurent, E. E.), *Rapports . . . sur les Indices des Crises Économiques* Paris, 1912.
France. Travail, Ministère du, *Annuaire,* 1923. Paris.
France. Travaux Publics, Ministère des, *Notice sur la Périodicité des Crises Économiques.* Paris, 1907.
French Year Book, The, 1919. Paris.
Great Britain. Overseas Trade Department, *Report on Economic Conditions in France,* 1923-1924. London.
Guerard, Albert L., *French Civilization in the Nineteenth Century.* London, 1914.
Guyot, Yves and Raffalovich, Arthur, "Crise." *Dictionnaire du Commerce,* p. 1127. Paris, 1898.
Hanotaux, Gabriel, *Contemporary France.* 4 vols. New York, 1903-1909.
Institut de Statistique de l'Université de Paris, *Indices du Movement Général des Affaires en France et en Divers Pays,* 1922-1926. Paris.
Journal des Économistes, 1841-1926. Paris.
Lampériere, Hippolyte, *Les Discussion sur les Crises de Surproduction dans les Premières Années du xixe Siècle.* Paris, 1912.
Lavisse, Ernest, *Histoire de France Contemporaine depuis la Revolution jusqu'a la Paix de 1919.* 10 vols. Paris, 1920-1922.
Levasseur, Émile, *Histoire des Classes Ouvrières et de l'Industrie en France de 1789 à 1870.* 2 vols. 2d ed. Paris, 1903-1904.
Liësse, André, *Evolution of Credit and Banks in France.* (United States. National Monetary Commission. 61st Congress, 2d Session, Senate Documents, vol. xxiv) Washington, 1909.
MacDonald, John R., *A History of France.* 3 vols. New York, 1915.
Newmarck, Alfred, *Finances Contemporaines.* 5 vols. Paris, 1902-1907.
Renard, Georges F., *La Republique de 1848 (1848-1852).* (Histoire Socialiste, 1789-1900. vol. ix) Paris, 1907.
Société d'Études et d'Informations Économiques, "L'Évolution de l'Activité Industrielle de la France Depuis l'Armistice." *Daily Bulletin, Supplement,* Dec. 17, 1923. Paris.

(i) Germany.

Anderson, Benjamin M., *German Business and Finance under the Dawes Plan.* (*The Chase Economic Bulletin,* April, 1926. vol. viii, no. 1) New York.
Annalen des Deutschen Reichs für Gesetzgebung, Verwaltung und Statistik, 1868-1877. Leipzig.
Basch, Julius, ed., *Wirtschaftliche Weltlage, Börse und Geldmarkt,* 1889, 1892-1902. Berlin.
Bücher, Hermann, *Finanz-, und Wirtschaftsentwicklung Deutschlands in den Jahren 1921 bis 1925.* Berlin, 1925.
Calwer, Richard, *Handel und Wandel,* 1900, 1901. Berlin.
Clapham, J. H., *The Economic Development of France and Germany 1815-1914.* Cambridge (Eng.), 1921.
Dawson, William H., *The German Empire, 1867-1914.* 2 vols. London, 1919.
Das Deutsche Wirtschaftsjahr. (Reviewed in *Jahrbücher für Nationalökonomie und Statistik*) 1880-1883. Jena.
Finanzpolitische Korrespondenz, 1925-1926. Berlin.
Frankfurter Societatsdruckerei, G. M. B. H., *Geschichte der Frankfurter Zeitung, 1856 bis 1906.* Frankfurt a. M., 1906.
Germany. Kriegslastenkommission, *Germany's Economy, Currency and Finance.* Berlin, 1924.
Germany. Reichsbank, *Verwaltungsbericht der Reichsbank,* 1920-1924. Berlin.
Germany. Statistisches Amt, *Statistisches Handbuch für das Deutsche Reich.* 2 vols. Berlin, 1907.
Germany. Statistiches Amt, *Statistisches Jahrbuch für das Deutsche Reich,* 1880-1923. Berlin.
Germany. Statistisches Amt, *Wirtschaft und Statistik,* 1921-1926. Berlin.
Gooch, George P., *Germany.* London, 1925.
Great Britain. Overseas Trade Department, *Report on the Economic and Financial Situation of Germany, 1923-1924.* London.
Hammerbacher, *Die Konjunkturen in der Deutschen Eisen-, und Maschinen-, Grossindustrie.* Munich, 1914.
Hansen, Alvin H., *Cycles of Prosperity and Depression in the United States, Great Britain and Germany. . . . 1902-1908.* (University of Wisconsin Studies in the Social Sciences and History, no. 5) Madison, 1921.
Howard, Earl D., *The Cause and Extent of the Recent Industrial Progress of Germany.* Boston, 1907.
Kuczynski, Robert R., *Postwar Labor Conditions in Germany.* (United States. Labor Statistics Bureau, Bulletin no. 380) Washington, 1925.
Lièsse, André, *The Reichsbank, 1876-1900.* (United States. National Monetary Commission. 61st Congress, 2d Session, Senate Documents, vol. 16) Washington, 1910.
May, R. E., *Das Grundgesetz der Wirtschaftskrisen.* Berlin, 1902.
Michaelis, Otto, *Die Handelskrisis von 1857.* (Volkswirtschaftliche Schriften, II) Berlin, 1873.
Neuwirth, Josef, *Die Speculationscrisis von 1873.* Leipzig, 1874.
Perrot, Franz, *Der Bank-, Börsen, und Actienschwindel.* 3 vols. Rostock, 1873-76.
Prussia. Statistisches Bureau, *Vergleichende Übersicht des Ganges der Industrie, des Handels und Verkehrs im Preussischen Staate,* 1859-1868. Berlin.
Reparations Commission, *Report of the Agent General for Reparation Payments, November 30, 1925.* Berlin, 1925.
Review of German Economic Conditions, 1925. New York.
Sartorius von Waltershausen, August, *Deutsche Wirtschaftsgeschichte 1815-1914.* Jena, 1920.
Saxony. Statistisches Bureau, *Statistisches Jahrbuch für das Königreich Sachsen.* II Teil, *Statistische Jahrbuch,* 1873-1890. Dresden.
Sayons, André E., *La Crise Allemande de 1900-1902.* Paris, 1903.
Schmitz, Otto, *Die Bewegung der Warenpreise.* Berlin, 1903.
Sombart, Werner, *Die Deutsche Volkswirtschaft im Neunzehnten Jahrhundert.* Berlin, 1913.

BIBLIOGRAPHY 369

Stern, Boris, *Works Council Movement in Germany*. (United States. Labor Statistics Bureau, Bulletin no. 383) Washington, 1925.
Störungen im Deutschen Wirtschaftsleben während der Jahre 1900 ff., Die. (Schriften des Vereins für Socialpolitik. vol. cv-cxii) Leipzig, 1903.
Vierteljahrschrift für Volkswirtschaft, Politik und Kulturgeschichte, 1863–1893. Berlin.
Ward, Adolphus W., *Germany, 1815–1890*. 3 vols. Cambridge (Eng.), 1916–1918.
Wirtschaftliche Bewegung von Handel und Industrie in Deutschland, Die (Reviewed in Jahrbücher für Nationalökonomie und Statistik), 1884–1888. Jena.
Wirtschaftsdienst, 1916–1926. Hamburg.
Wirtschaftskurve mit Indexzahlen der Frankfurter Zeitung, Die, 1924–1925. Frankfurt a. Main.
Wolff, Siegfried, *Das Grundungsgeschäft im Deutschen Bankegewerbe*. Stuttgart, 1915.

(j) Great Britain.

Acworth, A. W., *Financial Reconstruction in England, 1815–1822*. London, 1925.
Agricultural Gazette, 1852–1874.
Alison, Archibald, *England in 1815 and 1845 and the Monetary Famine of 1847*. 4th ed. London, 1847.
Alison, Archibald, *Free Trade And Protection*. Edinburgh, 1844.
Annual Register, The, 1790–1923. London.
Ashburton, Alexander Baring, *The Financial and Commercial Crisis Considered*. 3d ed. London, 1847.
Bagehot, Walter, *Lombard Street*. New York, 1873.
Barclays Bank, Limited, *Monthly Review*, 1923–1925. London.
Baring, Francis, *Observations on the Establishment of the Bank of England and on the Paper Circulation of the Country*. London, 1797.
Baxendale, A. S., *Currency: An Indictment*. London, 1925.
Bell, G. M., "History of English Panics." *Hunt's Merchants' Magazine and Commercial Review*, December, 1850. vol. xxiii, p. 605. New York.
Bouniatian, Mentor, *Geschichte der Handelskrisen in England, 1640–1840*. Munich, 1908.
Bowden, Witt, *Industrial Society in England towards the End of the Eighteenth Century*. New York, 1925.
Brassey, Thomas B., *Foreign Work and English Wages*. London, 1879.
Browning, G., *The Domestic and Financial Condition of Great Britain*. London, 1834.
Buchanan, David, *Inquiry into the Taxation and Commercial Policy of Great Britain*. Edinburgh, 1844.
Burke, Edmund, *Thoughts and Details on Scarcity*. London, 1800.
Caird, James, *The Landed Interest and The Supply of Food*. 4th ed. London, 1880.
Cannan, Edwin, ed., *The Paper Pound of 1797–1821*. (A reprint of the bullion report with editor's introduction) London, 1919.
Chalmers, George, *Considerations on Commerce, Bullion, etc*. London, 1811.
Cleghorn, James, *On the Depressed State of Agriculture*. Edinburgh, 1822.
Corrie, Edgar, *Considerations on the Corn Laws*. London, 1791.
Cunningham, William, *The Growth of English Industry and Commerce in Modern Times*. 3 vols. Cambridge (Eng.), 1903–1912.
Danson, J. T., *A Contribution Towards An Investigation of the Changes . . . from . . . 1839 to . . . 1847, etc*. London, 1848.
Dawson, William, *An Inquiry into the Causes of the General Poverty and Dependence of Mankind*. Edinburgh, 1814.
Droppers, Garrett, *Economic History in the Nineteenth Century*. New York, 1923.
Ellis, Arthur, *The Rationale of Market Fluctuations*. 4th ed. London, 1879.
Enderby, Charles, *The Distress of the Nation, its Causes and Remedies*. London, 1844.
Ernle, Rowland E. Prothero, *The Pioneers and Progress of English Farming*. London, 1888.

Evans, David M., *The Commercial Crisis 1847-48.* 2d ed. London, 1849.
Evans, David M., *The History of the Commercial Crisis, 1857-58.* London, 1859.
Financial Review, The, 1873-1921. New York.
Francis, John, *History of the Bank of England, its Times and Traditions.* 2 vols. 2d ed. London, 1867.
Gentleman's Magazine, The, 1790-1860. London.
Giffen, Robert, *Economic Inquiries and Studies.* 2 vols. London, 1904.
Gleichen, Edward, comp., *Great Britain.* (The Nations of To-Day.) 2 vols. London, 1923.
Great Britain. Bank Acts Committee, *Report from the Select Committee on Bank Acts, etc.* London, 1857.
Great Britain. Commercial Credit Committee, *Report from the Select Committee, etc., 29 April, 1793.* London, 1826.
Great Britain. Gold Bullion, Select Committee on the High Price of, *Report . . . from the Select Committee, etc.* London, 1810.
Great Britain. House of Lords, *The Lords' Report on Commercial Distress.* London, 1848.
Great Britain. Labour Ministry, *The Ministry of Labour Gazette,* 1893-1926. London.
Great Britain. Manufactures, Commerce and Shipping Committee, *Report from the Select Committee, etc., 1833.* London.
Great Britain. Poor Laws and Relief of Distress Commission, *Report of the Royal Commission, etc.,* part vi. London, 1909.
Great Britain. Statistical Department, *Statistical Abstract,* 1865-1924. London.
Great Britain. Trade and Industry Depression Commission, *Second Report of the Royal Commission.* London, 1886.
Great Britain. Trade Board. Statistical Department, *Tables of the Revenue, Population, Commerce, etc., of the United Kingdom and its Dependencies, 1850-1851.* London.
Greene, J. R., *A Short History of the English People.* 4 vols. New York, 1892.
Hansen, Alvin H., *Cycles of Prosperity and Depression in the United States, Great Britain and Germany . . . 1902-1908.* (University of Wisconsin Studies in the Social Sciences and History, no. 5) Madison, 1921.
Hassall, Arthur, *British History Chronologically Arranged.* London, 1920.
Hawtrey, R. G., *Currency and Credit.* London, 1919.
Hazell's Annual, 1886-1922. London.
Heckscher, Eli F., *The Continental System.* Oxford, 1922.
Hesketh, W. T., "Depression in Trade and its Causes." *Transactions of the Manchester Statistical Society,* March, 1909. p. 79. Manchester (Eng.).
Is Unemployment Inevitable? London, 1924.
Jevons, William S., *Investigations in Currency and Finance.* London, 1884.
Kirkaldy, Adam W., *British Finance during and after the War, 1914-1921.* (Publication of the British Association for the Advancement of Science) London, 1921.
Laing, Samuel, sr., *National Distress: Its Causes and Remedies.* London, 1844.
Late Commercial Crisis, The, by a Glasgow Manufacturer. Glasgow, 1839.
Layton, Walter T., *An Introduction to the Study of Prices.* London, 1920.
Levi, Leone, *History of British Commerce and of the Economic Progress of the British Nation.* London, 1872.
Long, Charles, *A Temperate Discussion of the Causes Which Have Led to the Present High Price of Bread.* London, 1800.
Lowe, David, *Appeal to the Common Sense of the Country.* Edinburgh and London, 1850.
Lowe, Joseph, *The Present State of England in regard to Agriculture, Trade and Finance.* 2d ed. London, 1823.
Loyd, Samuel J., *Reflections Suggested by a Perusal of J. Palmer's Pamphlet on the Causes and Consequences of the Pressure of the Money Market.* London, 1837.
Lyon, Charles E., *British Financial Conditions in 1924.* (United States Bureau of Foreign and Domestic Commerce, Trade Information Bulletin no. 336) Washington, 1925.

MacLeod, Henry D., "Crisis, Commercial." *A Dictionary of Political Economy.* p. 626. London, 1863.
Macpherson, David, *Annals of Commerce, etc.* 4 vols. London, 1805.
Marriott, John A. R., *England Since Waterloo.* London, 1913.
Martineau, Harriet, *History of England, A.D. 1800–1815.* London, 1878.
Martineau, Harriet, *History of the Peace, 1816–1854.* Boston, 1864–1866.
Mulhall, Michael G., *The Dictionary of Statistics.* 4th ed. London, 1903.
Norman, George W., *Remarks upon some Prevalent Errors, with respect to Currency and Banking.* London, 1838.
Page, William, ed., *Commerce and Industry.* 2 vols. London, 1919.
Palgrave, Robert H. I., ed., "Crises Commercial and Financial." "Crises, 1857–1866–1890." *Dictionary of Political Economy.* London, 1894–1899.
Palmer, John H., *The Causes and Consequences of the Pressure Upon the Money-Market.* London, 1837.
Peel, Robert, *Speech Delivered in House of Commons, Tuesday, 18th May, 1841.* Edinburgh, 1841.
Porter, George R., *The Progress of the Nation.* 3d ed. London, 1851.
Ricardo, David, *The High Price of Bullion, a Proof of the Depreciation of Bank Notes.* 3d ed. London, 1810.
Ricardo, Samson, *Observations on the Recent Pamphlet of J. Horsley Palmer, Esq., on the Causes and Consequences of the Pressure on the Money Market, etc.* London, 1837.
Rose, George, *A Brief Examination into the Increase of the Revenue, Commerce, and Manufactures of Great Britain, from 1792 to 1799.* London, 1799.
Sauerbeck, Augustus, "Prices of Commodities," articles published annually in *Journal of the Royal Statistical Society* and *The Bankers' Magazine,* 1885-1912. London.
Seeley, Robert B., *Memories of the Life and Writings of Michael Thomas Sadler.* London, 1842.
Sheffield, 1st Earl of, John B. H., *Remarks on the Deficiency of Grain.* London, 1800.
Silberling, Norman J., "British Prices and Business Cycles, 1779–1850." *Review of Economic Statistics, The. Supplement.* Oct. 1923. vol. v, p. 219. Cambridge.
Smart, William, *Economic Annals of the Nineteenth Century.* 2 vols. London, 1910, 1917.
Smith, John B., *Report to the Manchester Chamber of Commerce, 1839.* Manchester, 1840.
Stock Exchange Gazette, The, "Annual Financial and Commercial Review." 1920–1926. London.
Third Winter of Unemployment, The. London, 1923.
Thomas, Dorothy S., *Social Aspects of Business Cycles.* London, 1925.
Thoughts on the Causes of the Present Failures. 3d ed. London, 1793.
Tooke, Thomas, *A History of Prices and of the State of the Circulation from 1793–1856.* 6 vols. London, 1838–57.
Tougan-Baranowsky, Michel, *Les Crises Industrielles en Angleterre.* Paris, 1913.
Trevelyan, George M., *British History of the Nineteenth Century.* London, 1922.
Wade, John, *England's Greatness, Rise and Progress.* London, 1856.
Wallas, Graham, *The Life of Francis Place, 1771–1854.* London, 1898.
Watts, John, *The Facts of the Cotton Famine.* London, 1866.
Webb, Sidney and Webb, Beatrice, *The History of Trade Unionism.* Revised edition. London, 1920.
Western, Charles C., *A Letter on the Present Distress of the Country, Addressed to his Constituents.* Chelmsford, 1829.
Western, Charles C., *A Letter to Lord John Russell on his Proposed Alteration of the Corn Laws.* 2d ed. London, 1841.
Western, Charles C., *A Second Letter on the Present Distress of the Country, etc.* Chelmsford, 1830.
Western, Charles C., *A Supplement to Lord Western's Letter to Lord John Russell, Upon Corn Laws and Commercial Distress.* London, 1841.
Westminster Bank, Limited, *Westminster Bank Review,* 1920–1925. London.

Williams, Judith B., *A Guide to Some Aspects of English Social History 1750–1850.* New York, 1916.
Wilson, Robert, *An Enquiry into the Causes of the High Prices, etc.* Edinburgh, 1815.

(k) *India.*

Bombay (Presidency). Labour Office, *Labour Gazette,* 1921–1926. Bombay.
Brij Narayan, *Essay on Indian Economic Problems.* Lahore, 1922.
Chablani, H. L., *Indian Currency and Exchange.* Madras, 1925.
Commerce, 1925–1926. Calcutta.
Das, Rajani Kanta, *Production in India.* Calcutta, 1924.
Datta, K. L., *Report on the Enquiry into the Rise of Prices in India.* 4 vols. Calcutta, 1914.
Dutt, Romesh C., *The Economic History of India in the Victorian Age.* London, 1917.
Gadgil, Dhananjaya R., *The Industrial Evolution of India in Recent Times.* London, 1924.
Great Britain. India Office, *Statement Exhibiting the Moral and Material Progress and Condition of India,* 1888-1917. London.
Great Britain. India Office, *Statistical Abstract Relating to British India.* 1885–1920. London.
Great Britain. Overseas Trade Department, *Report on Some Aspects of British Trade in India,* 1921–1925. London.
Havell, Ernest B., *A Short History of India.* London, 1924.
India. Commercial Intelligence Department, *Financial and Commercial Statistics of British India.* Calcutta, 1904.
India. Commercial Intelligence Department, *Statistical Abstract for British India,* 1912-1922. Calcutta.
India. Industrial Commission, *Report, 1916–1918.* Calcutta, 1918.
India. Information, Director of, *India,* 1917–1925. Calcutta.
India. Statistics Department, *Index Numbers of Indian Prices, 1861–1918.* Calcutta, 1919.
India. Statistics Department, *Prices and Wages in India,* 1890–1920. Calcutta.
India. Statistics Department, *Review of the Trade of India,* 1895–1922. Calcutta.
India. Statistics Department, *Statistical Tables Relating to Wheat.* Calcutta, 1916.
Indian Annual Register, The, 1922–1923. Calcutta.
Indian Journal of Economics, 1916–1926. Allahabad.
Indian Year Book, 1914–1925. Bombay.
Kale, Vaman G., *Introduction to the Study of Indian Economics.* 2d ed. Poona (India), 1918.
Keynes, John M., *Indian Currency and Finance.* London, 1913.
Knowles, Lilian C. A., *The Economic Development of the British Overseas Empire.* New York, 1925.
Loveday, Alexander, *The History and Economics of Indian Famines.* London, 1914.
Malabari, Behramji M., *India in 1897.* Bombay, 1898.
Nash, Vaughan, "The Condition of India." *The Speaker,* July 14, 1900. N. s. vol. ii, p. 410. London.
Panandikar, S. G., *Some Aspects of the Economic Consequences of the War for India.* Bombay, 1921.
Pepper, Charles M., *Report on Trade Conditions in India.* Washington, 1907.
Sarkar, Jadunath, *Economics of British India.* London, 1920.
Shah, Khushal T., *Trade, Tariffs and Transport in India.* Bombay, 1923.
Smith, Vincent A., *The Oxford History of India.* Oxford, 1919.
Spalding, William F., *Eastern Exchange, Currency and Finance.* 4th ed. London, 1924.
United States. Foreign and Domestic Commerce Bureau, *British India.* (Special Consular Report, no. 72) Washington, 1915.
Vakil, C. N., *Financial Developments in Modern India, 1860–1924.* Bombay, 1924.
Wadia, P. A. and G. N. Joshi, *The Wealth of India, 1912–1922.* London, 1925.

(l) Italy.

Association of Italian Corporations, *Business and Financial Report*, 1923–1926. Rome.
Associazione fra le Società Italiane per Azioni, *Bolletino di Notizie Economiche*, 1925–1926. Rome.
Associazione fra le Società Italiane per Azioni, *Piccolo Annuario Statistica Italiano, 1925*. Rome.
Associazione Serica Italiana, *Notizie Statistiche sul Raccolto Bozzoli d'Italia del 1924*. Milan, 1925.
Bachi, Riccardo, ed., *L'Italia Economica*, 1909–1921. Turin.
Banca Commerciale Italiana, *Cenni Statistici sul Movimento Economico dell'Italia, 1916–1920*. Milan.
Banca Commerciale Italiana, *Statistical Summary of Economic Conditions in Italy*. Milan, 1919.
Bernardino, Anselmo *Rassegne di Economia e di Finanza*. Rome, 1925.
Chandler, Henry A. E., "Economic and Financial Progress of Italy." *Commerce Monthly*, Dec., 1925, vol. vii, no. 8. New York.
Credito Italiano, *The Economic Resources of Italy*. 2 vols. Milan, 1920.
Giornale Degli Economisti e Rivista di Statistica. Articles entitled "La Situazione del Marceto Monetaria." 1890–1924. Rome.
Gleichen, Edward, comp., *Italy*. (The Nations of To-day) London, 1923.
Great Britain. Overseas Trade Department, *General Report on the Commercial, Industrial and Economic Situation of Italy, 1920–1925*. London.
International Chamber of Commerce. Italian Section, *A Brief Survey of Italy's Economic Condition*. Rome, 1923.
Italian Industries, The General Confederation of, *Industrial Italy*. Rome, 1922.
Italy. Agricoltura, Industria e Commercio, Ministero di, *Il Frumento in Italia*. Rome, 1914.
Italy. Finanze, Ministero delle (Alberto de'Stefani), *Documenti Sulla Condizione Finanziaria ed Economia dell'Italia*. Rome, 1923.
Italy. Giunta Tecnica Interministeriale, *Data Regarding Italian Economics During the War with International Comparisons*. Rome, 1919.
Italy. Statistica, Direzione Generale della, *Annuario Statistico Italiano* 1890–1921. Rome.
King, Bolton, and Okey, Thomas, *Italy To-day*. London, 1901.
Lémonon, Ernest, *L'Italie Économique et Sociale (1861–1912)*. Paris, 1913.
Lémonon, Ernest, *L'Italie d'Apres Guerre (1914–1921)*. Paris, 1922.
MacLean, H. C., *Labor, Wages, and Unemployment in Italy*. (United States Bureau of Foreign and Domestic Commerce, Trade Information Bulletin, no. 337) Washington, 1925.
Marchetti, Livio, *The Economic Revival of Italy*. Turin, 1918.
Mortara, Giorgio, "Numeri Indici delle Condizioni Economiche d'Italia." *Giornali degli Economisti e Rivista di Statistica*. September, 1913. Third Series, vol. xlvii, p. 193. Rome.
Mortara, Giorgio, *Prospettive Economiche*, 1922–1925. Citta di Castello (Italy).
Pareto, Vilfredo, "La Crise Économique en Italie." *Journal des Économistes*, May, 1889. Four Series, vol. xlvi, p. 161. Paris.
Pietra, Gaetano, "Gli Indici del Movimento Economico in Italia." *Economia*, Jan., 1926. vol. iv, p. 23. Trieste.
Sullam, Angelo, *Die Wirtschaftliche Entwicklung Italiens in Jahre 1905*. Leipzig, 1906.
Trevelyan, Janet P., *A Short History of the Italian People*. New York, 1920.
Villari, Luigi, *The Awakening of Italy*. London, 1924.
Volta, Richard D., "The Italian Banking Crisis." *Journal of Political Economy*, Dec., 1893. vol. ii, p. 1. Chicago.

(m) Japan.

Asakawa, Kanichi, *The Russo-Japanese Conflict*. New York, 1904.
Butts, Halleck A., *Trends in Japan's Trade*. (United States Bureau of Foreign and Domestic Commerce, Trade Information Bulletin, no. 389) Washington, 1926.

Clement, Ernest W., *A Handbook of Modern Japan.* Chicago, 1904.
Dautremer, Joseph, *The Japanese Empire and its Economic Condition.* London, 1910.
Eastern Commerce, 1916–1923. Yokohama.
Great Britain. Overseas Trade Department, *Report on the Commercial, Industrial and Financial Situation of Japan,* 1919–1924. London.
Japan. Agriculture and Commerce Department, *Agricultural and Commercial Statistics,* 1919–1921. Tokyo.
Japan. Agriculture and Commerce Department, *Statistical Report,* 1915. Tokyo.
Japan. Agriculture and Commerce Department, *Statistics of Agriculture, Industries and Commerce,* 1922. Tokyo.
Japan. Finance Department, *Financial and Economic Annual of Japan,* 1901–1924. Tokyo.
Japan. Finance Department, *Latest Economic Condition of Japan Compared with the Previous Year,* 1915–1921. Tokyo.
Japan. Finance Department, *The Quarterly Economic Condition of Japan,* 1922–1924. Tokyo.
Japan Financial and Economic Monthly, The, 1907, 1911–1926. Tokyo.
King-Hall, Stephen, *Western Civilization and the Far East.* London, 1924.
Latourette, Kenneth S., *The Development of Japan.* New York, 1918.
Mitsu Bishi Goshi Kaisha, Economic Research Department, *Monthly Circular,* 1925–1926. Tokyo.
Okuma, Shigenobu, *Fifty Years of New Japan.* 2 vols. New York, 1909.
Ono, Giichi, *Expenditures of the Sino-Japanese War.* New York, 1922.
Porter, Robert P., *The Full Recognition of Japan.* London, 1911.
Sato, Shosuke, *Some Historical Phases of Modern Japan.* New York, 1916.
Spalding, William F., *Eastern Exchange, Currency, and Finance.* 4th ed. London, 1924.
Times, The London, *The Japanese Empire* (a reprint of *The Times,* Japanese edition, July 19, 1910) London, 1910.
Trans-Pacific, The, 1919–1926. Tokyo.
United States. Statistics Bureau, "Commercial Japan in 1900." *Monthly Summary of Commerce and Finance,* Dec., 1901. p. 2219. Washington.

(n) *Netherlands.*

Barnouw, Adriaan J., *Holland under Queen Wilhelmina.* New York, 1923.
Blok, Petrus J., *History of the People of the Netherlands.* 5 vols. New York, 1898–1912.
Bousquot, Georges H., *L'Évolution Sociale aux Pays-Bas.* Paris, 1923.
Economisch-Statistische Berichten, 1925–1926. Rotterdam.
Economist, De, 1888–1926. 's-Gravenhage.
Eisfeld, Curt, *Das Niederländische Bankwesen.* 2 vols. The Hague, 1916.
Great Britain. Overseas Trade Department, *General Report on the Economic, Financial and Industrial Conditions of the Netherlands,* 1919, 1921–1924. London.
Moore, Blaine F., *Economic Aspects of the Commerce and Industry of the Netherlands, 1912–1918.* (United States. Foreign and Domestic Commerce Bureau, Miscellaneous Series, no. 91) Washington, 1919.
Nederlandsche Bank, *Verslag van den President en de Commissarissen,* 1896–1907. Amsterdam.
Nederlandsche Financier, Dagelijksche Beurscourant, *De Financieel Jaarboek voor 1915.* Amsterdam.
Netherlands. Landbouw, Nijverheid en Handel, Departement van. Afdeeling van Handel, *Verslagen en Mededeelingen,* 1907–1913, 1919, 1920. 's-Gravenhage.
Netherlands. Statistiek, Centraal Bureau voor de, *Jaarcijvers, Binnenland,* 1892–1897. 's-Gravenhage.
Netherlands. Statistiek, Centraal Bureau voor de, *Jaarcijfers voor Nederland,* 1923–1924. 's-Gravenhage.
Netherlands. Statistiek, Centraal Bureau voor de, *Jaarcijvers, Rijk in Europa,* 1898–1922. 's-Gravenhage.

BIBLIOGRAPHY

Netherlands. Statistiek, Centraal Bureau voor de, *Maandschrift,* 1925–1926. 's-Gravenhage.
Rotterdamsche Bankvereeniging, *Monthly Review,* 1925–1926. Amsterdam.
Schoepp, F., *Economische Crises.* Groningen (Holland), 1909.
van der Flier, M. J., *War Finance in the Netherlands up to 1918.* Oxford, 1923.

(o) Russia.

Aleksinski, Grigori I., *Modern Russia.* London, 1913.
Arnot, R. Page, *The Russian Revolution.* London, 1923.
British Trades Union Delegation to Russia and Caucasia, 1924, *Russia.* London, 1925.
Commercial Year Book of the Soviet Union, 1925. New York, 1925.
Idelson, Wladimir and Lexis, Wilhelm H. R. A., *Organization of Banking in Russia.* (United States. National Monetary Commission. 61st Congress, 2d Session, Senate Documents, vol. xxxvii) Washington, 1911.
Katzenellenbaum, Zakharii S., *Russian Currency and Banking, 1914–1924.* London, 1925.
Köhler, Siegfried, *Die Russische Industriearbeiterschaft von 1905 bis 1917.* Leipzig, 1921.
League of Nations. Secretariat, *Report on the Economic Conditions in Russia.* Nancy, 1922.
Leites, K., *Recent Economic Developments in Russia.* Oxford, 1922.
Mavor, James, *An Economic History of Russia.* 2 vols. 2nd ed. London, 1925.
Pasvolsky, Leo, and Moulton, Harold G., *Russian Debts and Russian Reconstruction.* New York, 1924.
Planowoe Chasjaistwo, 1925–1926. Moscow.
Raffalovich, Arthur, ed., *Russia: Its Trade and Commerce.* London, 1918.
Russia. Finance, People's Commissariat of. Conjuncture Institute, *Economic Bulletin,* 1922–1925. Moscow.
Russia. Gosplan, *Kontrolnye Zifre Narodnawo Chasjaistwo, 1925–1926.* Moscow, 1925.
Russia. Statisticheski Komitet, *Annuaire Statistique de la Russie, 1896.* Moscow.
Russian Year Book, The, 1911–1916. London.
Skrine, Francis H. B., *The Expansion of Russia, 1815–1900.* Cambridge (Eng.), 1904.
Soviet Union Monthly, The, 1926. London.
Volkswirtschaft der Union der Sozialistischen Sowjet-Republiken, Die, 1926. Berlin.
Wallace, Donald M., *Russia.* New York, 1905.
Yurovsky, L. N., *Currency Problems and Policy of the Soviet Union.* London, 1925.

(p) South Africa.

Birchenough, Henry, *Report upon the Present Position and Future Prospects of British Trade in South Africa.* (Great Britain. Parliamentary Papers, 1904. vol. lxi. ed. 1844) London, 1904.
Bryce, James, *Impressions of South Africa.* New York, 1897.
Cape of Good Hope. Colonial Secretary's Office, *Statistical Register of the Colony of the Cape of Good Hope,* 1890–1892, 1894, 1897–1902. Cape Town.
Great Britain. Overseas Trade Department, *Report on the Economic and Financial Conditions of South Africa,* 1920–1923. London.
Great Britain. Trade Commissioner for South Africa, *Report to the Board of Trade,* 1911–1919. London.
Journal of the Institute of Bankers in South Africa, 1905–1925. Cape Town.
Kock, Michiel H. de, *Selected Subjects in the Economic History of South Africa.* Cape Town, 1924.
Lehfeldt, Robert A., *Gold, Prices, and the Witwatersrand.* London, 1919.
Lehfeldt, Robert A., *The National Resources of South Africa.* Johannesburg, 1922.
Nathan, Manfred, *The South African Commonwealth.* Johannesburg, 1919.
South African Year-Book, 1914. London.
Standard Bank of South Africa, Ltd., *Monthly Review,* 1920–1926. Cape Town.
Tilby, Aubrey W., *South Africa, 1486–1913.* (In his: *The English People Overseas,* vol. vi.) Boston, 1914.

Union of South Africa. Census and Statistics Office, *Monthly Bulletin of Union Statistics*, 1925–1926. Pretoria.
Union of South Africa. Census and Statistics Office, *Quarterly Abstract of Union Statistics*, 1922. Johannesburg.
Union of South Africa. Census and Statistics Office, *Official Year Book of the Union of South Africa*, 1917–1923. Pretoria.
Union of South Africa. Census and Statistics Office, *Social Statistics*, 1919–1923. Pretoria.
Union of South Africa. Census and Statistics Office, *Statistical Yearbook of the Union of South Africa*, 1912–1916. Johannesburg.
Union of South Africa. Finance Department. Kemmerer, Edwin W., and Vissering, Gerard, *Report on the Resumption of Gold Payments by the Union of South Africa*. Pretoria, 1925.
Union of South Africa. Labour Department, *Official Labour Gazette* (published jointly with the *South African Journal of Industries*), 1925. Pretoria.
Union of South Africa. Labour Department, *The Social and Industrial Review*, 1926. Pretoria.
Union of South Africa. Mines and Industries Department, *South African Journal of Industries*, 1918–1925. Pretoria.
Wilmot, Alexander, *The History of Our Own Times in South Africa, 1872–1898*. 3 vols. London, 1897–1899.
Worsfold, William B., *The Union of South Africa*. London, 1912.

(*q*) *Sweden.*

Affärsvärlden, 1925–1926. Stockholm.
Åkerman, Johan G., *En svensk Konjunkturindex, 1913–1922*. Stockholm, 1922.
Bain, Robert N., *Scandinavia*. Cambridge (Eng.), 1905.
Drachmann, Povl, *The Industrial Development and Commercial Policies of the Three Scandinavian Countries*. Oxford, 1915.
Flux, Alfred W., *The Swedish Banking System*. (United States. National Monetary Commission. 61st Congress, 2d Session, Senate Documents, vol xvii) Washington, 1910.
Great Britain. Overseas Trade Department, *Report on the Commercial and Industrial Situation of Sweden*, 1919–1924. London.
Guinchard, J., ed., *Sweden. Historical and Statistical Handbook*. 2 vols. 2d ed. Stockholm, 1914.
Key, Helmer, *La Vie Économique de la Suède*. Paris, 1913.
Skandinaviska Kreditaktiebolaget, *Quarterly Report*, 1920–1926. Stockholm.
Stockholms Enskilda Bank, *Direktions och Revisions-Berättelser för 1905 och 1912*. Stockholm.
Sveriges Riksbank, *Årsbok*, 1908–1915. Stockholm.
Sweden. Kommerskollegium, *Economisk Översikt*, 1921. Stockholm.
Sweden, Statistiska Centralbyrån, *Statistisk Årsbok för Sverige*, 1914–1925. Stockholm.
Swedish-American Trade Journal, The, 1925–1926. New York.
Swedish Board of Trade, *The Swedish Economic Review*, 1922–1925. Stockholm.
Swedish Export, 1925–1926. Stockholm.
Swedish Year Book, The, 1921–1925. Stockholm.

(*r*) *United States.*

Adams, Henry, *History of the United States of America*. 9 vols. New York, 1921.
Annalist, The, 1913–1926. New York.
Avery, Elroy M., *History of the United States and Its People*. 7 vols. Cleveland, 1901–1910.
Babson, Roger W., *Business Barometers*. 11th ed. Wellesley Hills, 1918.
Ballagh, James C., *Southern Economic History*. (The South in the Building of the Nation. vols. v, vi) Richmond, 1909.

BIBLIOGRAPHY 377

Barry, John S., *The History of Massachusetts.* 3 vols. Boston, 1855–1857.
Bassett, John S., *The Federalist System, 1789–1801.* (The American Nation: A History. vol. ii) New York, 1906.
Beard, Charles A., *Economic Origins of Jeffersonian Democracy.* New York, 1915.
Benton, Thomas H., *Thirty Years' View.* 2 vols. New York, 1886.
Bidwell, Percy W., and Falconer, John I., *History of Agriculture in the Northern United States 1620–1860.* Washington, 1925.
Bigelow, Erastus B., *The Tariff Question Considered in Regard to the Policy of England and the Interests of the United States.* Boston, 1862.
Bogart, Ernest L., and Rawles, W. A., *Trial Bibliography and Outline of Lectures on the Financial History of the United States.* (Oberlin College, Library Bulletin no. 5) Oberlin, 1901.
Bolles, Albert S., *The Financial History of the United States from 1789 to 1860 and from 1861–85.* 2 vols. New York, 1883–1886.
Bradford, Alden, *History of the Federal Government for Fifty Years from March, 1789, to March, 1839.* Boston, 1840.
Bradstreet's, 1879–1926. New York.
Burton, Theodore E., *Financial Crises and Periods of Industrial and Commercial Depression.* New York, 1902.
Callender, Guy S., *Selections from the Economic History of the United States, 1765–1860.* Boston, 1909.
Carey, Henry C., *Review of the Decade 1857–67.* Philadelphia, 1867.
Carey, Mathew, *Essays on Political Economy.* Philadelphia, 1822.
Carey, Mathew, *The New Olive Branch.* 2nd ed. Philadelphia, 1821.
Catterall, Ralph C. H., *The Second Bank of the United States.* Chicago, 1903.
Channing, Edward, *History of the United States.* 6 vols. New York, 1905–1925.
Clark, Victor S., *History of Manufactures in the United States 1607–1860.* Washington, 1916.
Clarkson, Grosvenor B., *Industrial America in the World War.* Boston, 1924.
Cole, Arthur H., "Wholesale Prices in the United States." *Review of Economic Statistics,* April, 1926. vol. viii, p. 69. Cambridge.
Commercial and Financial Chronicle, The, 1865–1926. New York.
Commons, John R., and others, ed., *A Documentary History of American Industrial Society.* 10 vols. Cleveland, 1910.
Commons, John R., and Saposs, David J., Sumner, Helen L., Mittelman, E. B., Hoagland, H. E., Andrews, John B., Perlman, Selig, *History of Labour in the United States.* 2 vols. New York, 1918.
Conant, Charles A., *A History of Modern Banks of Issue.* New York, 1915.
Cowdrick, Edward S., *Industrial History of the United States.* New York, 1923.
Coxe, Tench, *A View of the United States of America.* Philadelphia, 1794.
De Bow, J. D. B., *The Industrial Resources, etc., of the Southern and Western States.* 4 vols. New Orleans, 1852–1853.
Dewey, Davis R., *Financial History of the United States.* New York, 1903.
Droppers, Garrett, *Economic History in the Nineteenth Century.* New York, 1923.
Dunning, William A., *Reconstruction, Political and Economic, 1865–1877.* (The American Nation: A History. vol. xxii) New York, 1907.
Dun's Review, 1895–1926. New York.
Financial Age, The, 1926. New York.
Financial History Monthly, 1856–93.
Financial Review, The, 1860–1921. New York.
Findley, William, *History of the Insurrection, in the Four Western Counties of Pennsylvania in 1794.* Philadelphia, 1796.
Fite, Emerson D., *Social and Industrial Conditions in the North During the Civil War.* New York, 1910.
Fortnightly Review, The, 1866–1880. London.
Gibbs, George, *Memoirs of the Administrations of Washington and Adams.* 2 vols. New York, 1846.
Gordy, J. P., *A History of Political Parties in the United States.* 2 vols. New York, 1900–1902.

Gouge, William M., *A Short History of Paper Money and Banking in the United States.* Philadelphia, 1833.
Great Britain. Overseas Trade Department, *Report on the Finance, Industry and Commerce of the United States of America, 1922–1924.* London.
Hansen, Alvin H., *Cycles of Prosperity and Depression in the United States, Great Britain and Germany . . . 1902–1908.* (University of Wisconsin Studies in the Social Sciences and History. no. 5) Madison, 1921.
Hart, Albert B., ed., *The American Year Book,* 1925. New York.
Heckscher, Eli F., *The Continental System.* Oxford, 1922.
Hildreth, Richard, *Banks, Banking and Paper Currencies.* Boston, 1840.
Holdsworth, John T., and Dewey, Davis R., *The First and Second Banks of the United States.* (United States. National Monetary Commission. 61st Congress, 2d Session, Senate Documents. vol. iv) Washington, 1910.
Hosmer, James K., *Outcome of the Civil War, 1863–1865.* (The American Nation: A History. vol. xxi) New York, 1907.
Inquiry into the Causes of Public Distress (An). New York, 1834.
Jennings, Walter W., *The American Embargo 1807–1809.* (University of Iowa Studies in the Social Sciences. vol. viii, no. 1) Iowa City, 1921.
Jennings, Walter W., *A History of Economic Progress in the United States.* New York, 1926.
Johnson, Emory R., and Van Metre, T. W., Huebner, G. G., and Hanchett, D. S., *History of Domestic and Foreign Commerce of the United States.* 2 vols. Washington, 1915.
Juglar, Clément, and DeCourcy, W. Thom, *Brief History of Panics and Their Periodical Occurrence.* 3d ed. New York, 1916.
Kettell, Thomas P., "Commerce," in *Eighty Years' Progress of the United States.* Hartford, 1869.
Kinley, David, *The Independent Treasury of the United States and its Relations to the Banks of the Country.* (United States. National Monetary Commission. 61st Congress, 2d Session. Senate Document. vol. xxxviii) Washington, 1910.
Knox, John J., *A History of Banking in the United States.* New York, 1900.
Lambert, John, *Travels through Canada and the United States of North America, in the Years 1806, 1807 and 1808.* 2 vols. 2d ed. London, 1814.
Lewis, Lawrence, Jr., *A History of the Bank of North America.* Philadelphia, 1882.
Lightner, Otto C., *The History of Business Depressions.* New York, 1922.
Macdonald, William, *Select Documents Illustrative of the History of the United States, 1776–1861.* New York, 1898.
McGrane, Reginald C., *The Panic of 1837.* Chicago, 1924.
MacLeod, Henry D., "Banking in America." *A Dictionary of Political Economy.* London, 1863.
McMaster, John B., *History of the People of the United States from the Revolution to the Civil War.* 8 vols. New York, 1885–1913.
Manual of Statistics, The, 1884–1923. New York.
Martin, Joseph G., *History of the Boston Stock and Money Markets from January, 1798, to January, 1898.* Boston, 1898.
Merchants' Magazine and Commercial Review, 1839–1879. New York.
Meyer, Balthasar H., ed., *History of Transportation in the United States before 1860.* Washington, 1917.
Mitchell, Wesley C., *Gold, Prices, and Wages Under the Greenback Standard.* (University of California. Publications in Economics. vol. i.) Berkeley, 1908.
Mitchell, Wesley C., *A History of the Greenbacks.* (University of Chicago. The Decennial Publications. Series 2, vol. 9) Chicago, 1903.
Monthly Review of Credit and Business Conditions in the Second Federal Reserve District, 1924–1926. New York.
Morison, Samuel E., *The Maritime History of Massachusetts, 1783–1860.* Boston, 1921.
Moulton, R. K., *Legislative and Documentary History of the Banks of the United States.* New York, 1834.
New York (State) Chamber of Commerce, *Annual Report,* 1858-1925. New York.

New York. State Senate, *Message from the Governor on the Present State of Commercial Embarrassment.* . . . (Senate Document 105, March 24, 1834) Albany, 1834.
Niles' Weekly Register, 1811–1849. Baltimore.
Noyes, Alexander D., *Forty Years of American Finance, 1865–1907.* New York, 1909.
Oliver, Frederick S., *Alexander Hamilton.* London, 1915.
Persons, Warren M., Tuttle, Pierson M., Frickey, Edwin, "Business and Financial Conditions Following the Civil War in the United States." *Review of Economic Statistics, The,* Supplement, July, 1920. vol. ii, p. 1. Cambridge.
Paxson, Frederic L., *History of the American Frontier, 1763–1893.* Boston, 1924.
Phillips, Ulrich B., *Financial Crises in the Antebellum South* (in The South in the Building of the Nation, vol. v) Richmond, 1909.
Pitkin, Timothy, *A Statistical View of the Commerce of the United States of America.* New Haven, 1835.
Poor, Henry V., *History of the Railroads and Canals of the United States.* New York, 1860.
Poor's Manual of the Railroads of the United States, 1890. New York.
Proceedings of the General Convention of Agriculturists and Manufactures, and Others Friendly to the Encouragement and Support of the Domestic Industry of the United States. Held in Harrisburg, July 30–August 3, 1827.
Reed, John C., *The Economic Conditions in the South during the Civil War.* (The South in the Building of the Nation, vol. v) Richmond, 1909.
Richardson, James D., *A Compilation of the Messages and Papers of the Presidents, 1789–1908.* 11 vols. New York, 1908.
Ridpath, John C., *History of the United States.* 2 vols. Washington, 1900.
Rynar, Ira, *On the Crises of 1837, 1847, and 1857 in England, France and the United States.* (University of Nebraska Studies. vol. v, no. 2) Lincoln, Nebraska, 1905.
Schluter, William C., *The Pre-War Business Cycle.* (Columbia University Studies in History, Economic and Public Law. vol. cvii) New York, 1923.
Schwab, John C., *The Confederate States of America, 1861–1865.* New York, 1901.
Seybert, Adam, *Statistical Annals . . . of the United States of America.* Philadelphia, 1818.
Shepard, Edward M., *Martin Van Buren.* Boston, 1900.
Shipping and Commercial List and New York Price Current, 1826–1841. New York.
Smith, Theodore C., *Parties and Slavery, 1850–1859.* (The American Nation: A History. vol. xvii) New York, 1906.
Spaulding, E. G., *One Hundred Years of Progress in the History of Banking.* Buffalo, 1876.
Spectator, The, 1797–1804. New York.
Sprague, C. M. W., *History of Crises Under the National Banking System.* (United States. National Monetary Commission. 61st Congress, 2d Session, Senate Documents. vol. xxv) Washington, 1910.
Standard Statistics Company, *Standard Daily Trade Service,* 1917–1926. New York.
Stevens, Albert C., "Analysis of the Phenomena of the Panic in the United States in 1893." *Quarterly Journal of Economics,* Jan., 1894. vol. viii, p. 117. Boston.
Stevens, John A., *Albert Gallatin.* Boston, 1899.
Sumner, William G., *Alexander Hamilton.* New York, 1890.
Sumner, William G., *A History of Banking in the United States.* New York, 1896.
Sumner, William G., *A History of American Currency.* New York, 1876.
Tammany Society or Columbian Order, *Address of the Society to its Absent Members, and the Members of its Several Branches Throughout the United States.* New York, 1819.
Taussig, Frank W., *The Tariff History of the United States.* 7th ed. New York, 1923.
Tooke, Thomas, *A History of Prices and the State of the Circulation from 1793–1856.* 6 vols. London, 1838–1857.
Turner, Frederick J., *Rise of the New West, 1819–1829.* (The American Nation: A History. vol. xiv) New York, 1906.

United States. Agricultural Inquiry, Joint Commission of, *Report.* (United States. 67th Congress, 1st Session, House Reports. no. 3) 4 vols. Washington, 1921.
United States. Agriculture Department, *Year Book,* 1894–1924. Washington.
United States. Agriculture Department, *Annual Report of the Commissioner,* 1862–1880. Washington.
United States. Agriculture Department. Bureau of Statistics, *Cotton Crop of the United States 1790–1911.* Circular 32) Washington, 1912.
United States. Census Bureau, *Survey of Current Business,* 1921–1926. Washington.
United States. Commerce Department, *Annual Report of the Secretary of Commerce,* 1925. Washington.
United States. Federal Reserve Board, *Annual Report,* 1914–1925. Washington.
United States. Foreign and Domestic Commerce Bureau, *Statistical Abstract of the United States,* 1913–1924. Washington.
United States. Patent Office, *Annual Report of the Commissioner of Patents,* 1842–1849. Washington.
United States. Revenue Special Commissioner, *Annual Report,* 1866–1869. Washington.
United States. Statistics Bureau, *Annual Report on Commerce and Navigation,* 1821–1845. Washington.
United States. Statistics Bureau, *Statistical Abstract of the United States,* 1878–1912. Washington.
United States. Treasury Department, *Reports of the Secretary of the Treasury . . . 1790–1849.* 7 vols. Washington.
United States Economist, 1852–1859. New York.
United States Magazine and Democratic Review, The, 1837–1857. Washington.
Van Metre, Thurman W., *Economic History of the United States.* New York, 1921.
Ware, Norman, *The Industrial Worker, 1840–1860.* Boston, 1924.
Wells, David A., *Recent Economic Changes.* New York, 1891.
Wells, David A., *The Recent Financial, Industrial, and Commercial Experiences of the United States.* (The Financier Economic Series. no. 1) New York, 1872.
Wildman, Murray S., *Money Inflation in the United States.* Chicago, 1905.
Winterbotham, William, *An Historical, Geographical, Commercial and Philosophical View of the American United States.* 4 vols. London, 1795.
Wirth, Max, "The Crisis of 1890." *The Journal of Political Economy,* March, 1893. vol. i, p. 214. Chicago.
Wood, John, *The Suppressed History of the Administration of John Adams.* Philadelphia, 1846.

DATE DUE
~~NOV 11 1995~~
~~MAY 2 0 1997~~